Emotion and Psychopathology

Emotion and Psychopathology

BRIDGING AFFECTIVE AND CLINICAL SCIENCE

EDITED BY

Jonathan Rottenberg

Sheri L. Johnson

AMERICAN PSYCHOLOGICAL ASSOCIATION

WASHINGTON, DC

Published by
American Psychological Association
750 First Street, NE
Washington, DC 20002
www.apa.org

To order
APA Order Department
P.O. Box 92984
Washington, DC 20090-2984
Tel: (800) 374-2721; Direct: (202) 336-5510
Fax: (202) 336-5502; TDD/TTY: (202) 336-6123
Online: www.apa.org/books/
E-mail: order@apa.org

In the U.K., Europe, Africa, and the Middle East, copies may be ordered from
American Psychological Association
3 Henrietta Street
Covent Garden, London
WC2E 8LU England

Typeset in Goudy by AlphaWebTech, Mechanicsville, MD

Printer: Maple-Vail Book Manfacturing Group, Binghamton, NY
Cover Designer: Berg Design, Albany, NY
Technical/Production Editor: Harriet Kaplan

The opinions and statements published are the responsibility of the authors, and such opinions and statements do not necessarily represent the policies of the American Psychological Association.

Library of Congress Cataloging-in-Publication Data

Emotion and psychopathology : bridging affective and clinical science / edited by Jonathan Rottenberg and Sheri L. Johnson. — 1st ed.
    p. cm.
  Includes bibliographical references and index.
  ISBN-13: 978-1-59147-786-0
  ISBN-10: 1-59147-786-7
  1. Emotions. 2. Physiology, Pathological. 3. Affect (Psychology). I. Rottenberg, Jonathan. II. Johnson, Sheri L.
  [DNLM: 1. Emotions—physiology. 2. Affective Symptoms—physiopathology. 3. Mental Disorders—physiopathology. 4. Mental Disorders—therapy. 5. Psychophysiology—methods. WL 103 E533 2007]
  RC455.4.E46E38 2007
  616.89—dc22
                                                  2006032732

British Library Cataloguing-in-Publication Data
A CIP record is available from the British Library.

Printed in the United States of America
First Edition

CONTENTS

CONTRIBUTORS

John J. B. Allen, PhD, Department of Psychology, University of Arizona, Tucson

Jack J. Blanchard, PhD, Clinical Program, Department of Psychology, University of Maryland, College Park

Jaymee T. Carreño, MA, Department of Psychology, University of Maryland, College Park

Michael Chmielewski, MA, Department of Psychology, University of Iowa, Iowa City

Alex S. Cohen, Department of Psychology, University of Maryland, College Park

John J. Curtin, PhD, Department of Psychology, University of Wisconsin—Madison

Kari Merrill Eddington, PhD, Department of Psychology and Neuroscience, Duke University, Durham, NC

Lori R. Eisner, BA, Department of Psychology, University of Miami, Miami, FL

Frank J. Farach, MS, Department of Psychology, Yale University, New Haven, CT

James J. Gross, PhD, Department of Psychology, Stanford University, Stanford, CA

June Gruber, MA, Department of Psychology, University of California, Berkeley

Steven D. Hollon, PhD, Department of Psychology, Vanderbilt University, Nashville, TN

John Humrichouse, BA, Department of Psychology, University of Iowa, Iowa City

Sheri L. Johnson, PhD, Psychology Department, University of Miami, Coral Gables, FL

Dacher Keltner, PhD, Department of Psychology, University of California, Berkeley

Alan R. Lang, PhD, The R. Robert von Brüning Professor of Psychology, Department of Psychology, Florida State University, Tallahassee

Colin MacLeod, BSc, MPhil, DPhil, School of Psychology, University of Western Australia, Crawley

Megan C. McCrudden, MA, Department of Psychology and Neuroscience, Duke University, Durham, NC

Elizabeth A. McDade-Montez, MA, Department of Psychology, University of Iowa, Iowa City

Douglas S. Mennin, PhD, Department of Psychology and Yale Anxiety and Mood Services, Yale University, New Haven, CT

Arne Öhman, PhD, Psychology Section, Department of Clinical Neuroscience, Karolinska Institute and Hospital, Solna, Stockholm, Sweden

Christopher J. Patrick, PhD, Department of Psychology, and Clinical Science and Psychopathology Research Training Program, University of Minnesota, Minneapolis

Jonathan Rottenberg, PhD, Department of Psychology, University of South Florida, Tampa

Christian Rück, PhD, MD, Psychiatry Section, Department of Clinical Neuroscience, Karolinska Institute, Stockholm, Sweden

Craig Santerre, MA, Department of Psychology, University of Arizona, Tucson

Richard C. Shelton, MD, Department of Psychiatry, Vanderbilt University Medical School, Nashville, TN

Timothy J. Strauman, PhD, Department of Psychology and Neuroscience, Duke University, Durham, NC

Andrew J. Tomarken, PhD, Department of Psychology, Vanderbilt University, Nashville, TN

David Watson, PhD, F. Wendell Miller Professor, Department of Psychology, University of Iowa, Iowa City

Edward Wilson, PhD, School of Psychology, University of Western Australia, Crawley

Emotion and Psychopathology

INTRODUCTION: BRIDGING AFFECTIVE AND CLINICAL SCIENCE

JONATHAN ROTTENBERG AND SHERI L. JOHNSON

Part of being human is that we must often rely on our emotions. One might think of emotions as trusted counselors who urge us to do the right thing at the right time. Usually, this reliance is well placed: Fear helps prevent injury, love forges lasting bonds, and anger wards off attack. Although emotions can help us adapt successfully to the environment, psychopathology reveals the darker side of emotion.

On this darker side, emotional impulses are poorly tuned to the environment: They arise in the wrong contexts, build to the wrong intensity, and last for the wrong duration. When emotions go wrong, the consequences can be terrible. Anyone who has suffered from clinical depression or anxiety or who has cared for a person who suffers from these conditions, for example, knows full well that to lose purchase on one's emotions is not only debilitating but frightening.

In fact, emotional disturbance, in one form or another, is a central feature of psychopathology. A review of the main diagnostic handbook, the *Diagnostic and Statistical Manual of Mental Disorders* (American Psychiatric Association, 2000), reveals that most disorders are accompanied by emotional disturbances. Table 1 illustrates this point by listing 10 representative examples of emotional symptoms in psychopathology.

TABLE 1
Ten Examples of Emotional Symptoms in Psychopathology

Disorder	Symptom
Major depressive disorder	Sadness, guilt, anhedonia
Mania	Excessive euphoria, irritability
Schizophrenia	Flat affect, anhedonia
Panic disorder	Sudden unexplained bursts of fear
Specific phobia	Excessive fear of focal object
Obsessive–compulsive disorder	Repetitive anxious thoughts
Hypochondriasis	Persistent fear of serious disease
Pyromania	Pleasure from setting fires
Antisocial personality disorder	Irritability, aggressiveness, lack of guilt
Borderline personality disorder	Emotional instability, anger attacks

Emotions have historically been regarded as mysterious, even impenetrable to inquiry, and it has been left to poets and philosophers to marvel at their power to disrupt our affairs. Can contemporary science succeed where others have failed and bring conceptual order to the dark side of emotion? At first this task may seem daunting. Emotions can go wrong in so many ways, and these various forms of dysfunction are not easily described or arrayed into a meaningful scheme. Fortunately, however, a set of tools has been developed—which we refer to in this volume as *affective science*—that have tremendous potential to facilitate scientific work on the role of emotions in psychopathology. These new tools, which vary from techniques to measure emotion to procedures to elicit emotion in a laboratory setting, are already allowing researchers and clinicians to formulate more sophisticated conceptualizations that will enhance the capacity to diagnose and treat disorders. We hope that in communicating these advances, this book represents a small step in harnessing these tools to better understand both psychopathology and normal emotional variation.

WHY IS BRIDGING AFFECTIVE AND CLINICAL SCIENCE SO IMPORTANT?

We titled this volume *Emotion and Psychopathology: Bridging Affective and Clinical Science*. Arguably, the most salient of these eight words is *bridging*. In this introduction, we want to explain what bridging is and why it matters.

The fragmentation of modern scientific inquiry has been lamented in virtually every field of investigation—from astronomy to zoology. Scientific fragmentation has been acutely felt in the field of emotion, where there has been a wide gulf between "basic" research on normative emotion functioning and "applied" research on clinical disorders. Why the gulf between affective and clinical science? Undoubtedly, many factors have contributed to this separation, including old habits of thinking, the complexity of the phenomena under study, and differences in training and methodology. There are likely to be multiple payoffs for synthesizing affective and clinical science. Here we highlight three main reasons why the time is ripe to bridge basic research and clinical science in the study of emotion.

First, emotion is inherently a multifaceted construct. This is reflected both in definitions of emotion, which typically contain multiple elements such as subjective experience, cognition, behavior, and physiology, as well as in wider discussions of emotion, which often draw on molar concepts such as culture, development, evolution, or socialization. Thus, the pursuit of knowledge about emotion naturally takes one on an imperialistic venture, leading across established disciplinary boundaries.

Second, empirical research on emotion has veritably exploded in the past 3 decades, accompanied by new theories (e.g., evolutionary analyses of emotion), new methods (e.g., anatomically based systems for coding facial expressive behavior, brain imaging strategies), and new organizations (e.g., the International Society for Research on Emotion) and journals (e.g., the American Psychological Association journal *Emotion*). One particularly crucial methodological advance has been improved experimental paradigms for the standardized assessment of individual differences in emotional reactivity across multiple systems of response (i.e., neural, peripheral physiological, cognitive, and behavioral). From these paradigms, important findings have emerged that illuminate how emotion drives successful and unsuccessful adaptation. That is, the science of emotion is rapidly enriching our understanding of basic processes, and this knowledge is providing the foundation to analyze which processes go awry and at which times within different disorders.

Third, the integration of basic research on emotion with clinical science provides the potential for enhancing treatment for psychological disorders. Even before the advent of affective science, clinicians honored the importance of emotion in their work. For example, for psychoanalytic therapists, emotion is a powerful marker of the events of the unconscious. For cognitive therapists, emotional episodes provide telling clues for understanding a patient's faulty thinking. Recently, more explicitly emotion-focused treatment approaches have been developed and have gained research support and public recognition (Elliott, Greenberg, & Lietaer, 2003; Elliott, Watson, Goldman, & Greenberg, 2004), and the latest wave of cognitive–behavioral therapy manuals have also greatly expanded the focus on emotion and emotion regulation (Hayes & Strosahl, 2005; Linehan, 1993). These clinical approaches, however, have advanced in parallel, and at times separately, from the basic research that has addressed emotion processes with increasingly sophisticated methods and theories. The moment is upon us for the integration of these two rich streams of basic and applied work. In sum, affective and clinical scientists can no longer afford to ignore one another, because each group has the potential to gain from a synthesis of these research areas.

WHY IS BRIDGING AFFECTIVE AND CLINICAL SCIENCE SO CHALLENGING?

Despite the obvious benefits of bridging affective and clinical science, this synthesis has been slow to develop. Why? Synthesis across disciplines requires us not only to give up old habits of thought and training but also to develop new ones, with a shared conceptual framework and a common language as well as methodological paradigms. Synthesis is not a matter of snapping one's fingers; it is hard work that requires persistence.

It should also be kept in mind that emotion is a famously messy construct. Thus, synthesis, in the domain of emotion, has an extra degree of difficulty. The complexity of the emotion construct explains in part why the field has often been consumed with definitional issues such as what an emotion is, how many emotions there are, and how emotions can be differentiated from related constructs such as mood and temperament. Emotions are indeed an elusive object of study. In part, this elusiveness stems from a phenomenon that involves multiple response elements cutting across experience, behavior, cognition, and both central and peripheral nervous system activity. Indeed, each of these response elements alone is hard to study and requires mastering a set of conceptual and methodological issues. To make matters even more complicated, when emotions are activated, these response elements often do not operate in concert (e.g., one can feel emotion without displaying emotion on one's face).

Even with the difficulties of integrating affective and clinical science, a good deal of progress has been made thus far. This progress has been assisted by federal agencies, including the National Institutes of Health, which has provided generous financial support for translational research, enlarging a field that is explicitly devoted to developing a research framework that bridges applied questions and basic methodologies. We think the time is right to showcase leading examples of translational research. Therefore, this book highlights the progress that has been made to date in the synthesis of emotion and clinical science.

WHAT IS IN THIS BOOK?

Most centrally, we hope this book provides a concise guide for clinicians and researchers who seek information about the emerging field of translational research and about the clinical implications of this synthesis. In the interest of providing an efficient guide, we have chosen to be illustrative rather than comprehensive. In fact, with the explosion of viable methods for studying emotion, we had little choice in the matter! In particular, the neuroimaging of emotion has clearly spawned an important, complex, and rapidly evolving set of methods. Although this volume notes several key developments in neuroimaging methods and concepts, a detailed coverage of this massive area would exhaust the page constraints of a short book (the interested reader is referred to volumes focused on affective neuroscience, including Davidson, Scherer, & Goldsmith, 2003; Lane & Nadel, 2000; Panksepp, 1998).

More specifically, we had three aims that guided our selection of chapters for this book. Our first aim was to provide a clear overview of the best methodologies available. In Part I, leading experts provide a crisp set of chapters on major components of emotion, including self-report of experience, as well as behavior, cognition, and physiological response. In addition to a survey of the methods, readers will find a discussion of theoretical and pragmatic issues.

Our second aim was to illustrate how emotion research has the potential to provide understanding of key mechanisms in psychopathology. Chapters in Part II provide reviews of the literature on a handful of key psychopathologies. Although space precludes coverage of all disorders, readers will come to appreciate differences in the emotion mechanisms involved across these disorders. For example, research summarized in these chapters suggests that anxiety disorders involve anomalous reactivity to negative stimuli, bipolar disorders involve elevated reactivity to approach stimuli, and major depression involves a diminished reactivity to emotion stimuli of both valences. Research on schizophrenia provides an example of a disorder characterized by a lack of coherence across response elements, which illustrates the importance of measuring multiple facets of emotion. Research on alcohol abuse and dependence suggests the need to consider that alcohol may operate through multiple mechanisms on emotion processes. Research on psychopathy illustrates that understanding links between emotion and disorder may help us to reconceptualize diagnostic subtypes. To us, these differences are exciting because they paint a more sensitive picture of the array of potential emotion disturbances and how these could explain very different symptom profiles.

Our third aim was to illustrate how emotion theory can inform treatment. Although many treatment manuals include a focus on emotion and emotion regulation, the explicit use of emotion research to develop more effective treatments for psychopathology is in an early phase. Perhaps the best-developed example of how emotion can enrich psychotherapy comes from research on anxiety disorders, summarized in chapter 11 by Farach and Mennin. It is clear, however, that the amount to which findings from systematic emotion research have been integrated into treatment has varied. Tomarken, Shelton, and Hollon (chap. 12) provide an illustration of the gains that can be made by integrating emotion research into pharmacotherapy studies (drawing heavily from the study of antidepressants), in which much of this research has been conducted. Finally, Strauman, Eddington, and McCrudden (chap. 13) provide a road map for more creative integration of emotion research into treatment outcome and process research. Thus, Part III of the book not only provides examples of new advances but also focuses on future directions in applying emotion research to treatment.

Our goal, then, was to gather chapters from authors who succeed in the important but difficult task of bridging disciplines—scholars who are at the forefront of integrating work on emotion and psychopathology. This synthesis and, by extension, this book, reflect a work in progress, and we have not tried to hide the rough edges. For example, despite strong parallels, a careful reader will note that authors differ in how they define key terms across chapters. One of our overarching aims in selecting authors for this book was to find a critical mass of individuals who could communicate the excitement of this synthesis. Thus, we sought to identify authors who are known not only for their methodological rigor but also for their ability to relate nuances of emotion theory and psychopathology findings to the broadest possible audience of students, researchers, and clinicians.

WHO IS THIS BOOK FOR?

We believe many audiences will benefit from reading this book. Just as the understanding of normal brain function has been informed by the study of brain lesions, affective scientists have a profound opportunity to learn about the normal operation of emotion by studying emotion when it goes wrong. In turn, psychopathology researchers will learn about the recent gains in understanding different disorders. Clinical practitioners will benefit by gaining an understanding of how to apply affective science to several intervention contexts. Finally, treatment researchers will learn about ways that affective science could be integrated into future research on treatment.

The dark side of emotion is certainly a dense and tangled realm. There is little doubt that the profundity of emotional disturbance will continue to elicit films, novels, poems, religious teachings, and philosophy, all aimed at illuminating this aspect of the human experience. We believe the authors in this volume demonstrate the potential for scientific inquiry to reclaim this important subject. We hope this book highlights how insights onto disordered emotional states can speak to the complexity—and the fragility—of human emotion regulation. We hope that improved understanding of these complex phenomenon will shed light where darkness has existed and, in doing so, enable the development of better techniques to relieve human misery.

REFERENCES

American Psychiatric Association. (2000). *Diagnostic and statistical manual of mental disorders* (4th ed., text revision). Washington, DC: American Psychiatric Association.

Davidson, R. J., Scherer, K. R., & Goldsmith, H. H. (Eds.). (2003). *Handbook of affective sciences*. Oxford, England: Oxford University Press.

Elliott, R., Greenberg, L. S., & Lietaer, G. (2003). Research on experiential psychotherapies. In M. J. Lambert (Ed.), *Bergin and Garfield's handbook of psychotherapy and behavior change* (5th ed., pp. 493–540). New York: Wiley.

Elliott, R., Watson, J. C., Goldman, R. N., & Greenberg, L. S. (2004). *Learning emotion-focused therapy: The process-experiential approach to change*. Washington, DC: American Psychological Association.

Hayes, S. C., & Strosahl, K. D. (2005). *A practical guide to acceptance and commitment therapy*. New York: Springer Science & Business Media.

Lane, R. D., & Nadel, L. (Eds.). (2000). *Cognitive neuroscience of emotion*. New York: Oxford University Press.

Linehan, M. M. (1993). *Cognitive–behavioral treatment of borderline personality disorder*. New York: Guilford Press.

Panksepp, J. (1998). *Affective neuroscience: The foundations of human and animal emotions* (Series in affective science). New York: Oxford University Press.

I

ADVANCES IN BASIC
AFFECTIVE SCIENCE

1

AFFECT ASSESSMENT THROUGH SELF-REPORT METHODS

JOHN HUMRICHOUSE, MICHAEL CHMIELEWSKI,
ELIZABETH A. McDADE-MONTEZ, AND DAVID WATSON

Affect emerged as a central concept in psychology during the 1980s, and affective science has flourished ever since. To document this explosion of interest, we conducted a search of the PsycINFO database using the keywords *affect, emotion, emotions, emotional states,* and *mood.* This search generated 7,083 hits during the 5-year period from 1980 to 1984. Since 1984, the number has increased dramatically, rising to 11,374 (1985–1989), 16,478 (1990–1994), 24,602 (1995–1999), and finally to 33,828 during the most recent 5-year period (2000–2004).

The explosion of scientific interest has created an acute need for reliable and valid measures of affect. In this chapter, we provide a brief introduction to the self-report assessment of affect. The chapter is organized into three main sections. First, we define and distinguish among affective terms and address the basic underlying structure of affect. Second, we review and evaluate existing self-report measures of affect. Third, we discuss basic considerations in affect measurement (e.g., construct validity, reliability, and sources of measurement error) and make general recommendations about assessing affect through self-report methods.

Before one can assess affect intelligently, it is important to define several constructs that are relevant to this area of investigation (i.e., affect, emotions, and moods). *Affect* is a broad overarching construct, encompassing both emotions and moods. It is what one is experiencing or feeling, either pleasant or unpleasant, with varying levels of intensity, duration, and triggers or patterns of activation (Gray & Watson, in press). Watson (2000) argued that one's waking experience invariably is spent in some affective state and referred to this continuous affective experience as a "stream of affect [that] typically is experienced as mildly to moderately pleasant" (p. 15).

Within the domain of affect, *emotions* have been defined as biobehavioral systems comprising at least four core components: (a) a subjective experience, (b) a physiological reaction, (c) an expressive component (e.g., a facial expression), and (d) a behavioral response (Watson & Vaidya, 2003). For example, the emotion of fear comprises the subjective experience of apprehension, the physiological reaction of increased heart rate and general sympathetic activation, the facial expression of raised eyebrows and wide-open eyes, and the behavioral response of either freezing or fleeing. These components occur as part of an intense, coordinated response that lasts for a very brief period of time, usually for only a matter of seconds or minutes. Affective experiences comprising these four components have been conceptualized as basic emotions. Although there is no consensual taxonomy of basic emotions, most models include anger, disgust, fear, sadness, interest, joy, and surprise (Watson, 2000).

Moods are similar to the subjective components of emotions—they represent the subjective aspects of one's experience. Moods have an evaluative quality of being either positive or negative and can vary in relative intensity and duration. However, many mood states do not reflect basic emotional responses because they do not clearly exhibit all four components mentioned earlier (Watson, 2000; Watson & Vaidya, 2003). For example, the classic emotion of anger involves dramatic manifestations of all four components; in contrast, the experience of an irritable mood need not implicate the other three components (e.g., the face may not exhibit a prototypic anger expression). Additionally, the concept of mood includes an array of low-intensity states (e.g., calm, quiet, sleepy) and mixed states (e.g., nostalgia) that are not traditionally considered to represent emotions. Therefore, moods encompass a broader range of subjective states than classically defined emotions.

Whereas emotions are brief and intense, moods can be less dramatic and can last much longer. Considering that emotions are generally of greater relative intensity than moods, there are adaptive advantages (e.g., conservation of energy and bodily resources) to experiencing these states relatively infrequently (see Watson, 2000). Indeed, experiencing prolonged, intense emotional states may be maladaptive and indicative of psychopathology (Clark & Watson, 1994). For example, panic disorder is characterized by an intense negative emotional episode that essentially represents a prolonged (and situationally inappropriate) fear response.

On the basis of an analysis of thousands of momentary observations, Watson (2000) estimated that as little as 17% of our waking time may be spent experiencing intense affective states reflecting classical emotions. Therefore, moods comprise a much larger part of the continuous "stream of affect." Additional analyses have indicated that people show consistent and stable individual differences in their tendency to have both positive and negative mood states. These findings have led researchers to distinguish between *state affect* (i.e., current short-term fluctuations in mood) and *trait affect* (i.e., stable individual differences in the tendency to experience different types of mood; see Watson, 2000; Watson, Clark, & Tellegen, 1988).

Another distinction between emotions and moods lies in the activation or triggers of these affective states. Generally, emotions have an identifiable trigger or event that activates the coordinated response. On the other hand, moods often seem to arise without a clear trigger or reference point and later dissipate without a clear intervention or change in the environment. Thus, for instance, a person may experience a low, dysphoric mood without knowing why. One reason for this is that moods are strongly influenced by a variety of endogenous processes, such as circadian rhythms (see Watson, 2000, chap. 4; Watson, Wiese, Vaidya, & Tellegen, 1999). Likewise, psychopathology may involve strong affective responses without clear precipitants, as is seen in *generalized anxiety disorder*, which is defined by "prolonged, moderately intense anxiety in the absence of an overt stressor" (Clark & Watson, 1994, p. 135).

Researchers should consider how these key distinctions between mood and emotions (i.e., intensity, duration, and breadth of activation) may be relevant to particular investigations of affect and psychopathology. On the basis of the considerations we have discussed, most self-report measures of affect—regardless of their names or intended target constructs—are better viewed as assessing moods rather than emotions, because they invariably assess responses ranging widely in intensity and duration, even when administered in clinical samples. We emphasize, however, that emotions and moods are not mutually exclusive and that both may be influenced by similar processes and share some common components (Clark & Watson, 1999), an insight captured nicely by Davidson (1994): "It also appears to be the case that moods and emotions dynamically interact in important ways. Emotions can lead to particular moods and moods can alter the probability that particular emotions will be triggered" (p. 53).

THE STRUCTURE OF AFFECT

To optimally define and assess affective experiences, it is necessary to understand the underlying structure of affect. Historically, there have been two basic approaches to assessing the structure of affect: (a) discrete or specific affect models and (b) dimensional schemes. First, we briefly discuss discrete affect models and review issues associated with them. Next, we discuss the basic characteristics of dimensional models, focusing on two particularly popular schemes. Third, we describe an integrated three-level hierarchical model that neatly integrates all of these other schemes (Tellegen, Watson, & Clark, 1999).

Specific or Discrete Affect Models

Specific or discrete affect models posit the existence of specific types of affect and generally focus on emotions such as happiness, fear, anxiety, sadness, and anger (Gray & Watson, in press; Watson & Vaidya, 2003). This approach has been supported by a wide array of empirical evidence. Most notably, structural analyses of mood terms repeatedly have identified well-defined content factors corresponding to these specific affect states. Moreover, a common core of discrete affects—including fear, sadness, and anger—have emerged consistently in analyses based on widely varying item pools and diverse samples of respondents (Watson & Clark, 1997, 1999; Watson & Vaidya, 2003).

Having said that, however, we also must discuss two key problems associated with this approach. First, although a few core states are universally recognized, we still lack a compelling taxonomy of affect at the discrete, lower order level. That is, even after more than 50 years of study, affect researchers have not reached a consensus regarding the basic discrete states that must be included in any complete and comprehensive assessment of affect (see Watson & Clark, 1997; Watson & Vaidya, 2003). Second, structural analyses have established that measures created to assess specific affects typically show only limited discriminant validity (Watson & Clark, 1997). That is, measures of similarly valenced affects tend to be strongly intercorrelated, establishing a substantial level of nonspecificity in the data. For example, people who report feeling anxious also report feeling sad, angry, and guilty. In fact, multitrait–multimethod analyses consistently demonstrate much stronger evidence for nonspecificity (i.e., significant positive correlations among measures of different, similarly valenced affects) than for specificity (i.e., unique relations between different measures of the same target affect; Diener, Smith, & Fujita, 1995; Watson, 2000; Watson & Clark, 1992).

Dimensional Models of Affect

This evidence of strong nonspecificity indicates that mood can be characterized by a smaller number of general dimensions, thereby stimulating the development of dimensional models. Although three-dimensional schemes also have been proposed (see Watson & Tellegen, 1985), most attention has

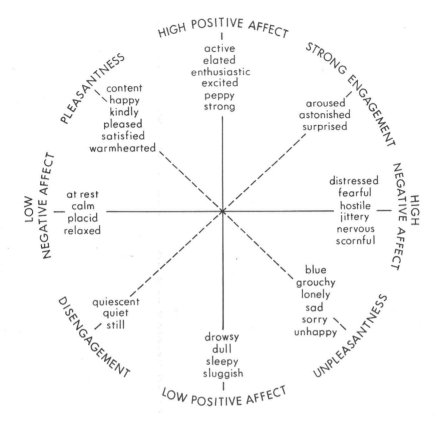

Figure 1.1. The two-factor structure of affect. From "Toward a Consensual Structure of Mood," by D. Watson and A. Tellegen, 1985, *Psychological Bulletin, 98,* p. 221. Copyright 1985 by the American Psychological Association.

been given to two-dimensional structures. On the basis of analyses of facial expressions and similarity ratings of mood terms, Russell (1980) proposed a two-factor dimensional model of affect that can be visually represented as a circumplex (i.e., mood terms mapped onto the perimeter of a circle within a two-dimensional space). In Russell's model, the circumplex is defined by two strongly bipolar dimensions: Pleasure–Displeasure and Arousal–Sleep. This model particularly emphasizes the bipolarity of the Pleasure–Displeasure dimension; that is, pleasant (e.g., happy, cheerful) and unpleasant (e.g., sad, lonely) affect are viewed as opposite ends of a single continuum. This model therefore suggests that one cannot simultaneously experience negative and positive affects and that the ends of the continuum should be highly negatively correlated.

On the basis of self-report data from several studies, Watson and Tellegen (1985) created a similar circumplex structure that is a rotational variant of Russell's model. Specifically, both schemes can be mapped onto a common circumplex structure with approximately a 45-degree rotation separating the two sets of reference axes (see Figure 1.1). Watson and Tellegen's model emphasized two factors—Positive Affect (PA; also labeled *Positive Activation*) and Negative Affect (NA; also called *Negative Activation*)—that are largely unipolar and independent of one another. PA comprises mood terms such as *active*, *excited*, *energetic*, and *strong*, whereas NA is defined by terms such as *distressed*, *guilty*, *hostile*, and *nervous*. This model, with the largely independent factors of PA and NA, allows for the simultaneous experience of positive affect states and negative affect states; thus, according to this scheme, a person can feel both nervous and enthusiastic at the same time.

Watson and Tellegen's (1985) model addresses the issues of discriminant validity and specificity by positing that (a) similarly valenced mood states (e.g., sad and fearful) will be substantially correlated, whereas (b) oppositely valenced mood states (e.g., fearful and energetic) will be only weakly related; it is the latter property that is largely responsible for the quasi-independence of the NA and PA dimensions. It should be noted, however, that the independence of PA and NA mainly applies to low-intensity states (Watson, 1988; Watson et al., 1999). When experiencing an extremely intense, negative emotional state (e.g., terror), it is highly unlikely that one would simultaneously be experiencing an intense, positive emotional state (e.g., elation). However, mood states are generally less intense and tend to last for greater lengths of time, thereby allowing for the simultaneous experience of positive and negative feelings.

The key distinction between the Russell and the Watson and Tellegen schemes appears to be in their conceptualization of positive and negative affect as either largely independent (Watson & Tellegen) or as opposite ends of a single bipolar continuum (Russell). This has led to some confusion in the recent literature. It must be emphasized, however, that bipolarity and independence actually are key features of both models. In fact, a close inspection of Figure 1 indicates that some positive and negative descriptors are placed 180 degrees apart and should be strongly negatively correlated (e.g., happy vs. sad), whereas others are only 90 degrees apart and should be very weakly related to one another (e.g., enthusiastic vs. fearful). Thus, the circumplex model actually hypothesizes both independence and bipolarity, depending on the descriptors involved; it should be noted, moreover, that these hypothesized relations have been consistently confirmed empirically (see Tellegen et al., 1999; Watson, 1988; Watson & Tellegen, 1999).

Furthermore, a diverse array of research has subsequently demonstrated the empirical and heuristic value of this proposed independence between positive and negative affect. Research on hemispheric asymmetry in the prefrontal cortex (Tomarken & Keener, 1998) has linked two key biobehavioral systems—the behavioral activation system (BAS) and the behavioral inhibition system (BIS)—to PA and NA, respectively. PA essentially can be viewed as the affective component of the BAS, which exists in synchrony with its other components (e.g., cognitive, biological, and behavioral) to motivate the organism to seek out pleasure or rewards. Conversely, NA, the affective component of the BIS, exists in synchrony with its other components to motivate the organism to avoid aversive stimuli or punishment (see Watson, 2000; Watson et al., 1999). In clinical research, the existence of these independent PA and NA dimensions has helped to elucidate the comorbidity of anxiety and depression (Watson, Clark, & Carey, 1988): Although both types of disorders are characterized by high negative affect, they show differential relations with positive affect (i.e., low positive affect is more prominent in depression than in anxiety).

Integrated Hierarchical Model

Thus far, we have treated discrete affect and dimensional models separately. Although these two approaches often are seen as antagonistic and incompatible, they actually can be integrated into a three-level hierarchical structure that incorporates key features from all of the models we have discussed (Tellegen et al., 1999). At its lowest or first-order level, this model includes nine specific affect dimensions (i.e., calm–ease, joy, interest, surprise, fear, anger–disgust–contempt, shame–guilt, sadness–distress, and low energy). The second-order level of this model consists of the relatively independent dimensions of PA and NA. Finally, at the highest or third-order level of this model is a bipolar happiness–unhappiness dimension that accounts for the bipolarity between pleasant and unpleasant affect.

One important implication of this hierarchical structure is that any complete examination of affect must model and assess it at both the discrete affect and dimensional levels; otherwise significant information likely will be lost. The relative importance of these levels will differ, however, according to the nature and goals of the research. For instance, the overarching Happiness dimension may be most relevant to the study of life satisfaction (Tellegen et al., 1999), whereas the second-level NA and PA dimensions may be more useful for many areas of personality and psychopathology research. Finally, a focus on at the lowest, discrete-affect level may be particularly informative in certain circumstances (e.g., in the study of self-esteem; see Watson, Suls, & Haig, 2002).

Affective Structure Across Samples

The bulk of the structural evidence we have reviewed is based on college student responses. This raises questions about the robustness of this structure across samples. In particular, psychopathology researchers may question whether these results will generalize to clinical samples. Accordingly, we present data to establish that the basic structure of affect is highly robust across samples. Table 1.1 shows correlations among four content-valid affect scales in four large samples: college students, psychiatric patients, community-dwelling adults, and high school students. The scales assess sad, depressed

TABLE 1.1
Correlations Between Mood Scales Created From the
Iowa Depression and Anxiety Scales Item Pool

Scale	1	2	3	4
College students (N = 673)				
1. Depression	(.88)			
2. Anxiety	.76	(.91)		
3. Anger	.72	.71	(.93)	
4. Well-Being	−.47	−.38	−.32	(.84)
Psychiatric patients (N = 353)				
1. Depression	(.91)			
2. Anxiety	.77	(.93)		
3. Anger	.55	.57	(.94)	
4. Well-Being	−.49	−.38	−.20	(.88)
Community adults (N = 362)				
1. Depression	(.92)			
2. Anxiety	.78	(.93)		
3. Anger	.69	.74	(.94)	
4. Well-Being	−.54	−.43	−.39	(.90)
High school students (N = 247)				
1. Depression	(.90)			
2. Anxiety	.78	(.90)		
3. Anger	.73	.72	(.94)	
4. Well-Being	−.52	−.40	−.37	(.86)

Note. Internal consistency reliabilities (coefficient alphas) are shown in parentheses. All correlations are significant at $p < .01$, two-tailed.

mood (Depression, 5 items; e.g., "I felt depressed"); anxious, fearful mood (Anxiety, 9 items; e.g., "I felt anxious"); angry, irritable mood (Anger, 11 items; e.g., "I felt irritable"); and pleasant, positive mood (Well-Being, 8 items; e.g., "I felt hopeful about the future"). All respondents rated the extent to which they experienced each item "during the past two weeks, including today" on a 5-point scale ranging from *not at all* to *extremely*.

Several aspects of these data are noteworthy. First, the overall pattern is highly consistent across the four samples, indicating that the structural evidence we have reviewed should generalize well to clinical populations. Second, the correlations among the Depression, Anxiety, and Anger scales consistently are high, demonstrating the strong influence of the general NA dimension. Third, the correlations among the Depression and Anxiety scales are particularly high, which has potentially important implications for our understanding of psychopathology. Most notably, they establish a strong link between sad–depressed mood (a core, defining element of the mood disorders) and fearful–anxious mood (a key feature of the anxiety disorders). On the basis of this and other evidence, Watson (2005) has suggested that the current distinction between the mood and anxiety disorders is not particularly useful and that it should be replaced by an empirically based taxonomy that reflects the actual similarities among disorders. Finally, the Well-Being scale consistently has significantly stronger negative correlations with Depression than with either Anxiety or Anger; this again establishes that (low) PA is more strongly linked to depression than to other types of negative affect.

SELF-REPORT MEASURES OF AFFECT

Because of the large number of self-report affect measures that currently are available, our review necessarily must be selective. We focus on those measures that are the most important, the most recent, or the most widely used; that have demonstrated expected patterns of correlations with psychopathology symptoms; and/or that show the best psychometric properties (see Table 1.2 for a summary of the reviewed measures). For a more detailed review of self-report measures, see Watson and Vaidya (2003) and Gray and Watson (in press).

Specific or Discrete Affect Measures

The Mood Adjective Check List (MACL; Nowlis, 1965) assesses 12 factor-analytically derived affects (e.g., Fatigue, Aggression, Surgency, Anxiety, Elation, Concentration, Social Affection, Sadness, Skepticism, Egotism, Vigor, and Nonchalance) using adjectives that are rated on a 4-point scale. The MACL was designed to assess current mood as well as to detect changes in mood. Although it had a highly influential role in the early literature on the structure and assessment of affect, the MACL failed to become a standard measure in the field, in part because its basic psychometric properties were never clearly established (see Watson & Vaidya, 2003).

The Profile of Mood States (POMS; McNair, Lorr, & Droppleman, 1971) consists of 65 adjectives that are rated on a 4- or 5-point scale. It assesses six specific affects: anger–hostility, vigor–activity, fatigue–inertia, confusion–bewilderment, tension–anxiety, and depression–dejection. The scale was originally created to assess mood fluctuations in psychiatric patients and has since been validated in other settings (Lane & Lane, 2002). Multiple short forms assessing fewer factors were subsequently created as well (e.g., Curran, Andrykowski, & Studts, 1995; Shacham, 1983). Evidence indicates that the POMS scales (a) demonstrate acceptable internal consistency reliabilities and moderate short-term stability, (b) are sensitive to changes due to therapy, and (c) show good concurrent and predictive valid-

TABLE 1.2
Self-Report Measures of Affect

Measure	State or trait	Reliability	Subscales
			Discrete measures
MACL	State	N/A	Fatigue, Aggression, Surgency, Anxiety, Elation, Concentration, Social Affection, Sadness, Skepticism, Egotism, Vigor, Nonchalance
POMS	Both	Moderate	Anger–Hostility, Vigor–Activity, Fatigue–Inertia, Confusion–Bewilderment, Tension–Anxiety, Depression–Dejection
DES	Both	Fair	Interest, Joy, Surprise, Sadness, Anger, Disgust, Contempt, Fear, Shame/Shyness, Guilt/Anxiety, Depression, Hostility, Positive Affect, Sensation Seeking
MAACL–R	Both	Good	
PANAS–X	Both	Good	Fear, Sadness, Guilt, Hostility, Joviality, Self-Assurance, Attentiveness, Shyness, Fatigue, Serenity, Surprise
			Dimensional measures
AD-ACL	State	Good	General Activation, Deactivation-Sleep, High Activation, General Deactivation
Affect Grid	State	N/A	Pleasure–Displeasure, Arousal–Sleep
CMQ	State	Fair–moderate	Pleasure–Displeasure, Arousal–Sleep
PANAS	Both	Good	Positive Affect, Negative Affect
UMACL	State	Good	Tense Arousal, Energetic Arousal, Hedonic Tone

Note. Reliability is internal consistency reliability. The rating scale is Poor, Fair, Moderate, or Good. MACL = Mood Adjective Check List; POMS = Profile of Mood States; DES = Differential Emotions Scale; MAACL–R = Multiple Affect Adjective Check List—Revised; PANAS–X = Positive and Negative Affect Schedule—Expanded Form; AD-ACL = Activation–Deactivation Adjective Check List; CMQ = Current Mood Questionnaire; PANAS = Positive and Negative Affect Schedule; UMACL = UWIST Mood Adjective Checklist.

ity (Lane & Lane, 2002; McNair & Lorr, 1964; Payne, 2001). However, the negative mood scales of the POMS are strongly intercorrelated and fail to demonstrate strong discriminant validity with one another (Watson & Clark, 1999).

The Differential Emotions Scale (DES; Izard, Libero, Putnam, & Haynes, 1993) originally was designed to measure 10 discrete emotions: interest, joy, surprise, sadness, anger, disgust, contempt, fear, shame/shyness and guilt. There are multiple versions of the DES using different response formats and instructions; depending on the instructions used, the DES can be modified to assess current, past week, or long-term affect. In its most recent version, the Differential Emotions Scale—IV, shyness and shame are measured separately and a new subscale, Inner-Directed Hostility, has been added, creating a total of 12 subscales (Izard et al., 1993). Although the subscales are stable over time, many of them show moderate to high intercorrelations and only low to moderate internal consistencies (see Watson & Vaidya, 2003), which is largely due to the low number of items per scale (typically only three apiece across the various versions of the instrument).

The Multiple Affect Adjective Check List—Revised (MAACL–R; Zuckerman & Lubin, 1985) assesses both state and trait affect. It contains five scales: Anxiety, Depression, Hostility, Positive Affect, and Sensation Seeking. The original MAACL (Zuckerman & Lubin, 1965) was revised in 1985 because of widespread evidence of poor discriminant validity among its Anxiety, Depression, and Hostility scales (despite these concerns, however, the original MAACL continues to be used and actually has been cited hundreds of times since the publication of the MAACL–R). The MAACL–R has many strong psychometric properties, including generally good coefficient alphas and test–retest reliability. Unfortunately, the negative affective scales continue to demonstrate high intercorrelations and questionable discriminant validity (Watson & Vaidya, 2003). Finally, it should be noted that one of the original authors has developed a short-form version of the MAACL–R (Lubin, Whitlock, Reddy, & Petren, 2001).

The Positive and Negative Affect Schedule—Expanded Form (PANAS–X; Watson & Clark, 1999) is a factor-analytically derived measure that assesses 11 specific affects; this includes four negative mood states (Fear, Sadness, Guilt, and Hostility), three positive mood states (Joviality, Self-Assurance, and Attentiveness), and four scales that are less consistently related to the higher order NA and PA dimensions (Shyness, Fatigue, Serenity, and Surprise). The PANAS–X contains mood terms rated on a 5-point scale ranging from *not at all* to *extremely*; instructions can be varied to assess either state or trait affect. Extensive reliability and validity data from multiple samples have been reported on the PANAS–X (Watson & Clark, 1997, 1999). The longer scales are highly reliable (e.g., coefficient alphas .83 or higher), and its shorter scales still consistently demonstrate adequate reliabilities (e.g., above .76).

Dimensional Affect Measures

The Activation–Deactivation Adjective Check List (AD-ACL; Thayer, 1967) is one of the earliest dimensional measures of affect. The AD-ACL was developed out of research using the MACL (Nowlis, 1965). The AD-ACL contains a series of affect adjectives that are rated on a 4-point scale. It consists of four factor-analytically derived factors: General Activation (Energy), Deactivation–Sleep, High Activation, and General Deactivation (Calmness). Further analyses have shown two higher order activation dimensions—Energy versus Tiredness and Tension versus Inactivation (Thayer, 1967, 1978)—that are broadly similar to PA and NA, respectively (Yik, Russell, & Feldman Barrett, 1999). The AD-ACL demonstrates excellent test–retest reliability and validity and can be administered in approximately 2 minutes (Thayer, 1978).

The Affect Grid (Russell, Weiss, & Mendelsohn, 1989) represents affect in the two-dimensional space representing Russell's version of the circumplex. The 9 × 9 grid contains affect descriptors in each corner and at each midpoint along the sides (i.e., in each cell). Respondents are asked to place a check in the cell that best captures their current affect. The descriptors, moving clockwise from the top left corner of the grid, include *stress, high arousal, excitement, pleasant feelings, relaxation, sleepiness, depression,* and *unpleasant feelings.* Thus, the two major dimensions of Pleasure–Displeasure and Arousal–Sleep are represented as bipolar opposites (see Russell, Weiss, & Mendelsohn, 1989, Figure 1, p. 494). The Affect Grid has demonstrated acceptable interrater reliability and good convergent validity with other dimensional measures of affect, and it is particularly well suited for quick and frequent assessment (Russell et al., 1989). However, one encounters obvious difficulties in assessing internal consistency reliability with single item measures; moreover, such instruments are likely more affected by systematic or random error than other types of affect scales.

The Current Mood Questionnaire (CMQ; Feldman Barrett & Russell, 1998) assesses all eight octants of Russell's circumplex using multiple response formats for each dimension; the inclusion of multiple measures for each construct allows researchers to use structural equation modeling to correct for both random and systematic error (Feldman Barrett & Russell, 1998). The CMQ was developed to test key aspects of Russell's model, particularly the assertion that the dimensions of pleasure versus displeasure and arousal versus sleep are fully bipolar. The CMQ scales demonstrate good convergent and discriminant validity, and the Pleasure–Displeasure scale consistently demonstrates acceptable internal consistency reliability (Feldman Barrett & Russell, 1998; Watson & Vaidya, 2003). However, the Arousal–Sleep dimension shows less acceptable internal consistency, and the scales defining this factor do not appear to be fully bipolar (Watson & Vaidya, 2003). In addition, the use of multiple response formats makes the CMQ longer to complete and more cumbersome than the other dimensional measures included in this review; this, in turn, makes it less attractive for use in many contexts. Recent CMQ citations are low in number relative to other dimensional measures of affect.

The Positive and Negative Affect Schedule (PANAS; Watson et al., 1988)—which later was subsumed into the PANAS–X (see Watson & Clark, 1997, 1999)—is a brief measure of the two major dimensions in the Watson and Tellegen model and can be used to assess either state or trait affects with a slight modification in instructions. The PANAS was factor-analytically derived from Zevon and Tellegen's (1982) set of 60 adjectives. PA and NA are each assessed with 10 adjectives, which participants rate on a 5-point scale. The scales show excellent internal consistency and convergent and discriminant validity.

The UWIST Mood Adjective Checklist (UMACL; Matthews, Jones, & Chamberlain, 1990) was designed to synthesize the competing structural models proposed by Watson and Tellegen (1985), Russell (1980), and Thayer (1986). The UMACL includes adjectives rated on a 4-point response scale that tap the affective dimensions of tense arousal, energetic arousal (reflecting constructs from both the Thayer and Watson and Tellegen models), and hedonic tone (i.e., Russell's pleasure–displeasure dimension). In addition, the adjectives can also be scored to yield a General Arousal Index, corresponding to Russell's arousal–sleep dimension. Most of the UMACL scales show excellent internal consistency and convergent and discriminant validity, although the arousal scales correlate moderately with hedonic tone.

BASIC CONSIDERATIONS IN AFFECT MEASUREMENT

In many ways, the basic considerations involved in assessing affect are the same as those involved in measuring any psychological construct. Any construct must be assessed in a way that is both valid and reliable. However, because of the internal and subjective nature of affect, measurement in this area also faces some unique assessment issues. For example, to provide valid assessments, participants must be able to both (a) synthesize information regarding their affective experiences and then (b) accurately report that information. In the following section, we outline the evidence supporting the validity and reliability of affect measurement and report on some factors that contribute to measurement error.

CONSTRUCT VALIDITY OF TRAIT AFFECT MEASURES

Self–Other Agreement of Trait Affect

Personality researchers have long used self–other agreement, that is, the convergence between a self-rating and a peer rating of the same target (e.g., Person A's self-rating vs. Person B's ratings of Person A), as evidence for the validity of personality measures. Until recently, few studies have examined self–other agreement in trait affect. This neglect can be attributed to the *trait visibility effect* (i.e., highly observable traits will yield better self–other agreement than more internalized traits; see Watson et al., 2000). Affective experiences are highly internal and subjective, and thus researchers anticipated finding relatively poor convergence because of this effect. However, recent studies consistently have found significant correlations between self- and other-ratings of trait affect (Diener et al., 1995; Watson, Hubbard, & Wiese, 2000). Watson and Vaidya (2003) reported PANAS–X data from four samples: 279 friendship dyads, 68 dating couples, 136 dating couples, and 74 married couples. The PANAS–X scales (with the single exception of Surprise) consistently showed significant, moderate levels of convergent validity (weighted mean correlations across the samples ranged from .25 to .42.) Furthermore, there was clear evidence of the *acquaintanceship effect*, that is, the tendency for individuals who know each other well to generate higher self–other agreement correlations; thus, higher convergent correlations were found in the married couples than in the dating samples, whereas the dating couples tended to produce higher correlations than the friendship dyads. These results help to establish the construct validity of trait measures of affect.

Although these correlations are encouraging, it is interesting to note that they tend to be lower than those of standard personality measures. For instance, scales assessing the Big Five personality traits had agreement correlations ranging from .42 to .53 in three of these same samples (see Watson et al., 2000). Even though affective experiences are less "visible" than most personality traits, the trait visibility effect cannot fully explain the differences in self–other agreement found between neuroticism and trait negative affect. These two constructs are highly correlated; the mean correlation between neuroticism and the PANAS–X Negative Affect scale was .60 (self-ratings) and .69 (other-ratings) in the three samples reported in Watson et al. (2000). Nevertheless, the neuroticism scales produced higher self–other agreement correlations in all three groups (.37–.59) than did PANAS–X Negative Affect (.20–.44). This cannot be attributed to differences in the internal consistency of the scales (Watson et al., 2000; Watson & Vaidya, 2003) and becomes even more intriguing when one considers their content. For instance, the Neuroticism scale of the Big Five Inventory (BFI; John & Srivastava, 1999) is strongly affective in character (Pytlik Zillig, Hemenover, & Dienstbier, 2002); nevertheless, it consistently shows better self–other agreement than the PANAS–X Negative Affect scale.

Temporal Stability of Trait Affect

Temporal stability is a necessary property of any construct that is defined as a trait. Watson (2004) examined both short-term stability (2 months; 465 students) and stability over a much longer time span (approximately 2.5

years; 392 participants). Strong retest correlations were found for the PANAS–X in the short-term stability study; coefficients ranged from .67 to .76, with a mean of .70 for the negative affect scales and .71 for the positive affect scales (Watson, 2004). The data from the long-term study demonstrated that trait affect as measured by the PANAS–X is moderately stable over a 2.5-year period; correlations ranged from .46 to .55, with mean coefficients of .49 (negative affect scales) and .51 (positive affect scales; Watson, 2004). These data enhance the construct validity of trait affect measures by demonstrating that they have a stable dispositional component.

Paralleling the self–other agreement data, however, the temporal stabilities of trait affect measures are lower than those of standard personality scales. For example, in these same two studies, Watson (2004) reported that the short-term BFI retest correlations ranged from .79 to .89 (mean r = .82), whereas the long-term BFI stabilities ranged from .59 to .72 (mean r = .64). Many of these correlations are significantly higher than those of the PANAS–X. This pattern is not entirely unexpected (see Watson, 2004) and, in general, could be explained by systematic differences in content between these scales. However, we again see a puzzling discrepancy between the BFI Neuroticism and PANAS–X Negative Affect scales: Watson (2004) found that BFI Neuroticism was significantly more stable in both the long- and short-term retests than PANAS–X Negative Affect. Given that this discrepancy cannot be attributed to differences in internal consistency reliability or item content, other, more subtle factors must be responsible.

Retrospective Recall of Affective States

We now turn our attention to possible sources of measurement error that potentially could lessen the validity and reliability of self-report affect scales. One potential problem with the measurement of longer term affect (e.g., mood rated over the past week, past month, or in general) is its retrospective nature. Participants have to remember their past experiences and recall their previous affective states, which could lead to several problems. For example, raters could experience *duration neglect*, that is, they could be relatively insensitive to how long a particular affect lasted and instead give more attention to the overall intensity of the experience. They may also be influenced by the *recency effect*, that is, the tendency for individuals to weight recent experiences more heavily than earlier experiences. Furthermore, there is evidence indicating that a person's current, momentary mood at the time of assessment may influence his or her retrospective ratings of past affective experiences (see Stone, Shiffman, & deVries, 1999). Given these problems, several researchers have advocated an alternative method for assessing trait affect. Specifically, they have proposed that a large number of state affect ratings be aggregated into one composite score (i.e., averaging several ratings of current mood assessed across time; see Stone et al., 1999).

In general, this process results in aggregated ratings that display moderate to strong levels of convergence with traditional, global measures of trait affect. Watson and Vaidya (2003) reported convergent correlations ranging from .37 to .60 (Mdn = .51) with aggregated daily ratings and from .45 to .64 (Mdn = .53) with aggregated weekly ratings. Although these correlations demonstrate that the two approaches converge well, the correlations are far from +1.00. This, then, raises an interesting question: Which type of rating is more valid? We already have discussed the potential problems associated with retrospective ratings of longer term affect; it must be emphasized, however, that the aggregation of state ratings produces problems of its own. The most serious problem is the reduced discriminant validity of aggregated measures of specific, lower order affects. Diener et al. (1995) were the first to demonstrate this effect. They collected global ratings of four negative affects (fear, anger, sadness, shame) and corresponding aggregated daily ratings from 212 participants. Although the convergence between the two methods was strong (mean r = .62), there was a striking difference in discriminant validity across the two methods. In the global ratings, correlations among the four negative affect scales ranged from .54 to .61, with a mean value of .58; in marked contrast, the corresponding correlations in the aggregated ratings ranged from .70 to .79, with a mean value of .75. Watson and Tellegen (2002) replicated this finding with the PANAS–X scales and also extended it by demonstrating that the same pattern emerged using positive affect scales.

The most likely explanation for this phenomenon is that systematic measurement errors (e.g., acquiescence) are inflated during the aggregation process; this, in turn, artificially increases the correlations between scales assessing similarly valenced constructs (e.g., fear and sadness; see Watson & Tellegen, 2002; Watson & Vaidya, 2003). This may seem counterintuitive, given that one of the frequently touted advantages of aggregation is that it reduces measurement error. However, this is only true when the errors are random and, therefore, increasingly cancel each other out with repeated assessment. When the errors are instead systematic, they can be correlated across the assessments; therefore, instead of neutralizing systematic error, aggregation will actually increase it in some cases. Furthermore, it appears that this same basic process also is responsible for the almost complete lack of bipolarity in aggregated affect ratings (Watson & Tellegen, 2002). In light of these data, we conclude that although aggregated ratings may be advantageous in some contexts, global trait ratings generally are superior and should be the preferred method (see also Watson & Tellegen, 2002; Watson & Vaidya, 2003).

Unidentified Sources of Error

With a few exceptions, affect researchers have given little attention to the response formats of their measures or to the specific instructions that are given to participants. Recent data strongly suggest that these issues may play an important role in the reliability and validity of affect measures. There is increasing evidence that different information processing systems—such as schematic memory, semantic memory, and autobiographical–episodic memory—may be activated depending on the specific assessment approach taken (Robinson & Clore, 2002). In this regard, Watson (2004) showed that highly correlated measures of obsessive–compulsive disorder symptoms, dissociative tendencies, personality traits, and trait affectivity yielded significantly different levels of stability over a 2-month period. Furthermore, broad differences in item content could not account for the discrepancy in stability between matched pairs of scales. This evidence of differential stability becomes even more important when one considers the short retest interval (i.e., 2 months) between assessments in this study; this makes it unlikely that these effects are due to true changes on these dimensions. It therefore seems likely that this differential stability results from different levels of measurement error across instruments. This, in turn, leads to the intriguing possibility that subtle differences between scales (e.g., instructions, response formats, wording effects) can lead to varying amounts of error variance.

To investigate this idea, Watson (2004) created the Temperament and Emotion Questionnaire (TEQ) by taking PANAS–X items and embedding them in sentences. For example, the PANAS–X item "sad" became "I often feel a bit sad." In addition, the response format was changed to a 5-point agree–disagree scale. This process ensured that the TEQs content was extremely similar to the PANAS–X. Furthermore, strong convergent correlations between corresponding PANAS–X and TEQ scales (mean $r = .70$) demonstrated that these instruments are assessing the same basic affective constructs. Nevertheless, the 2-month stability correlations for the TEQ negative affect scales were higher than those of their PANAS–X counterparts; these differences were statistically significant for the Fear, Sadness, and Hostility scales. These results suggest that, in some cases, measurement error can be reduced simply by embedding standard affect descriptors in sentences; however, the BFI Neuroticism scale still was significantly more stable than the TEQ Negative Affect scale. Therefore, other subtle differences also contribute to the increased error variance in standard measures of trait affect. We are currently investigating these differences in new studies of temporal stability and self–other agreement.

The Influence of Social Desirability

Because self-report affect measures almost invariably contain face-valid items whose content is not hidden, it is possible that participants could respond in a manner that is not entirely accurate. For example, participants may respond defensively and distort their answers (either consciously or unconsciously) in a self-enhancing manner. One way to investigate the extent to which social desirability is a problem in affect measurement is by obtaining other-ratings from judges who know the target individual well. Because others should not be as inclined to rate targets in a socially desirable manner, comparisons of other-ratings with the targets' own self-ratings help to determine the extent to which social desirability introduces error into mood measurement. Thus, if social desirability were a significant problem, then self-ratings would be expected to yield lower levels of negative affect and higher levels of positive affect (e.g., responses in the socially desirable direction) than other-ratings. To investigate this issue, Watson and Vaidya (2003) analyzed self- and other-ratings of the trait version of the PANAS–X from friendship, dating, and married dyads. Comparisons of the self- and other-ratings indicated that social desirability does not play a substantial role in self-ratings of affect.

Reducing Error and Improving Measurement

Given the findings we have examined, we believe it is essential that affect researchers pay careful attention to measurement-related issues. We especially encourage studies that allow for side-by-side comparisons of scales that tap the same (or very similar) constructs. Comparing the reliabilities and validities of similar scales in the same sample enables researchers to identify the measures that best suit their needs. Furthermore, such comparisons enhance our understanding of the issues that influence validity and reliability. Too often, researchers view stability and validity as dichotomous, "either–or" properties; they are eager to conclude that their instruments are adequate or satisfactory without giving these issues much real thought (see Watson, 2004). A more nuanced dimensional approach in which researchers investigate how specific factors influence validity, reliability, and error would lead to the creation of more valid and reliable assessment instruments.

CONCLUSION

We conclude this brief introduction to the assessment of self-rated affect by emphasizing several basic points. First, affect assessment should be guided by a thorough understanding of the underlying structure of this domain. As we have discussed, any complete and comprehensive assessment should acknowledge the hierarchical structure of this domain and, accordingly, should include measures of both general dimensions and specific, discrete affects. Second, researchers can choose between instruments that show very different psychometric properties. We therefore urge investigators to examine these properties carefully—including internal consistency, test–retest reliability, and convergent and discriminant validity—before selecting instruments for their research. Third, we now have extensive evidence establishing the reliability and construct validity of commonly used self-report measures. As we have discussed, however, measures of longer term affect, including both global and aggregated ratings, are subject to a variety of forces that may lessen their reliability and validity. Further research is needed to identify specific sources of measurement error that, if minimized, will enable researchers to create a new generation of even better self-report affect measures.

REFERENCES

Clark, L. A., & Watson, D. (1994). Distinguishing functional from dysfunctional affective responses. In P. Ekman & R. J. Davidson (Eds.), *The nature of emotion: Fundamental questions* (pp. 131–136). New York: Oxford University Press.

Clark, L. A., & Watson, D. (1999). Temperament: A new paradigm for trait psychology. In L. Pervin & O. John (Eds.), *Handbook of personality: Theory and research* (2nd ed., pp. 399–423). New York: Guilford Press.

Curran, S. L., Andrykowski, M. A., & Studts, J. L. (1995). Short form of the Profile of Mood States (POMS–SF): Psychometric information. *Psychological Assessment, 7,* 80–83.

Davidson, R. J. (1994). On emotion, mood and related affective constructs. In P. Ekman & R. J. Davidson (Eds.), *The nature of emotion: Fundamental questions* (pp. 51–55). New York: Oxford University Press.

Diener, E., Smith, H., & Fujita, F. (1995). The personality structure of affect. *Journal of Personality and Social Psychology, 69,* 130–141.

Feldman Barrett, L., & Russell, J. A. (1998). Independence and bipolarity in the structure of current affect. *Journal of Personality and Social Psychology, 74,* 967–984.

Gray, E. K., & Watson, D. (in press). Assessing positive and negative affect via self report. In J. J. B. Allen & J. A. Coan (Eds.), *The handbook of emotion elicitation and assessment.* New York: Oxford University Press.

Izard, C. E., Libero, D. Z., Putnam, P., & Haynes, O. M. (1993). Stability of emotion expression experiences and their relations to traits of personality. *Journal of Social and Personality Psychology, 64,* 847–860.

John, O. P., & Srivastava, S. (1999). The Big Five trait taxonomy: History, measurement, and theoretical perspectives. In L. A Pervin & O. P. John (Eds.), *Handbook of personality* (2nd ed., pp. 102–138). New York: Guilford Press.

Lane, A. M., & Lane, H. J. (2002). Predictive effectiveness of mood measures. *Perceptual and Motor Skills, 94,* 785–791.

Lubin, B., Whitlock, R. V., Reddy, B., & Petren, S. (2001). A comparison of the short and long forms of the Multiple Affect Adjective Check List—Revised (MAACL–R). *Journal of Clinical Psychology, 57,* 411–416.

Matthews, G., Jones, D. M., & Chamberlain, A. G. (1990). Refining the measurement of mood: The UWIST Mood Adjective Checklist. *British Journal of Psychology, 81,* 17–42.

McNair, D. M., & Lorr, M. (1964). An analysis of mood in neurotics. *Journal of Abnormal and Social Psychology, 69,* 620–627.

McNair, D. M., Lorr, M., & Droppleman, L. F. (1971). *Manual: Profile of Mood States.* San Diego, CA: Educational and Industrial Testing Service.

Nowlis, V. (1965). Research with the Mood Adjective Check List. In S. S. Tompkins & C. E. Izard (Eds.), *Affect, cognition, and personality: Empirical studies* (pp. 352–389). New York: Springer Publishing Company.

Payne, R. (2001). Measuring emotions at work. In R. L. Payne & C. L. Cooper (Eds.), *Emotions at work: Theory, research and applications in management* (pp. 107–129). West Sussex, England: Wiley.

Pytlik Zillig, L. M., Hemenover, S. H., & Dienstbier, R. A. (2002). What do we assess when we assess a Big 5 trait? A content analysis of the affective, behavior, and cognitive processes represented in Big 5 personality inventories. *Personality and Social Psychology Bulletin, 28,* 847–858.

Robinson, M. D., & Clore, G. L. (2002). Belief and feeling: Evidence for an accessibility model of emotional self-report. *Psychological Bulletin, 128,* 934–960.

Russell, J. A. (1980). A circumplex model of affect. *Journal of Personality and Social Psychology, 39,* 1161–1178.

Russell, J. A., Weiss, A., & Mendelsohn, G. A. (1989). Affect Grid: A single-item scale of pleasure and arousal. *Journal of Personality and Social Psychology, 57,* 493–502.

Shacham, S. (1983). A shortened version of the Profile of Mood States. *Journal of Personality Assessment, 47,* 305–306.

Stone, A. A., Shiffman, S. S., & deVries, M. W. (1999). Ecological momentary assessment. In D. Kahneman, E. Diener, & N. Schwarz (Eds.), *Well-being: The foundations of hedonic psychology* (pp. 26–29). New York: Russell Sage Foundation.

Tellegen, A., Watson, D., & Clark, L. A. (1999). On the dimensional and hierarchical structure of affect. *Psychological Science, 10,* 297–303.

Thayer, R. E. (1967). Measurement of activation through self-report. *Psychological Reports, 20,* 663–678.

Thayer, R. E. (1978). Factor analytic and reliability studies on the Activation–Deactivation Adjective Check List. *Psychological Reports, 42,* 747–756.

Thayer, R. E. (1986). Activation–Deactivation Adjective Check List: Current overview and structural analysis. *Psychological Reports, 58,* 607–614.

Tomarken, A. J., & Keener, A. D. (1998). Frontal brain asymmetry and depression: A self-regulatory perspective. *Cognition and Emotion, 12,* 387–420.

Watson, D. (1988). The vicissitudes of mood measurement: Effects of varying descriptors, time frames, and response format on measures of positive and negative affect. *Journal of Personality and Social Psychology, 55,* 128–141.

Watson, D. (2000). *Mood and temperament.* New York: Guilford Press.

Watson, D. (2004). Stability versus change, dependability versus error: Issues in the assessment of personality over time. *Journal of Research in Personality, 38,* 319–350.

Watson, D. (2005). Rethinking the mood and anxiety disorders: A quantitative hierarchical model for DSM–V. *Journal of Abnormal Psychology, 114,* 122–136.

Watson, D., & Clark, L. A. (1992). Affects separable and inseparable: On the hierarchical arrangements of the negative affects. *Journal of Personality and Social Psychology, 62,* 489–505.

Watson, D., & Clark, L. A. (1997). Measurement and mismeasurement of mood: Recurrent and emergent issues. *Journal of Personality Assessment, 68,* 267–296.

Watson, D., & Clark, L. A. (1999). *The PANAS–X: Manual for the Positive and Negative Affect Schedule—Expanded Form.* Retrieved September 8, 2006, from http://www.psychology.uiowa.edu/Faculty/Watson/Watson.html

Watson, D., Clark, L. A., & Carey, G. (1988). Positive and negative affectivity and their relation to anxiety and depressive disorders. *Journal of Abnormal Psychology, 97,* 346–353.

Watson, D., Clark, L. A., & Tellegen, A. (1988). Development and validation of brief measures of positive and negative affect: The PANAS scales. *Journal of Personality and Social Psychology, 54,* 1063–1070.

Watson, D., Hubbard, B., & Wiese, D. (2000). Self–other agreement in personality and affectivity: The role of acquaintanceship, trait visibility, and assumed similarity. *Journal of Personality and Social Psychology, 78,* 546–558.

Watson, D., Suls, J., & Haig, J. (2002). Global self-esteem in relation to structural models of personality and affectivity. *Journal of Personality and Social Psychology, 83,* 185–197.

Watson, D., & Tellegen, A. (1985). Toward a consensual structure of mood. *Psychological Bulletin, 98,* 219–235.

Watson, D., & Tellegen, A. (1999). Issues in the dimensional structure of affect—Effects of descriptors, measurement error, and response formats: Comment on Russell and Carroll (1999). *Psychological Bulletin, 125,* 601–610.

Watson, D., & Tellegen, A. (2002). Aggregation, acquiescence, and the assessment of trait affectivity. *Journal of Research in Personality, 38,* 589–597.

Watson, D., & Vaidya, J. (2003). Mood measurement: Current status and future directions. In J. A. Schinka & W. Velicer (Eds.), *Comprehensive handbook of psychology: Vol. 2. Research methods* (pp. 351–375). New York: Wiley.

Watson, D., Wiese, D., Vaidya, J., & Tellegen, A. (1999). The two general activation systems of affect: Structural findings, evolutionary considerations, and psychobiological evidence. *Journal of Personality and Social Psychology, 76,* 820–838.

Yik, M. S. M., Russell, J. A., & Feldman Barrett, L. (1999). Structure of self-reported current affect: Integration and beyond. *Journal of Personality and Social Psychology, 77,* 600–619.

Zevon, M. A., & Tellegen, A. (1982). The structure of mood change: An idiographic/nomothetic analysis. *Journal of Personality and Social Psychology, 43,* 111–122.

Zuckerman, M., & Lubin, B. (1965). *Manual for the Multiple Affect Adjective Check List.* San Diego, CA: Educational and Industrial Testing Service.

Zuckerman, M., & Lubin, B. (1985). *Manual for the MAACL–R: The Multiple Affect Adjective Check List—Revised.* San Diego, CA: Educational and Industrial Testing Service

2

EMOTIONAL BEHAVIOR AND PSYCHOPATHOLOGY: A SURVEY OF METHODS AND CONCEPTS

JUNE GRUBER AND DACHER KELTNER

Here we encounter remarkable possibilities: facial expressions of sadness (i.e., "grief muscles") lasting for extended periods of times, perhaps even months; weeping for no reason; expressive behavior revealing depressed states of mind and the predilection to suicide.
—Darwin (1872/1997, p. 184)

Charles Darwin (1872/1997) advocated that the unregulated emotions of the mentally ill provided rich examples of the universal expressions that he sought and so successfully described. Darwin's accounts of expressive behavior drew attention to the potential importance of emotional expression in psychopathology. In the opening quote to this chapter, Darwin described what appear to be individuals suffering from depression, exhibiting sadness and grief that exceeded the typical duration of these emotions and seemed often to occur without obvious cause. Darwin also noted individuals whose absence of expressive behavior was equally revealing of the underlying mental condition: "Many idiots are morose, passionate, restless, in a painful state of mind, or utterly stolid, and these never laugh" (p. 196). In these cases, the relative absence of expression—blushing or laughing—is just as dysfunctional, and a sign of the individual's inability to participate in typical social encounters. At the heart of these observations is the idea that a person's functioning in life, and clues to his or her state of mind and character might be revealed in specific patterns of expressive behavior. Does emotional behavior provide a window onto psychopathology? What evidence is there for this provocative idea?

Empirical science has only recently begun to catch up with Darwin's prescient observations (e.g., Keltner & Kring, 1998). The purpose of this chapter is to provide an overview of the emergent methodologies used to study emotional behavior and of the empirical insights these methods have yielded. In the first half of the chapter, we focus on methods relevant to four channels of behavioral communication. Specifically, we review methods for analyzing facial expressions of emotion and the vocal and acoustic properties of speech during the expression of emotional states. Next, we consider narrative approaches, a behaviorally rich source of idiographic emotional information. We end by reviewing recent advances in research on touch and tactile behaviors intended to convey emotions to others.

Following this review, we turn to three themes for considering the empirical relationship between psychopathology and emotional behavior. The first theme is that certain psychopathologies involve an excess of emotional behaviors. The second, seemingly opposite, theme is that psychopathologies often involve noteworthy absences of emotional behavior. Our final theme is that psychopathologies involve disjunctions between emotional behavior and other emotional response components that are normally well coordinated.

FOUR METHODOLOGIES CENTRAL TO THE STUDY OF EMOTIONAL BEHAVIOR

Emotions are multifaceted phenomena, involving multiple response systems that each can be measured in a variety of ways (see, e.g., chap. 1, on self-report methods, and chap. 3, on the psychophysiology of emotions, this volume). The study of emotional behavior is complex compared with other channels, such as self-report, in part because of the seemingly limitless ways to parse the behavioral stream. This chapter discusses four methodologies that researchers have identified as particularly meaningful to measure behavioral activity. Thus, in this chapter, we focus specifically on facial expression, vocal cues, touch, and narrative behavior—all of which are response systems central to emotional communication. We focus on these four aspects because the empirical literature has shown that they are a richer source of emotional information compared with other behavioral responses (e.g., postural behavior; Keltner, Ekman, Gonzaga, & Beer, 2003). Furthermore, deficits in emotional communication have been theorized as integral to the social difficulties and dysfunction at the heart of numerous psychopathologies (Keltner & Kring, 1998). Emotional behavior is important to study in the context of psychopathology because the use of naturalistic measures allows researchers to assess emotions online and unobtrusively within the stream of spontaneous interactions (this is often not possible with, e.g., self-report measures). Furthermore, the methods we detail in this chapter to measure emotional behavior in the face, voice, touch, and narrative all provide data that robustly discriminate among discrete emotions (e.g., anger vs. disgust; compassion vs. love). To the extent that a line of inquiry seeks to document fairly specific relations between a clinical disorder and a distinct emotion (e.g., fear in anxiety disorders), the measures we detail here will be the most sensitive. Finally, the measures of emotional behavior that we discuss can be exported to other cultures or ethnic groups without significant translation difficulties, thus allowing for cross-cultural and cross-ethnic comparisons.

Facial Behavior and the Expression of Emotion

Facial expressions are rightly considered a grammar of the elementary social interactions of human social life and, by implication, psychopathology (Eibl-Eibesfeldt, 1989). Facial expressions are central to parent–child attachment dynamics and to how parents communicate to offspring about objects in the environment. They are part of how adolescents negotiate positions within social hierarchies. Facial expressions are central to the often unspoken flirtations between potential romantic partners. The face includes 43 sets of facial muscles; these muscles can combine into thousands of facial configurations. Of the many possible muscular configurations, only a limited set communicate emotion (e.g., Ekman, 1993). Some configurations, such as smiles or deferential displays of embarrassment, occur relatively frequently during social interaction and appear to be especially critical for adaptation.

Several characteristics have been identified that differentiate emotional expressions from other nonverbal behavior, such as gestures or emblems (e.g., Frank & Ekman, 1993). First, facial expressions of emotion (and vocal expressions as well) tend to be fairly brief, typically lasting between 1 and 10 seconds (Bachorowski, Smoski, & Owren, 2001). For example, a smile accompanying enjoyment will typically start and stop within a span of 5 seconds; nonemotional smiles of politeness, in contrast, can be exceptionally brief or quite long in duration. Second, facial expressions of emotion often involve involuntary muscle actions that most people cannot intentionally produce or suppress (Dimberg, Thunberg, & Grunedal, 2002). Facial expressions of anger, for example, most typically involve the action of the muscle that tightens around the mouth, which most people cannot produce voluntarily. In fact, the neuroanatomical pathways for generating involuntary emotional expressions can be distinguished from those of voluntary facial actions, such as the furrowed brow or lip press (Rinn, 1984).

Here we concentrate on two approaches oriented toward identifying discrete occurrences of emotion in the face. We should first, however, mention a widely used technique, electromyography (EMG), to record the activation of certain muscle movements, most notably the *corrugator* (brow tighten) and *zygomatic major* (lip corner pull). EMG has the advantage of sensitively recording movements of these muscles, even those that are not visible to the human eye (and thus not codeable in the two systems we describe subsequently). However, EMG is less useful for measurement of emotional behavior because it does not provide differentiated measurement of negative (e.g., the corrugator is involved in numerous negative emotions, such as anger, fear, and sadness) and positive emotions.

One widely used approach that is well suited for studying specific emotional expressions is the Emotion Facial Action Coding System (EMFACS). EMFACS is a restricted application of the Facial Action Coding System (FACS), developed by Ekman and Friesen (1978) to code all visible facial muscle movements. Specifically, EMFACS codes emotion-relevant facial muscle movements derived from a previous theory using a rigorous, anatomically based approach (e.g., Ekman, 1992; Ekman, Friesen, & Hager, 2002; Ekman & Rosenberg, 1997). Learning FACS requires 80 to 100 hours. To achieve acceptable interrater reliability between two coders, a ratio can be used on overlapping data coded whereby the number of action units is multiplied by 2 and then divided by the total number of action units scored (e.g., Keltner & Bonanno, 1997). This agreement ratio can then be calculated for each event code by one or both of the coders. The elegance of EMFACS lies in its ability to translate coded facial muscle movements into a variety of discrete negative and positive emotional expressions, including anger, compassion, desire, disgust, pain, sadness, shame, embarrassment, enjoyment (i.e., Duchenne smiles), and amusement (e.g., Keltner & Bonanno, 1997). With the addition of specific postural and gestural movements, one can also identify displays of pride and love.

Another important system for coding discrete emotional expressions in the face is the Emotional Expressive Behavior (EEB) coding system (Gross & Levenson, 1993). Whereas EMFACS and other FACS-based systems code specific units of observable muscle action, EEB is more global and codes a broader range of behaviors. EEB includes rated intensities on a 0 (*slight*) to 3 (*strong*) scale for Disgust, Confusion, Fear, Sadness, Happiness and Amusement, Interest, Surprise, and Sleepiness. These intensity scales are applied to a predefined epoch of behavior (15–30 seconds is probably optimal). EEB also includes other behavioral codes such as yawns, face touching, and degree of body movement.

Comparing these two approaches, the strength of EMFACS is its precision: It allows researchers to identify the frame-by-frame unfolding of the specific muscle actions involved in emotion. This allows psychopathology researchers to identify specific millisecond occurrences of emotion as well as small but potentially important variations in emotional expression. For example, in EMFACS, more than 60 variations of anger have been documented, and one may speculate that some of these expressions systematically covary with specific emotional disorders. By contrast, in EEB, observers rate the overall emotional pleasantness, intensity, and attentiveness–engagement at the end of a designated trial. The strength of EEB, with its use of global codes, is its ease and economy of use relative to EMFACS. EEB is also easier to learn and takes less time to code data.

Communication of Emotion With the Voice

The richness of the voice as a source of information about emotional behavior was not widely appreciated until recently. Unlike facial expression, the voice can communicate emotion when communicator and recipient are not looking at one another, even over great physical distances. Researchers who study vocal communication of emotion rely on more than 20 properties of speech to make inferences regarding the occurrence of emotion (for a catalog of acoustic markers, see Bachorowski, 1999; Scherer, 1986). These markers include speech rate and fluency, including number of syllables per second; syllable duration; and number and duration of pauses. To study the extent to which people can communicate emotions with the voice, researchers have asked people to express different emotions in the voice while reading nonsense syllables or relatively neutral text passages (e.g., Banse & Scherer, 1996; Klasmeyer & Sendlmeier, 1997). These vocal expressions are then presented to listeners, who select from a series of options to identify the term that best matches the emotion conveyed. In a review, Juslin and Laukka (2001) concluded that hearers can judge five emotions in the voice—anger, fear, happiness, sadness, and tenderness—with accuracy rates that approach 70%, comparable to the accuracy rates observed in facial judgment studies. Within these and other reviews, researchers have detailed the specific vocal markers of distinct emotions, which are intuitive categories and fairly easy to translate to empirical use.

One additional advantage of studying the voice is that it is fairly easy to establish the extent to which vocalizations of one person are contingent on the vocalizations of another. This aspect of studying vocalization derives from the continuous nature of many vocal cues (e.g., pitch) and allows researchers to investigate the social contingencies of emotion-related vocalizations. Bachorowski and colleagues have mapped acoustic characteristics of different laughs, for example, and their functions (e.g., Bachorowski et al., 2001). There are cackles; hisses; breathy pants; snorts and grunts; and voiced or songlike laughs, which include vowel-like sounds and pitch modulation. Smoski and Bachorowski (2003) have found that friends are likely to engage in antiphonal laughter, in which the two individuals overlap in their bouts of laughter. Social contingent laughter, then, is often a behavioral cue of relational closeness, and inversely, the absence of such laughter may afford a clue into disrupted relational bonds characteristic of some clinical disorders. Claims about the social disconnectedness of different disorders (e.g., autism, depression) could readily be assessed with these techniques.

Narratives and Communication of Emotion

People most frequently communicate emotion with words. The study of *emotion-related narratives*, which we define as stories people tell in spontaneous speech about their emotional experiences, offers several distinct advantages within the study of emotion-related communication. A first advantage of these narratives is that they allow researchers to move beyond general categories of emotional communication (e.g., "anger," "compassion") to the study of more nuanced, idiographic emotion that emerges out of an individual's particular life circumstances. For example, measures of facial expression provide indexes of an individual's anger, disgust, or shame; narrative techniques provide additional data about the history in which the emotion is embedded; the social context of the emotion; the individual's interpretation of the causes, origins, and associations of the emotion; and his or her evaluation of the emotion.

A second advantage of narrative techniques is closely related to the first: Narrative techniques allow researchers to identify spontaneous appraisals within a stream of emotional behavior. A central assumption in the field of affective science is that emotions are the products of meaning making and construal processes, which affective scientists most typically refer to with the rubric *appraisal* (e.g., Smith & Lazarus, 1993). Narrative techniques allow researchers to identify emotion-related appraisals, such as "injustice," "uncertainty," "loss," or "connection" within steams of emotional behavior (e.g., Bonanno & Keltner, 2004).

A third advantage to the use of narrative techniques, unlike the other channels of emotional communication that we have considered thus far, is that they provide a window into the study of the metarepresentational processes, or the representation of experience from other than the first-person perspectives in different linguistic forms, such as fictional simulation, story, metaphor, or poetic image, that accompany so many emotional experiences. The study of emotion narratives, in more pragmatic terms, focuses on the storytelling of an emotional event, such as a loss or turning point in life, with a specific emphasis on how semantic elements are temporally sequenced, how these propositions and elements are evaluated by the narrator, and which specific words are used.

A select review of different theoretically relevant categories reveals the rich psychological data latent in emotion-related narratives. These include references to core appraisal themes definitive of different emotions (e.g., Bonanno & Keltner, 2004; Capps & Bonanno, 2000), metaphor analysis (Kovesces, 2000; Lakoff & Johnson, 1980), language dysfluencies and disturbances (e.g., Docherty, Rhinewine, Nienow, & Cohen, 2001; Tannen, 1993), and computerized analysis of word usage within a narrative (e.g., Pennebaker, Francis, & Booth, 2001). In this brief review, we highlight emotion-relevant findings, which attest to the likely fruits of studying how people describe their emotional experiences.

First, appraisal themes within the stream of narrative behavior are important in predicting psychological outcomes, such as increased long-term adjustment. For example, in one study, Capps and Bonanno (2000) identified self-construals of agentic action—so central to human emotion—within bereaved individuals' narratives of their experience of loss. Markers of their experience of agency included explicit references to feeling out of control, passive grammatical constructions, and verbs of necessity (*have to, need to*). It is remarkable that individuals who expressed diminished agentive roles in the language they used to describe their profound loss, beyond the effect of negative thoughts and feelings, suffered more persistent grief symptoms 2 years following the loss. This is one of the few studies in the field to link a spontaneous appraisal of agency—central to the experience of emotions like sadness, anger, guilt, and shame (e.g., Smith & Ellsworth, 1985)—to a significant life outcome.

Second, metaphors for emotions serve to structure experience of emotions within alternative, nonliteral representations (Lakoff & Johnson, 1980). For example, metaphors for anger (e.g., "blew his fuse" and "boiling with anger") may actually reflect the physiological phenomenon (i.e., increased body temperature) that one associates with anger. Metaphors may be labels of subjective emotional experience guided by patterns of autonomic activation. Further evidence by Fainsilber and Ortony (1987) suggests that metaphors may also be a marker of intensity of experience whereby frequency of metaphor use increases with the intensity of the emotion described. Thus, metaphor use may both capture and increase understanding of the intensity and possible physiological sensations of emotion in everyday language in a way that minimizes demand characteristics.

Third, Pennebaker et al. (2001) have developed ways to explore differences in word usage within narratives using a computer-based text analysis program called Linguistic Inquiry and Word Count (LIWC). LIWC has been used to track language use within classical literature, press conferences, everyday conversations, and personal narratives. Within more than 70 linguistic dimensions, LIWC can code both positive and negative emotion-relevant word usage. It also enables researchers to create their own theory-driven word categories. Pennebaker, Kiecolt-Glaser, and Glaser (1988) demonstrated that individuals who constructed a coherent narrative of a negative life event, incorporating aspects of negative emotion and increased cognitive processing, showed enhanced immune functioning and reported fewer medical visits. Thus, carefully attending to the specific words people use when constructing meaningful events may yield novel insights about the processes that promote physical and mental health.

Communication of Emotion Through Touch

Touch is the most developed sensory modality at birth, contributing to cognitive and socioemotional development throughout infancy and childhood (e.g., Field, 2001; Hertenstein, 2002; Stack, 2001) and likely has an abiding importance throughout the life course. In this section, we describe several emotion-based functions that touch provides, stressing the importance of touch in emotional behavior and the cultivation of social relationships.

A first is that certain types of touches can soothe. For example, in one study, infants held by their mothers during a painful medical procedure cried 82% less and had decreased heart rate during the procedure compared with those who were not held by their mothers (Gray, Watt, & Blass, 2000). A second function of touch is to signal safety. Theorists have observed that a primary need of infants is to know whether the environment is safe. For example, Anisfeld, Casper, Nozyce, and Cunningham (1990) discovered that infants who were carried next to their parents' bodies were more likely to be judged later as securely attached than infants carried less close to parents. A third function of touch is that it reinforces reciprocity. That is, the act of touching produces compliance, sharing, and cooperation (e.g., Willis & Hamm, 1980). A fourth function of touch is to provide pleasure. The simple touch of the arm with a soft velvety cloth activates the region of the prefrontal cortex that is involved in the processing of rewards such as pleasurable tastes and smells (Berridge, 2003). Finally, people can communicate emotions with touch. In fact, Hertenstein and Keltner (2005) recently found that people can communicate several emotions with touch, including anger, disgust, fear, sadness, love, compassion, and gratitude.

Although still in its infancy, the empirical study of touch has identified several measurable properties of tactile communication. The first is the social semantics of the tactile act. Tactile acts can be coded in terms of whether they are hits, squeezes, pinches, strokes, shakes, or rubs. A second is the temporal dynamics of the tactile act; that is, the duration and rapidity of onset and offset of the touch. Finally, there is the location on the recipient's body where the touch occurs.

William James (1890/1981) acknowledged the centrality of touch to the health of bonds between individuals. Few data, if any, exist with respect to how touch is involved in psychological disorder. The same could be said of the manner in which individuals interpret touch, that is, how they derive emotional meaning from others' tactile communication. These are two open areas of inquiry that we believe will yield significant results concerning the origins, manifestation, and maintenance of specific psychopathologies. Touch may be a good place to discern behaviorally the social dysfunction common to many disorders, perhaps through decreased soothing behaviors between caregivers with depression and their offspring, fewer touching behaviors as evidence of social withdrawal in depression or perhaps social anxiety, or the absence of touching as an index of marital and family discord in bipolar disorder (Miklowitz & Goldstein, 1997).

Taken together, the study of facial expression, vocalization, narrative emotional behavior, and touch provide the tools to identify distinct emotions as they occur in the flow of social interaction. Each method has its advantages and disadvantages, as we have tried to highlight in our brief review. These methods are especially useful to the study of emotion (and psychological disorders). We now consider three insights regarding the relation between emotion and psychopathology that the use of these methods has generated.

THEMES IN STUDYING EMOTIONAL BEHAVIOR: EXTREMES, ABSENCES, AND DISJUNCTIONS

Theme 1: Look for Extremes

Extremes in emotional behavior can be indexed in several ways. They may be evident in the intensity of the behavior, such as an anger display that involves maximal contractions of the emotion-relevant facial actions. Extremes can be evident in the duration of the behavior or its frequency across some epoch of time. Within a social functional approach to emotion, which has guided much of this chapter, emotional extremes are likely to be highly dysfunctional within relationships, and specific types of emotional extremes (e.g., extreme sadness vs. extreme anger) may be markers of different psychopathologies.

Externalization and Extreme Anger Displays

Anger may be the most destructive emotion. It is associated with harmful intent and action toward others (Berkowitz, 1989), problems within interpersonal relationships, and risky perceptions and behaviors (e.g., Lerner & Keltner, 2001). One relevant study investigated facial expressions young boys displayed during an interactive IQ test that were coded using FACS. Specifically, measures of the extremity of facial expression were derived for each emotion by finding the product of the mean intensity of emotion-relevant muscle action and the frequency of emotional display. The IQ test produced frequent embarrassment, anger, and fear as the boys made intellectual mistakes in front of an authority figure. Consistent with the hypothesis that extremes of anger relate to antisocial behavior, the externalizers displayed the most anger (Keltner, Moffitt, & Stouthamer-Loeber, 1995). Furthermore, these boys displayed the least embarrassment compared with control participants and those who internalized their emotions. This latter finding is important given the claim that individuals who are less inclined toward self-conscious emotions (i.e., embarrassment, shame, or guilt), which motivate the adherence to social norms, are more prone to antisocial behavior.

We contend that these findings reveal important guidelines for studying relations between emotional extremes and psychopathology. One does not need to sample extensive amounts of behavior; Keltner et al. (1995) found behavioral markers of antisocial tendencies using only 2 minutes of IQ test behavior. The context for the behavior also matters. Anger in response to an authority figure is a telling and maladaptive response for young boys. Dysfunctional emotion, therefore, is especially problematic in terms of social implications vis-à-vis the specifics of the social context.

Extreme Socially Inappropriate Behaviors in Orbitofrontal Patients

In similarly motivated research, Beer, Heerey, Keltner, Scabini, and Knight (2003) have looked at the self-conscious emotion of individuals with damage to the orbitofrontal region of the frontal lobes. The orbitofrontal region of the frontal lobes, which rests behind the eye orbits (i.e., Brodmann's areas 11, 12, 14, 47), is involved in the regulation of social behavior. Patients with orbitofrontal damage have been observed to greet strangers by kissing them on the cheek and hugging them (e.g., Rolls, Hornak, Wade, & McGrath, 1994), engage in inappropriate joking (Stuss & Benson, 1984), and inappropriately disclose personal information to a stranger (Beer, 2002).

In one study that examined inappropriately extreme emotion, patients with orbitofrontal damage and age-matched control participants were asked to tease a stranger. More specifically, participants were given two initials (e.g., "H.F.") and asked to generate a nickname for the stranger in the study and tease that person on the basis of the nickname. Patients' nonverbal displays of embarrassment and pride were coded based on a modified version of EMFACS. This demonstrated how EMFACS reveals important clues to emotion behavior. Specifically, patients, unlike control participants, exhibited inappropriate self-conscious emotion: They displayed increased pride and reduced embarrassment, even given the fact that they teased in overly forward and even sexually suggestive ways. Extremes of emotion—in this case, pride—reveal specific psychological deficits. Here again, there are normative expectations, as in the IQ test, for emotion: Teasing a stranger is a certain source of embarrassment for most. Not so for these patients.

Theme 2: Look for Notable Absences

As William James (1890/1981) and Charles Darwin (1872/1997) long ago observed, relative absence of emotion can also be unsettling and ultimately dysfunctional. We saw this to be the case with externalizing boys and with the patients with orbitofrontal damage, who showed a relative absence of embarrassment behavior in contexts in which the emotion was normative. The absence of emotional expression is also revealing of depression.

Depression and the Absence of Emotional Responding

Although most studies of depression and emotional disturbance have concentrated on emotional experience, mounting evidence suggests that people with major depression exhibit limited emotional behavior in response to a variety of stimuli (Rottenberg, 2005). For example, compared with nondepressed control participants, people with depression have been found to exhibit fewer facial expressions, especially in positive emotion contexts (e.g., Berenbaum & Oltmanns, 1992; Gotlib & Robinson, 1982; Pogue-Geile & Harrow, 1984). These notable absences in emotional facial behaviors resonate with findings on vocal affect and communication of emotion in depression. Caregivers with depression, for example, have been found to exhibit relatively flat vocal affect, with minimal emotional intonation (Bettes, 1988). Given the importance of pronounced vocal stimulation as a source of stimulation and learning for infants, these deficits are likely to have lasting implications for subsequent development. The study of narrative behavior has also yielded important insights into the absence of emotional responses in patients with depression; Bucci and Freedman (1981) found that individuals with depression exhibited greater speech dysfluencies when discussing positive emotional topics. Other theories posit a negative self-referentiality in the narrative behavior of people with depression (e.g., Rude, Gortner, & Pennebaker, 2004), with increased usage of negatively valenced and self-referential word usages, pointing to a provocative thesis that depression represents a notable absence of positive emotion representation in vocal affect and speech content. Thus, evidence from multiple behavioral response systems (facial behavior, vocal properties of speech, and narrative) converges on the theme of notable absence in depression.

Absence of Self-Conscious Emotions in Autism

One of the central social disturbances associated with autism is difficulties with theory of mind (e.g., Capps & Sigman, 1996). Theory of mind involves an appreciation of social norms and the awareness of others' evaluations. One might therefore expect deficits in theory of mind to relate to deficits in self-conscious emotions requiring these skills, such as embarrassment and shame, and recognizing self-conscious facial behavior in others. Here we highlight how the narrative and facial behavior approaches yield information about the absence of self-conscious emotions in children with autism. Few studies have specifically investigated embarrassment and shame among children with this condition. When asked to provide narratives of these emotions, children with autism have difficulty, providing general, factual knowledge rather than accounts of personal experiences (Capps, Yrimiya, & Sigman, 1992). Capps et al. (1992) concluded that self-conscious emotions are problematic for children with autism because of their decreased ability to engage in social referencing and perspective taking.

The recognition of self-conscious emotion involves the understanding of violations of social norms and negative social evaluations, both important aspects of theory of mind. When asked to judge emotions depicted in photos of human facial expressions, children with autism were impaired in the recognition of self-conscious emotional expressions specifically, because they performed comparably to control participants on the identification of non-self-conscious emotions such as anger or fear (Heerey, Keltner, & Capps, 2003). Children with autism tended to confuse embarrassment with "happy," whereas they tended to describe shame as "sleepy." Thus, absences of self-conscious emotions were most fruitfully understood using multiple avenues of behavioral data, including narratives to understand the lack of self-conscious emotional experience and facial behaviors to see a failure even to perceive these emotional states in others.

Theme 3: Disjunction and Malfunction

Within the study of emotion, it is assumed that the many response systems (e.g., communication, physiology, expressive behavior) are modestly interrelated. Empirical reviews of studies of university students have typically found that the report of emotional experience and the expression of emotion in the face correlate at about $r = .3$ (e.g., Matsumoto, 1987). This correlation makes sense within a functional analysis of display: Displays of emotion are more evocative of responses in others and thereby regulate interactions in adaptive ways when the expressions covary with experience. A nonverbal display of romantic love or of anger, for example, is likely to have much greater potency when accompanied by the experience of the specific emotion.

Historically, diminished emotional expressiveness, or flat affect, has been considered a prominent emotional feature of schizophrenia (e.g., Bleuler, 1911/1950; Kraepelin, 1919/1971). Modern experimental investigations using emotionally evocative stimuli have found that patients with schizophrenia are less facially expressive than nonpatients in response to emotional films (e.g., Berenbaum & Oltmanns, 1992; Kring & Neale, 1996), cartoons (Dworkin, Clark, Amador, & Gorman, 1996), and during social interactions (Krause, Steimer, Sänger-Alt, & Wagner, 1989). If one were to discuss emotions in schizophrenia simply in terms of behavior, we would conclude that patients with schizophrenia are simply less facially expressive across a variety of emotion elicitors and consider this as an example of a "notable absence."

In the case of schizophrenia, a richer story unfolds when experiential data are included with behavioral measures. Specifically, research suggests that patients with schizophrenia exhibit significantly fewer positive and negative facial expressions in response to emotionally evocative pictures and film clips compared with healthy controls, yet these patients report having levels of emotion in response to emotional stimuli that are similar to or greater than those of nonpsychiatric control participants. Schizophrenia thus involves an unusual disjunction between experiential and behavioral response systems (e.g., Berenbaum & Oltmanns, 1992; Kring & Neale, 1996).

These findings raise intriguing questions about other kinds of disjunctions that might be observed in psychopathology. One might examine disjunctions between emotional display and other channels, such as physiological response. This kind of inquiry applied to depression or bipolar disorder (Gruber, Johnson, Oveis, & Keltner, 2006) would help ascertain whether their disjunctions reflect some general incoherence in emotional response.

CONCLUSIONS AND FUTURE DIRECTIONS

Pioneers in the field of psychology were drawn to the question of how emotions are involved in psychopathology. They pursued this line of inquiry for a very good reason: The study of emotion and psychopathology offers the promise of several conceptual gains in the two fields (e.g., Keltner & Kring, 1998). For affective scientists, study of the relations between emotions and psychopathology still remains one of the clearest routes to understanding the function of a particular emotion. For example, in this review, we have discussed findings showing that the relative absence of embarrassment is associated with a chronic tendency to engage in antisocial behavior, as is evident in externalizing disorders and in patients with orbitofrontal damage. Hence, by studying dysfunction, we learn about function (Oatley & Jenkins, 1992).

For clinical scientists, the kind of research we have detailed here offers similar promise for understanding the social expression and underpinnings of various disorders. More generally, individual differences in emotional behavior, present early in life, may help to explain the life course of the individual, problems the person systematically encounters, and the person's relational difficulties (e.g., Malatesta, 1990). This framework, which treats emotional behavior as one mediator between person and environment, could readily be extended to the study of specific psychopathologies.

The four methodologies of measuring emotional communication that we have detailed—facial expression, vocalization, narrative, and touch—are likely to be central to the manner in which psychopathologies shape the environment and the life course. In the case of schizophrenia, defined by decreased outward displays of emotion, interventions that help patients to match their internal feelings with their outward displays may therefore have positive effects on interpersonal adjustment. To the extent that there prove to be fairly specific expressive markers of a particular disorder—say, reduced embarrassment with autism (e.g., Heerey et al., 2003)—researchers might be better able to identity individuals prone to the disorder earlier in development using markers of emotional behavior (e.g., Kagan, Reznick, & Gibbons, 1989). Studies of emotional expression and psychological disorder, still in a nascent stage, could help refine the classification, understanding, and treatment of individuals with various disorders.

REFERENCES

Anisfeld, E., Casper, V., Nozyce, M., & Cunningham, N. (1990). Does infant carrying promote attachment? An experimental study of the effects of increased physical contact on the development of attachment. *Child Development, 61*, 1617–1627.

Bachorowski, J.-A. (1999). Vocal expression and perception of emotion. *Current Directions in Psychological Science, 8*, 53–57.

Bachorowski, J.-A., Smoski, M. J., & Owren, M. J. (2001). The acoustic features of human laughter. *Journal of Acoustical Society of America, 110*, 1581–1597.

Banse, R., & Scherer, K. R. (1996). Acoustic profiles in vocal emotion expression. *Journal of Personality and Social Psychology, 70*, 614–636.

Beer, J. S. (2002). Positive illusions about the self: Short-term benefits and long-term costs. *Journal of Personality and Social Psychology, 80*, 340–352.

Beer, J. S., Heerey, E. H., Keltner, D., Scabini, D., & Knight, R. T. (2003). The regulatory function of self-conscious emotion: Insights from patients with orbitofrontal damage. *Journal of Personality and Social Psychology, 85*, 594–604.

Berenbaum, H., & Oltmanns, T. (1992). Emotional experience and expression in schizophrenia and depression. *Journal of Abnormal Psychology, 101*, 37–44.

Berkowitz, L. (1989). The frustration–aggression hypothesis: Examination and reformulation. *Psychological Bulletin, 106*, 59–73.

Berridge, K. C. (2003). Pleasures of the brain. *Brain and Cognition, 52*, 106–128.

Bettes, B. (1988). Maternal depression and motherese: Temporal and intonational features. *Child Development, 59*, 1089–1096.

Bleuler, E. (1950). *Dementia praecox or the group of schizophrenias* (J. Zinkin, Trans.). New York: International Universities Press. (Original work published 1911)

Bonanno, G. A., & Keltner, D. (2004). The coherence of emotion systems: Comparing "online" measures of appraisal and facial expressions and self-report. *Cognition and Emotion, 18*, 431–444.

Bucci, W., & Freedman, N. (1981). The language of depression. *Bulletin of the Menninger Clinic, 45*, 334–358.

Capps, L. M., & Bonanno, G. A. (2000). Narrating bereavement: Thematic and grammatical predictors of adjustment to loss. *Discourse Processes, 30*, 1–25.

Capps, L. M., & Sigman, M. (1996). Autistic aloneness. In R. D. Kavanaugh, B. Zimmerberg, & S. Fein (Eds.), *Emotion: Interdisciplinary perspectives* (pp. 273–296). Mahwah, NJ: Erlbaum.

Capps, L. M., Yrimiya, N., & Sigman, M. (1992). Understanding of simple and complex emotions in non-retarded children with autism. *Journal of Child Psychology and Psychiatry, 33*, 1169–1182.

Darwin, C. (1997). *The expression of the emotions in man and animals.* London: Murray. (Original work published 1872)

Dimberg, U., Thunberg, M., & Grunedal, S. (2002). Facial reactions to emotional stimuli: Automatically controlled emotional responses. *Cognition and Emotion, 16,* 449–471.

Docherty, N. M., Rhinewine, J. P., Nienow, T. M., & Cohen, S. (2001). Affective reactivity of language symptoms, startle responding, and inhibition in schizophrenia. *Journal of Abnormal Psychology, 110,* 194–198.

Dworkin, R. H., Clark, S. C., Amador, X. F., & Gorman, J. M. (1996). Does affective blunting in schizophrenia reflect affective deficit or neuromotor dysfunction? *Schizophrenia Research, 20,* 301–306.

Eibl-Eibesfeldt, I. (1989). *Human ethology.* New York: Aldine de Gruyter.

Ekman, P. (1992). An argument for basic emotions. *Cognition and Emotion, 6,* 169–200.

Ekman, P. (1993). Facial expressions and emotion. *American Psychologist, 48,* 384–392.

Ekman, P., & Friesen W. V. (1978). *Facial Action Coding System: A technique for the measurement of facial movement.* Palo Alto, CA: Consulting Psychologists Press.

Ekman, P., Friesen, W. V., & Hager, J. C. (2002). *Facial Action Coding System* (2nd ed.). London: Weidenfeld & Nicolson.

Ekman, P., & Rosenberg, E. L. (1997). *What the face reveals: Basic and applied studies of spontaneous expression using the Facial Action Coding System (FACS).* New York: Oxford University Press.

Fainsilber, L., & Ortony, A. (1987). Metaphorical uses of language in the expression of emotions. *Metaphor and Symbolic Activity, 2,* 239–250.

Field, T. (2001). Touch therapy effects on development. *International Journal of Behavioral Development, 22,* 779–798.

Frank, M. G., & Ekman, P. (1993). Not all smiles are created equal: The differences between enjoyment and nonenjoyment smiles. *Humor: International Journal of Humor Research, 6,* 9–26.

Gotlib, I. H., & Robinson, L. A. (1982). Responses to depressed individuals: Discrepancies between self-report and observer-rated behavior. *Journal of Abnormal Psychology, 91,* 231–240.

Gray, L., Watt, L., & Blass, E. M. (2000). Skin-to-skin contact is analgesic in healthy newborns. *Pediatrics, 105,* 110–111.

Gross, J. J., & Levenson, R. W. (1993). Emotional suppression: Physiology, self-report, and expressive behavior. *Journal of Personality and Social Psychology, 64,* 970–986.

Gruber, J., Johnson, S. L., Oveis, C., & Keltner, D. (2006). *Mania vulnerability and dysfunctional positive emotion.* Manuscript under review.

Heerey, E. A., Keltner, D., & Capps, L. M. (2003). Making sense of self-conscious emotion: Linking theory of mind and emotion in children with autism. *Emotion, 3,* 394–400.

Hertenstein, M. J. (2002). Touch: Its communicative functions in infancy. *Human Development, 45*, 70–94.

Hertenstein, M. J., & Keltner, D. (2005, May). *Touch: Evidence for a new signaling system of emotion.* Presented at the 17th Annual Convention of the American Psychological Society, Chicago.

James, W. (1981). *The principles of psychology.* Cambridge, MA: Harvard University Press. (Original work published 1890)

Juslin, P. N., & Laukka, P. (2001). Impact of intended emotion intensity on cue utilization and decoding accuracy in vocal expression of emotion. *Emotion, 1*, 381–412.

Kagan, J., Reznick, J. S., & Gibbons, J. (1989). Inhibited and uninhibited types of children. *Child Development, 60*, 838–845.

Keltner, D., & Bonanno, G. (1997). A study of laughter and dissociation: Distinct correlates of laughter and smiling during bereavement. *Journal of Personality and Social Psychology, 73*, 687–702.

Keltner, D., Ekman, P., Gonzaga, G. C., & Beer, J. (2003). Facial expressions of emotion. In R. J. Davidson, H. Goldsmith, & K. R. Scherer (Eds.). *Handbook of the affective sciences* (pp. 415–432). New York: Oxford University Press.

Keltner, D., & Kring, A. M. (1998). Emotion, social function, and psychopathology. *Review of General Psychology, 2*, 320–342.

Keltner, D., Moffitt, T. E., & Stouthamer-Loeber, M. (1995). Facial expressions of emotion and psychopathology in adolescent boys. *Journal of Abnormal Psychology, 104*, 644–652.

Klasmeyer, G., & Sendlmeier, W. F. (1997). The classification of different phonation types in emotional and neutral speech. *Forensic Linguistics, 1*, 104–124.

Kovesces, Z. (2000). *Metaphor and emotion: Language, culture, and body in human feeling.* Cambridge, England: Cambridge University Press

Kraepelin, E. (1971). *Dementia praecox and paraphrenia* (R. M. Barclay, Trans.). Huntington, NY: Krieger. (Original work published 1919)

Krause, R., Steimer, E., Sänger-Alt, C., & Wagner, G. (1989). Facial expression of schizophrenic patients and their interaction partners. *Journal for the Study of Interpersonal Processes, 52*, 1–12.

Kring, A. M., & Bachorowski, J.-A. (1999). Emotions and psychopathology. *Cognition and Emotion, 13*, 575–599.

Kring, A. M., & Neale, J. M. (1996). Do schizophrenic patients show a disjunction among expressive, experiential, and psychophysiological components of emotion? *Journal of Abnormal Psychology, 105*, 249–257.

Lakoff, G., & Johnson, M. (1980). *Metaphors we live by.* Chicago: University of Chicago Press.

Lerner, J. S., & Keltner, D. (2001). Fear, anger, and risk. *Journal of Personality and Social Psychology, 81*, 146–159.

Malatesta, C. Z. (1990). The role of emotions in the development and organization of personality. In A. T. Ross (Ed.), *Nebraska Symposium on Motivation* (Vol. 36, pp. 1–56). Lincoln: University of Nebraska Press.

Matsumoto, D. (1987). The role of facial response in the experience of emotion: More methodological problems and a meta-analysis. *Journal of Personality and Social Psychology, 52*, 769–774.

Miklowitz, D. J., & Goldstein, M. J. (1997). *Bipolar disorder: A family-focused treatment approach.* New York: Guilford Press.

Oatley, K., & Jenkins, J. M. (1992). Human emotions: Function and dysfunction. *Annual Review of Psychology, 43*, 55–85.

Pennebaker, J. W., Francis, M. E., & Booth, R. J. (2001). Linguistic inquiry and word count: LIWC2001 [Computer software]. Mahwah, NJ: Erlbaum.

Pennebaker, J., Kiecolt-Glaser, J. K., & Glaser, R. (1988). Disclosure of traumas and immune function: Health implications for psychotherapy. *Journal of Consulting and Clinical Psychology, 56*, 239–245.

Pogue-Geile, M. F., & Harrow, M. (1984). Negative and positive symptoms in schizophrenia and depression: A follow-up. *Schizophrenia Bulletin, 10*, 371–387.

Rinn, W. E. (1984). The neuropsychology of facial expression. *Psychological Bulletin, 95*, 52–77.

Rolls, E. T., Hornak, J., Wade, D., & McGrath, J. (1994). Emotion-related learning in patients with social and emotional changes associated with frontal lobe damage. *Journal of Neurology, Neurosurgery, and Psychiatry, 57*, 1518–1524.

Rottenberg, J. (2005). Mood and emotion in major depression. *Current Directions in Psychological Science, 14*, 167–170.

Rude, S. G., Gortner, E., & Pennebaker, J. W. (2003). Language use of depressed and depression vulnerable college students. *Cognitive Therapy and Research, 27*, 415–429.

Scherer, K. R. (1986). Vocal affect expression: A review and model for future research. *Psychological Bulletin, 99*, 143–165.

Smith, C. A., & Ellsworth, P. C. (1985). Patterns of cognitive appraisal in emotion. *Journal of Personality and Social Psychology, 48*, 813–838.

Smith, C. A., & Lazarus, R. S. (1993). Appraisal components, core relational themes, and emotions. *Cognition and Emotion, 7*, 233–269.

Smoski, M. J., & Bachorowski, J. A. (2003). Antiphonal laughter between friends and strangers. *Cognition and Emotion, 17*, 327–340.

Stack, D. M. (2001). The salience of touch and physical contact during infancy: Unraveling some of the mysteries of the somaesthetic sense. In G. Bremner & A. Fogel (Eds.), *Blackwell handbook of infant development: Part II. Social, emotional and communicative development* (pp. 351–378). Oxford, England: Blackwell.

Stuss, D. T., & Benson, D. F. (1984). Neuropsychological studies of the frontal lobes. *Psychological Bulletin, 95*, 3–28.

Tannen, D. (1993). What's in a frame? Surface evidence for underlying expectations. In D. Tannen (Ed.), *Framing in discourse* (pp. 14–56). Oxford University Press.

Willis, F., & Hamm, H. (1980). The use of interpersonal touch in securing compliance. *Journal of Nonverbal Behavior, 5,* 49–55.

3

METHODS FOR STUDYING THE PSYCHOPHYSIOLOGY OF EMOTION

CRAIG SANTERRE AND JOHN J. B. ALLEN

More than a century ago, William James (1890/1950) noted that emotional stimuli "not only prompt a man to outward deeds, but provoke characteristic alterations in his attitude and visage, and affect his breathing, circulation, and other organic functions in specific ways" (p. 442). This statement anticipated the contemporary idea that emotions are multicomponential responses (e.g., Frijda, 2000) involving not only the subjective aspect but also cognitive appraisals, behavioral action tendencies, and physiological fluctuations, reflecting that emotions are embodied phenomena.

Psychophysiological methods are central to the measurement of emotions. First, because emotions are multifaceted, the measurement of physiological responses to psychological manipulations (and vice versa) allows researchers to include additional observations in the validation of emotion constructs; these measurements can complement subjective and behavioral data. Additionally, psychophysiological measures can circumvent some of the problems inherent in other measures of emotion (e.g., the fallibility of self-report, social [un]desirability of reporting certain emotions). For example, Gross and Levenson (1993) observed that participants who suppressed their emotional expressions while watching an emotional film did not alter their reported subjective experiences; however, the manipulation did increase physiological activity.

Another benefit of using psychophysiological methods to measure emotion is the possibility that psychophysiological indicators of emotion may identify aberrant patterns of responding that increase risk for psychopathology. Such measures may themselves serve as an indicator or risk or as an endophenotype (Gottesman & Gould, 2003; Iacono, 1998), measurable endogenous characteristics of an individual that are related to underlying mechanisms conferring risk. Such risk may stem from genetic or environmental factors, or their interaction, but in all cases the purpose of the endophenotype is to provide a relatively easily measured correlate of underlying mechanisms of risk, a correlate that ideally can be identified in at-risk individuals regardless of whether they are currently symptomatic. Such a marker may prove useful in identifying a subset of those at risk for developing particular forms of psychopathology and may ultimately assist in identifying the underlying mechanisms that may point to new treatments and preventions. The rationale for exploring endophenotypes is that these markers are more elementary than the specialized phenotypical behaviors of a disorder and hence may be controlled by fewer genes, thus also aiding in the quest to identify the links between specific genes and risk for psychopathology. Finally, psychophysiological measures of emotion may tap mechanisms relevant to the etiology of or treatment or prognosis for a given form of psychopathology.

The goal of this chapter is to survey selected psychophysiological methods used to measure emotion and to illustrate their application in psychopathology research. This chapter is intended to be sufficient to guide the reader to appropriate and specific psychophysiological measures, including the following popular psychophysiological methods: electrodermal activity, cardiovascular activity, brain electrical activity, and facial muscular activity (including the startle eyeblink reflex). Because of space constraints, this chapter is not intended to be a complete manual for conducting research. Please note that essential in-depth guidelines papers (see http://www.sprweb.org/journal.html) are marked in the reference section with an asterisk, and several other sources from the Web site noted here provide excellent coverage of specific measures (Andreassi, 2000; Cacioppo, Tassinary, & Berntson, 2000a; Hugdahl, 2001; Stern, Ray, & Quigley, 2000) as well as the pragmatics of setting up a psychophysiological laboratory (Curtin, Lozano, & Allen, in press).

ELECTRODERMAL ACTIVITY

Electrodermal activity (EDA) may be the most widely used psychophysiological measure and that with the longest history. In the late 19th century, a colleague of French neurologist Jean Charcot used tonic skin resistance levels from various patient groups as a clinical marker (Vigouroux, 1888). Since EDA was first recognized, this response system has been associated with psychological concepts such as emotion, arousal, and attention and hence is an invaluable tool for the affective scientist.

The skin is a selective barrier that aids in the maintenance of water balance in the body as well as regulating core body temperature. Eccrine sweat glands within the skin cover most of the body but are most dense on the palms and on the soles of the feet. Their primary function is thermoregulation, although on the palmar and plantar surfaces, these glands provide moisture to improve grasping behavior. Eccrine glands in these locations are of primary interest to psychophysiologists because they respond more to psychological and emotional situations than to thermal stimuli.

Electrodermal activity is measured by passing a small current through a pair of electrodes attached to the skin. When sweat fills the pores, there is a more conductive path through the relatively electrically resistant outer layer of skin. The sweat glands function like a set of variable resistors wired in parallel, which influence the electrical current depending on the quantity of sweat and the number of glands that are active. If a constant voltage is applied, the skin's resistance will vary with the sweat gland activity and can be quantified with Ohm's law: voltage (V) = resistance (R) × current (I). Although early studies measured skin resistance, contemporary studies prefer to measure conductance (the reciprocal of resistance) because changes are more linear across a broad range of responses, and the measured conductance is linearly related to actual sweat secretion. The tonic level of skin conductance at rest, free from episodic fluctuations or averaged across such fluctuations, is referred to as *skin conductance level* (SCL). Perturbations superimposed on the tonic level are referred to as *skin conductance responses* (SCRs). Phasic SCRs are usually small compared with the tonic level and have been likened to waves riding on the tidal drifts of SCL.

To measure EDA, two electrodes are most commonly placed on the thenar eminences of the palms or the volar surface of the medial or distal phalanges of the fingers. Electrodes are easily attached using adhesive collars, which also help to control the area of skin that comes in contact with the measuring device. This is a critical parameter because a difference in number of exposed sweat glands (or parallel resistors) would affect the conductance values. Choosing the appropriate electrode paste is also an important concern. Fowles et al. (1981) recommend using an electrode paste that closely approximates the salinity of human sweat (0.05 NaCl). This procedure preserves the properties of the bioelectric signals of interest, whereas typical electrocardiogram (EKG) or electroencephalogram (EEG) pastes (which contain near-saturation levels of NaCl) would markedly inflate EDA values.

Electrodermal activity provides a direct measure of sympathetic activity. The eccrine sweat glands have predominantly cholinergic innervation from sudomotor fibers that originate in the sympathetic chain; therefore, increases in SCL or SCR are due to increases in tonic or phasic sympathetic activation. Central control of the sympathetic nervous system is distributed in various parts of the brain, making it difficult to determine which specific brain center and pathway is causing the EDA activity. Several relatively independent pathways have been proposed (for reviews, see Boucsein, 1992; Hugdahl, 2001).

To ensure that EDA changes reflect specific emotional or psychological processes, one must tightly control the experimental conditions and environment (e.g., ambient noise, temperature). EDA responds to a wide range of stimuli, many of which are easily confounded (e.g., task significance, emotional content, stimulus novelty, intensity), and therefore caution must be used when interpreting the cause of its activation. Additionally, EDA is a relatively slow-moving response system. The latency of a skin conductance response is typically about 1 second to 3 seconds; this measure thus has limited utility for tracking rapidly occurring changes in sympathetic activity. Moreover, the system is slow to recover, and multiple stimuli in rapid succession will not produce continued responding. Stimuli must be separated in time (i.e., by 20 seconds or more) to increase the likelihood of continued responding. When quantifying EDA, numerous issues that are beyond the scope of this section must be considered. The interested reader should consult Dawson, Schell, and Filion (2000) for a detailed review.

A common paradigm in emotion research involves the presentation of a discrete stimulus to determine its impact on EDA. For example, Greenwald, Cook, and Lang (1989) presented participants with pictures from the International Affective Picture System (see Lang, Bradley, & Cuthbert, 2005) that varied in arousal and valence and measured their skin conductance responses. Results showed that the SCR increased linearly as ratings of arousal increased, regardless of emotional valence: Reactivity was generally higher for pleasant and unpleasant pictures compared with neutral ones. Manning and Melchiori (1974) observed similar patterns of SCRs when the stimuli were words rated as highly pleasant and unpleasant compared with neutral words. Campos, Marcos, and Gonzalez (1999) investigated how SCR related to different qualities of displayed words, and they found that 30% of the variance in SCR was explained by imagery and subject-rated emotionality of the displayed words.

The body's physiological response to emotionally arousing stimuli is the cornerstone of Damasio's (1994) somatic marker hypothesis. This theory posits that physiological "marker" signals (conscious or unconscious) arise during emotional processes and are critical in guiding responses to various situations. SCR is often used as an index of somatic activation. For example, Bechara, Damasio, Tranel, and Damasio (1997) measured SCRs while participants performed a gambling task, which involved choosing from a "good" or "bad" deck of cards to maximize monetary gains and minimize monetary losses. Healthy participants were able to choose advantageously before they were able to consciously verbalize the correct strategy; moreover, they demonstrated an anticipatory SCR when they considered a choice that would be risky. In a rather different experiment, Patrick, Cuthbert, and Lang (1994) demonstrated that psychopathic individuals were deficient in the physiological arousal that normally accompanies emotional imagery. When imagining a fearful scene, psychopathic participants self-reported equivalent amounts of fearfulness and imagery experience; however, they showed deficits in SCRs compared with nonpsychopathic control participants. These experiments suggest that physiological responses can provide information about emotional processes that may be dissociated from conscious verbal knowledge.

Another experimental paradigm that often depends on SCRs to discrete stimuli is classical conditioning. In a classic study, Öhman, Ericksson, and Olofsson (1975) conditioned SCRs to visual images by pairing electric shocks (unconditional stimulus) with specific pictures (conditioned stimuli). Some pictures were of neutral objects (e.g., flowers, mushrooms), and some were of "potentially phobic" objects—images that a person may be biologically prepared to fear, such as spiders and snakes. Results showed that it was more difficult to extinguish the SCRs conditioned to the fearful images than the neutral images. Öhman and Dimberg (1978) found the same effect for pictures of angry versus happy faces. It is interesting to note that Soares and Öhman (1993) reported that conditioned SCRs to fear-relevant stimuli (e.g., snakes, angry faces) persist even when the stimuli are subsequently presented in a masked fashion. In another variation that did not use classical conditioning, Öhman and Soares (1994) found that participants with snake and spider phobias showed an enhanced SCR to their masked specific fear-relevant stimuli. The SCRs elicited by the masked stimuli were equivalent to the SCRs elicited by recognizable stimuli. These experiments demonstrate how the measurement of electrodermal responses support the hypothesis that emotion can activate preattentive processes (Öhman, Flykt, & Esteves, 2001).

Numerous studies have used SCR as a marker for arousal during emotional processing. This paradigm is not limited to the presentation of discrete stimuli. Many studies use measures of SCLs over longer time periods to measure the impact of repeated stimuli (for a review, see Dawson et al., 2000). Measuring individual differences in electrodermal responding has often proved fruitful in investigations of emotion and psychopathology. For example, Bernstein et al. (1982) noted that a high proportion of individuals with schizophrenia have hypoactive SCRs. Sponheim, Allen, and Iacono (1995) reviewed the findings that phasic and tonic electrodermal activity is markedly diminished in depressed patients. Rottenberg, Gross, Wilhelm, and Gotlib (2002) noted less EDA during depressed patients' crying episodes than during healthy control participants' crying. Roedema and Simons (1999) observed less EDA in participants with alexithymia compared with control participants who watched emotion-eliciting color slides.

In sum, EDA is a valuable method for indexing sympathetic nervous system activity and has widespread applicability to emotion research. This method is easy to use; relatively inexpensive; and sensitive to many important variables—although this last point can also be a disadvantage, because EDA may respond to potentially confounding variables. Finally, EDA is a relatively slow-moving response system and is therefore limited in its ability to track moment-to-moment changes in sympathetic activity.

CARDIOVASCULAR ACTIVITY

Poets and scientists have long observed that the heart can race, pound, or flutter depending on the emotion elicited; hence, measuring cardiovascular activity has been an essential psychophysiological method. Multiple techniques are available for measuring cardiac function (for a detailed review, see Brownley, Hurwitz, & Schneiderman, 2000), and there are many medical purposes for its measurement. For publication guidelines for heart rate studies, see Jennings et al. (1981). This discussion, however, focuses on issues and measures of particular interest to emotion researchers, including measures of heart rate, variability, and contractility.

To measure EKG, psychophysiologists typically use bipolar recordings between pairs of limbs according to Einthoven's triangle (Einthoven, Fahr, & de Waart, 1913). Electrode placements may be a "right arm–left arm" (Lead I), a "right arm–left leg" (Lead II), or a "left arm–left leg" (Lead III) configuration. An EKG measures voltage changes associated with various phases of the cardiac cycle, with a characteristic waveform that has peaks and valleys associated with the timing of atrial and ventricular depolarization and repolarization. As depicted in Figure 3.1, accurate identification of the QRS complex of an EKG, associated with ventricular depolarization, provides an easy to identify and reliable index of cardiac timing. By assessing the *interbeat interval* (IBI), the elapsed time between two consecutive heartbeats, measured in milliseconds, a continuous measure of heart rate (HR) is obtained, where HR in beats per minute = $1/\text{IBI} \times 60{,}000$. Changes in the HR and IBI can be due to emotional processes as well as to metabolic and cognitive processes.

Cardiac activity is regulated by both the sympathetic and parasympathetic division of the autonomic nervous system. Under normal conditions, both divisions regulate the heart, with the parasympathetic division supplying inhibitory control and the sympathetic division supplying excitatory control. Parasympathetic fibers decelerate the HR by releasing acetylcholine from nerves that innervate the heart via the vagus nerve. Sympathetic fibers in the heart accelerate the HR by releasing norepinephrine. Because of the heart's dual innervation, changes in HR could be caused by the influence of either sympathetic or parasympathetic activity, although the parasympathetic divi-

EKG Waveform

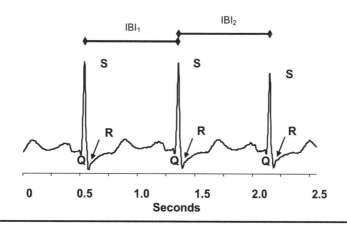

Beat-to-Beat Variability

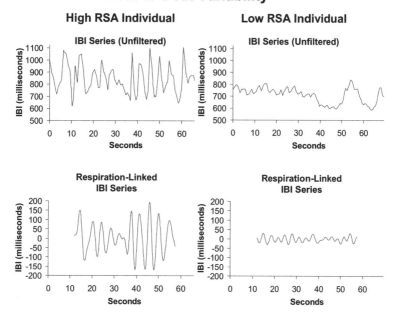

Figure 3.1. Top panel shows a prototypic electrocardiogram (EKG) waveform for three consecutive heartbeats. The QRS complex is identified, with the prominent R spike used to identify the interbeat interval (IBI). Bottom panel shows the IBI series for two individuals, one high in respiration-linked IBI variability and one low in respiration-linked IBI variability. The upper two graphs in this bottom panel show the raw unfiltered IBI series, and the lower panels show the same data filtered to include only frequencies within the respiratory band. Note that the filter results in a loss of 12 seconds of data at both ends of the series. The variability in the lower panels represents that portion of the total variability that reflects vagal influence. Note that the variability seen in the latter portion of the raw series for the low-RSA individual was not in synch with respiration and therefore was not conclusively vagally mediated.

sion typically has a much larger impact on cardiac chronotropy (i.e., rate) than the sympathetic division (Henning, Khalil, & Levy, 1990).

Measures of cardiac chronotropy can reflect changes over short intervals, such as the few seconds preceding (Hare, 1965) or following (Bradley, Lang, & Cuthbert, 1993) a stimulus, or they can reflect estimates of rate or variability summarized over a longer interval, such as while viewing an emotional film or a series of pictures, performing a stressful task, or even during a "resting" condition. The latter assessments of baseline or resting EKG across several minutes form the basis for assessing individual differences in HR variability.

Measuring Parasympathetic Influence

Respiratory sinus arrhythmia (RSA) is a measure of HR variability and provides a noninvasive index of parasympathetic control over the heart (see lower panel of Figure 3.1). RSA reflects the influence of the respiratory processes on the cardiovascular system. Inspiration and expiration lead to HR acceleration and deceleration, respectively. This HR variability, or *arrhythmia*, is controlled by the vagus nerve: Vagal efferent traffic to the heart occurs primarily in phase with expiration and is absent or attenuated during inspiration. Further evidence supporting that RSA is under vagal control comes from studies using atropine, an anticholinergic drug that inhibits vagal influence at the sinoatrial node of the heart, that have found atropine abolishes RSA (Berntson, Cacioppo, Binkley, & Uchino, 1994).

Various methods are used to compute RSA, all of which involve estimating the variability in HR that is tied to the respiratory cycle. There is no consensus, however, as to which method is most accurate. J. J. B. Allen (2002) reviewed the logic and procedures of several popular metrics of cardiac chronotropy and also provided a computer program (CMet) that calculates many of the metrics given a series of IBIs. J. J. B. Allen showed that under laboratory conditions, the various metrics are highly intercorrelated (typically $r > .8$), although some authors have argued that RSA may provide a misleading index of vagal influence under conditions in which breathing rate varies considerably (Berntson et al., 1997; Grossman, Karemaker, & Wieling, 1991). It is also critical to ensure that beats are accurately identified because either missing a beat or erroneously identifying an extra (nonexistent) beat in the IBI series will grossly distort the estimates of variability (Berntson & Stowell, 1998).

Cardiac vagal tone is inferred from RSA and serves as a particularly important physiological variable for emotion researchers because of its relationship to psychological processes. Vagal tone is most often construed as an individual difference variable and reflects the primary peripheral output from a series of cortical and subcortical structures known as the *central autonomic network* (CAN; Thayer & Lane, 2002). These structures are reciprocally connected such that information travels centrally–peripherally and vice versa, and thus the CAN is directly linked to HR variability. Proper functioning of this system allows an organism to regulate its behavior in response to changing environmental demands. Flexible attention is required for an organism to shift from relevant to irrelevant information in the environment. If this neurovisceral feedback system is either uncoupled or rigidly coupled, it may lead to abnormal affective processing.

It is important to note that vagal tone can serve as an index of functioning between the CAN and peripheral neural feedback. Specifically, high vagal tone is associated with the ability to demonstrate greater behavioral flexibility and adaptability in a changing environment, and low vagal tone is associated with poor self-regulation, deficits in attention modulation, and a lack of behavioral flexibility (Porges, 1992). Measurement of vagal tone has provided considerable evidence that disruption of the CAN is associated with affective disorders and perseverative responses (Friedman & Thayer, 1998) as well as many other forms of psychopathology (Beauchaine, 2001).

For example, Thayer, Friedman, and Borkovec (1996) investigated the relationship between vagal tone and generalized anxiety disorder (GAD). Worry, the essential component of GAD, involves excessive, unrealistic apprehension and also attentional alterations such as hypervigilance, scanning, and a preattentive bias for threat information (Mathews, 1990). When comparing persons with GAD and nonanxious control participants in a worry and relaxation condition, two main effects were revealed. First, persons with GAD had lower vagal tone compared with control participants in all conditions including baseline. Second, worry in both the GAD and nonanxious control group members was associated with a reduction in vagal tone. Disruptions in vagal tone have been associated with a number of other conditions and disorders, including panic disorder (Klein, Cnaani, Harel, Braun, & Ben-Haim, 1995; Friedman & Thayer, 1998), posttraumatic stress disorder (Cohen et al., 1997), hostility (Sloan et al., 2001), and depression (Rechlin, Weis, Spitzer, & Kaschka, 1994; also see Rottenberg, Wilhelm, Gross, & Gotlib, 2002).

Measuring Sympathetic Influence

In addition to measures of chronotropy, which reflect primarily parasympathetic influence, measures of *inotropy* (contractility) are useful as indices of sympathetic influences on cardiac function. Greater sympathetic activity is reflected in greater contractility of the ventricles, essentially a more forceful and rapid ejection of blood. Ventricular contractility is measured indirectly by examining the *preejection period* (PEP), the interval between the onset of ventricular depolarization and the onset of ventricular ejection. Lower PEP intervals reflect faster contraction and greater sympathetic influence. Cardiac contractility can be measured noninvasively with impedance cardiography. In this technique, a constant low-voltage alternating current is passed through the chest. The current follows the path of least resistance, which is the red blood cells; therefore, changes in resistance are associated with changes in thoracic blood volume. The output voltage generated by impedance cardiography corresponds to beat-by-beat changes in stroke volume. In addition to PEP, impedance cardiography can also be used to generate several other indices of sympathetic myocardial drive. The interested reader should see Brownley et al. (2000) for a detailed review of these calculations and also several limitations associated with impedance cardiography, as well as Sherwood et al. (1990) for methodological guidelines. Also see Newlin and Levenson (1979) for a technologically simple but slightly more labor-intensive method of measuring PEP.

Measuring sympathetic nervous system effects on cardiac function has been incorporated into the research of emotion processes and individual differences in emotion variables. In a common protocol, impedance cardiography is measured while participants engage in a laboratory stressor task, and the changes observed in PEP during stress are considered to reflect predominantly sympathetic effects on the heart (Cacioppo, Uchino, & Berntson, 1994). Combining this methodology with an emotional variable, Light, Kothandapadi, and Allen (1998) tested the hypothesis that individuals with depressive symptoms would respond to a laboratory stressor task with exaggerated cardiovascular and sympathetic nervous system activity. Consistent with this hypothesis, a shorter PEP (indexing greater sympathetic activation) was observed among individuals with depressive symptoms compared with control participants. Burns, Friedman, and Katkin (1992) continuously measured impedance cardiography while undergraduate men performed a mental arithmetic task and found a significant correlation between the change in PEP from baseline and participants' self-reported anger. In another study, Gross and Levenson (1993) investigated the effects of emotional suppression on behavioral and physiological variables. Sympathetic activity was indexed by measuring an EKG and the peripheral pulse at the finger and then calculating the pulse transmission time to the finger, a statistic that is correlated with the PEP (Newlin, 1981). Compared with participants who did not suppress their emotions, suppressors showed several indices of increased sympathetic nervous system activity.

ELECTROENCEPHALOGRAM

The EEG is a noninvasive measurement of the brain's electrical activity from the surface of the scalp. This psychophysiological method is a valuable tool for measuring various emotional processes. This section reviews basic descriptive characteristics of EEG, general issues in recording and measurement, and its strengths and limitations as well as a selected current research application to emotion. (For a detailed examination of other theoretical and practical issues, see Davidson, Jackson, & Larson, 2000; for recording and quantification guidelines, see Pivik et al., 1993.)

Most researchers now agree that EEG measured at the scalp surface derives from summated postsynaptic potentials in the brain. Conceptually, the EEG signal is primarily composed of rhythmic sinusoidal patterns of electrical activity that are most commonly characterized by frequency and amplitude parameters. The frequency of the signal can range from very slow (<1 Hz) to very fast (80 Hz). A power spectral analysis of the processed EEG signal is performed to compute the power of each underlying sine wave constituent. A fast Fourier transform can decompose the signal into specific frequencies, which are then often summed into traditional EEG frequency bands: delta (1–4 Hz), theta (5–7 Hz), alpha (8–13 Hz), and beta (13–30 Hz). Differences in behavioral states can be compared based on the frequency and amplitude of these EEG bands. For example, in normal adults, deep sleep has been associated with large and very slow waves in the delta frequency range, whereas drowsiness has been associated with low-amplitude theta activity and delta waves. Alpha activity has often been characterized as "relaxed wakefulness," and "alert attentiveness" is mainly characterized by low-amplitude activity in the beta range.

Despite the widespread use of EEG recording, there is considerable variability in its basic methodology. Typically, recording electrodes resemble small cups or hollow disks that are to be filled with conducting gel before being applied to the head. The electrodes may be applied singly with an adhesive material or as a group using a net or cap. The placement of the electrodes should evenly sample the scalp surface, and the 10-20 system (Jasper, 1958) has been the traditional means of achieving this goal. The 10-20 system positions specific electrodes on the basis of fixed cranial landmarks (e.g., inion, nasion), and then the remaining electrodes are placed on the basis of standardized distances from these coordinates. It is important to note that the EEG signal from a single site is actually a bipolar recording and reflects the potential difference between the "active" site and a reference site. There are multiple options for choosing a reference site or configuration (for more information about this important issue, see J. J. B. Allen, Coan, & Nazarian, 2004; Davidson et al., 2000).

A key advantage of recording EEG is that it has very good temporal resolution. Changes in neuronal activity are reflected immediately in the EEG signal, which is a significant advantage over other hemodynamic measures of brain activity such as functional magnetic resonance imaging and positron emission tomography. Thus, the EEG is well suited for measuring electrical brain activity that changes rapidly with behavioral or emotional states. For example, Davidson, Ekman, Saron, Senulis, and Friesen (1990) recorded the continuous EEG of participants and video recorded their facial behavior so that it could be coded for emotional expressions. Because of the

EEG's temporal resolution, it was possible to observe changes in brain electrical activity that was coincident with even fleeting facial expressions.

A major limitation of EEG is its poor spatial resolution. Davidson et al. (2000) described three reasons in particular for this problem. First, even large-channel (e.g., 128 or 256 sites) EEG recording is considerably coarser than what is achieved with functional imaging techniques. Second, the EEG signal passes through the skull, which is highly resistant and acts like a low-pass spatial filter that distorts the electrical activity over a relatively large region of the scalp. Third, even high-density EEG recordings provide only two-dimensional data on the scalp. Inferring the intracerebral source of that electrical activity is problematic because there is no unique solution to the pattern of observed signals. The scalp potentials could be produced by many combinations of underlying sources. Mathematical techniques are used to model the location, orientation, and strength of the hypothetical source; even a good model fit, however, does not ensure the results are valid. If the generator is likely to be a single source (e.g., during simple sensory and motor processes), then the source localization technique may be useful. However, when the EEG is being used to measure complex cognitive or emotional processes that are likely to have several source generators, localization techniques are more problematic. The validity of such modeling ultimately depends on the anatomical plausibility given what is known about the function of the identified regions and on corroborative findings from other spatially precise (but temporally less precise) methods such as functional magnetic resonance imaging or positron emission tomography.

Event-Related Brain Potentials

Event-related brain potentials (ERPs) are an application of EEG that take advantage of its temporally precise resolution. ERPs reflect brainwave activity that is time locked to specific stimuli or events; the waveform is usually regarded as signifying a psychological process that may have occurred in preparation for or in response to the specific event (for a review, see Kok, 1997). An ERP is relatively small, typically less than 10 μV, whereas the ongoing EEG signal is about 50 μV. The ERP can be extracted from this background activity by averaging multiple segments of the EEG that are time locked to a particular event (see Figure 3.2), but such events must occur with temporal precision (e.g., a printed word or picture on a computer screen but not a video clip). The resulting ERP waveform typically contains a number of positive and negative peaks that are graphed as a voltage × time function, which is obtained for each electrode site, with peaks labeled for polarity (P = positive, N = negative) and sequence (e.g., P3 is the third major positive peak). The label may also refer to the psychological or experimental condition that elicited the potential (e.g., the error-related negativity [ERN]). A component is best considered a construct, with the construct validity of a

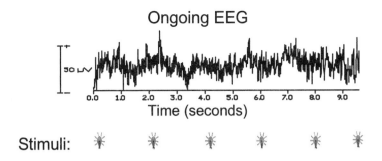

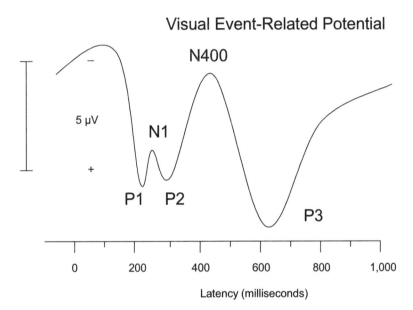

Figure 3.2. The relation between ongoing electroencephalographic (EEG) activity (top) and event-related potential (ERP; bottom). The top panel depicts voltage changes in the range of 50 µV to 100 µV that occur across several seconds. Beneath the ongoing EEG is depicted a series of stimuli presented approximately once every 2 seconds. As can be seen from the figure, no visually discernable changes occur in the EEG as a result of the stimulus presentation. When the EEG activity surrounding multiple presentations is averaged together, however, the ERP in the lower panel emerges. The ERP represents voltage changes on the order of 5 µV to 20 µV that occur across a 1-second (1,000-milliseconds) interval. Positive is plotted downward, and peaks are labeled for polarity and latency or for their sequential appearance. P = positive; N = negative; P1 = the first major positive peak; P3 = the third positive peak; N400 = the negative peak appearing at 400 milliseconds.

component deriving from a combination of polarity, latency, scalp topography, and response to experimental manipulations.

Historically, ERP research has focused more on cognitive and sensory processes, although applications are increasingly popular in emotion research.

For example, the P3 is a positive peak in the ERP that typically results from the detection of a deviant or "meaningful" stimulus, indicating an orientation of attention (Halgren & Marinkovic, 1995). Applying this cognitive process to a study of emotion and psychopathology, Deldin, Keller, Gergen, and Miller (2001) examined the P3 of individuals with depression during the encoding and recognition of emotional words. Control participants showed an enhanced P3 during encoding and a reduced P3 during recognition of positive words. Individuals with depression lacked this bias for positive information, and a substantial portion of the P3 variance was related to clinical scale scores.

A new but promising family of ERP components, the ERN, and a related feedback negativity often termed the *medial-frontal negativity* (MFN), has become of interest to emotion researchers. The ERN is a negative component that peaks at frontocentral scalp sites approximately 100 milliseconds after an individual commits an overt error, and the MFN is a similar appearing negative component but time locked to feedback informing subjects that they have made an incorrect response (e.g., Miltner, Braun, & Coles, 1997). Examining the MFN, Tucker, Luu, Frishkoff, Quiring, and Poulsen (2003) demonstrated that brain systems generating the ERN and MFN may also reflect biases in the expectation of negative outcomes, and thus individuals with clinical depression may show exaggerated MFNs in response to negative feedback compared with control participants.

For a detailed review of ERP methodology, see Fabiani, Gratton, and Coles (2000), and for a recording and publication guidelines article, see Picton et al. (2000). The remainder of this section reviews one widely used application of EEG to emotion and psychopathology.

Frontal Electroencephalogram Asymmetry and Emotion

Asymmetrical frontal brain activity is a reliable and reasonably stable individual difference variable that appears to index risk for depression and possibly anxiety, as well as to moderate emotional and motivational constructs in populations as diverse as human infants, adults, and nonhuman primates (for a review, see Coan & Allen, 2003, 2004). Frontal EEG asymmetry is measured by quantifying alpha power (8–13 Hz) over the scalp. Oscillations in the alpha band are thought to be inversely related to active cortical processing, such that less alpha activity is thought to be indicative of greater cortical activity (J. J. B. Allen, Urry, Hitt, & Coan, 2004). In calculating the asymmetry score, alpha power is compared at pairs of symmetrical sites across the scalp, typically by taking a natural log-transformed difference score (i.e., ln[Right]–ln[Left]). Higher scores on this metric thus reflect relatively greater right than left alpha power, indicative of relatively greater left than right cortical activity. A more comprehensive review of methods for recording and analyzing EEG asymmetry data has been provided by J. J. B. Allen, Coan, and Nazarian (2004).

Findings from more than 40 studies suggest that resting frontal EEG activity may serve as an indicator of a traitlike diathesis to respond to emotional situations with a characteristic pattern of emotional negativity and behavioral withdrawal. Studies assessing resting EEG activity reveal that relatively less left than right frontal brain activity characterizes individuals with depression both when symptomatic and when euthymic (J. J. B. Allen, Iacono, Depue, & Arbisi, 1993; Gotlib, Ranganath, & Rosenfeld, 1998; Henriques & Davidson, 1990), although not without exception (Reid, Duke, & Allen, 1998). Such findings suggest that frontal EEG asymmetry may be more than simply a correlate of a depressive episode, potentially serving as a liability marker for the development of depression or other emotion-related psychopathology (J. J. Allen, Urry, Hitt, & Coan, 2004; Coan & Allen, 2004), and similar findings have been observed in panic disorder (Wiedemann et al., 1999) and anxiety (Davidson, Marshall, Tomarken, & Henriques, 2000).

Conceptual models of frontal brain asymmetry posit that asymmetry may underlie fundamental dimensions of approach and withdrawal motivations and actions (e.g., Coan & Allen, 2003). According to Davidson's (1993, 1998) approach–withdrawal model of frontal EEG asymmetry, relatively greater left frontal activity should generally result in either an approach orientation or an approach-oriented action, and relatively greater right frontal activity should generally result in either a withdrawal orientation or a withdrawal-oriented action. This approach–withdraw model parallels the behavioral activation and behavioral inhibition systems proposed by Gray (1987, 1994). In support of these models, three studies have identified that relatively greater left frontal EEG activity characterizes those higher in behavioral activation system sensitivity using self-report scales (Coan & Allen, 2003; Harmon-Jones & Allen, 1997; Sutton & Davidson, 1997). Also, greater left frontal EEG activity has been associated with higher trait-positive affect (Tomarken, Davidson, Wheeler, & Kinney, 1992), and higher trait anger (Harmon-Jones & Allen, 1998).

Resting frontal asymmetry has also predicted emotional responding. Individuals with greater relative right frontal EEG activity exhibited greater negative affect in response to disgusting and fearful films; they also exhibited less positive affect in response to happy films (Tomarken, Davidson, & Henriques, 1990; Wheeler, Davidson, & Tomarken, 1993). Additionally, and consistent with the motivational model of asymmetry, individuals with greater relative left frontal EEG activity reported greater anger and exhibited more aggressive behavior following an insult manipulation (Harmon-Jones & Sigelman, 2001).

Frontal EEG asymmetry has also been associated with state emotional changes. For example, relative left frontal activity was found to increase when individuals voluntarily produced smiles indicating enjoyment (Ekman & Davidson, 1993). Similarly, Coan, Allen, and Harmon-Jones (2001) found greater left frontal activity when individuals produced facial movements that mimicked a joyful expression compared with relatively less left frontal activity when the individuals' movements mimicked a fearful expression. Thus, frontal EEG consistently exhibits sensitivity to facial expressions of emotion (Coan & Allen, 2004); surprisingly few studies have suggested that frontal EEG asymmetry is sensitive to other manipulations of valence, such as valenced picture viewing, unless highly personally relevant and intense pictorial stimuli are used (Harmon-Jones, Lueck, Fearn, & Harmon-Jones, 2006).

Although asymmetrical frontal brain activity holds promise as a marker of risk for depression, superimposed on the traitlike stability are fluctuations that vary as a function of occasion of assessment or experimentally manipulated emotion. Estimates of the stability of frontal EEG asymmetry are in the range of .60 (J. J. B. Allen, Urry, et al., 2004; Hagemann, Naumann, Thayer, & Bartussek, 2002), suggesting that trait factors are substantial but that variation across assessments may limit the utility of asymmetrical frontal brain activity as a traitlike risk indicator for depression. The predictive ability of frontal EEG asymmetry may be enhanced by observing not simply resting states, as is often the case, but instead examining individual differences in state-elicited EEG asymmetry (Coan, Allen, & McKnight, 2006).

FACIAL ELECTROMYOGRAPHY

The electrophysiological signals that emanate from active muscles are another important aspect of behavioral and psychological processes. Surface electromyography (EMG) is a noninvasive means of measuring this muscle activity, with facial expressions of particular interest to emotion researchers for more than 100 years (Darwin, 1872/1998; Duchenne, 1862/1990).

Facial muscle regions of particular interest to emotion researchers are the *corrugator supercilii* and the *depressor supercilii*, which are used to lower and contract the brow; the *zygomaticus major*, which pulls the corner of the mouth during a smile or grimace; and the *orbicularis oculi*, the circular band of muscles that make the eyes seem to smile when someone experiences happiness and that can contract defensively to close the eye quickly during a startle reflex. Although muscle contractions are required to achieve facial expressions, facial muscles can flex in the absence of any obvious facial display (Tassinary & Cacioppo, 1992). Even visually imperceptible contractions of the facial musculature create motor action potentials that can be recorded in response to stimuli (Cacioppo, Tassinary, & Fridlund, 1990), with mildly evocative emotional stimuli capable of producing effects on facial EMG that were not detectable with skin conductance measurement (Cacioppo, Petty, Losch, & Kim, 1986). Thus, a major advantage of facial EMG measures is the ability to record muscle activity associated with affective processes even when it is subtle and visually imperceptible to others.

For a review of the details concerning the measurement of facial EMG, see Tassinary and Cacioppo (2000), and for EMG guidelines see Fridlund and Cacioppo (1986). The remainder of this section highlights the application of facial EMG to emotion research, emphasizing an additional facial EMG method: the eyeblink startle response.

Facial Muscles and Emotion

Corrugator muscles furrow the brow, a facial display that provides an index of distress (Fridlund & Izard, 1983). This muscle group should be active when a person encounters an unpleasant stimulus. Zygomatic muscles produce a smile response, and activity in this muscle group increases while viewing stimuli that individuals rate as pleasant (Lang, Greenwald, Bradley, & Hamm, 1993); however, for pictures that are rated as most unpleasant (e.g., scenes of mutilation) there is also a tendency for increased zygomatic activity. This activation usually occurs in addition to significant corrugator activity and suggests a facial grimace in response to highly aversive material.

The predicted relationship between facial EMG and emotional stimuli was supported by experiments using valenced pictures (Lang et al., 1993) and during mental imagery (Schwartz, Fair, Salt, Mandel, & Klerman, 1976). Cacioppo, Martzke, Petty, and Tassinary (1988) demonstrated that facial EMG activity covaried with subtle variations in specific emotions during an interview even when overt facial expressions did not distinguish them. Jäncke (1994) measured facial EMG while eliciting anger responses from participants and also found patterns of EMG activation specific to the emotional display.

Using Electromyography to Measure Emotion-Modulated Startle

The startle–eyeblink reflex is another electromyographic measure that is of considerable interest to emotion researchers. The eyeblink reflex is a reliable component of the behavioral cascade that constitutes the startle pattern and likely serves as a protective function to avoid injury to the eye, but which is also influenced by emotional processes. The eyeblink reflex can be elicited by brief and intense auditory, visual, or tactile stimuli, but the most typical procedure is a 50-millisecond burst of white noise at approximately 95 dB. The magnitude of the blink can be measured by placing two electrodes over the orbicularis oculi muscle, one just below the lower eyelid, centered under the pupil, and the second electrode placed 1 centimeter laterally. Greater detail on signal acquisition and analysis is available in the guidelines article of Blumenthal et al. (2005).

The startle reflex appears to be potentiated during anxiety or fear states, and this pattern has been observed in animals (Davis, 1986) as well as humans (Grillon & Davis, 1997). In the typical experiment, a conditioned stimulus (e.g., light) that was previously paired with an unconditional stimulus (e.g., electric shock) is used as a context for measuring the startle reflex. The startle response is greater in the presence of the light than in its absence.

Extensive research on the neural circuitry of the startle response has identified primary pathways as well as secondary circuits affecting the primary reflex (see Davis, 1989). The amygdala is a critical component to the modulation of the primary startle response. Activation of this subcortical circuitry should prime defensive reflexes (i.e., enhance eyeblink reflex), whereas activation of appetitive–approach circuitry should inhibit defensive responding (i.e., attenuate eyeblink reflex). Hence, measurement of the eyeblink reflex provides emotion researchers with a highly useful probe of the activation of defensive motivational systems.

Lang (1995) reviewed eyeblink startle data that demonstrated support for the motivational priming hypothesis. The blink response to startle probes was potentiated during unpleasant pictures and inhibited during pleasant pictures. The startle reflex was modulated by the affective valence of the picture regardless of whether the probe was visual, acoustic, or tactile (Bradley, Cuthbert, & Lang, 1990). As reviewed by Bradley, Cuthbert, and Lang (1999), affective stimuli other than pictures (e.g., films, odors, sound clips) have also been shown to modulate the startle reflex. The startle response has been modulated as soon as 500 milliseconds after stimulus presentation and maintained throughout a 6-second viewing interval; the modulation can persist up to 3 seconds even if the affective stimulus is removed after 500 milliseconds.

The eyeblink startle reflex has also been used to investigate emotional processes in a wide range of clinical populations, including an accentuated startle reflex during anticipation of aversive stimuli in patients with panic disorder (Grillon, Ameli, Goddard, Woods, & Davis, 1994) and posttraumatic stress disorder (Grillon & Morgan, 1996). Abnormal startle reflexes have also been reported in patients with major depression (N. B. Allen, Trinder, & Brennan, 1999) and schizophrenia (Schlenker, Cohen, & Hopmann, 1995), individuals with specific phobias who were exposed to pictures and imagery of their feared objects (de Jong, Visser, & Merckelback, 1996; Vrana, Constantine, & Westman, 1992), and psychopathic individuals with criminal records (Patrick, Bradley, & Lang, 1993).

In sum, facial expressions and reflexes are an important component to the experience of an emotion, and facial EMG is relatively easy to implement. It provides fine sensitivity, especially considering that subtle changes in facial musculature are difficult to detect from the third-person vantage, and they may be absent from first-person self-report.

CONCLUSION

Psychophysiological variables appeared as the dependent measure in many of the studies reviewed in this chapter; however, they are not limited to this role. As an independent variable, psychophysiological patterns have the potential to identify individuals who are at risk for various disorders (e.g., Finn, Kessler, & Hussong, 1994), they can act as moderator variables for other dependent measures (e.g., Coan et al., 2001), and they can be used as a marker for clinical outcome studies (e.g., Lang, Cuthbert, & Bradley, 1998).

Gaining the full value of psychophysiological measures also requires appreciating their limitations. A critical issue that confronts psychophysiological research is one of inference. Much of the research presented here highlighted only a single psychophysiological variable reported in the experiment, but actually in most cases several other variables were also tested. To optimize the interpretability of a psychophysiological experiment, it is highly desirable to assess multiple systems (e.g., EKG, SCR, and EEG) and to integrate data from multiple levels of analysis with the hope that convergence and divergence across these measures will allow for accurate interpretation of the results. As Cacioppo, Tassinary, and Berntson (2000b) noted, establishing that a psychological manipulation leads to a particular physiological response or profile of responses is not logically sufficient to infer that the physiological event will be a strong predictor of the psychological element of interest; base-rate information about the occurrence of the physiological event across situations must also be considered. To avoid the logical flaw of "affirming the consequent," the researcher must be aware that a wide range of complex relationships may exist between psychological and physiological phenomena. Carefully constructed experimental designs that hold constant alternative explanations are essential to determining the results' range of validity. An appreciation of both the advantages and limitations of psychophysiological measures will lead to the most fruitful use of these valuable methods for measuring emotion.

Psychophysiology is now a mainstream research tool. A half century ago, psychophysiological tools were used by a group of scientists with highly specialized training and esoteric laboratories that resembled an electronics parts emporium. Today, nonspecialists treat these tools as just one of many means for addressing their research questions comprehensively. This chapter is offered in the hope of furthering this trend.

REFERENCES

References marked with an asterisk are considered essential resources.

Allen, J. J. B. (2002). Calculating metrics of cardiac chronotropy: A pragmatic overview. *Psychophysiology, 39,* S18.

Allen, J. J. B., Coan, J. A., & Nazarian, M. (2004). Issues and assumptions on the road from raw signals to metrics of frontal EEG asymmetry in emotion. *Biological Psychology, 67,* 183–218.

Allen, J. J. B., Iacono, W. G., Depue, R. A., & Arbisi, P. (1993). Regional electroencephalographic asymmetries in bipolar seasonal affective disorder before and after exposure to bright light. *Biological Psychiatry, 33,* 642–646.

Allen, J. J. B., Urry, H. L., Hitt, S. K., & Coan, J. A. (2004). The stability of resting frontal electroencephalographic asymmetry in depression. *Psychophysiology, 41,* 269–280.

Allen, N. B., Trinder, J., & Brennan, C. (1999). Affective startle modulation in clinical depression: Preliminary findings. *Biological Psychiatry, 46,* 542–550.

Andreassi, J. L. (2000). *Psychophysiology: Human behavior and physiological response* (4th ed.). Hillsdale, NJ: Erlbaum.

Beauchaine, T. (2001). Vagal tone, development, and Gray's motivational theory: Toward an integrated model of autonomic nervous system functioning in psychopathology. *Development and Psychopathology, 13,* 183–214.

Bechara, A., Damasio, H., Tranel, D., & Damasio, A. R. (1997, February 28). Deciding advantageously before knowing the advantageous strategy. *Science, 275,* 1293–1295.

Bernstein, A., Frith, C., Gruzelier, J., Patterson, T., Straube, E., Venables, P., et al. (1982). An analysis of the skin conductance orienting response in samples of American, British, and German schizophrenics. *Biological Psychology, 14,* 155–211.

*Berntson, G. G., Bigger, J. T., Jr., Eckberg, D. L., Grossman, P., Kaufmann, P. G., Malik, M., et al. (1997). Heart rate variability: Origins, methods, and interpretive caveats. *Psychophysiology, 34,* 623–648.

Berntson, G. G., Cacioppo, J. T., Binkley, P. F., & Uchino, B. N. (1994). Autonomic cardiac control: III. Psychological stress and cardiac response in autonomic space as revealed by pharmacological blockades. *Psychophysiology, 31,* 599–608.

Berntson, G. G., & Stowell, J. R. (1998). ECG artifacts and heart period variability: Don't miss a beat! *Psychophysiology, 35,* 127–132.

*Blumenthal, T. D., Cuthbert, B. N., Filion, D. L., Hackley, S., Lipp, O. V., & van Boxtel, A. (2005). Committee report: Guidelines for human startle eyeblink electromyographic studies. *Psychophysiology, 42,* 1–15.

Boucsein, W. (1992). *Electrodermal activity.* New York: Plenum Press.

Bradley, M. M., Cuthbert, B. N., & Lang, P. J. (1990). Startle reflex modification: Emotion or attention? *Psychophysiology, 27,* 513–523.

Bradley, M. M., Cuthbert, B. N., & Lang, P. J. (1999). Affect and the startle reflex. In M. E. Dawson, A. M. Schell, & A. H. Böhmelt (Eds.), *Startle modification: Implications for neuroscience, cognitive science, and clinical science* (pp. 157–183). New York: Cambridge University Press.

Bradley, M. M., Lang, P. J., & Cuthbert, B. N. (1993). Emotion, novelty, and the startle reflex: Habituation in humans. *Behavioral Neuroscience, 107,* 970–980.

Brownley, K. A., Hurwitz, B. E., & Schneiderman, N. (2000). Cardiovascular psychophysiology. In J. T. Caccioppo, L. G. Tassinary, & G. G. Berntson (Eds.), *Handbook of psychophysiology* (2nd ed., pp. 224–264). Cambridge, England: Cambridge University Press.

Burns, J. W., Friedman, R., & Katkin, E. S. (1992). Anger expression, hostility, anxiety, and patterns of cardiac reactivity to stress. *Behavioral Medicine, 18,* 71–78.

Cacioppo, J. T., Martzke, J. S., Petty, R. E., & Tassinary, L. G. (1988). Specific forms of facial EMG response index emotions during an interview: From Darwin to the continuous flow hypothesis of affect-laden information processing. *Journal of Personality and Social Psychology, 54*, 592–604.

Cacioppo, J. T., Petty, R. E., Losch, M. E., & Kim, H. S. (1986). Electromyographic activity over facial muscles regions can differentiate the valence and intensity of affective reactions. *Journal of Personality and Social Psychology, 50*, 260–268.

Cacioppo, J. T., Tassinary, L. G., & Berntson, G. G. (Eds.). (2000a). *Handbook of psychophysiology* (2nd ed.). Cambridge, England: Cambridge University Press.

Cacioppo, J. T., Tassinary, L. G., & Berntson, G. G. (2000b). Psychophysiological science. In J. T. Cacioppo, L. G. Tassinary, & G. G. Berntson (Eds.), *Handbook of psychophysiology* (2nd ed., pp. 3–23). Cambridge, England: Cambridge University Press.

Cacioppo, J. T., Tassinary, L. G., & Fridlund, A. J. (1990). The skeletomotor system. In J. T. Cacioppo & L. G. Tassinary (Eds.), *Principles of psychophysiology: Physical, social, and inferential elements* (pp. 325–384). New York: Cambridge University Press.

Cacioppo, J. T., Uchino, B. N., & Berntson, G. G. (1994). Individual differences in the autonomic origins of heart rate reactivity: The psychometrics of respiratory sinus arrhythmia and preejection period. *Psychophysiology, 31*, 412–419.

Campos, A., Marcos, J. L., & Gonzalez, M. A. (1999). Relationship between properties of words and elicitation of skin conductance responses. *Psychological Reports, 85*, 1025–1030.

Coan, J. A., & Allen, J. J. B. (2003). Frontal EEG asymmetry and the behavioral activation and inhibition systems. *Psychophysiology, 40*, 106–114.

Coan, J. A., & Allen, J. J. B. (2004). Frontal EEG asymmetry as a moderator and mediator of emotion. *Biological Psychology, 67*, 7–50.

Coan, J. A., Allen, J. J. B., & Harmon-Jones, E. (2001). Voluntary facial expression and hemispheric asymmetry over the frontal cortex. *Psychophysiology, 38*, 912–925.

Coan, J. A., Allen, J. J. B., & McKnight, P. E. (2006). A capability model of individual differences in frontal EEG asymmetry. *Biological Psychology, 72*, 198–207.

Cohen, H., Kotler, M., Matar, M. A., Kaplan, Z., Miodownik, H., & Cassuto, Y. (1997). Power spectral analysis of heart rate variability in posttraumatic stress disorder patients. *Biological Psychiatry, 41*, 627–629.

Curtin, J. J., Lozano, D., & Allen, J. J. B. (in press). The psychophysiological laboratory. In J. A. Coan & J. J. B. Allen (Eds.), *The handbook of emotion elicitation and assessment*. New York: Oxford University Press.

Damasio, A. R. (1994). *Descartes' error: Emotion, reason, and the human brain.* New York: Grosset/Putnam.

Darwin, C. (1998). *The expression of the emotions in man and animals.* London: HarperCollins. (Original work published 1872)

Davidson, R. J. (1993). Parsing affective space: Perspectives from neuropsychology and psychophysiology. *Neuropsychology, 7,* 464–475.

Davidson, R. J. (1998). Affective style and affective disorders: Perspectives from affective neuroscience. *Cognition and Emotion, 12,* 307–330.

Davidson, R. J., Ekman, P., Saron, C. D., Senulis, J. A., & Friesen, W. V. (1990). Approach–withdrawal and cerebral asymmetry: Emotional expression and brain physiology: I. *Journal of Personality and Social Psychology, 58,* 330–341.

Davidson, R. J., Jackson, D. C., & Larson, C. L. (2000). Human electroencephalography. In J. T. Cacioppo, L. G. Tassinary, & G. G. Berntson (Eds.), *Handbook of psychophysiology* (2nd ed., pp. 27–52). Cambridge, England: Cambridge University Press.

Davidson, R. J., Marshall, J. R., Tomarken, A. J., & Henriques, J. B. (2000). While a phobic waits: Regional brain electrical and autonomic activity in social phobics during anticipation of public speaking. *Biological Psychiatry, 47,* 85–95.

Davis, M. (1986). Pharmacological and anatomical analysis of fear conditions using the fear-potentiated startle paradigm. *Behavioral Neuroscience, 100,* 814–824.

Davis, M. (1989). Sensitization of the acoustic startle reflex by foot shock. *Behavioral Neuroscience, 10,* 495–503.

Dawson, M. E., Schell, A. M., & Filion, D. L. (2000). The electrodermal system. In J. T. Cacioppo, L. G. Tassinary, & G. G. Berntson (Eds.), *Handbook of psychophysiology* (2nd ed., pp. 200–223). Cambridge, England: Cambridge University Press.

de Jong, P., Visser, S., & Merckelback, H. (1996). Startle and spider phobia: Unilateral probes and the prediction of treatment effects. *Journal of Psychophysiology, 10,* 150–160.

Deldin, P. J., Keller, J., Gergen, J. A., & Miller, G. A. (2001). Cognitive bias and emotion in neuropsychological models of depression. *Cognition and Emotion, 15,* 787–802.

Devinsky, O., Morrell, M., & Vogt, B. (1995). Contributions of anterior cingulate cortex to behaviour. *Brain, 118,* 279–306.

Duchenne, G.-B. (1990). *The mechanism of human facial expression* (R. A. Cuthbertson, Ed. & Trans.). New York: Cambridge University Press. (Original work published 1862)

Einthoven, W., Fahr, G., & de Waart, A. (1913). Uber die Richtung und die manifeste Grosse der Pontetialschwankungen in menchlichen Herzen und uber den Einfluss der Herzlage auf die Form des Elecktrokardiogramms [On the direction and manifest size of the variations of potential in the human heart and on the influence of the position of the heart on the form of the electrocardiogram]. *Pflügers Archiv European Journal of Physiology, 150,* 275–315.

Ekman, P., & Davidson, R. J. (1993). Voluntary smiling changes regional brain activity. *Psychological Science, 4,* 342–345.

Fabiani, M., Gratton, G., & Coles, M. G. (2000). Event-related brain potentials. In J. T. Cacioppo, L. G. Tassinary, & G. G. Berntson (Eds.), *Handbook of psycho-*

physiology (2nd ed., pp. 53–84). Cambridge, England: Cambridge University Press.

Finn, P. R., Kessler, D. N., & Hussong, A. M. (1994). Risk for alcoholism and classical conditions to signals for punishment: Evidence for a weak behavioral inhibition system. *Journal of Abnormal Psychology, 103,* 293–301.

*Fowles, D., Christie, M. J., Edelberg, R., Grings, W. W., Lykken, D. T., & Venables, P. H. (1981). Publication recommendations for electrodermal measurements. *Psychophysiology, 18,* 232–239.

*Fridlund, A. J., & Cacioppo, J. T. (1986). Guidelines for human electromyographic research. *Psychophysiology, 23,* 567–589.

Fridlund, A. J., & Izard, C. E. (1983). Electromyographic studies of facial expressions of emotion and patterns of emotion. In J. T. Cacioppo & R. E. Petty (Eds.), *Social psychophysiology* (pp. 243–280). New York: Guilford Press.

Friedman, B., & Thayer, J. (1998). Autonomic balance revisited: Panic anxiety and heart rate variability. *Journal of Psychosomatic Research, 44,* 133–151.

Frijda, N. H. (2000). The psychologists' point of view. In M. Lewis & J. M. Haviland-Jones (Eds.), *Handbook of emotions* (pp. 59–74). New York: Guilford Press.

Gotlib, I. H., Ranganath, C., & Rosenfeld, J. P. (1998). Frontal EEG alpha asymmetry, depression, and cognitive functioning. *Cognition and Emotion, 12,* 449–478.

Gottesman, I. I., & Gould, T. D. (2003). The endophenotype concept in psychiatry: Etymology and strategic intentions. *American Journal of Psychiatry, 160,* 636–645.

Gray, J. A. (1987). *The psychology of fear and stress* (2nd ed.). Cambridge, England: Cambridge University Press.

Gray, J. A. (1994). Three fundamental emotion systems. In P. Ekman & R. J. Davidson, (Eds.), *The nature of emotion* (pp. 243–247). New York: Oxford University Press.

Greenwald, M. K., Cook, E. W., III, & Lang, P. J. (1989). Affective judgment and psychophysiological response: Dimensional covariation in the evaluation of pictorial stimuli. *Journal of Psychophysiology, 3,* 51–64.

Grillon, C., Ameli, R., Goddard, A., Woods, S., & Davis, M. (1994). Baseline and fear-potentiated startle in panic disorder patients. *Biological Psychiatry, 35,* 431–439.

Grillon, C., & Davis, M. (1997). Fear-potentiated startle conditioning in humans: Explicit and contextual cue conditioning following paired vs. unpaired training. *Psychophysiology, 34,* 451–458.

Grillon, C., & Morgan, C. A. (1996). Fear-potentiated startle conditioning to explicit and contextual cues in Gulf War veterans with posttraumatic stress disorder. *Journal of Abnormal Psychology, 108,* 134–142.

Gross, J. J., & Levenson, R. W. (1993). Emotional suppression: Physiology, self-report, and expressive behavior. *Journal of Personality and Social Psychology, 64,* 970–986.

Grossman, P., Karemaker, J., & Wieling, W. (1991). Prediction of tonic parasympathetic cardiac control using respiratory sinus arrhythmia: The need for respiratory control. *Psychophysiology, 28,* 201–216.

Hagemann, D., Naumann, E., Thayer, J. F., & Bartussek, D. (2002). Does resting electroencephalograph asymmetry reflect a trait? An application of latent state–trait theory. *Journal of Personality and Social Psychology, 82,* 619–641.

Halgren, E., & Marinkovic, K. (1995). Neurophysiological networks integrating human emotions. In M. Gazzaniga (Ed.), *Cognitive neurosciences* (pp. 1137–1151). Cambridge, MA: MIT Press.

Hare, R. D. (1965). Temporal gradient of fear arousal in psychopaths. *Journal of Abnormal Psychology, 70,* 442–445.

Harmon-Jones, E., & Allen, J. J. B. (1997). Behavioral activation sensitivity and resting frontal EEG asymmetry: Covariation of putative indicators related to risk for mood disorders. *Journal of Abnormal Psychology, 106,* 159–163.

Harmon-Jones, E., & Allen, J. J. B. (1998). Anger and frontal brain activity: EEG asymmetry consistent with approach motivation despite negative affective valence. *Journal of Personality and Social Psychology, 74,* 1310–1316.

Harmon-Jones, E., Lueck, L., Fearn, M., & Harmon-Jones, C. (2006). The effect of personal relevance and approach-related action expectation on relative left frontal cortical activity. *Psychological Science, 17,* 434–440.

Harmon-Jones, E., & Sigelman, J. (2001). State anger and frontal brain activity: Evidence that insult-related relative left prefrontal activation is associated with experienced anger and aggression. *Journal of Personality and Social Psychology, 80,* 797–803.

Henning, R. J., Khalil, I. R., & Levy, M. N. (1990). Vagal stimulation attenuates sympathetic enhancement of left ventricular function. *American Journal of Physiology, 258,* 1470–1475.

Henriques, J. B., & Davidson, R. J. (1990). Regional brain electrical asymmetries discriminate between previously depressed and healthy control subjects. *Journal of Abnormal Psychology, 99,* 22–31.

Hugdahl, K. (2001). *Psychophysiology: The mind–body perspective.* Cambridge, MA: Harvard University Press.

Iacono, W. G. (1998). Identifying psychophysiological risk for psychopathology: Examples from substance abuse and schizophrenia research. *Psychophysiology, 35,* 621–637.

James, W. (1950). *The principles of psychology* (Vol. 2). New York: Dover. (Original work published 1890)

Jäncke, L. (1994). An EMG investigation of the coactivation of facial muscles during the presentation of affect-laden stimuli. *Journal of Psychophysiology, 8,* 1–10.

Jasper, H. H. (1958). The ten-twenty electrode system of the International Federation. *Electroencephalography and Clinical Neurophysiology, 10,* 371–375.

*Jennings, J. R., Berg, W. K., Hutcheson, J. S., Obrist, P., Porges, S., & Turpin, G. (1981). Publication guidelines for heart rate studies in man. *Psychophysiology, 18,* 226–231.

Klein, E., Cnaani, E., Harel, T., Braun, S., & Ben-Haim, S. A. (1995). Altered heart rate variability in panic disorder patients. *Biological Psychiatry, 37,* 18–24.

Kok, A. (1997). Event-related potential (ERP) reflections of mental resources: A review and synthesis. *Biological Psychology, 45,* 19–56.

Lang, P. J. (1995). The emotion probe: Studies of motivation and attention. *American Psychologist, 50,* 372–385.

Lang, P. J., Bradley, M. M., & Cuthbert, B. N. (2005). *International affective picture system (IAPS): Affective ratings of pictures and instruction manual* (Technical Report A-6). Gainesville: University of Florida.

Lang, P. J., Cuthbert, B. N., & Bradley, M. M. (1998). Measuring emotion in therapy: Imagery, activation, and feeling. *Behavior Therapy, 29,* 655–674.

Lang, P. J., Greenwald, M. K., Bradley, M. M., & Hamm, A. O. (1993). Looking at pictures: Affective, facial, visceral, and behavioral reactions. *Psychophysiology, 30,* 261–273.

Light, K. C., Kothandapani, R. V., & Allen, M. T. (1998). Enhanced cardiovascular and catecholamine responses in women with depressive symptoms. *International Journal of Psychophysiology, 28,* 157–166.

Manning, S. K., & Melchiori, M. P. (1974). Words that upset urban college students: Measured with GSRs and rating scales. *Journal of Social Psychology, 94,* 305–306.

Mathews, A. (1990). Why worry? The cognitive function of anxiety. *Behaviour Research and Therapy, 28,* 455–468.

Miltner, W. H. R., Braun, C. H., & Coles, M. G. H. (1997). Event-related brain potentials following incorrect feedback in a time-estimation task: Evidence for a "generic" neural system for error detection. *Journal of Cognitive Neuroscience, 9,* 787–797.

Newlin, D. B. (1981). Relationships of pulse transmission times to pre-ejection period and blood pressure. *Psychophysiology, 18,* 316–321.

Newlin, D. B., & Levenson, R. W. (1979). Pre-ejection period: Measuring beta-adrenergic influences upon the heart. *Psychophysiology, 16,* 546–553.

Öhman, A., & Dimberg, U. (1978). Facial expressions as conditioned stimuli for electrodermal responses: A case of "preparedness"? *Journal of Personality and Social Psychology, 36,* 1251–1258.

Öhman, A., Eriksson, A., & Olofsson, C. (1975). One-trial learning and superior resistance to extinction of autonomic responses conditioned to potentially phobic stimuli. *Journal of Comparative and Physiological Psychology, 88,* 619–627.

Öhman, A., Flykt, A., & Esteves, F. (2001). Emotion drives attention: Detecting the snake in the grass. *Journal of Experimental Psychology: General, 130,* 466–478.

Öhman, A., & Soares, J. J. (1994). "Unconscious anxiety": Phobic responses to masked stimuli. *Journal of Abnormal Psychology, 103,* 231–240.

Patrick, C. J., Bradley, M. M., & Lang, P. J. (1993). Emotion in the criminal psychopath: Startle reflex modulation. *Journal of Abnormal Psychology, 102,* 82–92.

Patrick, C. J., Cuthbert, B. N., & Lang, P. J. (1994). Emotion in the criminal psychopath: Fear imaging processing. *Journal of Abnormal Psychology, 103,* 523–534.

*Picton, T. W., Bentin, S., Berg, P., Donchin, E., Hillyard, S. A., Johnson, R., Jr., et al. (2000). Guidelines for using human event-related potentials to study cognition: Recording standards and publication criteria. *Psychophysiology, 37*, 127–152.

*Pivik, R. T., Broughton, R. J. H., Coppola, R., Davidson, R. J., Fox, N., & Nuwer, M. R. (1993). Guidelines for the recording and quantitative analysis of electroencephalographic activity in research contexts. *Psychophysiology, 30*, 547–558.

Porges, S. W. (1992). Autonomic regulation and attention. In B. A. Campbell, H. Hayne, & R. Richardson (Eds.), *Attention and information processing in infants and adults* (pp. 201–223). Hillside, NJ: Erlbaum.

Rechlin, T., Weis, M., Spitzer, A., & Kaschka, W. P. (1994). Are affective disorders associated with alterations of heart rate variability? *Journal of Affective Disorders, 32*, 271–275.

Reid, S. A., Duke, L. M., & Allen, J. J. (1998). Resting frontal electroencephalographic asymmetry in depression: Inconsistencies suggest the need to identify mediating factors. *Psychophysiology, 35*, 389–404.

Roedema, T. M., & Simons, R. F. (1999). Emotion-processing deficit in alexithymia. *Psychophysiology, 36*, 379–387.

Rottenberg, J., Gross, J. J., Wilhelm, F. H., & Gotlib, I. H. (2002). Crying threshold and intensity in major depressive disorder. *Journal of Abnormal Psychology, 111*, 302–312.

Rottenberg, J., Wilhelm, F. H., Gross, J. J., & Gotlib, I. H. (2002). Respiratory sinus arrhythmia as a predictor of outcome in major depressive disorder. *Journal of Affective Disorders, 71*, 265–272.

Schlenker, R., Cohen, R., & Hopmann, G. (1995). Affective modulation of the startle reflex in schizophrenic patients. *European Archives of Psychiatry and Clinical Neuroscience, 245*, 309–318.

Schwartz, G. E., Fair, P. L., Salt, P., Mandel, M. R., & Klerman, G. L. (1976, April 30). Facial muscle patterning to affective imagery in depressed and nondepressed subjects. *Science, 192*, 489–491.

*Sherwood, A., Allen, M. T., Fahrenberg, J., Kelsey, R. M., Lovallo, W. R., & van Doornen, L. J. P. (1990). Methodological guidelines for impedance cardiography. *Psychophysiology, 27*, 1–23.

Sloan, R. P., Bagiella, E., Shapiro, P. A., Kuhl, J. P., Chernikhova, D., Berg, J., et al. (2001). Hostility, gender, and cardiac autonomic control. *Psychosomatic Medicine, 63*, 434–440.

Soares, J. J., & Öhman, A. (1993). Backward masking and skin conductance responses after conditioning to nonfeared but fear-relevant stimuli in fearful subjects. *Psychophysiology, 30*, 460–466.

Sponheim, S. R., Allen, J. J., & Iacono, W. G. (1995). Selected psychophysiological measures in depression: The significance of electrodermal activity, electroencephalographic asymmetries, and contingent negative variation to behavioral and neurobiological aspects of depression. In G. A. Miller (Ed.), *The behavioral high-risk paradigm in psychopathology* (pp. 222–249). New York: Springer-Verlag.

Stern, R. M., Ray, W. J., & Quigley, K. S. (2000). *Psychophysiological recording*. Cambridge, England: Oxford University Press.

Sutton, S. K., & Davidson, R. J. (1997). Prefrontal brain asymmetry: A biological substrate of the behavioral approach and inhibition systems. *Psychological Science, 8*, 204–210.

Tassinary, L. G., & Cacioppo, J. T. (1992). Unobservable facial actions and emotion. *Psychological Science, 3*, 28–33.

Tassinary, L. G., & Cacioppo, J. T. (2000). The skeletomotor system: Surface electromyography. In J. T. Cacioppo, L. G. Tassinary, & G. G. Berntson (Eds.), *Handbook of psychophysiology* (2nd ed., pp. 163–199). Cambridge, England: Cambridge University Press.

Thayer, J. F., Friedman, B. H., & Borkovec, T. D. (1996). Autonomic characteristics of generalized anxiety disorder and worry. *Biological Psychiatry, 39*, 255–266.

Thayer, J. F., & Lane, R. D. (2002). Perseverative thinking and health: Neurovisceral concomitants. *Psychology and Health, 17*, 685–695.

Tomarken, A. J., Davidson, R. J., & Henriques, J. B. (1990). Resting frontal brain asymmetry predicts affective responses to films. *Journal of Personality and Social Psychology, 59*, 791–801.

Tomarken, A. J., Davidson, R. J., Wheeler, R. E., & Kinney, L. (1992). Psychometric properties of resting anterior EEG asymmetry: Temporal stability and internal consistency. *Psychophysiology, 29*, 576–592.

Tucker, D. M., Luu, P., Frishkoff, G., Quiring, J., & Poulsen, C. (2003). Frontolimbic response to negative feedback in clinical depression. *Journal of Abnormal Psychology, 112*, 667–678.

Vigouroux, R. (1888). The electrical resistance considered as a clinical sign. *Progres Medicale, 3*, 87–89.

Vrana, S. R., Constantine, J. A., & Westman, J. S. (1992). Startle reflex modification as an outcome measure in the treatment of phobia: Two case studies. *Behavioral Assessment, 14*, 279–291.

Wheeler, R. E., Davidson, R. J., & Tomarken, A. J. (1993). Frontal brain asymmetry and emotional reactivity: A biological substrate of affective style. *Psychophysiology, 30*, 82–89.

Wiedemann, G., Pauli, P., Dengler, W., Lutzenberger, W., Birbaumer, N., & Buchkremer, G. (1999). Frontal brain asymmetry as a biological substrate of emotions in patients with panic disorders. *Archives of General Psychiatry, 56*, 78–84.

4

METHODS FOR STUDYING COGNITIVE ASPECTS OF EMOTION

EDWARD WILSON AND COLIN MacLEOD

The breadth of work dedicated to defining and accounting for variation in emotional experience amply indicates that emotions are complex constructs that involve an interactive relationship between behavioral, somatic, and cognitive factors (see Lambie & Marcel, 2002). The cognitive aspects of the emotions, which are the focus of this chapter, may be studied from at least two perspectives. The focus of study may be either the subjective cognitive contents associated with different emotions or the individual differences in styles of selective information processing, which may plausibly give rise to such cognitive content. In modern psychological science, cognitive explanations of emotions extend as far back as the work of Arnold (1960) and are underpinned by the premise that the manner in which any situation is subjectively represented will determine the nature and intensity of the resulting emotional response (e.g., Lazarus, 1968, 1991). Cognitive accounts of affective psychopathology similarly suggest that idiosyncratic styles of attribution and inference may underlie proneness to such psychopathology. For example, Beck and his colleagues (e.g., Beck, 1976, 1985) argued that clinical depression and anxiety disorders result, at least in part, from an inflated tendency to construe life experiences as having negative meanings and implications.

The negative emotional states associated with these disorders may thus represent appropriate emotional responses to inappropriate mental representations of events.

Such models often have adopted concepts from cognitive psychology in order to construct explanations for individual differences in susceptibility to the negative emotions and to related affective psychopathology (e.g., Mathews & Mackintosh, 1998; Williams, Watts, MacLeod, & Mathews, 1997). Many of these models initially focused on depression and anxiety, although more recent variants have been put forward to account for variations in vulnerability to other emotions such as anger (e.g., Power & Dalgleish, 1997). These models emphasize the importance of low-level processing biases in operations, such as the original encoding of emotionally laden information and its subsequent retrieval from memory, in determining idiosyncrasies in emotional reaction to a particular situation. Thus, elevated vulnerability to depression or anxiety may be underpinned by a biased tendency to selectively encode and/or retrieve emotionally negative information (e.g., Williams et al., 1997). A central distinction in this chapter—that between initial encoding of perceptual stimuli on one hand and subsequent memory for such stimuli on the other—originated in mainstream cognitive psychology. Application of this distinction to the study of individual differences in processing of emotional stimuli has proven fruitful, with particular kinds of emotional vulnerability appearing to be more closely associated with variations in either selective encoding or retrieval processes.

Determining the relevance of such processing biases to variations in emotional vulnerability and, by extension, affective psychopathology, represents a key challenge for investigators working within this field of inquiry (see Mathews & MacLeod, 2005). To meet these challenges, researchers have developed a range of experimental methodologies designed to reveal objectively various aspects of biases in the selective processing of emotional information. Our goal within this chapter is to provide the reader with a brief overview of such methodologies together with an appreciation of their various strengths and limitations.

We begin by reviewing the methods that have been used to examine the cognitive contents of depression and anxiety as well as the inferences that may produce such emotional contents. Our focus will then shift to the methods used to examine lower level processing biases in the selective encoding and retrieval of emotional information. Finally, we consider some of the most recent methodologies that have been developed to illuminate the causal contribution of processing biases to emotional vulnerability. These involve task variants designed to manipulate processing biases systematically to examine their emotional consequences (see MacLeod, Campbell, Rutherford, & Wilson, 2004; Mathews, 2004). Such techniques have the potential to test empirically the hypothesis that biases in the encoding and retrieval of emotional information causally underpin emotional vulnerability.

METHODS FOR STUDYING THE COGNITIVE CONTENT OF EMOTIONAL EXPERIENCE

A range of methodologies have been developed to investigate the se-mantic content of cognitions associated with elevated levels of emotional vulnerability and associated psychopathologies. Some methods of assessing cognitive content rely purely on participants' own reports of their conscious thoughts. For example, naturalistic techniques such as thought sampling have been used to obtain measures of thought content (see Hurlburt, 1997). How-ever, researchers more often have used retrospective questionnaire-based tech-niques to investigate such phenomena. In the case of depression and anxiety, such standardized questionnaires itemize a range of possible depressive or anxious thoughts and require individuals to endorse the frequency or inten-sity with which they experience each thought. The Automatic Thoughts Questionnaire (Hollon & Kendall, 1980) assesses depressive cognitive con-tents by requiring participants to indicate the frequency with which specific thoughts (e.g., "It's just not worth it") come to mind. Similar scales have been developed to assess the frequency of anxiety-related cognitions and of both anxious and depressive cognitions (e.g., Beck, Brown, Steer, Eidelson, & Riskind, 1987).

Self-report methodologies designed to assess the thought content asso-ciated with anxiety and depression typically shed little light on the processes that give rise to this content. More refined assessment approaches have been developed, however, to test the hypothesis that such negative thinking in emotionally vulnerable individuals reflects their inflated tendency to draw emotionally negative inferences from ambiguous information. One of the most commonly used methods of assessing inferential bias involves provid-ing participants with textual descriptions of emotionally ambiguous situa-tions and asking them to indicate their preferred interpretation of each situ-ation. In an early study (Butler & Mathews, 1983), patients with anxiety and clinical depression and nonclinical control participants were presented with a series of ambiguous scenarios, each of which permitted both a negative and a neutral interpretation (e.g., "Suppose you wake with a start in the middle of the night thinking you heard a noise, but all is quiet. What do you suppose woke you up?"). Participants first provided an unconstrained explanation of each scenario that was later rated for emotional valence. They also selected their preferred interpretation from among three provided alternatives, only one of which was negative. The clinical patients demonstrated a preference for producing and endorsing the more negative inferences, a pattern that has since been replicated in clinically anxious participants (e.g., Casey, Oei, Newcombe, & Kenardy, 2004) and clinically depressed patients (Nunn, Mathews, & Trower, 1997).

Although such procedures offer the promise of illuminating the infer-ential biases that may underpin negative thought content in anxiety and depression, they are constrained by their continued reliance on self-report data. Even fairly simple inferential processes that operate within the cognitive system are potentially inaccessible to introspection (see Nisbett & Wilson, 1977; see also Prinz, 2004). Thus, self-reports of inferential style may well be inaccurate. In addition, differences between the reports of affectively disordered patients and control participants could well be accommodated by demand–effect explanations. The hypothesis that such disorders are associated with negative inference may well be obvious to participants, and it is not implausible that clinical patients may simply report the inferential preferences that they believe researchers expect of them.

To reduce this problematic reliance on introspection, several alternative methodologies have been designed to assess inferential processing indirectly using simple task performance measures. In the frequently employed homophone spelling task (e.g., Blanchette & Richards, 2003; Terry & Burns, 2001), participants are presented auditorily with a series of homophones, each of which possesses differentially valenced meanings that are distinguished by different spellings (e.g., *dye* and *die*). Participants are led to believe that they are taking part in a spelling test and are instructed to write down each word they hear. The interpretation that the participants impose on each homophone is revealed by the spelling that they use.

For example, Mogg, Baldwin, Brodrick, and Bradley (2004) used the homophone spelling task to contrast individuals with generalized anxiety disorder (GAD) and control participants. Compared with the control group, the GAD group provided a greater number of threatening homophone spellings. Thus, the investigators concluded that individuals with GAD were indeed more likely than control participants to impose threatening interpretations on such ambiguous information. Unfortunately, this task has not yet been used to examine individuals with clinical depression.

Advantages of the homophone spelling task include its ease of administration and relatively low demand characteristics. However, one drawback of the task is that production of negative spellings could result from an emotion-linked response bias rather than from a true interpretive bias. Specifically, the possibility cannot be excluded that in some cases both meanings of a homophone are accessed, and individuals with anxiety may simply choose to respond with the more negative spelling under such circumstances. To overcome the potential influence of response bias, methodological approaches have been developed that do not infer interpretation from the relative likelihood of emitting alternative responses. Priming methodologies represent an example of this approach. In such priming tasks, ambiguous items such as words or sentences are presented as initial primes, which are then followed by target words related either to their threatening or their nonthreatening meanings. Participants perform some simple task on each target word, such as naming it aloud or verifying its lexical status, which yields a measure of how readily this target can be processed. It is assumed that to the extent a particular meaning of the prime has been accessed, so the processing of the target related to that meaning will be facilitated (in comparison with a baseline condition in which no prime precedes the target). The priming approach can overcome the response bias difficulty associated with the homophone spelling methodology because the measure of interpretation is provided by the degree to which the same response is facilitated for a given type of target word, on primed compared with unprimed trials.

Using the priming methodology, Richards and French (1992) presented high and low anxiety-vulnerable individuals with homograph primes that each permitted differentially threatening interpretations (e.g., "stroke"). These were followed 750 milliseconds later by a target word about which participants were required to make a rapid lexical decision. In the primed condition, the target was related to one meaning of the ambiguous prime; in the unprimed condition, target and prime were unrelated. To the extent that participants imposed a threatening interpretation on the prime, it was assumed that they would be disproportionately faster, in the primed relative to the unprimed condition, to determine the lexical status of target words related to this threat meaning as opposed to the nonthreat meaning of the prime. This was indeed found to be the case. The more anxiety-prone individuals displayed relatively enhanced priming effects for threat-related targets compared with non-threat-related targets, suggesting that they imposed negative interpretations on the ambiguous prime word stimuli. Other studies have obtained similar patterns of findings in populations of individuals diagnosed with anxiety-related pathology, such as patients with social phobia (e.g., Hirsch & Mathews, 2000). In contrast, priming studies have not provided evidence that vulnerability to depression is characterized by a negative inferential bias (e.g., Pury, 2004).

Researchers have employed these various methodologies to reveal the relationship between inferential biases and affective tendencies in nonclinical as well as clinical samples. Although there has been interest in a range of emotional dispositions, such as the tendency to experience anger and hostility (e.g., Chen & Matthews, 2003), the majority of studies involving nonclinical groups have concentrated on variations in inference associated with trait anxiety. Like clinically anxious individuals, individuals with high trait anxiety but without anxiety pathology are more likely than individuals with low trait anxiety to provide the threatening spellings of homophones (e.g., Dalgleish, 1994), suggesting that they too may be more likely to impose negative interpretations on such stimuli. The magnitude of the spelling bias shown by individuals with nonclinical high trait anxiety falls midway between that evidenced by control participants with low trait anxiety and by individuals with clinical anxiety (Mathews, Richard, & Eysenck, 1989). Similarly, individuals with social anxiety but without a social phobia diagnosis (Hirsch & Mathews, 1997), like patients with social phobia (Hirsch & Mathews, 2000), display patterns of priming effects that suggest a heightened tendency to impose negative interpretations on ambiguous social stimuli.

In summary, a wide range of methodologies have been used to reveal the cognitive content associated with emotional vulnerability and to illuminate the inferential biases that might serve to influence this cognitive content. Although self-report techniques are perhaps the easiest types of assessment to administer, the validity of the resulting data is questionable, especially when participants are required to access their own inferential processing introspectively. Many researchers therefore prefer assessment techniques that use performance measures to permit conclusions concerning inferential bias. The homophone spelling task is one such example, although priming methodologies yield data that are less susceptible to alternative explanations such as participant response bias. In general, the most rigorous methodologies have tended to reveal more consistent evidence of a negative interpretive bias in anxiety than in depression.

METHODS FOR STUDYING THE SELECTIVE ENCODING OF EMOTIONAL INFORMATION

As noted earlier, a premise common to many cognitive accounts of emotional vulnerability is that elevated vulnerability to negative emotions is associated with a selective encoding bias favoring negative information. Selective encoding can here be understood to imply that some information, after its initial sensation (visual, auditory, or other), receives further cognitive processing, whereas other information that was initially registered may be ignored or inhibited. A number of methodologies have been used to determine the degree to which such selective encoding is associated with vulnerability to anxiety and/or depression. Each of these alternatives is characterized by differing strengths and limitations.

Early methods designed to examine biased encoding of emotional information involved assessing participants' capacity to explicitly identify valenced stimuli presented under conditions designed to make such identification difficult. Powell and Hemsley (1984), for example, assessed the degree to which individuals with and without depression could identify negative and neutral words presented for very brief durations. Compared with the control group, the participants with depression showed a disproportionate ability to identify negative, relative to neutral, words, suggesting enhanced encoding of negative stimulus information. Parallel findings have been obtained for individuals with clinical anxiety in studies using similar methodologies (e.g., Burgess, Jones, Robertson, Radcliffe, & Emerson, 1981).

However, with such methodologies, it remains possible that the superior identification of negative stimulus words could result from an emotionally linked response bias and not from a genuine encoding bias. Rather than being distinguished by a genuine tendency to preferentially encode negative information, vulnerable individuals may simply be more willing to make negatively toned guesses, resulting in higher hit rates for negative targets. One means of overcoming this response bias problem involves eliminating the need for participants to report stimulus identity. Instead, the degree to which emotionally negative stimuli interfere with performance on a central task, when these stimuli are presented as irrelevant distracters, is taken as an index of encoding bias favoring negative information. Such tasks are known as interference tasks, and the most commonly used variant is the emotional Stroop task (see MacLeod, 2004). In this task, each participant is presented with a series of colored words, some of which are neutral and some of which are emotionally negative in content. The participant's task is to name the color of each word as quickly as possible while simultaneously ignoring its meaning. To the extent that processing is directed toward encoding the semantic content of a word stimulus rather than its color, this is expected to slow down color naming. Thus, any tendency to encode negative information selectively is revealed by disproportionate slowing to color name negative words. In an example of this approach, Becker, Rinck, Margraf, and Roth (2001) presented patients with GAD and nonanxious control participants with threatening and nonthreatening words. Unlike the nonanxious control participants, the participants in the GAD group were slower to color name the threatening words compared with the nonthreatening words. Similar findings have been obtained for other clinically anxious populations, such as individuals with posttraumatic stress disorder (e.g., McNeil, Tucker, Miranda, Lewin, & Nordgren, 1999) and panic disorder (e.g., Buckley, Blanchard, & Hickling, 2002). Although comparable findings have sometimes been obtained for clinically depressed patients (e.g., Gotlib & Cane, 1987), these have not been replicated consistently (e.g., Bradley, Mogg, Millar, & White, 1995; see Mogg & Bradley, 2005).

The Stroop task is the methodology most commonly used to assess the selective encoding of emotional information, perhaps in part because it can be readily administered in a card-based format, with minimal need for technical resources. Despite its high degree of practical utility and its resistance to the response bias problem discussed earlier, one problem with the Stroop task, and indeed with the use of any interference task, is that impaired performance on a central task provides at best only an indirect measure of what information is actually encoded. For example, participants may be slow to color name a threatening word not because they selectively processed its semantic content but because they directed encoding resources away from this stimulus altogether, thereby impairing apprehension of its color.

A more direct measure of selective encoding has been provided by the attentional probe methodology. In this approach, participants are first briefly presented with a pair of differentially valenced stimuli. Following the offset of this stimulus pair, a probe appears in the vicinity of either stimulus. The participant is required to discriminate the probe stimulus and respond with a button press. It is assumed that probe discrimination latencies will be shortest when probes appear within the attended areas of the display. Thus, speeding to discriminate probes in the vicinity of negative stimuli, compared with those in the vicinity of neutral stimuli, is taken as an indicator of the participant's tendency to encode negative information selectively.

In the original attentional probe task variant (MacLeod, Mathews, & Tata, 1986), patients with GAD and nonanxious control participants were presented with word pairs that consisted of a threat word and a neutral word. One word from each pair was presented in an upper screen location, and the other appeared in a lower screen location. A small visual probe sometimes appeared 500 milliseconds later in the vicinity of either the threat word or the neutral word. Participants were required to press a response key as soon as they detected the probe. Unlike the control participants, the patients with GAD displayed speeded detection of probes in the vicinity of threat words, suggesting attentional orientation toward threat stimuli. Similar findings have since been obtained for patients with other anxiety disorders, such as panic disorder (Horenstein & Segui, 1997) and obsessive–compulsive disorder (e.g., Tata, Leibowitz, Prunty, Cameron, & Pickering, 1996). In contrast, studies of clinical depression have not consistently shown this effect (Musa, Lepine, Clark, Mansell, & Ehlers, 2003).

Each of these various methodologies, developed initially to reveal the patterns of selective encoding associated with affective pathology, has also been used to illuminate the patterns of selective encoding associated with normal variations in emotional disposition. Like patients with anxiety disorders, individuals with high trait anxiety, compared with individuals with low trait anxiety, display slowing to color name threatening rather than non-threatening words, especially when state anxiety is elevated (e.g., Egloff & Hock, 2001). Similarly, individuals with high trait anxiety show more rapid detection of probes presented in the vicinity of threatening compared with neutral words (e.g., Bradley, Mogg, & Lee, 1997, Experiment 2), and again this group difference is most pronounced when state anxiety is also elevated (e.g., Broadbent & Broadbent, 1988). Thus, these findings are consistent with the conclusion that individuals with high trait anxiety demonstrate a tendency to encode threat information selectively, particularly under conditions of elevated state anxiety.

Although the methodologies described in this section were originally developed to examine the patterns of selective encoding associated with anxiety and depression, they have also been used to reveal the patterns of encoding selectivity associated with variations in proneness to other emotions, such as anger or hostility. For example, individuals with high trait anger have been found to display a disproportionate slowing to color name anger-related information (e.g., Putnam, Hermans, & van Honk, 2004; van Honk, Tuiten, de Haan, van den Hout, & Stam, 2001).

To summarize, early methods of assessing the selective encoding of emotional information, which required participants to report the identity of such stimuli, have largely been replaced by interference or attentional probe methodologies. In general, the findings have revealed more consistent evidence of a selective encoding advantage for negative emotional information in individuals with a heightened vulnerability to anxiety rather than to depression.

METHODS FOR STUDYING THE SELECTIVE RETRIEVAL OF EMOTIONAL INFORMATION

A number of approaches have been developed to examine the association between emotional vulnerability and the selective retrieval of negative information from memory. At the more naturalistic end of the spectrum lie methodologies designed to assess the affective tone of autobiographical memories reported by individuals who differ in emotional vulnerability. Typically, participants may be asked to describe autobiographical memories brought to mind by neutral cue words, and these memories are rated for emotional tone (e.g., Burke & Mathews, 1992; Clark & Teasdale, 1982; Field, Psychol, & Morgan, 2004). For example, Burke and Mathews (1992) found that relative to nonanxious control participants, patients with GAD reported a greater number of negatively toned memories. Clark and Teasdale (1982) conducted similar work with clinically depressed patients and nondepressed control participants and found that the patients diagnosed with depression also reported a disproportionate number of emotionally negative personal memories. A related approach involves presenting participants with a series of emotionally toned cue words and directing them to retrieve autobiographical memories of this specified affective valence. The speed with which specific autobiographical memories can be produced in response to these cue words provides a measure of the retrievability of these memories. Depressed patients demonstrate a slowing in retrieval of positive memories compared with negative memories (e.g., Williams & Scott, 1988). In contrast, such studies have revealed no similar effect in patients with anxiety disorders such as social phobia (e.g., Wenzel, Jackson, & Holt, 2002) or obsessive–compulsive disorder (e.g., Wilhelm, McNally, Baer, & Florin, 1997). Thus, it appears that a negative retrieval bias may be associated with depression but not anxiety.

It would be imprudent to conclude that these performance differences on autobiographical memory tasks necessarily imply the existence of biased retrieval, however, because these could equally well result from differences in the actual frequency of negative life experiences. People with heightened vulnerability to anxiety or depression may simply have experienced more emotionally negative events and hence have a greater store of negative memories on which to draw. To overcome this problem, it has become common to assess memory for emotional materials that are experimentally delivered. One of the most common variants of this approach involves an encoding phase within which participants are presented with a series of differentially valenced words, followed after a short interval by a retrieval phase, in which participants are directed to recall as many words as possible. For example, Sefarty et al. (2002) auditorily presented a series of negative and positive words to participants with and without clinical depression and required them to judge whether each item was self-descriptive. Following a brief interval, participants were instructed to recall these words. Unlike the nondepressed control participants, the depressed patients recalled more negative than positive words. This pattern of findings has replicated consistently in individuals with clinical depression (see Gotlib & Neubauer, 2000; Matt, Vazquez, & Campbell, 1992). In contrast, this methodology has revealed no convincing evidence of a similar negative memory bias in most anxiety disorders (see MacLeod & Mathews, 2004).

Although the use of experimentally presented stimulus materials excludes the possibility that variations in memory performance result from different opportunities to encode emotional information, performance on such tasks still can be influenced by response bias. More emotionally vulnerable individuals, when striving to recall forgotten material, may be disproportionately more likely to generate negative guesses, thereby artificially inflating their apparent capacity to recall negative stimuli that were previously presented. For this reason, researchers have attempted to differentiate between an actual retrieval advantage and a response bias by using recognition memory tasks to yield signal detection measures. In such studies, participants are presented with items that were not previously presented (i.e., foils) and with items that were presented during the encoding phase (targets). Hit and false-alarm rates then are used to calculate measures of memory sensitivity (i.e., d') and of response bias (i.e., beta) for stimuli of each valence (e.g., Dunbar & Lishman, 1984; Ridout, Astell, Reid, Glen, & O'Carroll, 2003). In an early example of this approach, Dunbar and Lishman (1984) presented a series of negative, positive, and neutral words to individuals with clinical depression and nondepressed control participants in an initial encoding task. On a subsequent recognition memory task, measures of d' and beta revealed evidence of greater memory sensitivity for negative than for positive items among depressed individuals but not among control participants (see also Ridout et al., 2003). In contrast, studies that have used this approach to compare individuals with clinical anxiety and nonanxious control participants have not consistently revealed evidence of differential memory sensitivity for threatening, relative to nonthreatening, stimuli (e.g., Coles & Heimberg, 2005).

Many of the methodologies discussed here have also been extended to investigate whether biased patterns of memory are associated with heightened emotional vulnerability in nonclinical populations. A small number of such studies have used these procedures to examine the memorial correlates of individual differences in proneness to emotions other than depression and anxiety, such as hostility (e.g., Allred & Smith, 1991). More often, however, researchers have concentrated on nonclinical elevation in vulnerability to anxiety and depression. The findings from such studies have typically been consistent with the clinical literature. Methodologies assessing the recall of experimentally presented material have revealed no consistent evidence of a threat-related recall bias among nonclinical participants who report elevated trait anxiety levels (see MacLeod & Rutherford, 2004). There is, however, good evidence that elevated depression among nonclinical participants is associated with the enhanced recall of negative information. Induced depressed mood gives rise to a recall advantage for negative autobiographical memories in nondepressed participants, with this effect most pronounced in individuals with heightened vulnerability to depression (e.g., Josephson, Singer, & Salovey, 1996). Individual differences in naturally occurring depressed mood within the nonclinical population also are associated with differential recall and recognition memory for negative words exposed earlier in the experimental session (e.g., Gilboa, Roberts, & Gotlib, 1997). Matt et al. (1992) concluded from a meta-analysis of studies that although clinically depressed individuals reliably recall a greater number of negative than positive trait adjectives, dysphoric individuals not meeting criteria for clinical diagnosis are more likely to display the absence of the superior recall of positive trait adjectives that is characteristic of healthy individuals who report low levels of dysphoria.

In general, therefore, across a diverse range of methodologies, and regardless of whether clinical disorders or normal emotional variability are considered, there has been more consistent evidence of a negative memory bias in depression than in anxiety.

METHODS FOR STUDYING THE CAUSAL ROLE OF SELECTIVE PROCESSING BIASES

Studies that serve only to demonstrate the existence of an association between emotional vulnerability and selective processing bias cannot serve to establish the causal nature of this association. The premise that such processing biases contribute causally to emotional vulnerability is central to a range of cognitive accounts of emotional vulnerability (e.g., Beck & Clark, 1997; Power & Dalgleish, 1997; Williams et al., 1997). To determine more directly the degree to which this direction of causation actually operates, experimental tasks have been developed to manipulate patterns of processing selectivity and thus to determine whether this serves to modify emotional vulnerability. In such studies, training contingencies are introduced into tasks previously designed only to assess selective processing, with the goal of encouraging the induction of target processing biases. The emotional consequence of such bias modification is then assessed by examining the intensity of emotional reactions to a subsequent stressor. For example, to create a task capable of inducing biased interpretations, Grey and Mathews (2000) modified the priming methodology that Richards and French (1992) had used previously to assess anxiety-linked interpretive bias. In Grey and Mathew's (2000) training version of this task, following each homograph prime, participants were presented with a word fragment derived from a word related to either the threatening or the nonthreatening meaning of the homograph. They were instructed to use the prime as a clue to help complete the fragment quickly and were assigned to one of two training conditions. In the training condition designed to encourage the development of negative interpretive bias, all the fragments could be completed only to yield words related to the threatening meanings of the preceding homograph primes. Thus, for participants who received this training, it was always advantageous to access the threatening meaning of each homograph because only this meaning could assist in completion of the target fragment. In contrast, for participants assigned to the training designed to reduce negative interpretive bias, all fragments could be completed only to yield words related to the nonthreatening meanings of the homograph primes. For these participants, it therefore was never advantageous to access threatening meanings of the ambiguous primes, and it was expected that this would encourage the development of a bias favoring nonthreatening interpretations of ambiguity. Following 120 such training trials, induced interpretive bias was revealed using an assessment version of the task from which the training contingency was eliminated. This confirmed that the two training groups did indeed come to differ in terms of their relative speed to complete fragments related to negative and neutral meanings of the homographs in precisely the manner that would be expected from the successful induction of the intended patterns of interpretive bias. Most important, the experimental induction of differential interpretive bias does appear to have modified emotional experience. Participants induced using a similar approach to acquire a negative interpretive bias later reported higher levels of anxious mood state than did participants induced to acquire the opposing interpretive bias (Mathews & Mackintosh, 2000), and they demonstrated an increased tendency to experience elevated anxiety and depression in response to subsequent exposure to stressful video clips (Wilson, MacLeod, Mathews, & Rutherford, 2006). The finding that the manipulation of interpretive bias affects emotional vulnerability supports the hypothesis that interpretive bias causally contributes to emotional vulnerability.

A similar methodological approach has been taken to determine the causal status of selective encoding bias. MacLeod, Rutherford, Campbell, Ebsworthy, and Holker (2002) developed a training methodology based on the attentional probe approach to manipulate selective encoding of emotional information. As in the original version of this task, on each trial, a threat–nonthreat word pair first appeared briefly, followed by a visual probe that appeared in the vicinity of either word. Participants were assigned to one of two training conditions. For one group of participants, the probes always appeared in the vicinity of the threat words, with the intention of encouraging the selective allocation of encoding resources toward this threat information. For the other group of participants, the probes always appeared in the vicinity of nonthreatening words, with the aim of encouraging the selective allocation of encoding resources away from threat. Following several hundred such training trials, a conventional assessment version of the dot probe task revealed that the procedure did indeed successfully induce the intended group difference in the selective encoding of emotionally valenced stimuli. Furthermore, consistent with the hypothesis that encoding bias plays a causal role in emotional vulnerability, the groups also differed in their emotional reactivity to a subsequent stressor. Specifically, those participants trained to acquire an encoding bias away from threat information showed attenuated anxious and depressive reactions to a later stressful anagram task.

Extended versions of these same training procedures have now been developed to examine whether they can reduce existing elevated levels of trait anxiety. For example, extended exposure to the dot-probe training has been delivered to individuals with high trait anxiety to assess its impact on their trait anxiety scores (Campbell, Rutherford, & MacLeod, 2002). In two studies, Campbell et al. (2002) provided a total of 6,000 to 7,000 training trials to individuals with high trait anxiety across a series of sessions completed over a 3-week period. In each study, half of the participants were assigned to an avoid-threat training condition in which the probes always appeared in the location of nonthreat words; for the remaining participants, there was no training contingency, and probes appeared equally often in the location of threat and nonthreat words. In both studies, those participants assigned to the no-contingency control condition displayed no change in encoding bias across the course of the training and did not show any change in level of trait anxiety. In contrast, those assigned to the avoid-threat training condition displayed a reduced tendency to allocate encoding resources to threat and also showed a significant decline in their level of trait anxiety across the course of the training. These findings support the hypothesis that encoding selectivity can contribute causally to anxiety vulnerability outside of the laboratory. Yiend and Mackintosh (2004) adopted a parallel approach designed to assess whether the manipulation of interpretive bias could reduce anxiety symptoms in participants with high trait anxiety. These researchers provided their participants with either four sessions of training designed to encourage positive inferential bias or four sessions of a control condition involving no inferential training. Relative to the control group, the participants exposed to the inferential training procedure developed an increasingly positive inferential bias across the course of the training. This group also showed reduced levels of anxiety across the training period, indicating that inferential bias, like encoding bias, can make a causal contribution to real-life anxiety outside the laboratory.

These demonstrations that the amelioration of negative processing biases in nonclinical samples serve to reduce apparent emotional vulnerability have led researchers to examine the therapeutic consequences of such training for individuals suffering from emotional psychopathology. In addition to extending theoretical understanding by illuminating the causal role played by selective processing in the manifestation of affective psychopathology, such research carries the applied promise of providing clinicians with a new therapeutic tool that may assist in the treatment of such conditions. MacLeod et al. (2004) described a study in which patients with social phobia were exposed to an online attentional training procedure for reducing selective encoding bias. Half these individuals were assigned to an avoid-threat training condition, and the remainder were assigned to a no-training control condition. Whereas the control group reported no change in social phobia symptoms across the 2-week training period, those individuals who received the avoid-threat training evidenced a significant reduction of phobic symptomatology. Other researchers have also had success in ameliorating anxiety symptoms using a similar training approach with GAD patients and with participants with pathological worry (Elias, Beard, & Amir, 2003; Vasey, Hazen, & Schmidt, 2002). Such findings suggest that extended training regimes, designed to reduce negative processing biases, can indeed have a significant therapeutic impact on affective psychopathology.

In general, training procedures to modify emotional processing biases are at an early stage of development. However, this approach holds much promise for future research, providing not only a means to assess the causal role of selective processing biases but also the potential to play a role in the treatment of emotional dysfunction. The results of such studies are likely to have reciprocal benefit for both theory and clinical practice, bearing on the hypothesis that such biases play a causal role in emotional vulnerability and carrying direct implications for the therapeutic modification of such vulnerability.

CONCLUSION

In this chapter, we have attempted to familiarize the reader with some of the most common experimental techniques that have been used to investigate the patterns of biased cognitive content and processing associated with individual differences in vulnerability to experience anxiety and depression. As we have indicated, studies using these methodologies have revealed that the various dimensions of emotional vulnerability are each associated with distinctive profiles of processing selectivity. Elevated anxiety vulnerability is reliably characterized by an inflated tendency to encode threatening information selectively and to draw threatening inferences from ambiguous information. In contrast, elevated vulnerability to depression is most convincingly associated with enhanced explicit memory for negatively valenced information.

We have illustrated how the consistent improvement of methodological techniques has served both to exclude alternative explanations of earlier data and to increase understanding of the specific cognitive mechanisms that underpin such processing selectivity. The consequent theoretical advances have permitted the generation of more sophisticated hypotheses, which in turn have stimulated the further refinement of experimental methodologies. We have no doubt that this reciprocal relationship between methodological and theoretical progress will continue to expand our understanding of the cognitive mechanisms that govern both normal variability in emotional temperament and heightened susceptibility to emotional pathology. We are equally confident that the productive partnership that has recently developed between experimental researchers investigating basic affective processes and clinical scientists seeking to enhance the treatment of emotional disorders will contribute greatly to such future advancement. This partnership has entered a new phase of collaboration within which the therapeutic value of theoretical models represents a shared focus of interest. By further strengthening the important bridge between affective and clinical science, these developments promise to enrich comprehension of both normal emotion and affective psychopathology.

REFERENCES

Allred, K. D., & Smith, T. W. (1991). Social cognition in cynical hostility. *Cognitive Therapy and Research, 15*, 399–412.

Arnold, J. R. (1960). *Emotion and personality.* New York: Columbia University Press.

Beck, A. T. (1976). *Cognitive therapy and the emotional disorders.* Oxford, England: International Universities Press.

Beck, A. T. (1985). Theoretical perspectives on clinical anxiety. In A. H. Tuma & J. D. Maser (Eds.), *Anxiety and the anxiety disorders* (pp. 183–196). Hillsdale, NJ: Erlbaum.

Beck, A. T., Brown, G., Steer, R. A., Eidelson, J. I., & Riskind, J. H. (1987). Differentiating anxiety and depression: A test of the cognitive content-specificity hypothesis. *Journal of Abnormal Psychology, 96*, 179–183.

Beck, A. T., & Clark, D. A. (1997). An information processing model of anxiety: Automatic and strategic processes. *Behaviour Research and Therapy, 35*, 49–58.

Becker, E. S., Rinck, M., Margraf, J., & Roth, W. T. (2001). The emotional Stroop effect in anxiety disorders: General emotionality or disorder specificity? *Journal of Anxiety Disorders, 15*, 147–159.

Blanchette, I., & Richards, A. (2003). Anxiety and the interpretation of ambiguous information: Beyond the emotion-congruent effect. *Journal of Experimental Psychology: General, 132,* 294–309.

Bradley, B. P., Mogg, K., & Lee, S. C. (1997). Attentional biases for negative information in induced and naturally occurring dysphoria. *Behaviour Research and Therapy, 35,* 911–927.

Bradley, B. P., Mogg, K., Millar, N. H., & White, J. (1995). Selective processing of negative information: Effects of clinical anxiety, concurrent depression, and awareness. *Journal of Abnormal Psychology, 104,* 532–536.

Broadbent, D., & Broadbent, M. (1988). Anxiety and attentional bias: State and trait. *Cognition and Emotion, 2,* 165–183.

Buckley, T. C., Blanchard, E. B., & Hickling, E. J. (2002). Automatic and strategic processing of threat stimuli: A comparison between PTSD, panic disorder, and nonanxiety controls. *Cognitive Therapy and Research, 26,* 97–115.

Burgess, I. S., Jones, L. M., Robertson, S. A., Radcliffe, W. N., & Emerson, E. (1981). The degree of control exerted by phobic and non-phobic verbal stimuli over the recognition behaviour of phobic and non-phobic subjects. *Behaviour Research and Therapy, 19,* 233–243.

Burke, M., & Mathews, A. (1992). Autobiographical memory and clinical anxiety. *Cognition and Emotion, 6,* 23–35.

Butler, G., & Mathews, A. (1983). Cognitive processes in anxiety. *Advances in Behaviour Research and Therapy, 5,* 51–62.

Campbell, L., Rutherford, E. M., & MacLeod, C. (2002, November). *Practice makes perfect: The reduction of trait anxiety through extended retraining of attentional response to threat.* Paper presented at the 36th Annual Convention of the Association for Advancement of Behavior Therapy, Reno, NV.

Casey, L. M., Oei, T. P. S., Newcombe, P. A., & Kenardy, J. (2004). The role of catastrophic misinterpretation of bodily sensations and panic self-efficacy in predicting panic severity. *Journal of Anxiety Disorders, 18,* 325–340.

Chen, E., & Matthews, K. A. (2003). Development of the cognitive appraisal and understanding of social events (CAUSE) videos. *Health Psychology, 22,* 106–110.

Clark, D. M., & Teasdale, J. D. (1982). Diurnal variation in clinical depression and accessibility of memories of positive and negative experiences. *Journal of Abnormal Psychology, 91,* 87–95.

Coles, M. E., & Heimberg, R. G. (2005). Recognition bias for critical faces in social phobia: A replication and extension. *Behaviour Research and Therapy, 43,* 109–120.

Dalgleish, T. (1994). The relationship between anxiety and memory biases for material that has been selectively processed in a prior task. *Behaviour Research and Therapy, 32,* 227–231.

Dunbar, G. C., & Lishman, W. A. (1984). Depression, recognition memory, and hedonic tone: A signal detection analysis. *British Journal of Psychiatry, 144,* 376–382.

Egloff, B., & Hock, M. (2001). Interactive effects of trait anxiety and state anxiety on emotional Stroop interference. *Personality and Individual Differences, 31*, 875–882.

Elias, J., Beard, C., & Amir, N. (2003, November). *Ideographic training of attention disengagement in individuals with generalised anxiety disorder*. Paper presented at the Association for Advancement of Behavior Therapy Annual Convention, Boston, MA.

Field, A. P., Psychol, C., & Morgan, J. (2004). Post-event processing and the retrieval of autobiographical memories in socially anxious individuals. *Journal of Anxiety Disorders, 18*, 647–663.

Gilboa, E., Roberts, J. E., & Gotlib, I. H. (1997). The effects of induced and naturally occurring dysphoric mood on biases in self-evaluation and memory. *Cognition and Emotion, 11*, 65–82.

Gotlib, I. H., & Cane, D. B. (1987). Construct accessibility and clinical depression: A longitudinal investigation. *Journal of Abnormal Psychology, 96*, 199–204.

Gotlib, I. H., & Neubauer, D. L. (2000). Information-processing approaches to the study of cognitive biases in depression. In S. L. Johnson, A. M. Hayes, T. M. Field, N. Schneiderman, & P. M. McCabe (2000). *Stress, coping, and depression* (pp. 117–143). Mahwah, NJ: Erlbaum.

Grey, S., & Mathews, A. (2000). Effects of training on interpretation of emotional ambiguity. *Quarterly Journal of Experimental Psychology: Human Experimental Psychology, 53*, 1143–1162.

Hirsch, C., & Mathews, A. (1997). Interpretative inferences when reading about emotional events. *Behaviour Research and Therapy, 12*, 1123–1132.

Hirsch, C., & Mathews, A. (2000). Impaired positive inferential bias in social phobia. *Journal of Abnormal Psychology, 109*, 705–712.

Hollon, S. D., & Kendall, P. C. (1980). Cognitive self-statements in depression: Development of an automatic thoughts questionnaire. *Cognitive Therapy and Research, 4*, 383–395.

Horenstein, M., & Segui, J. (1997). Chronometrics of attentional processes in anxiety disorders. *Psychopathology, 30*, 25–35.

Hurlburt, R. T. (1997). Randomly sampling thinking in the natural environment. *Journal of Consulting and Clinical Psychology, 65*, 941–949.

Josephson, B. A., Singer, J. A., & Salovey, P. (1996). Mood regulation and memory: Repairing sad moods with happy memories. *Cognition and Emotion, 10*, 437–444.

Lambie, J. A., & Marcel, A. J. (2002). Consciousness and the varieties of emotion experience: A theoretical framework. *Psychological Review, 109*, 219–259.

Lazarus, R. S. (1968). Emotions and adaptation: Conceptual and empirical relations. In W. J. Arnold (Ed.), *Nebraska Symposium on Motivation* (Vol. 16, pp. 175–266). Lincoln: University of Nebraska Press.

Lazarus, R. S. (1991). *Emotion and adaptation*. New York: Oxford University Press.

MacLeod, C. (2004). The Stroop task in clinical research. In A. Wenzel & D. C. Rubin (Eds.), *Cognitive methods and their application to clinical research* (pp. 41–62). Washington, DC: American Psychological Association.

MacLeod, C., Campbell, L., Rutherford, E. M., & Wilson, E. (2004). The causal status of anxiety-linked attentional and interpretive bias. In J. Yiend (Ed.), *Cognition, emotion and psychopathology: Theoretical, empirical, and clinical directions* (pp. 172–189). Cambridge, England: Cambridge University Press.

MacLeod, C., & Mathews, A. (2004). Selective memory effects in anxiety disorders: An overview of research findings and their implications. In D. Reisberg & P. Hertel, (Eds.), *Memory and emotion* (pp. 155–185). London: Oxford University Press.

MacLeod, C., Mathews, A., & Tata, P. (1986). Attentional bias in emotional disorders. *Journal of Abnormal Psychology, 95,* 15–20.

MacLeod, C., & Rutherford, E. M. (2004). Information-processing approaches: Assessing the selective functioning of attention, interpretation, and retrieval. In R. G. Heimberg, C. L. Turk, & D. S. Mennin (Eds.), *Generalized anxiety disorder: Advances in research and practice* (pp. 109–142). New York: Guilford Press.

MacLeod, C., Rutherford, E., Campbell, L., Ebsworthy, G., & Holker, L. (2002). Selective attention and emotional vulnerability: Assessing the causal basis of their association through the experimental manipulation of attentional bias. *Journal of Abnormal Psychology, 111,* 107–123.

Mathews, A. (2004). On the malleability of emotional encoding. *Behaviour Research and Therapy, 42,* 1019–1036.

Mathews, A., & Mackintosh, B. (1998). A cognitive model of selective processing in anxiety. *Cognitive Therapy and Research, 22,* 539–560.

Mathews, A., & Mackintosh, B. (2000). Induced emotional interpretation bias and anxiety. *Journal of Abnormal Psychology, 109,* 602–615.

Mathews, A., & MacLeod, C. (2005). Cognitive approaches to the emotional disorders. *Annual Review of Clinical Psychology, 1,* 167–196.

Mathews, A., Richards, A., & Eysenck, M. (1989). Interpretation of homophones related to threat in anxiety states. *Journal of Abnormal Psychology, 98,* 31–34.

Matt, G. E., Vazquez, C., & Campbell, W. K. (1992). Mood-congruent recall of affectively toned stimuli: A meta-analytic review. *Clinical Psychology Review, 12,* 227–255.

McNeil, D. W., Tucker, P., Miranda, R., Lewin, M. R., & Nordgren, J. C. (1999). Response to depression and anxiety Stroop stimuli in posttraumatic stress disorder, obsessive–compulsive disorder, and major depressive disorder. *Journal of Nervous and Mental Disease, 187,* 512–516.

Mogg, K., Baldwin, D. S., Brodrick, P., & Bradley, B. P. (2004). Effect of short-term SSRI treatment on cognitive bias in generalised anxiety disorder. *Psychopharmacology, 176,* 466–470.

Mogg, K., & Bradley, B. P. (2005). Attentional bias in generalized anxiety disorder versus depressive disorder. *Cognitive Therapy and Research, 29,* 29–45.

Musa, C., Lepine, J.-P., Clark, D. M., Mansell, W., & Ehlers, A. (2003). Selective attention in social phobia and the moderating effect of a concurrent depressive disorder. *Behaviour Research and Therapy, 41*, 1043–1054.

Nisbett, R. E., & Wilson, T. D. C. (1977). Telling more than we can know: Verbal reports on mental processes. *Psychological Review, 84*, 231–259.

Nunn, J. D., Mathews, A., & Trower, P. (1997). Selective processing of concern-related information in depression. *British Journal of Clinical Psychology, 36*, 489–503.

Powell, M., & Hemsley, D. R. (1984). Depression: A breakdown of perceptual defence? *British Journal of Psychiatry, 145*, 358–362.

Power, M., & Dalgleish, T. (1997). *Cognition and emotion: From order to disorder.* Hove, England: Psychology Press.

Prinz, J. J. (2004). The fractionation of introspection. *Journal of Consciousness Studies, 11*, 40–57.

Pury, C. L. S. (2004). Low positive affect and less extreme emotional encoding. *Cognition and Emotion, 18*, 149–158.

Putman, P., Hermans, E., & van Honk, J. (2004). Emotional Stroop performance for masked angry faces: It's BAS, not BIS. *Emotion, 4*, 305–311.

Richards, A., & French, C. C. (1992). An anxiety-related bias in semantic activation when processing threat/neutral homographs. *Quarterly Journal of Experimental Psychology, 45*, 503–525.

Ridout, N., Astell, A. J., Reid, I. C., Glen, T., & O'Carroll, R. E. (2003). Memory bias for emotional facial expressions in major depression. *Cognition and Emotion, 17*, 101–122.

Sefarty, M. A., Bothwell, R., Marsh, R., Ashton, H., Blizard, R., & Scott, J. (2002). Event-related potentials and cognitive processing of affectively toned words in depression. *Journal of Psychophysiology, 16*, 56–66.

Tata, P. R., Leibowitz, J. A., Prunty, M. J., Cameron, M., & Pickering, A. D. (1996). Attentional bias in obsessional compulsive disorder. *Behaviour Research and Therapy, 34*, 53–60.

Terry, W. S., & Burns, J. S. (2001). Anxiety and repression in attention and retention. *Journal of General Psychology, 128*, 422–432.

van Honk, J., Tuiten, A., de Haan, E., van den Hout, M., & Stam, H. (2001). Attentional biases for angry faces: Relationships to trait anger and anxiety. *Cognition and Emotion, 15*, 279–297.

Vasey, M. W., Hazen, R., & Schmidt, N. B. (2002, November). *Attentional retraining for chronic worry and generalised anxiety disorder.* Paper presented at the Annual Convention of the Association for Advancement of Behavior Therapy, Reno, NV.

Wenzel, A., Jackson, L. C., & Holt, C. S. (2002). Social phobia and the recall of autobiographical memories. *Depression and Anxiety, 15*, 186–189.

Wilhelm, S., McNally, R. J., Baer, L., & Florin, I. (1997). Autobiographical memory in obsessive–compulsive disorder. *British Journal of Clinical Psychology, 36*, 21–31.

Williams, J. M. G., & Scott, J. (1988). Autobiographical memories in depression. *Psychological Medicine, 18*, 689–695.

Williams, J. M. G., Watts, F. N., MacLeod, C., & Mathews, A. (1997). *Cognitive psychology and emotional disorders* (2nd ed.). Chichester, England: Wiley.

Wilson, E., MacLeod, C., Mathews, A. M., & Rutherford, E. M. (2006). The causal role of interpretive bias in anxiety reactivity. *Journal of Abnormal Psychology, 115*, 103–111.

Yiend, J., & Mackintosh, B. (2004). The experimental modification of processing biases. In J. Yiend (Ed.), *Cognition, emotion and psychopathology* (pp. 130–148). Cambridge, England: Cambridge University Press.

II

APPLICATIONS TO PSYCHOPATHOLOGY

5

EMOTION AND SCHIZOPHRENIA

JACK J. BLANCHARD, ALEX S. COHEN, AND JAYMEE T. CARREÑO

Schizophrenia is a disorder characterized by abnormalities in perception, thought, language, behavior, and emotion. Although features of psychosis (including delusions, hallucinations, and thought disorder) often dominate descriptions of schizophrenia, this disorder is also characterized by profound changes in emotion. This review provides a summary of historical and diagnostic descriptions of emotion in schizophrenia and then focuses on contemporary research examining trait dimensions of emotion, experience sampling studies, and laboratory mood induction studies. This is followed by a discussion of challenges and future directions in understanding emotion within schizophrenia.

HISTORICAL AND THEORETICAL PERSPECTIVES

In the earliest descriptions of schizophrenia, emotional changes were a prominent feature of this disorder. Bleuler (1911/1950) observed that "the fundamental affective symptoms often dominate the picture from the very start, in that the patients become increasingly indifferent and apathetic" (p. 254). Bleuler also noted the interpersonal consequences of such emotional changes. He described how individuals with schizophrenia had extreme difficulty in establishing a personal relationship and referred to this as a "defect in emotional rapport" (p. 322).

Kraepelin (1919/1971) also provided rich early description of emotional changes in schizophrenia. He noted that "profound damage occurs as a rule in the emotional life of our patients" (p. 32). Similar to Bleuler (1911/1950), Kraepelin noted that these emotional changes were evident within the relationships of individuals with schizophrenia. Kraepelin described "the extinction of affection for relatives and friends" (p. 33) and noted that

> even the fate of his nearest relatives affect the patient little or not at all. He receives visits without a greeting or other sign of emotion, does not enquire how they are, takes no share in their joys or sorrows. (p. 33)

Emotional changes take a prominent role in theories about the development of schizophrenia. Rado (1962) proposed that schizophrenia arose from genetic factors and, borrowing from genetic terminology, coined the term *schizotype* to refer to the phenotype that was expressed. Specifically, *schizotypy* referred to a personality organization that emerges in an individual with the genetic liability for schizophrenia, although the person may not have the full clinical manifestation of the disorder. Pathological traits associated with schizotypy included a "pleasure deficiency" that was defined as a decreased capacity to experience pleasure, or *anhedonia* (Rado, 1962). This pleasure deficiency was theorized to lead to changes in other positive affective states, including reduced intensity of desire, joy, affection, and love. Given this diminishment in pleasurable feelings, Rado proposed that the "emergency emotions" of fear, rage, and associated negative feeling states would grow in strength.

Influenced by Rado's (1962) work, Meehl (1962) proposed that anhedonia was a "quasi-pathognomonic sign" of schizophrenia. Anhedonia was conjectured to be a primary underlying cause of social isolation, social difficulties, and cognitive deviance. In a later work, Meehl (2001) noted a preference for the term *hypohedonia* to reflect that the capacity to experience pleasure is not entirely lacking and to refer more accurately to a dimensional individual difference in hedonic experience (with *anhedonia* continuing to be an acceptable term when referring to individuals at the extreme of this continuum). Meehl (2001) later clarified that hypohedonia may manifest either as a primary deficit (of genetic origins) arising from aberrations in the limbic system or as a secondary hypohedonia that may become evident later in the course of development.

Secondary hypohedonia was postulated to be a consequence of other factors, including negative affective states. That is, Meehl (1962, 1990, 2001) also discussed *aversive drift*, or the tendency for activities, people, and places "to take on a burdensome, threatening, gloomy, negative emotional charge" (Meehl, 1990, p. 21) among people with schizophrenia. Meehl (2001) described aversive drift as states of intense negative affect and proposed that these potentially unique negative affective experiences were pathognomonic of schizophrenia.

In summary, theoretical models of schizophrenia have placed great emphasis on emotional characteristics in both individuals with the disorder and those at genetic risk (schizotypy) for it. Rado (1962) and Meehl (1962, 2001) described an extreme diminution in pleasurable affect. These theorists also emphasized the elevation in negative affective states occurring in schizophrenia. Thus, these models appear to depict schizophrenia as involving significant changes across affective valence, including hypohedonia and increased negative affect. These affective changes were also conjectured to be stable individual differences in affective experience, or traitlike dispositions. Contemporary evidence regarding clinical phenomenology and diagnostic aspects of emotion are reviewed in the next section.

PHENOMENOLOGY AND DIAGNOSIS

Research on schizophrenia symptomatology has provided empirical support for the importance of affective features in schizophrenia. In particular, many people with schizophrenia experience negative symptoms (Andreasen, 1985), which have been defined as reduced pleasure from social and other activities (*anhedonia*), lowered drive and interest in one's environment (*avolition* and *apathy*, respectively), diminished emotional expression (*blunted* or *flat* affect), and diminished speech (*alogia*). Negative symptoms are represented in the diagnostic criteria for schizophrenia, per the *Diagnostic and Statistical Manual of Mental Disorders* (4th ed.; American Psychiatric Association, 1994). Specifically, affective flattening, alogia, and avolition are included within the characteristic symptoms of schizophrenia. The *Diagnostic and Statistical Manual* also noted that other affective changes can include diminished emotional intensity or the loss of feelings.

Multiple factor-analytic studies have demonstrated that negative symptoms are distinct from other symptoms of schizophrenia, including positive symptoms (characterized by delusions and hallucinations) and conceptual disorganization (involving thought disorder and disorganized behavior; e.g., Grube, Bilder, & Goldman, 1998). Even in more complex factorial solutions (e.g., four- or five-factor models), negative symptoms consistently emerge as a factor separate from other symptoms (e.g., Emsley, Rabinowitz, & Torreman, 2003; Mueser, Curran, & McHugo, 1997; White, Harvey, Opler, & Lindenmayer, 1997). In addition to structural validity, negative symptoms such as anhedonia and blunted affect have been shown to be uniquely associated with social functioning deficits, neurocognitive impairments, and neurobiological abnormalities not characteristic of other schizophrenia symptoms (e.g., see the review by Earnst & Kring, 1997).

Negative symptoms have served as the basis for identifying subtypes within schizophrenia, including the selection of patients with enduring primary negative symptoms, referred to as the *deficit syndrome* (Carpenter, Heinrichs, & Wagman, 1988; Kirkpatrick, Buchanan, Ross, & Carpenter, 2001). Furthermore, the structure of negative symptoms appears to be consistent with the existence of a distinct subtype of schizophrenia (Blanchard, Horan, & Collins, 2005). These results suggest that emotional changes characterized by diminished experience of pleasure and diminished affective expression are independent of psychosis and other symptoms and may represent the manifestation of independent etiological processes (Kirkpatrick et al., 2001). These findings also highlight the heterogeneity in disease process across schizophrenia, with some individuals with the diagnosis presenting with profound negative symptoms and others showing less pronounced negative symptoms (and thus fewer of the emotional characteristics associated with these symptoms).

The foregoing discussion demonstrates that schizophrenia is characterized by marked changes in the experience (anhedonia) and expression (blunted affect) of emotion. We now turn to a review of studies that have sought to examine more systematically the nature of emotion in schizophrenia by examining whether the changes in emotion noted by Meehl (1962) and others represent enduring individual differences (i.e., traits).

TRAIT DIMENSIONS OF EMOTION

As noted above, clinical observations and symptom assessments have described reduced pleasurable affect (anhedonia) and increased negative affect (aversive drift) in schizophrenia. Meehl (1962) posited that anhedonia was a personality trait arising from the genetic liability for schizophrenia. Clinical observations also support altered emotion-related personality features in the prodrome of individuals developing schizophrenia and in unaffected family members of individuals with schizophrenia (for a review, see Berenbaum & Fujita, 1994). Drawing on theory and clinical observations, researchers have examined how schizophrenia and risk for schizophrenia might relate to trait measures of affectivity (Watson & Tellegen, 1985; Watson, Wiese, Vaidya, & Tellegen, 1999; Zevon & Tellegen, 1982). We begin by reviewing the literature on anhedonia and then review research on the broader traits of positive affectivity (PA) and negative affectivity (NA).

Anhedonia

Traitlike anhedonia has been assessed using a variety of methods including clinical interviews and self-report questionnaires. Although each method has demonstrated reliability and validity (Horan, Kring, & Blanchard,

2006), this review focuses on findings based on self-report assessments of hedonic capacity. Informed by Meehl's (1962) model of schizotypy and anhedonia, Chapman, Chapman, and Raulin (1976) developed separate self-report scales to measure diminished pleasure from physical experiences (e.g., touch, sight, smell, sound, taste) and social interactions. These self-report measures have been used to study schizophrenia, schizotypy, and other disorders, including depression. These trait measures have repeatedly shown that compared with nonpsychiatric samples, people with schizophrenia report elevated physical and social anhedonia (Berenbaum & Oltmanns, 1992; Blanchard, Bellack, & Mueser, 1994; Blanchard, Horan, & Brown, 2001; Blanchard, Mueser, & Bellack, 1998; Chapman et al., 1976; Cohen et al., 2005; Katsanis, Iacono, & Beiser, 1990). Consistent with the conjecture that anhedonia reflects an enduring traitlike deficit, people with schizophrenia have been found to report stable levels of anhedonia over 90 days (Blanchard et al., 1998) and over a 1-year period (Blanchard et al., 2001).

Despite the evidence that anhedonia is a feature of schizophrenia, it is also clear that anhedonia may not be unique to this disorder. Anhedonia is elevated among people with current affective disorders (Berenbaum & Oltmanns, 1992; Katsanis et al., 1990; Schuck, Leventhal, Rothstein, & Irizarry, 1984). However, anhedonia appears to be a reflection of current symptoms in affective disorders as opposed to a trait disposition. Anhedonia in these disorders appears secondary to depressed mood (Blanchard et al., 1994, 2001; Katsanis, Iacono, Beiser, & Lacey, 1992) and decreases as depressive symptoms remit (Blanchard et al., 2001). Thus, anhedonia is an enduring individual difference within schizophrenia that appears independent of affective and psychotic symptoms, whereas anhedonia in depression is only manifested during symptomatic periods.

Anhedonia has also been examined as an indicator of schizotypy and as a risk marker for developing schizophrenia-spectrum disorders. Anhedonia has been found to be elevated in family members of individuals with schizophrenia (Kendler, Thacker, & Walsh, 1996). Additionally, nonclinical individuals (generally college students, but see Collins, Blanchard, & Biondo, 2005) with markedly elevated social anhedonia scores have been reported to exhibit clinical, cognitive, and physiological characteristics similar to those seen in individuals at known genetic risk for schizophrenia. Specifically, cross-sectional studies have shown that individuals with elevated social anhedonia scores demonstrate clinical characteristics consistent with schizophrenia-spectrum disorders, including schizoid social withdrawal (Mishlove & Chapman, 1985); elevated schizotypal, schizoid, and paranoid personality disorder symptoms (Gooding, Tallent, & Matts, 2005; Kwapil, Crump, & Pickup, 2002); interpersonal behavioral signs of schizoidia and schizotypy (Collins et al., 2005); increased psychotic-like experiences (Gooding, Kwapil, & Tallent, 1999; Kwapil et al., 2002; Mishlove & Chapman, 1985); and cognitive slippage (Gooding, Tallent, & Hegyi, 2001). Neuropsychological deficits and psychophysiological abnormalities consistent with schizotypy have also been observed in individuals with extreme social anhedonia, including deficits in working memory (Tallent & Gooding, 1999), visuospatial reconstruction and recall (Cohen, Leung, Saperstein, & Blanchard, 2006; Gooding & Braun, 2004), executive functioning (Gooding et al., 1999; Tallent & Gooding, 1999), and psychophysiological abnormalities in the visual system (Cohen, Leung, et al., 2006; Gooding, 1999; Gooding et al., 2000). Consistent with Meehl's (1962) conjecture that schizotypy is taxonic, the latent structure of social anhedonia has also been found to be taxonic (Blanchard, Gangestad, Brown, & Horan, 2000; Horan, Blanchard, Gangestad, & Kwapil, 2004).

Longitudinal results have also provided compelling evidence for the predictive validity of social anhedonia. In a 10-year longitudinal study, Kwapil (1998) demonstrated that individuals with social anhedonia were much more likely than control participants to be diagnosed with a schizophrenia-spectrum personality disorder at the 10-year follow-up (24% vs. 1%, respectively). At follow-up, individuals with social anhedonia also endorsed high rates of psychotic-like experiences, and they evidenced poorer overall functioning and lower rates of marriage compared with control participants (Kwapil, 1998). These findings have now been replicated in an independent 5-year follow-up study (Gooding et al., 2005), with social anhedonia participants exceeding control participants in the endorsement of psychotic-like experiences and in the proportion of participants meeting diagnostic criteria for a schizophrenia spectrum personality disorder (15.6% vs. 0%, respectively).

In summary, trait measures indicate that schizophrenia is characterized by enduring anhedonia. This anhedonia is unlike state-dependent reductions in hedonic capacity observed in other disorders such as depression. In nonclinical samples, anhedonia may serve as a marker for those individuals at risk for the development of schizophrenia spectrum disorders. Although anhedonia suggests reductions in the capacity to experience pleasure, the preceding summary does not directly address broader affective features of schizophrenia. The following section reviews trait assessments specifically targeting affect.

Broad Affective Traits of Positive and Negative Affectivity

Research on the structure of affect has identified two broad domains consisting of PA and NA (e.g., Watson et al., 1999; Watson & Tellegen, 1985). Trait PA reflects enduring individual differences in the experience of positive mood states, including enthusiasm and cheerfulness. Trait NA reflects the dispositional tendency to experience negative emotional states, including fear, sadness, and anger. At the trait level, PA and NA are strongly associated with the "Big Two" of personality, extraversion and neuroticism, respectively (Watson et al., 1999; see also chap. 1, this volume). A number of researchers have examined levels of PA and NA among people with schizophrenia.

Berenbaum and Fujita (1994) conducted a meta-analysis of personality studies involving schizophrenia. A robust finding was that individuals with schizophrenia had diminished extraversion and elevated neuroticism. Subsequent research has found that compared with nonclinical comparison groups, individuals with schizophrenia show diminished scores on markers of trait PA–Extraversion and elevations on markers of trait NA–Neuroticism (Bagby et al., 1997; Blanchard et al., 1998; Cohen et al., 2005; Gurrera, Nestor, & O'Donnell, 2000; Horan & Blanchard, 2003a; Lysaker, Bell, Kaplan, & Bryson, 1998; Suslow, Roestel, Ohrmann, & Arolt, 2003). This pattern of diminished PA and elevated NA has been found to be temporally stable in schizophrenia (Blanchard et al., 1998), even in the context of changes in hospitalization status and improving symptomatology (Blanchard et al., 2001).

The study of trait dimensions of affectivity may be informative for understanding individual differences in the functional outcomes observed in schizophrenia (Fowles, 1992). Environmental stressors, in particular a hostile and critical family environment, have proven to be a robust predictor of relapse in schizophrenia (Butzlaff & Hooley, 1998). However, it is important to note that many individuals exposed to such interpersonal stressors do not relapse (Kavanagh, 1992; Ventura, Nuechterlein, Lukoff, & Hardesty, 1989). Might it be the case that trait affectivity, such as elevated trait NA, can help clarify who might be most vulnerable to the effects of stress within schizophrenia? Horan and Blanchard (2003a) examined the role of individual differences in trait affectivity in predicting affective responding to a simulated social encounter. In patients with schizophrenia, trait NA was a significant predictor of negative affect following the social task even after controlling for baseline mood, current symptoms, and neuropsychological impairment. This demonstrates the potential utility of examining trait differences in affect to better understand individual differences in outcome.

EXPERIENCE SAMPLING METHODS

Although symptom and trait measures of emotion in schizophrenia are highly informative, they are limited in that they fail to address the actual experience of emotion as people navigate their daily lives. The experience sampling method (ESM) was developed to examine the covariance between daily life experiences and emotion (see Csikszentmihalyi & Larson, 1987). Individuals typically respond to random beeps (provided via wristwatch alarms or using personal digital assistants) and record their ongoing activities, current mood, and other aspects of functioning of interest to the researcher. This methodology permits for momentary assessment that may be less vulnerable to distortion in recall that might occur when using symptoms assessments or trait measures.

In one of the first studies to apply ESM to schizophrenia, Myin-Germeys, Delespaul, and deVries (2000) found that compared with control participants, patients reported less positive mood and greater negative mood over the course of a week. Comparison of patients with blunted and nonblunted schizophrenia indicated no difference in emotional experiences between these two groups (Myin-Germeys et al., 2000). In sum, these results are consistent with the trait data reflecting lower PA and increased NA in schizophrenia and indicate that blunted emotional expression (rated with symptom scales) is not related to daily emotional experience in schizophrenia.

In a subsequent ESM study of a psychotic sample (largely comprising individuals with schizophrenia and schizoaffective disorders), patients were compared with their first-degree family members and control participants (Myin-Germeys, Van Os, Schwartz, Stone, & Delespaul, 2001). Psychotic patients demonstrated lower positive mood and higher negative mood compared with control participants and family members, who did not differ. Additionally, patients reported more intense negative affective reactions to stress compared with control participants. Relatives of psychotic patients were also found to have greater stress reactivity than control participants, suggesting that vulnerability to psychosis may manifest in greater emotional reactions to daily life stress (Myin-Germeys et al., 2001).

Although ESM is a powerful approach to understanding emotional responding in schizophrenia, it is limited in addressing hypotheses about whether patients have a true decreased capacity to experience pleasure. That is, lowered PA may be the outcome of either dispositional differences in hedonic capacity or of less rewarding environments (e.g., see Myin-Germeys, Krabbendam, Delespaul, & Van Os, 2003). Thus, one is faced with the difficulty of accounting for differences in the environments to which individuals are exposed and how those environments influence emotional experience. Laboratory studies may serve to address this issue more directly because evocative stimuli can be held constant.

LABORATORY STUDIES

Contemporary models suggest that emotion involves activity across three domains, including expression, experience, and physiology (see Lang, 1995, for a review). Although studies employing clinical assessments, trait-based questionnaires, and ESM have been informative for understanding how emotion is disturbed in schizophrenia, findings from these studies fail to address fundamental issues about how emotional abnormalities manifest across expression, experience, and physiology. Laboratory-based studies have been invaluable for carefully assessing expression, experience, and physiology.

Moreover, laboratory-based studies afford the opportunity to examine emotion with stimulus properties held constant across individuals.

Laboratory studies of emotional expressivity have afforded a more sophisticated understanding of blunted or flat affect in schizophrenia. Generally speaking, the findings from this body of literature are concordant with those from studies using clinical ratings. Compared with control participants, patients show diminished levels of expressiveness across multiple communicative channels and in response to a variety of evocative stimuli. For example, individuals with schizophrenia have shown fewer emotional expressions than nonpsychiatric control participants in reaction to neutral, positive, and negatively valenced stimuli, such as flavored drinks (Berenbaum & Oltmanns, 1992), still pictures (Dworkin, Clark, Amador, & Gorman, 1996), and film clips (Berenbaum & Oltmanns, 1992; Kring, Kerr, Smith, & Neale, 1993; Kring & Neale, 1996). Similar reduced expressivity in schizophrenia is evident in other paradigms, including recounting of affectively valenced memories (Brozgold et al., 1998) and being involved in social interactions (Aghevli, Blanchard, & Horan, 2003). Moreover, patients have shown markedly attenuated levels of *speech prosody* (emphasis and intonation in speech) compared with nonpatient control participants in both neutral (Cohen, Alpert, Nienow, Dinzeo, & Docherty, 2006) and affectively valenced (Alpert, Rosenberg, Pouget, & Shaw, 2000) conditions. It is noteworthy that some of these studies were conducted with unmedicated patients (e.g., Kring et al., 1993; Kring & Neale, 1996), suggesting that diminished expressivity can occur independent of medication side effects.

Given that individuals with schizophrenia show relatively global expressivity deficits in laboratory experiments, an important issue arises concerning the degree to which schizophrenia is associated with complementary deficits in the experiential and physiological responses to evocative stimuli. To date, a number of laboratory studies have addressed this topic, and the general corpus of findings suggests that in schizophrenia, self-reported experience and physiological reaction are not consistent with diminished emotional expression. Individuals with schizophrenia and control participants have shown equivalent self-reported reactions to a wide array of positive and negatively valenced stimuli (Berenbaum & Oltmanns, 1992; Earnst & Kring, 1999; Horan & Blanchard, 2003b; Kring et al., 1993; Kring & Neale, 1996), even though patients show diminished facial expressivity. Similarly, patients with high levels of clinically rated blunted affect have not differed from other nonblunted patients or control participants in self-reported experience (Berenbaum & Oltmanns, 1992; Earnst & Kring, 1999) and have not differed in the number of emotionally valenced words used while recounting emotionally valenced memories (Alpert et al., 2000; Cohen, Alpert, et al., 2006).

Consistent with these findings of normative emotional experience in laboratory paradigms, individuals with schizophrenia have shown equivalent levels of physiological activation compared with nonpsychiatric comparison groups. For example, individuals with schizophrenia have shown similar or more intense electrodermal activity (Taylor, Liberzon, Decker, & Koeppe, 2002; Volz, Hamm, Kirsch, & Rey, 2003; Williams et al., 2004; but see Curtis, Lebow, Lake, Katsanis, & Iacono, 1999) and startle response (Curtis et al., 1999; Schlenker, Cohen, & Hopmann, 1995; Volz et al., 2003) compared with control participants in response to a variety of evocative stimuli. Perhaps most informative to this discussion are studies that have simultaneously measured emotion across all three domains. In several studies (Kring & Neale, 1996; Sison, Alpert, Fudge, & Stern, 1996), individuals with schizophrenia have exhibited markedly diminished levels of expressiveness yet have had experiential reports and physiological reactions that were similar to or greater than those of control participants. This pattern of findings was observed regardless of the affective valence of the condition (i.e., neutral, positive, or negative). Taken as a whole, findings from laboratory studies confirm that individuals with schizophrenia show relatively global expressive deficits but suggest that the capacity to experience emotion is preserved. These findings raise questions about the nature of the anhedonic deficits revealed in studies employing clinically rated and trait-affect-based instruments.

When interpreting the findings from laboratory studies, it is important to note that there is some inconsistency across studies in how patients have responded to positively valenced stimuli. Some investigations have found that patients rated positively valenced stimuli as being significantly less positive than control participants (Curtis et al., 1999; Paradiso et al., 2003; Quirk, Strauss, & Sloan, 1998; Schneider, Gur, Gur, & Shtasel, 1995; Taylor, Phan, Britton, & Liberzon, 2005). The nature of this inconsistency in findings from laboratory studies of schizophrenia is unclear. However, these data do suggest that entirely normative emotional responding to positive stimuli may not be found in all samples or methods. As noted later, aspects of the stimuli used in laboratory assessment need to be considered so that the most appropriate procedures are used to investigate affective responding in schizophrenia. An interesting area to consider in future studies is affective responding to olfactory cues. Olfaction may be an important domain given links between olfactory nerves and the limbic system as well as ties between olfaction and social behavior (Malaspina & Coleman, 2003). Using olfactory stimuli, patients with schizophrenia have been found to report attenuated ratings of pleasantness (Crespo-Facorro et al., 2001; Moberg et al., 2003), and olfactory deficits have been tied to diminished social drive in schizophrenia (Malaspina & Coleman, 2003).

INTEGRATION AND FUTURE DIRECTIONS

In examining the paradigms used to study emotion in schizophrenia, one sees some striking inconsistencies in results across methods. Relying on clinical assessment, self-report trait questionnaires, and experience sampling, it appears that schizophrenia is indeed characterized by diminished hedonic capacity. However, divergent conclusions are reached when examining laboratory studies where many (but not all) studies have failed to find group differences in emotional responding and instead report that self-rated mood and physiological responding to affect-eliciting stimuli appears normal in schizophrenia. These findings might suggest that laboratory methods provide a more valid characterization of emotion in schizophrenia. However, a potential constraint of laboratory studies concerns the types of evocative stimuli that have been used.

Laboratory studies have typically involved film clips, photos, and food to arouse mood states. Moreover, in evoking positive mood states, films have been largely selected for inducing "amusement" as evident in comedy film selections (e.g., Kring & Neale, 1996). One serious limitation of these studies is that they do not use social affiliative stimuli, which might be more effective in evoking emotional deficits among people with schizophrenia. Meehl (1962) originally observed that "schizoid anhedonia is mainly interpersonal" (p. 833). Similarly, Meehl (1990) indicated that even in the most deteriorated cases, individuals with schizophrenia can achieve pleasure from a few sources such as smoking or watching television. Morrone-Strupinsky and Depue (2004) demonstrated the importance of using films that uniquely induce warmth and affection versus other positive affective processes, showing that a trait measure of social affiliation was related to emotional responding to an affiliation film but not to another film eliciting positive affect. Thus, future research should examine the use of social affiliative stimuli in studies of social anhedonia and emotional responding in schizophrenia. Such social stimuli may provide for more compelling examination of potential individual differences in affective responding within schizophrenia.

In addition to examining the use of affiliative stimuli, it might be informative to consider how affective features of the illness manifest within a social context. For example, blunted or flat affect may have important implications for understanding how individuals with schizophrenia evoke responses from others. Affective expression serves an important communicative role that has critical implications for social relationships. Research with nonclinical samples indicates that lowered expressivity of positive emotions relates to lower likeability by peers and observers (Gross & John, 1998). Experimentally manipulated expressive suppression reduces rapport and inhibits relationship formation (Butler et al., 2003). Given these findings, might blunted affect in part contribute to nonrewarding social interactions experienced by those with schizophrenia? Patients may evoke social responses that are less pleasant, and this lack of affiliative response may underlie subsequent reports of social anhedonia. In schizophrenia, anhedonia and blunted affect, measured as clinical symptoms, are highly correlated and cohere in the broad factor of negative symptoms (Blanchard & Cohen, 2006). It is interesting to note that this is not unique to schizophrenia; indices of diminished expression and social anhedonia have been found to be correlated in nonclinical samples as well. In a validational study of a dispositional measure of generalized emotional expressivity, Kring, Smith, and Neale (1994) found that social anhedonia was significantly negatively correlated with self-reported expressiveness. We have replicated this finding (Blanchard, 2005) with a similarly robust correlation between social anhedonia and the Kring et al. (1994) measure of expressivity. Behavioral coding of social interactions has also shown that individuals high in social anhedonia have less facial affect and less verbal expression compared with control participants (Collins et al., 2005). Thus, greater social anhedonia appears associated with diminished emotional expressivity across clinical, nonclinical, and at-risk samples. Given the relevance of emotional expression to establishing rewarding social relations (Butler et al., 2003; Gross & John, 1998), social anhedonia may, in part, reflect the nonrewarding social environments that individuals evoke through their own diminished expressivity.

In attempting to integrate findings across the methodologies described in this chapter, it may be the case that only a particular aspect of hedonic experience is altered in schizophrenia. Specifically, hedonic experience can be parsed into "appetitive or anticipatory pleasure," which involves the anticipation of an activity that is enjoyable, and "consummatory pleasure," which represents the pleasure experienced from participation in the activity. Kring (Germans & Kring, 2000; Kring, 1999) has proposed that the hedonic deficit in schizophrenia may be specific to anticipatory pleasure (thus being reflected within interviews and trait measures asking about expected pleasure), whereas consummatory or "in the moment" pleasure is intact (as manifested in normative responding when exposed to laboratory stimuli). Additional research is required to determine how best to disentangle these aspects of emotion, but recent work is promising (see summary in Horan, Kring, & Blanchard, 2006).

Another factor that has been considered in attempting to understand the conflicting findings from emotion research within schizophrenia is the contribution of cognitive deficits. Schizophrenia is characterized by a range of cognitive impairments in domains such as memory, attention, and executive functioning (Blanchard et al., 1994; Heinrichs & Zakzanis, 1998; Horan & Blanchard, 2003a). Might individuals with schizophrenia not recall hedonic experiences and thus underreport these experiences within clinical interviews and on trait measures? To address this issue, a recent study (Horan, Green, Kring, & Nuechterlein, 2006) examined immediate and delayed recall of affective experience in schizophrenia. Consistent with prior studies, individuals with schizophrenia demonstrated affective responses that were similar to those of control participants, and this was evident both immediately following stimulus exposure and after a brief (4-hour) delayed recall. These results suggest that encoding and short-term retention of pleasurable affect is intact within schizophrenia (Horan, Green, et al., 2006). However, cognitive ability was not directly assessed in this study, and the delay was relatively brief. Thus, cognitive variables may affect emotional experience or the assessment of emotion in ways that are not yet fully understood.

As researchers plan future studies of emotion in schizophrenia, it will be necessary to address the vexing heterogeneity of this disorder. Although reviews of the literature typically make broad generalizations regarding anhedonia and other emotional features in schizophrenia (as done here), these statements reflect group results and do not accurately represent the range of responding within schizophrenia. It should be emphasized that not all individuals with schizophrenia are anhedonic, nor do all experience diminished trait PA and elevated levels of trait NA. The acknowledgment of this variability in emotion may permit the study of how these individual differences are related to other aspects of the illness, such as stress reactivity (e.g., Cohen, Docherty, Nienow, & Dinzeo, 2003; Horan & Blanchard, 2003a) and social functioning (e.g., Blanchard et al., 1998; Cohen et al., 2005).

One approach to dealing with the heterogeneity of schizophrenia is to study subtypologies on the basis of symptoms. The most compelling contemporary approach involves the identification of subtypes using negative symptoms (including anhedonia and blunted affect). This strategy is perhaps most clearly reflected in the proposal that enduring primary negative symptoms within schizophrenia identify a separate disease within this disorder, the deficit syndrome (e.g., Kirkpatrick et al., 2001). There is an accumulation of evidence supporting the validity of this typology (see Blanchard & Cohen, 2006), and some evidence suggests that the deficit syndrome involves deficits in both emotion expressivity and experience (e.g., Cohen & Docherty, 2004; Cohen et al., 2003; Horan & Blanchard, 2003b; Kirkpatrick & Buchanan, 1990).

Beyond issues of heterogenity, emotion deficits may not be adequately assessed within existing measures of negative symptoms. Horan, Kring, and Blanchard (2006) noted that current symptom assessments of anhedonia may actually fail to measure appropriately the experience of pleasure and instead reflect functional impairment. Thus, ratings of the symptom of anhedonia may actually reflect social isolation and not the experience of pleasure tied to social interaction. If this is the case, then comparing subgroups of individuals with schizophrenia on the basis of these symptom scales may not accurately represent comparisons on the construct of reduced hedonic capacity. Research strategies will need to consider carefully the assessment approaches used and whether they actually tap the emotion constructs that an investigator is interested in studying.

CLINICAL IMPLICATIONS

Although the affective abnormalities in schizophrenia are not yet fully understood, sufficient progress has been realized to suggest clinical implications. First, given the accumulation of research on negative symptoms, including anhedonia and blunted affect, it is clear that any clinical assessment of individuals with schizophrenia should include these symptom domains. Knowledge of these affective features of the disorder can be used to better characterize an individual's clinical state and functional impairments and thus inform treatment needs. Apart from symptoms, assessment of individual differences in affectivity may be informative in understanding individual vulnerability to stress (e.g., Horan & Blanchard, 2003a). Second, with regard to intervention, emotion research can be used to educate family members about the illness. Evidence suggests that negative symptoms may contribute to attributions that underlie critical or hostile attitudes of family members (e.g., Hooley, 1985; Weisman, Nuechterlein, Goldstein, & Snyder, 1998). Appropriate education about the negative symptoms and associated affective changes may serve to address these attitudes. For example, relatives could be informed that loss of pleasure, diminished drive, and blunted expression are features of the illness and do not merely reflect voluntary choices of the individual suffering from schizophrenia. Similarly, it might be informative for family members to be aware of the disconnect between emotional expression and experience in schizophrenia (i.e., a lack of expression associated with blunted affect does not reflect a paucity of emotional experience).

SUMMARY

Schizophrenia is characterized by profound changes in the expression and experience of emotion. At the symptom or trait level, this disorder appears to involve diminished pleasure or anhedonia, increased negative affectivity, and the blunted expression of affect. An important challenge faced by emotion researchers is trying to understand these findings in light of other evidence that individuals with schizophrenia report normative subjective responses to laboratory stimuli. Future research will need to examine carefully issues of heterogeneity within this disorder as well as features of the evocative stimuli used in laboratory studies to allow a better understanding of these results. In particular, we will need to pay closer attention to how emotion evolves within a social context so that we can appreciate the full complexities of emotional experience and links to social impairment within schizophrenia.

REFERENCES

Aghevli, M. A., Blanchard, J. J., & Horan, W. P. (2003). The expression and experience of emotion in schizophrenia: A study of social interactions. *Psychiatry Research, 119*, 261–270.

Alpert, M., Rosenberg, S. D., Pouget, E. R., & Shaw, R. J. (2000). Prosody and lexical accuracy in flat affect schizophrenia. *Psychiatry Research, 97*, 107–118.

American Psychiatric Association. (1994). *Diagnostic and statistical manual of mental disorders* (4th ed.). Washington DC: Author.

Andreasen, N. C. (1985). Positive vs. negative schizophrenia: A critical evaluation. *Schizophrenia Bulletin, 11*, 380–389.

Bagby, R. M., Bindseil, K. D., Schuller, D. R., Rector, N. A., Young, L. T., Cooke, R. G., et al. (1997). Relationship between the five-factor model of personality and unipolar, bipolar and schizophrenic patients. *Psychiatry Research, 70*, 83–94.

Berenbaum, H., & Fujita, F. (1994). Schizophrenia and personality: Exploring the boundaries and connections between vulnerability and outcome. *Journal of Abnormal Psychology, 103*, 148–158.

Berenbaum, H., & Oltmanns, T. F. (1992). Emotional experience and expression in schizophrenia and depression. *Journal of Abnormal Psychology, 101*, 37–44.

Blanchard, J. J. (2005, August). *Anhedonia revisited: What can hedonic capacity tell us about schizophrenia?* Paper presented at the 113th Annual Convention of the American Psychological Association, Washington, DC.

Blanchard, J. J., Bellack, A. S., & Mueser, K. T. (1994). Affective and social-behavioral correlates of physical and social anhedonia in schizophrenia. *Journal of Abnormal Psychology, 103*, 719–728.

Blanchard, J. J., & Cohen, A. S. (2006). The structure of negative symptoms in schizophrenia: Implications for assessment. *Schizophrenia Bulletin, 32*, 238–245

Blanchard, J. J., Gangestad, S. W., Brown, S. A., & Horan, W. P. (2000). Hedonic capacity and schizotypy revisited: A taxometric analysis of social anhedonia. *Journal of Abnormal Psychology, 109*, 87–95.

Blanchard, J. J., Horan, W. P., & Brown, S. A. (2001). Diagnostic differences in social anhedonia: A longitudinal study of schizophrenia and major depressive disorder. *Journal of Abnormal Psychology, 110*, 363–371.

Blanchard, J. J., Horan, W. P., & Collins, L. M. (2005). Examining the latent structure of negative symptoms: Is there a distinct subtype of negative symptom schizophrenia? *Schizophrenia Research, 77*, 151–165.

Blanchard, J. J., Mueser, K. T., & Bellack, A. S. (1998). Anhedonia, positive and negative affect, and social functioning in schizophrenia. *Schizophrenia Bulletin, 24*, 413–424.

Bleuler, E. (1950). *Dementia praecox or the group of schizophrenias* (J. Zinkin, Trans.). New York: International Universities Press. (Original work published 1911)

Brozgold, A. Z., Borod, J. C., Martin, C. C., Pick, L. H., Alpert, M., & Welkowitz, J. (1998). Social functioning and facial emotional expression in neurological and psychiatric disorders. *Applied Neuropsychology, 5*, 15.

Butler, E. A., Egloff, B., Wilhelm, F. H., Smith, N. C., Erickson, E. A., & Gross, J. J. (2003). The social consequences of expressive suppression. *Emotion, 3*, 48–67.

Butzlaff, R. L., & Hooley, J. M. (1998). Expressed emotion and psychiatric relapse: A meta-analysis. *Archives of General Psychiatry, 55,* 547–552.

Carpenter, W. T., Jr., Heinrichs, D. W., & Wagman, A. M. (1988). Deficit and nondeficit forms of schizophrenia: The concept. *American Journal of Psychiatry, 145,* 578–583.

Chapman, L. J., Chapman, J. P., & Raulin, M. L. (1976). Scales for physical and social anhedonia. *Journal of Abnormal Psychology, 85,* 374–382.

Cohen, A. S., Alpert, M., Nienow, T. M.., Dinzeo, T. J., & Docherty, N. M. (2006). *Computerized measurement of negative symptoms in schizophrenia.* Manuscript submitted for publication.

Cohen, A. S., Dinzeo, T. J., Nienow, T. M., Smith, D. A., Singer, B., & Docherty, N. M. (2005). Diminished emotionality and social functioning in schizophrenia. *Journal of Nervous and Mental Diseases, 193,* 796–802.

Cohen, A. S., & Docherty, N. M. (2004). Affective reactivity of speech and emotional experience in patients with schizophrenia. *Schizophrenia Research, 69,* 7–14.

Cohen, A. S., Docherty, N. M., Nienow, T., & Dinzeo, T. (2003). Self-reported stress and the deficit syndrome of schizophrenia. *Psychiatry, 66,* 308–316.

Cohen, A. S., Leung, W. W., Saperstein, A. M., & Blanchard, J. J. (2006). *Schizophrenia Research, 85,* 132–141.

Collins, L. M., Blanchard, J. J., & Biondo, K. M. (2005). Behavioral signs of schizoidia and schizotypy in social anhedonics. *Schizophrenia Research, 78,* 309–322.

Crespo-Facorro, B., Paradiso, S., Andreasen, N. C., O'Leary, D. S., Watkins, G. L., Ponto, L. L., & Hichwa, R. D. (2001). Neural mechanisms of anhedonia in schizophrenia: A PET study of response to unpleasant and pleasant odors. *JAMA, 286,* 427–435.

Csikszentmihalyi, M., & Larson, R. (1987). Validity and reliability of the experience-sampling method. *Journal of Nervous and Mental Disease, 175,* 526–536.

Curtis, C. E., Lebow, B., Lake, D. S., Katsanis, J., & Iacono, W. G. (1999). Acoustic startle reflex in schizophrenia patients and their first-degree relatives: Evidence of normal emotional modulation. *Psychophysiology, 36,* 469–475.

Dworkin, R. H., Clark, S. C., Amador, X. F., & Gorman, J. M. (1996). Does affective blunting in schizophrenia reflect affective deficit or neuromotor dysfunction? *Schizophrenia Research, 20,* 301–306.

Earnst, K. S., & Kring, A. M. (1997). Construct validity of negative symptoms: An empirical and conceptual review. *Clinical Psychology Review, 17,* 167–189.

Earnst, K. S., & Kring, A. M. (1999). Emotional responding in deficit and nondeficit schizophrenia. *Psychiatry Research, 88,* 191–207.

Emsley, R., Rabinowitz, J., & Torreman, M. (2003). The factor structure for the Positive and Negative Syndrome Scale (PANSS) in recent-onset psychosis. *Schizophrenia Research, 61,* 47–57.

Fowles, D. C. (1992). Schizophrenia: Diathesis–stress revisited. *Annual Review of Psychology, 43,* 303–336.

Germans, M. K., & Kring, A. M. (2000). Hedonic deficit in anhedonia: Support for the role of approach motivation. *Personality and Individual Differences, 28,* 659–672.

Gooding, D. C. (1999). Antisaccade task performance in questionnaire-identified schizotypes. *Schizophrenia Research, 35,* 157–166.

Gooding, D. C., & Braun, J. G. (2004). Visuoconstructive performance, implicit hemispatial inattention, and schizotypy. *Schizophrenia Research, 68,* 261–269.

Gooding, D. C., Kwapil, T. R., & Tallent, K. A. (1999). Wisconsin Card Sorting Test deficits in schizotypic individuals. *Schizophrenia Research, 40,* 201–209.

Gooding, D. C., Miller, M. D., & Kwapil, T. R. (2000). Smooth pursuit eye tracking and visual fixation in psychosis-prone individuals. *Psychiatry Research, 93,* 41–54.

Gooding, D. C., Tallent, K. A., & Hegyi, J. V. (2001). Cognitive slippage in schizotypic individuals. *Journal of Nervous and Mental Disease, 189,* 750–756.

Gooding, D. C., Tallent, K. A., & Matts, C. W. (2005). Clinical status of at-risk individuals 5 years later: Further validation of the psychometric high-risk strategy. *Journal of Abnormal Psychology, 114,* 170–175.

Gross, J. J., & John, O. P. (1998). Mapping the domain of expressivity: Multimethod evidence for a hierarchical model. *Journal of Personality and Social Psychology, 74,* 170–191.

Grube, B. S., Bilder, R. M., & Goldman, R. S. (1998). Meta-analysis of symptom factors in schizophrenia. *Schizophrenia Research, 31,* 113–120.

Gurrera, R. J., Nestor, P. G., & O'Donnell, B. F. (2000). Personality traits in schizophrenia: Comparison with a community sample. *Journal of Nervous and Mental Disease, 188,* 31–35.

Heinrichs, R. W., & Zakzanis, K. K. (1998). Neurocognitive deficit in schizophrenia: A quantitative review of the evidence. *Neuropsychology, 12,* 426–445.

Hooley, J. M. (1985). Expressed emotion: A review of the critical literature. *Clinical Psychology Review, 5,* 119–139.

Horan, W. P., & Blanchard, J. J. (2003a). Emotional responses to psychosocial stress in schizophrenia: The role of individual differences in affective traits and coping. *Schizophrenia Research, 60,* 271–283.

Horan, W. P., & Blanchard, J. J. (2003b). Neurocognitive, social, and emotional dysfunction in deficit syndrome schizophrenia. *Schizophrenia Research, 65,* 125–137.

Horan, W. P., Blanchard, J. J., Gangestad, S. W., & Kwapil, T. R. (2004). The psychometric detection of schizotypy: Do putative schizotypy indicators identify the same latent class? *Journal of Abnormal Psychology, 113,* 339–357.

Horan, W. P., Green, M. F., Kring, A. M., & Nuechterlein, K. H. (2006). Does anhedonia in schizophrenia reflect faulty memory for subjectively experienced emotions? *Journal of Abnormal Psychology, 115,* 496–508.

Horan, W. P., Kring, A. M., & Blanchard, J. J. (2006). Anhedonia in schizophrenia: A review of assessment strategies. *Schizophrenia Bulletin, 32,* 259–273.

Katsanis, J., Iacono, W. G., & Beiser, M. (1990). Anhedonia and perceptual aberration in first-episode psychotic patients and their relatives. *Journal of Abnormal Psychology, 99,* 202–206.

Katsanis, J., Iacono, W. G., Beiser, M., & Lacey, L. (1992). Clinical correlates of anhedonia and perceptual aberration in first-episode patients with schizophrenia and affective disorder. *Journal of Abnormal Psychology, 101,* 184–191.

Kavanagh, D. J. (1992). Recent developments in expressed emotion and schizophrenia. *British Journal of Psychiatry, 160,* 601–620.

Kendler, K. S., Thacker, L., & Walsh, D. (1996). Self-report measures of schizotypy as indices of familial vulnerability to schizophrenia. *Schizophrenia Bulletin, 22,* 511–520.

Kirkpatrick, B., & Buchanan, R. W. (1990). Anhedonia and the deficit syndrome of schizophrenia. *Psychiatry Research, 31,* 25–30.

Kirkpatrick, B., Buchanan, R. W., Ross, D. E., & Carpenter, W. T., Jr. (2001). A separate disease within the syndrome of schizophrenia. *Archives of General Psychiatry, 58,* 165–171.

Kraepelin, E. (1971). *Dementia praecox and paraphrenia* (R. M. Barclay, Trans.). Huntington, NY: Krieger. (Original work published 1919)

Kring, A. M. (1999). Emotion in schizophrenia: Old mystery, new understanding. *Current Directions in Psychological Science, 8,* 160–163.

Kring, A. M., Kerr, S. L., Smith, D. A., & Neale, J. M. (1993). Flat affect in schizophrenia does not reflect diminished subjective experience of emotion. *Journal of Abnormal Psychology, 102,* 507–517.

Kring, A. M., & Neale, J. M. (1996). Do schizophrenic patients show a disjunctive relationship among expressive, experiential, and psychophysiological components of emotion? *Journal of Abnormal Psychology, 105,* 249–257.

Kring, A. M., Smith, D., & Neale, J. (1994). Individual differences in dispositional expressiveness: Development and validation of the Emotional Expressivity Scale. *Journal of Personality and Social Psychology, 66,* 934–949.

Kwapil, T. R. (1998). Social anhedonia as a predictor of the development of schizophrenia-spectrum disorders. *Journal of Abnormal Psychology, 107,* 558–565.

Kwapil, T. R., Crump, R. A., & Pickup, D. R. (2002). Assessment of psychosis proneness in African-American college students. *Journal of Clinical Psychology, 58,* 1601–1614.

Lang, P. J. (1995). The emotion probe. Studies of motivation and attention. *American Psychologist, 50,* 372–385.

Lysaker, P. H., Bell, M. D., Kaplan, E., & Bryson, G. (1998). Personality and psychosocial dysfunction in schizophrenia: The association of extraversion and neuroticism to deficits in work performance. *Psychiatry Research, 80,* 61–68.

Malaspina, D., & Coleman, E. (2003). Olfaction and social drive in schizophrenia. *Archives of General Psychiatry, 60,* 578–584.

Meehl, P. E. (1962). Schizotaxia, schizotypy, schizophrenia. *American Psychologist, 17,* 827–838.

Meehl, P. E. (1990). Toward an integrated theory of schizotaxia, schizotypy, and schizophrenia. *Journal of Personality Disorders, 4,* 1–99.

Meehl, P. E. (2001). Primary and secondary hypohedonia. *Journal of Abnormal Psychology, 110,* 188.

Mishlove, M., & Chapman, L. J. (1985). Social anhedonia in the prediction of psychosis proneness. *Journal of Abnormal Psychology, 94,* 384–396.

Moberg, P. J., Arnold, S. E., Doty, R. L., Kohler, C., Kanes, S., Seigel, S., et al. (2003). Impairment of odor hedonics in men with schizophrenia. *American Journal of Psychiatry, 160,* 1784–1789.

Morrone-Strupinsky, J. V., & Depue, R. A. (2004). Differential relation of two distinct, film-induced positive emotional states to affiliative and agentic extraversion. *Personality and Individual Differences, 36,* 1109–1126.

Mueser, K. T., Curran, P. J., & McHugo, G. J. (1997). Factor structure of the brief psychiatric rating scale in schizophrenia. *Psychological Assessment, 9,* 196.

Myin-Germeys, I., Delespaul, P. A., & deVries, M. W. (2000). Schizophrenia patients are more emotionally active than is assumed based on their behavior. *Schizophrenia Bulletin, 26,* 847–854.

Myin-Germeys, I., Krabbendam, L., Delespaul, P. A. E. G., & Van Os, J. (2003). Do life events have their effect on psychosis by influencing the emotional reactivity to daily life stress? *Psychological Medicine, 33,* 327–333.

Myin-Germeys, I., Van Os, J., Schwartz, J. E., Stone, A. A., & Delespaul, P. A. (2001). Emotional reactivity to daily life stress in psychosis. *Archives of General Psychiatry, 58,* 1137–1144.

Paradiso, S., Andreasen, N. C., Crespo-Facorro, B., O'Leary, D. S., Watkins, G. L., Boles Ponto, L. L., & Hichwa, R. D. (2003). Emotions in unmedicated patients with schizophrenia during evaluation with positron emission tomography. *American Journal of Psychiatry, 160,* 1775–1783.

Quirk, S. W., Strauss, M. E., & Sloan, D. M. (1998). Emotional response as a function of symptoms in schizophrenia. *Schizophrenia Research, 32,* 31–39.

Rado, S. (1962). *Psychoanalysis of behavior: Collected papers: Vol. 2. 1956–1961.* New York: Grune & Stratton.

Schlenker, R., Cohen, R., & Hopmann, G. (1995). Affective modulation of the startle reflex in schizophrenic patients. *European Archives of Psychiatry and Clinical Neuroscience, 245,* 309–318.

Schneider, F., Gur, R. C., Gur, R. E., & Shtasel, D. L. (1995). Emotional processing in schizophrenia: Neurobehavioral probes in relation to psychopathology. *Schizophrenia Research, 17,* 67–75.

Schuck, J., Leventhal, D., Rothstein, H., & Irizarry, V. (1984). Physical anhedonia and schizophrenia. *Journal of Abnormal Psychology, 93,* 342–344.

Sison, C. E., Alpert, M., Fudge, R., & Stern, R. M. (1996). Constricted expressiveness and psychophysiological reactivity in schizophrenia. *Journal of Nervous and Mental Disease, 184,* 589–597.

Suslow, T., Roestel, C., Ohrmann, P., & Arolt, V. (2003). The experience of basic emotions in schizophrenia with and without affective negative symptoms. *Comprehensive Psychiatry, 44,* 303–310.

Tallent, K. A., & Gooding, D. C. (1999). Working memory and Wisconsin Card Sorting Test performance in schizotypic individuals: A replication and extension. *Psychiatry Research, 89*, 161–170.

Taylor, S. F., Liberzon, I., Decker, L. R., & Koeppe, R. A. (2002). A functional anatomic study of emotion in schizophrenia. *Schizophrenia Research, 58*, 159–172.

Taylor, S. F., Phan, K. L., Britton, J. C., & Liberzon, I. (2005). Neural response to emotional salience in schizophrenia. *Neuropsychopharmacology, 30*, 984–995.

Ventura, J., Nuechterlein, K. H., Lukoff, D., & Hardesty, J. P. (1989). A prospective study of stressful life events and schizophrenic relapse. *Journal of Abnormal Psychology, 98*, 407–411.

Volz, M., Hamm, A. O., Kirsch, P., & Rey, E. R. (2003). Temporal course of emotional startle modulation in schizophrenia patients. *International Journal of Psychophysiology, 49*, 123–137.

Watson, D., & Tellegen, A. (1985). Toward a consensual structure of mood. *Psychological Bulletin, 98*, 219.

Watson, D., Wiese, D., Vaidya, J., & Tellegen, A. (1999). The two general activation systems of affect: Structural findings, evolutionary considerations, and psychobiological evidence. *Journal of Personality and Social Psychology, 76*, 820.

Weisman, A. G., Nuechterlein, K. H., Goldstein, M. J., & Snyder, K. S. (1998). *Journal of Abnormal Psychology, 107*, 355–359.

White, L., Harvey, P. D., Opler, L., & Lindenmayer, J. P. (1997). Empirical assessment of the factorial structure of clinical symptoms in schizophrenia. A multisite, multimodel evaluation of the factorial structure of the Positive and Negative Syndrome Scale. The PANSS study group. *Psychopathology, 30*, 263–274.

Williams, L. M., Das, P., Harris, A. W., Liddell, B. B., Brammer, M. J., Olivieri, G., et al. (2004). Dysregulation of arousal and amygdala–prefrontal systems in paranoid schizophrenia. *American Journal of Psychiatry, 161*, 480–489.

Zevon, M. A., & Tellegen, A. (1982). The structure of mood change: An idiographic/nomothetic analysis. *Journal of Personality and Social Psychology, 43*, 111–122.

6

EMOTION AND BIPOLAR DISORDER

SHERI L. JOHNSON, JUNE GRUBER, AND LORI R. EISNER

The countless hypomanias, and mania itself, all have brought into my life a different level of sensing and feeling and thinking. Even when I have been most psychotic—delusional, hallucinating, frenzied—I have been aware of finding new corners in my heart and mind. Some of those corners were incredible and beautiful and took my breath away and made me feel as though I could die right then and the images would sustain me.

—Jamison (2004, pp. 218–219)

Bipolar disorder (BPD) is one of the most debilitating of psychiatric disorders. In those who are affected, divorce, unemployment, and hospitalization are all too common (Mitchell, Slade, & Andrews, 2004), and suicide is approximately 12 to 15 times higher than in the general population (Angst, Stausen, Clayton, & Angst, 2002). To improve intervention efforts, we need to understand the basic mechanisms involved in bipolar disorder. Here, we review evidence that one mechanism underlying bipolar disorder involves disturbed emotional responses.

We begin by defining key terms used throughout this chapter. According to the *Diagnostic and Statistical Manual of Mental Disorders* (4th ed., text rev.; American Psychiatric Association, 2000), a *manic episode* is defined as an elated or irritable mood lasting at least 1 week, accompanied by three associated symptoms (four if mood is irritable only), such as a decreased need for sleep and an elevated sense of self-esteem. *Bipolar I disorder* is a mood disorder defined by one or more lifetime episode(s) of mania (or a mixed episode, which involves simultaneous manic and depressive symptoms). Although depression is not required to receive a diagnosis of bipolar I disorder, many people who experience manic episodes also experience depressive episodes. The presence of two distinct mood poles certainly complicates the study of bipolar illness. A variety of milder forms of disorder have also been defined, such as bipolar II disorder and cyclothymia. Because bipolar I disorder has been studied more extensively, it is our major focus in this chapter.

In addition to clinically diagnosable forms of BPD, several scales have been designed to identify people at risk for development of BPD on the basis of subsyndromal symptoms of mania. The General Behavior Inventory (Depue, Krauss, Spoont, & Arbisi, 1989) and the Hypomanic Personality Scale (Eckblad & Chapman, 1986) are two well-validated instruments used in analog studies discussed in this chapter.

The depressive and manic episodes of BPD involve disordered mood states. It is important to acknowledge that moods are distinct from emotions. Whereas *moods* are thought to be long-lasting, diffuse, and not tied to a specific trigger, *emotions* are regarded as transient, acute responses to specific environmental stimuli that involve coordinated subjective, behavioral, and physiological components (Ekman, 1994). Although emotion theorists distinguish between moods and emotions, these constructs are interrelated because moods typically facilitate emotions of a similar valence and inhibit emotions of a dissimilar valence (Rosenberg, 1998). Researchers must consider the influence of mood episode status on emotional response. Because we would expect emotional responses in BPD to differ depending on the mood episode status (depressive or manic), we consider evidence that BPD is related to emotion disturbances separately for depression, mania, and well periods.

There is a widespread assumption that BPD, which is defined by severe mood changes, will involve intense emotions. Beyond the assumption that BPD will be tied to greater emotional responsivity to both positive and negative stimuli, a set of models over the past 30 years have emphasized that BPD is especially associated with greater reactivity to incentive, or rewarding, stimuli (Depue, Kleiman, Davis, Hutchinson, & Krauss, 1985; Johnson, 2005). There is surprisingly little research on emotion in BPD. Because of the gaps in emotion research, we review findings from several disparate subfields that provide indirect evidence concerning patterns of emotional disturbance in BPD. We then discuss the available emotion research in the field and, more broadly, studies examining responses to standardized stimuli.

INDIRECT EVIDENCE FOR HEIGHTENED EMOTION RESPONSIVITY IN BIPOLAR I DISORDER

We first review socioenvironmental, neurobiological, and temperament research on BPD. These studies provide indirect support for the idea that people with BPD might experience more intense emotional reactions than people without BPD.

First, socioenvironmental research suggests people with remitted BPD become symptomatic after positive and negative environmental events, a pattern that might be explained by disturbances in emotional responsivity. For example, people with BPD are vulnerable to depressive symptoms after family criticism and negative life events (Johnson, Winett, Meyer, Greenhouse, & Miller, 1999; Miklowitz & Johnson, 2006). People with BPD also appear vulnerable to increases in manic symptoms after major successes (Johnson et al., 2000). In sum, socioenvironmental findings are consistent with the idea that BPD might involve exaggerated emotional responsivity.

Second, neuroimaging findings link BPD to changes in brain pathways related to emotion responsivity (George & Ketter, 1994; Leibenluft, Charney, & Pine, 2003; Phillips, Drevets, Rauch, & Lane, 2003). For example, basic research among nondisturbed populations has suggested that the amygdala guides emotional responsivity to both negative and positive stimuli. Most neuroimaging studies have found that BPD is associated with larger amygdala volume and greater amygdala activity during cognitive tasks (Berns, Martin, & Proper, 2002; Kruger, Seminowicz, Goldapple, Kennedy, & Mayberg, 2003; Phillips et al., 2003; Strakowski et al., 1999; but see also Chen et al., 2004). Basic research also suggests that other regions, including the hippocampus, prefrontal cortex, and anterior cingulate, support planning and goal pursuit in the context of emotion (see Phillips et al., 2003). Activity in these regions appears diminished among people with BPD (Phillips et al., 2003; Strakowski et al., 1999). Hence, the heightened amygdala activity among people with BPD might be expected to produce greater responsivity to emotionally relevant stimuli, whereas diminished responsivity of other regions may interfere with the regulation of emotion.

Third, a set of findings suggests that mania may be more specifically tied to brain regions involved in regulating responses to reward cues rather than cues of either valence. For example, BPD appears to be associated with enhanced sensitivity of dopaminergic pathways from the basal ganglia and ventral tegmental area, pathways that are intricately involved in reward sensitivity (cf. Depue et al., 1985; Johnson, 2005). When confronted with an incentive stimulus, these pathways are thought to trigger positive affect (PA; e.g., hope, elation, excitement), approach motivation (e.g., a feeling of desire), and approach behavior. These "system outputs" serve to increase the probability of incentive acquisition (Depue & Zald, 1993). It has been noted that the outputs of this system closely mirror the symptoms of mania (Depue et al., 1985). Consistent with the hypersensitivity of these pathways, people with remitted BPD have been found to show atypically large behavioral responses to amphetamine, which increases levels of dopamine (Anand et al., 2000). In addition, mania has been found to be associated with more activity in the basal ganglia (Blumberg et al., 2000; Caliguiri et al., 2003).

Fourth, literature on affective temperament indicates that people with remitted BPD describe experiencing greater dispositional PA than do people without BPD (Bagby et al., 1996; Lovejoy & Steuerwald, 1995). Parallel findings have emerged in studies of students at risk for BPD (Hofmann & Meyer,

2006). Students with high mania risk, for example, demonstrated elevated resting levels (while watching a neutral film clip) of PA, as well as elevated cardiac vagal tone, a related phenomenon (Gruber, Johnson, Oveis, & Keltner, 2006). A few studies have used self-report measures of how people tend to react to cues of reward. In those studies, people with remitted BPD and those vulnerable to BPD report that they experience more excitement and enthusiasm in the context of opportunities to earn rewards and pursue goals than do people without BPD (Meyer, Johnson, & Carver, 1999; Meyer, Johnson, & Winters, 2001). Studies have found that levels of PA (Strakowski, Stoll, Tohen, Faedda, & Goodwin, 1993) and reward responsivity (Meyer et al., 2001) both predict a more severe course of mania among people diagnosed with BPD.

Despite the findings for PA, however, people with BPD do not report that they experience more negative affect (NA) during remission than do people without BPD, when asked about either personality traits relevant to NA (Klein, Durbin, Shankman, & Santiago, 2002; Lozano & Johnson, 2001) or their responses to daily stressors (Lovejoy & Steuerwald, 1995; see Hofmann & Meyer, 2006, for one exception). Similarly, people with BPD do not describe themselves as more emotionally responsive to negative stimuli on self-report measures during periods of remission (Meyer et al., 2001). Some research suggests that NA is associated not with a history of mania per se but rather with severity of current depressive symptoms in a state-dependent manner (Lozano & Johnson, 2001; Meyer et al., 2001). When present, however, elevated NA does predict worsening of depressive symptoms (Heerlein, Richter, Gonzalez, & Santander, 1998; Lozano & Johnson, 2001).

In sum, socioenvironmental research suggests that people with BPD experience strong reactions to negative and positive life events. Imaging research suggests a number of neural correlates of the disorder that are also consistent with greater emotional responsivity in BPD and with specific sensitivity to cues of reward. People with BPD and those vulnerable to mania report elevated dispositional PA even during remission, whereas elevated NA appears linked to depressive symptoms in BPD. Each of these findings seems consistent with the idea of heightened emotional responsivity in BPD, at least for approach-relevant stimuli. With these patterns as background, we now discuss emotion research that assesses responses to specific stimuli.

DIRECT EVIDENCE OF HEIGHTENED EMOTIONAL RESPONSIVITY IN BIPOLAR I DISORDER

In considering responses to specific emotionally evocative stimuli, we review measures of self-reported affect (the subjective experience of emotion), cognitive and behavioral responses, psychophysiological measures, and regional brain activity. Because most studies do not consider these components of emotional responses conjointly, we evaluate the findings separately for each component. We note in advance that there have been some disparities in the findings across these components, a theme we return to in our summary.

In preparing this review, we quickly realized that if we were to consider only studies with conventional measures of emotion, there would be a dearth of studies to review. Given the preliminary nature of the field, we also consider measures that are somewhat broader than traditional emotional reactivity measures (e.g., changes in cortisol, confidence, and neural activity after exposure to emotionally evocative stimuli). We also include studies that presented a wide range of stimuli, including words or pictures that might only elicit mild emotion, as a way to consider responses to valenced stimuli more generally.

We organize our findings according to two broad dimensions of emotion-eliciting stimuli: *approach-relevant stimuli* and *threat stimuli*. Although many researchers tend to focus on positive stimuli, we believe that approach-relevant stimuli (incentive cues), and responses to them, are important in light of theories that place emphasis on neurobiological reward pathways in BPD (Depue et al., 1985; Johnson, 2005). It is worth noting that neurobiological pathways involved in reward sensitivity are thought to generate more than just positive affective experiences. When the pursuit of rewards is thwarted, high activity in this system is thought to generate frustration and anger. This is particularly relevant in mania because episodes are defined by the presence of either extreme euphoria or irritability. Although these may seem like disparate mood states, consider the example of a person who is highly motivated to achieve a goal. When progress toward his or her goal is proceeding well, elation might be expected. By contrast, when goal progress is thwarted, anger or irritability may ensue (Carver & Scheier, 1998). Hence, we consider the presence and blocking of incentive cues.

We first begin by discussing the research on emotional responsivity in BPD during remission, or asymptomatic periods. We then turn toward studies (albeit, few) that measure responsivity during periods of depressive and manic symptoms.

Emotional Responsivity During Remission

A number of laboratory studies have examined responses to approach-relevant stimuli (see Table 6.1).

Responses to Approach Stimuli During Remission

No laboratory studies have identified group differences in self-reported affect. Keep in mind that many people with BPD have experienced heights of PA that most of us will never experience, as illustrated in the quote by Kay

TABLE 6.1

Laboratory Studies Examining Responses to Approach-Relevant Stimuli

Study	Participants	Mood state assessments	Stimulus presented	Emotional response components measured	Responses to approach stimuli	Responses to threat stimuli
Responses during remission						
Chang et al., 2004	12 youth with BPD I and at least 1 parent with BPD I or II; 10 youths with no BPD Dx confirmed with Kiddie SADS Stimulants, not other medications, discontinued 24 hours before task	Euthymic as indicated by YMRS and Childhood Depression Inventory	Working memory task: 2-back visuospatial working memory task Rate valence of positive, negative, and neutral photos	fMRI	No group differences in picture ratings BPD showed greater activation in the bilateral caudate, thalamus, left middle and superior frontal gyrus, and left anterior cingulate cortex compared with control participants	No group differences in ratings of pictures BPD showed greater activation in the bilateral dorsolateral prefrontal cortex, inferior frontal gyrus, and right insula, and less activation in the right posterior cingulate gyrus
Cuellar, 2005	35 BPD I and 35 healthy control participants with no mood or psychotic disorder; dx by SCID	BRMS < 7 and Modified HAM-D < 10 Current symptoms did not predict reactions to criticism	A stooge listened to the participant describe a personally challenging issue and	Affective reactivity and recovery	n/a	BPD = non-BPD on reactivity and regulation of negative affect after exposure to the negative criticism Medications were unrelated to

			then expressed blame and criticism			responses to the criticism
Gruber, Johnson, Oveis, & Keltner, 2006	34 high- and 83 low-risk participants defined by HPS	Current manic (Altman Self-Rating Scale for Mania) and depressive (BDI) symptoms	Film clips (3 positive, 2 negative, and 1 neutral)	Affect, facial expressions, and vagal tone at baseline and after each clip	High-risk participants reported elevated positive affect after all clips but no elevated responsivity to specific film clips compared with low-risk group	No group differences in reactivity to negative film clips on subjective affect, facial behavior, or psychophysiology
Harmon-Jones et al., 2002	72 college students with no psychiatric history; high- and low-risk groups defined by General Behavior Inventory	n/a	Anger-evoking task: listening to editorial regarding possible tuition increase at students' college	Subjective affect: 8 1-minute electroencephalogram epochs	Groups did not differ on anger after challenge. High-risk group showed higher relative left frontal activation than low-risk group	n/a
Johnson, Ruggero, & Carver, 2005	Students with high and low HPS scores	No more than mild symptoms of mania and depression, controlled for in analyses	Participants completed a button-pressing task, and then were	Subjective affect and confidence	Students with high risk demonstrated more confidence	n/a

continues

TABLE 6.1(Continued)

Study	Participants	Mood state assessments	Stimulus presented	Emotional response components measured	Responses to approach stimuli	Responses to threat stimuli
					after success feedback than those with low risk did, but not more PA	
Lawrence et al., 2004	12 medicated BPD I patients with no episodes for 6 months; 9 MDD patients; 11 healthy controls Groups matched on age and gender Excluded left-handed individuals and those with head injury, substance abuse, and comorbidity	All BRMS scores ≤7 BDI scores: MDD > BP> control	Viewed happy, sad, fearful, and neutral faces for 2 seconds each, with intensities manipulated to 50% or 100% of a prototypical face; identified the gender of the face	fMRI (1.5T)	Compared with depressed and control participants, participants with BPD showed greater reactivity in left amygdala, caudate nucleus, and putamen after mildly happy faces Compared with control patients BPD patients showed greater ventral prefrontal cortex activity	Compared with depressed and control participants, participants with BPD showed greater reactivity in right globus pallidus and thalamus to mild fear and left amygdala and ventrolateral prefrontal cortex to intense fear Compared with controls, participants BPD showed greater ventral prefrontal cortex to sadness Each type of medication related to differences between

Study	Sample		Task	Findings
				... after viewing mildly happy faces participants with BPD and controls
				No group differences
Stern & Berrenberg, 1979	Undergraduates with high and low scores on a measure of hypomanic symptoms 6 weeks before testing	Not assessed	Participants were given false success feedback or false failure feedback. Confidence ratings of likelihood of guessing a coin-toss outcome	Participants with high symptoms at Time 1 showed more increase in confidence after success feedback than those with low symptoms
Sutton & Johnson, 2002	Undergraduates with high (>30) and low (<25) HPS scores	Not assessed	Positive, negative, and neutral pictures. Eyeblink reflex as measured by electromyogram responses to a loud acoustic probe	No group differences. Participants with high HPS scores showed a more pronounced response (greater startle attenuation) after viewing positive pictures than did participants with low HPS scores
Yurgelun-Todd et al., 2000	14 BPD affective disorder. YMRS scores from 2 to 29		Silently identify the facial fMRI	No activations to happy faces. Among females, greater activation of

continues

TABLE 6.1 (Continued)

Study	Participants	Mood state assessments	Stimulus presented	Emotional response components measured	Responses to approach stimuli	Responses to threat stimuli
	patients with no current Axis I comorbid condition; 10 nonpsychiatric control participants with no Axis I condition Dx by SCID Excluded left-handed patients and those with organic brain disorder, head injury, or current substance abuse	HAM-D scores from 4 to 24	expression shown in a set of happy and fearful faces		were seen in either group	the amygdala in response to fearful faces for BPD than control; no differences among males Among males only, chlorpromazine equivalent doses were related to less amygdala activation in response to fearful faces
Responses during periods of depressive symptoms						
Depue, Kleiman, Davis, Hutchinson, & Krauss, 1985	15 medicated cyclothymic students; 7 control students with no history of psychiatric disorder	Varied measured with the BDI	Challenging math test	Measured cortisol at baseline, after the challenge test, and 3 hours after challenge	n/a	Groups did not differ in subjective stress rating of math challenge Cyclothymic > control on

Study	Sample/Method	Results	Stimuli	Measure	Findings
	Used GBI to screen, confirmed dx with SADS. Excluded those with neurological diagnoses, drug abuse, or those taking medications related to cortisol				• cortisol level across 3 hours • intraindividual variance in cortisol • time until reduction of cortisol after math challenge Among cyclothymic participants, BDI correlated with cortisol recovery and intraindividual variation
Forbes, Miller, Cohn, Fox, & Kovacs, 2005	38 BP I and II participants with childhood onset depression; 38 MDD participants with childhood onset; 60 adults with no history of psychiatric disorder. Dx with semistructured interviews	Participants with BPD and MDD obtained significantly higher BDI scores than controls	Positive, negative, and neutral pictures	Eyeblink reflex as measured by electromyogram responses to a loud acoustic probe	BPD and control groups did not differ in response during negative pictures; participants with MDD showed less of an increased startle response to negative pictures than did other groups Only the participants with MDD showed differential responses during positive pictures compared with negative pictures

(continues)

TABLE 6.1 (Continued)

Study	Participants	Mood state assessments	Stimulus presented	Emotional response components measured	Responses to approach stimuli	Responses to threat stimuli
Kruger, Seminowicz, Goldapple, Kennedy, & Mayberg, 2003	9 BPD remitted for at least 6 months; 11 BPD with current major depressive disorder Dx by SCID Excluded neurological or psychiatric comorbidities, head trauma, substance abuse, and medications other than mood stabilizers	Remission defined by HAM-D < 6 Depression defined by DSM–IV criteria. M HAM-D = 26	Participants created scripts describing personally sad events During positron emission tomography, sad script was projected on a computer screen for 5 minutes; participants rated sadness and anxiety during and after script presentation	Regional blood flow using positron emission tomography	n/a	In response to the sadness induction, both BPD groups showed decreases in dorsal ventral medial frontal cortices; depressed BPD group showed diminished in prefrontal cortex activity; and remitted BPD group showed elevated activity in the orbitofrontal cortex, dorsal anterior cingulate, and premotor cortex
Malhi et al., 2004b	10 participants with BPD, current major depression, comorbid Axis I	BPD higher than controls on the BDI, HAM-D,	Patients viewed photos for 9 seconds that were	fMRI (1.5T)	In response to positive pictures, BPD showed widespread	In response to negative pictures, BPD showed less widespread cortical activation, but did

Study	Sample	Measures	Task/stimuli		Findings
	& II excluded; 10 age-matched control participants with no personal or family psychiatric Axis I history Dx by SCID All right-handed females	Montgomery-Åsberg Depression Rating Scale, YMRS, and lower on Fawcett–Clarke Pleasure Scale	relatively neutral (e.g., picture of woman opening letter) but with negative (e.g., "She failed her exams"), positive, and neutral captions		cortical activation, more subcortical activation than controls	display more subcortical activation than controls
Ruggero & Johnson, 2006	28 BPD I; 40 control participants with no mood or psychotic disorder Dx by SCID Those in full episodes were excluded, but not those with mild symptoms	BRMS and Modified HAM-D <15 (no current episodes) Controlled for in analyses	Learned helplessness paradigm involving 0, 1, or 4 failures	Subjective affect and cognitive performance on an anagram task after feedback	n/a	Groups did not differ on subjective affect after failure After 1 failure, BPD participants showed more deficits in anagram performance than control participants did Medications were not correlated with performance

Responses during manic episodes

Study	Sample	Measures	Task/stimuli		Findings
Elliott et al., 2004	7 currently manic participants and 1 hypomanic participant as	M YMRS = 28.1 among BPD	Go/no no task with neutral, positive, and negative	fMRI	Group differences were most apparent in	In response to sad versus neutral distractor words, BPD showed

(continues)

TABLE 6.1 (Continued)

Study	Participants	Mood state assessments	Stimulus presented	Emotional response components measured	Responses to approach stimuli	Responses to threat stimuli
	confirmed by SADS; healthy controls screened with BDI and unspecified verbal interview No history of substance abuse, not left-handed, no comorbidities		words (respond quickly to target stimuli, withhold responses to distractor stimuli)		responses to emotional (positive or negative) versus neutral distractors BPD participants showed attenuated orbitofrontal response and enhanced response of left ventrolateral prefrontal cortex during trials in which they were to ignore emotionally valenced distractors compared with controls	elevated activity in the ventrolateral prefrontal cortex; controls did not
Lennox et al., 2004	10 inpatients with current mania; 12 age-	n/a	Pictures of faces in four intensities	Event-related fMRI	No group differences on neural or	BPD participants reported lower subjective ratings of

Study	Sample	Measures	Task/Stimuli	Imaging	Results
	matched control participants with no personal or family history of mental illness Dx by standardized clinical interview Groups were matched on facial recognition memory	ranging from 0% to 125% of sadness and happiness; participants rated how happy or how sad faces were			subjective responses to happy faces / sadness for the most sad faces than did comparison participants. In response to sad faces, BPD participants showed less activation of subgenal anterior cingulate cortex and amygdala and more activation of the posterior cingulate cortex and posterior insula than did controls
Malhi et al., 2004a	10 medicated outpatients with current hypomania and no comorbid Axis I or II condition; 10 control participants with no personal or family psychiatric history Dx confirmed with SCID	M YMRS for BPD = 24.3, M for control = 0.9. No group differences on Fawcett–Clarke Pleasure Scale, Montgomery–Asberg Depression scale, BDI, or State–Trait Anxiety Inventory	Patients viewed photos for 9 seconds that were relatively neutral (e.g., picture of woman opening letter) but with negative (e.g., "She failed her exams"),	fMRI	No group differences in self-reported emotion to positive photos When compared with neutral photos, participants with BPD and controls showed similar patterns of activation to positive photos, / No group differences in self-reported emotion to negative photos When compared with neutral photos, participants with BPD showed no cortical activation to negative pictures compared with controls, who showed widespread subcortical and cortical activation in response to

(continues)

TABLE 6.1 (Continued)

Study	Participants	Mood state assessments	Stimulus presented	Emotional response components measured	Responses to approach stimuli	Responses to threat stimuli
	All were right-handed females		positive, and neutral captions; rated positivity and negativity of photos		including precuneus, superior, and middle frontal and inferior parietal gyri	negative photos. Only region common to controls was superior frontal gyrus

Note. BPD = bipolar disorder; dx = diagnosis; SADS = Schedule for Affective Disorders and Schizophrenia; YMRS = Young Mania Rating Scale; fMRI = functional magnetic resonance imaging; BDI = Beck Depression Inventory; SCID = Structured Clinical Interview for *DSM–IV*; BRMS = Bech–Rafaelsen Mania Scale; HAM-D = Hamilton Rating Scale for Depression; HPS = Hypomanic Personality Scale; MDD = major depressive disorder; *DSM–IV = Diagnostic and Statistical Manual of Mental Disorders* (4th ed.); n/a = not assessed.

Jamison at the outset of this chapter. Asking them to rate whether a good mood is intense, then, may invoke a different subjective scale than that used by people without BPD. Thus, it is crucial to examine emotion responding without reliance on self-ratings of the intensity of affect.

Even when considering other channels of response, findings have varied. Previous reviews of stressor tasks have suggested that tasks involving personal engagement and performance feedback may yield more intense responses than those involving passive exposure to stimuli (Dickerson & Kemeny, 2004). Consistent with this point, findings in nonclinical samples using passive tasks have yielded mixed findings. One study that examined reactivity to positive film clips found no differences as a function of BPD risk across channels of emotional response (i.e., reported experience, facial expressions, vagal tone, heart rate, or skin conductance; Gruber, Johnson, Oveis, & Keltner, 2006). In contrast, high-risk participants have been found to exhibit greater startle modulation after viewing positive pictures than do participants with low manic risk (Sutton & Johnson, 2002).

Despite these mixed findings, studies that have used more engaging tasks have yielded more consistent group differences. For example, Harmon-Jones et al. (2002) found that students with high risk of mania demonstrated increased approach motivation, as measured by greater relative left frontal activation using an electroencephalogram (Harmon-Jones et al., 2002). Whereas most studies of approach stimuli consider how people react to positive words, film clips, or pictures, this work also considered how people respond when goals are thwarted. Findings suggested that approach motivation among the high-risk sample was specifically heightened after a challenge to goal pursuit, in which participants read about a potential increase in tuition at their school.

Cognitive and neural responses to positive stimuli in at-risk participants have also been investigated using less traditional measures of emotion. For example, two other studies have examined cognitive responses to success among students at risk for mania. In an initial test, Stern and Berrenberg (1979) found that participants with a history of mild hypomanic symptoms overestimated their ability to guess the outcome of a coin toss after false success feedback, whereas those without a history of hypomanic symptoms did not. Johnson, Ruggero, and Carver (2005) extended this study to examine other cognitive implications of false success feedback. In their study, students at risk for hypomania were asked to complete a button-pressing task. Then, they were given false success feedback and paid $3 as a reward for their fast responses. As an outcome measure, they were asked to choose the difficulty level of the next task, an unspecified eye–hand task. Vulnerability to mania was related to choosing a harder version of the task. In sum, among nonclinical samples, studies that have used personally engaging tasks have found that people at high risk for BPD are more responsive to approach-relevant stimuli than those who are at low risk.

These findings have been extended to clinically diagnosed BPD. For example, using the same button-pressing paradigm, Johnson, Ruggero, and Laurenceau (2006) asked people with and without BPD to choose the difficulty of a task after they were given success feedback. People with BPD chose a harder task after success feedback than did people without mood disorders, suggesting that people with BPD may become more confident after success than others.

Several researchers have examined neural activity in response to positive facial expressions. Both Lawrence et al. (2004) and Chang et al. (2004) found that people with BPD demonstrated greater neural reactivity to happy faces than did people without BPD. It should be noted, however, that Yurgelun-Todd et al. (2000) found that neither bipolar nor nonbipolar participants demonstrated changes in neural activity after viewing happy faces. As mentioned earlier, passively viewing facial expressions may not evoke the same levels of responsivity as more personally engaging tasks.

In sum, BPD is unrelated to self-reported PA after positive stimuli, probably because of problems in measuring subjective affect in a population that is defined by experiences of extreme affective states. Similarly, research has been mixed regarding whether BPD relates to elevated reactivity to passively viewed stimuli. Hence, in a less severe population, it may be important to use personally engaging tasks to capture emotional responsivity. In clinical studies and those using personally engaging tasks, BPD is associated with elevated neural and psychophysiological response to approach-relevant stimuli as well as greater confidence and goal engagement. That is, research supports the idea of BPD being linked to elevated responsivity to approach stimuli but only with personally engaging tasks or more severe levels of disorder.

Responses to Threat Stimuli During Remission

Although many have assumed that BPD involves exaggerated responses to threat stimuli, most studies do not support this idea. As Table 6.1 shows, researchers have evaluated responses to various forms of standardized threat stimuli, including failure feedback, interpersonal criticism, negative film clips, and challenging math tests. Regardless of the paradigm, no studies have found that people diagnosed with or vulnerable to episodes of mania actually endorse elevations in self-reported affect after exposure to threat stimuli. Even people with a history of depression (in addition to mania) have not been found to show greater self-reported reactivity to negative emotional stimuli during inter-episode periods (Cuellar, 2005; Ruggero & Johnson, 2006). Similarly, when behavioral (Gruber et al., 2006), physiological (Sutton & Johnson, 2002), or cognitive (Stern & Berrenberg, 1979) components of emotion responding are assessed in response to these various types of negative stimuli, no group differences emerge.

We have described here evidence of greater resting activity in brain regions involved in emotional responsivity among people with BPD. Given this, one might expect greater neural responsivity to negative stimuli within BPD as well. Nonetheless, findings of studies of neural responses to threatening stimuli have provided inconsistent evidence. Yurgelun-Toff et al. (2000) found that among patients with remitted BPD, women, but not men, demonstrated greater amygdala activation after viewing sad faces than nonpsychiatric control participants did. In contrast, Lawrence et al. (2004) found that people with remitted BPD demonstrated greater subcortical and ventral prefrontal cortex activation to negative faces compared with people without BPD. Chang et al. (2004) examined brain activation patterns among pediatric patients with remitted BPD who also had a parent diagnosed with BPD. Compared with healthy control participants, children with BPD demonstrated more robust activation in response to threatening pictures in cortical regions implicated in regulating emotional responses. But children with BPD also showed greater activation in these regions in response to cognitive tasks that did not involve emotion-relevant stimuli. Hence, the greater activation among patients with BPD in this study could be a reflection of stronger task involvement rather than specific emotional responsivity. The neural findings are not consistent; only 1 of 3 studies found a group effect in which patients with BPD demonstrated more activation specifically to emotional stimuli. Despite neurobiological models of greater emotional responsivity, described earlier, these findings do not indicate that neural responses to specific aversive stimuli are larger than those seen in the general population.

In sum, despite conventional wisdom that BPD involves elevated emotional responsivity, no studies have found that people with remitted BPD or those at risk differ in their emotion responses to negative stimuli on experiential, behavioral, cognitive, or psychophysiological measures. Studies of neural responses to negative stimuli provide, at best, mixed findings.

Responses to Valenced Stimuli During Periods of Depressive Symptoms

People with BPD describe themselves as more sensitive to threats and less sensitive to rewards as depression increases (Meyer et al., 2001). We can identify only one study of responsivity to standardized stimuli during episodes of bipolar depression. Malhi et al. (2004b) found that people with bipolar depression demonstrated more widespread subcortical activation in response to both positive and negative pictures than did control participants, consistent with enhanced emotional responsivity to stimuli of either valence.

Three studies intriguingly suggest that greater responsivity to negative stimuli may become apparent even with mild subsyndromal symptoms of depression (although these studies relied on nontraditional emotion measures). Each study included participants with BPD who were experiencing subsyndromal depressive symptoms at the time of testing and compared them to healthy control participants. One study found that BPD was associated with performance deficits on a cognitive task after failure feedback (Ruggero & Johnson, 2006). Another found that cyclothymia was related to poor cortisol regulation 3 hours after a challenging math test and that current depressive symptoms were generally correlated with poor cortisol regulation (Depue et al., 1985). A third found that among juveniles with bipolar spectrum disorder, current depressive symptoms were related to greater sensitivity to risk taking in a game with potential to earn money (Ernst et al., 2004). Hence, people with BPD may demonstrate elevated responsivity to negative stimuli even during periods of mild depression. This is consistent with findings, discussed earlier, that heightened NA may be specific to depressive periods within BPD.

Only one study is available that has used a traditional emotion paradigm to study responses of people with BPD during periods of depressive symptoms. This study, unlike other studies during depressive periods, found no evidence of greater reactivity to negative or positive stimuli among participants with BPD compared with healthy control participants when using acoustic startle eyeblink magnitude as an index (Forbes, Miller, Cohn, Fox, & Kovacs, 2005). Hence, even though some studies document greater negative reactivity associated with BPD, findings are not entirely consistent.

Responses to Valenced Stimuli During Manic Episodes

Relatively few researchers have examined emotional responses during mania, perhaps because of the difficulties in asking a person with acute mania to complete experimental tasks requiring sitting still and attending carefully to stimuli. There is indirect evidence from cognitive and behavioral studies that mania is associated with decreased reactivity to negative stimuli compared with positive stimuli. For example, cognitive studies indicate that during mania, people are more likely to remember positive self-descriptive words than people with no disorder or those with bipolar depression (Lyon, Startup, & Bentall, 1999) and to demonstrate greater difficulty in inhibiting attention to positive versus sad words compared with participants with bipolar depression (Murphy et al., 1999). The actions of people who are manic also appear to be guided more by potential rewards than dangers (Swann, Dougherty, Pazzaglia, Pham, & Moeller, 2004). For example, Clark, Iversen, and Goodwin (2001) used the Iowa Gambling Task to examine how people weighed the potential to win versus lose fake money. People who were manic were more likely to draw cards from a risky deck (higher payment for winning cards but even higher costs for losing cards) than control participants. In a similar task used with juvenile BPD, manic symptoms were related to less worry about losing money (Ernst et al., 2004). Even perception of cues may become impaired—people who are manic have been found to be less accurate in identifying negative facial expressions compared with people with remitted BPD (Lembke & Ketter, 2002).

Researchers using neuroimaging have also examined responses to positive and negative stimuli during mania. To date, people who are manic have not been found to demonstrate greater neural response to positive pictures than healthy control participants (Lennox, Jacob, Calder, Lupson, &

Bullmore, 2004; Malhi, Lagopoulos, Sachdev, et al., 2004). People who are manic, by contrast, demonstrate less neural activation of the amygdala in response to negative pictures than do control participants (Lennox et al., 2004). Hence, early studies indicate that when manic, people demonstrate poor responsivity to negative stimuli compared with positive stimuli.

Deficits in Cortical Activation During Both Manic and Depressive Episodes

In healthy individuals, cortical brain regions such as the anterior cingulate and the prefrontal cortex appear to be involved in regulation of emotions (Phillips et al., 2003). Activity within these regions appears to diminish during depressive and manic episodes of BPD while viewing valenced stimuli in functional magnetic resonance imaging studies (Elliott et al., 2004; Malhi, Lagopoulos, Sachdev, et al., 2004; Mahli, Lagopoulos, Ward, et al., 2004). Activity in these regions also appears diminished during sad moods among people with BPD (Kruger et al., 2003). Hence, early research suggests diminished activity in cortical regions involved in emotional regulation during depression and mania.

Summary of Emotion Research Findings

Before considering the pattern of findings, it is important to comment on limitations in the research. Because few studies of emotion in BPD are available, we cast a broad net by reviewing studies that included analog samples, mild emotion-eliciting stimuli, and nontraditional outcome measures. Several difficulties pervade this body of research. For example, most studies included only healthy control participants as a comparison. Research is needed to compare emotional responsivity to threat stimuli with that seen among people with depressive and anxiety disorders that involve high levels of NA and to compare the levels of responsivity to approach stimuli with that seen among people with psychopathy, gambling, and other disorders that involve high levels of impulsivity. Beyond the need for better comparison groups, few studies have controlled for medications in analyses (for exceptions, see Cuellar, Johnson, & Winters, 2005; Ruggero & Johnson, 2006), even though almost all clinically diagnosed participants were taking psychotropic medications at the time of testing. Illustrating this concern, psychotropic medications have been shown to confound studies of the neural response to emotion stimuli (see chap. 12, this volume; Lawrence et al., 2004; Yurgelun-Toff et al., 2000).

Beyond these issues, no studies have documented enhanced emotional responsivity among bipolar participants with subjective affect measures. This is not surprising given that BPD is diagnosed on the basis of extremes of mood that would shift the way people label emotional states. This raises the need to consider scaling issues (Bartoshuk, Fast, & Snyder, 2005).

Studies focused on other types of responses, however, have yielded an intriguing pattern of findings. People with BPD do appear to demonstrate elevated responsivity to approach stimuli. Elevated responsivity to approach stimuli is apparent during euthymic states, among clinical and at-risk samples, and across cognitive and psychophysiological indices. Some, but not all, neural studies also support this greater responsivity to approach stimuli. One exception to this pattern emerges from a study of nonclinical participants using stimuli that were not personally engaging. One would expect nonclinical samples to demonstrate less powerful responsivity, however, and so the types of stimuli used to elicit emotion will need to be considered carefully in such studies. Most studies, though, find that people with BPD are overly responsive to approach stimuli, even during remission. These findings, then, add to a small literature concerning psychological traits that characterize people with remitted BPD (Balanza-Martinez et al., 2005; Gotlib, Traill, Montoya, Joormann, & Chang, 2005).

In contrast to the approach-relevant findings, people with BPD show normative emotional responsivity to threat stimuli in the absence of depressive symptoms. Responsivity to threat stimuli is highly state-dependent. As depressive symptoms emerge, some studies document heightened responsivity to threat stimuli. As mania emerges, deficits in responsivity to threat stimuli become apparent. During manic and depressive episodes, activity in cortical regions diminishes, potentially interfering with the effortful control of emotion.

FUTURE DIRECTIONS

Two goals appear particularly important for future research. First, researchers need to dissect which aspects of emotions are most involved in BPD. For example, few studies have examined the time course of emotion responses (i.e., affective chronometry) in BPD using psychophysiological indices. In one such study, group differences in responses to positive stimuli did not emerge until 2 seconds after stimulus presentation (Sutton & Johnson, 2002), suggesting that it may be important to study postreward responses. Nonetheless, researchers have not studied anticipation of reward nor have they disentangled *emotional reactivity* (immediate response) from *emotion regulation* ("tuning down" of emotion over time).

Second, researchers need to consider how emotional responsivity helps predict the course of the disorder. Researchers have found that self-reported sensitivity to approach-relevant stimuli predicts increases in mania over time (Meyer et al., 2001). It is quite striking that we cannot identify a single study that has used emotion research to predict the course and recurrence of BPD. One might expect that people who are more responsive to approach stimuli would be particularly vulnerable to manic symptoms after major successes in life. Beyond episode recurrence, researchers could examine whether reward responsivity predicts the onset of BPD.

CLINICAL IMPLICATIONS

Although there is a need for more basic research, findings to date have clinical implications. We focus here on the implications of emotional responsivity to approach stimuli. In a recent review, Johnson (2005) suggested that several facets of emotional reactivity to reward and success might lead to a spiral into mania. That is, people with BPD appear to be characterized by a traitlike investment in achieving goals and successes. In the context of success, they may experience a more profound shift in affect and confidence than others might, which promotes setting ambitious goals. Other research has shown that self-reported engagement in goal pursuit, such as setting higher goals and spending more time pursuing those goals, predicts increases in manic symptoms over time (Lozano & Johnson, 2001).

Drawing on this model, one intervention goal is to help people modulate initial responses to reward. Effective intervention will depend on identifying cognitive and behavioral coping strategies that do improve regulation after people are exposed to positive stimuli. There is an extensive history of research on emotion regulation strategies (see Gross & John, 2003). Most of this research has focused on negative emotion regulation, and with good reason—outside of the context of mania, few people wish to dampen positive emotions. Available research, however, finds that strategies differ in their effectiveness for PA and NA (Gross, 2002).

Rather than drawing on emotion regulation research on NA, there is a need to understand the strategies that people naturalistically choose to diminish or enhance PA. Feldman, Joormann, and Johnson (in press) found that undergraduates who responded to positive moods by thinking about how well they would do in the future were more likely to report current hypomanic symptoms. Consistent with the idea that people with BPD should not focus too much on the potential for future successes, Lam, Wong, and Sham (2001) asked people with BPD about the strategies they use in response to early signs of hypomania. People with BPD endorsed that it was helpful for them to decrease overly stimulating activities and goal-relevant activities. In sum, researchers have begun to consider how coping strategies could help modulate initial emotional responses to success and reward, perhaps to help prevent spiraling into severe mania.

Johnson, Greenhouse, McMurrich, and Ruggero (2005) have developed an intervention designed to prevent manic episodes. The intervention draws on findings regarding reward sensitivity. Components of the intervention include psychoeducation about the nature of emotional reactivity, helping patients learn to monitor for mood changes as well as triggers of those moods, and teaching skills for mood regulation. Over the course of 12 weeks, clients are taught a variety of cognitive and behavioral tools for self-monitoring and mood regulation. Although early results are promising, interventions such as these will be improved by greater knowledge of which aspects of emotion dysregulation are most impaired within BPD.

REFERENCES

American Psychiatric Association. (2000). *Diagnostic and statistical manual of mental disorders* (4th ed., text revision). Washington, DC: Author.

Anand, A., Verhoeff, P., Seneca, N., Zoghbi, S. S., Seibyl, J. P., Charney, D. S., & Innis R. B. (2000). Brain SPECT imaging of amphetamine-induced dopamine release in euthymic bipolar disorder patients. *American Journal of Psychiatry, 157,* 1109–1114.

Angst, F., Stausen, H. H., Clayton, P. J., & Angst, J. (2002). Mortality of patients with mood disorders: Follow-up over 34 to 38 years. *Journal of Affective Disorders, 68,* 167–181.

Bagby, R. M., Young, L. T., Schuller, D. R., Bindseil, K. D., Cooke, R. G., Dickens, S. E., et al. (1996). Bipolar disorder, unipolar depression and the Five-Factor Model of Personality. *Journal of Affective Disorders, 41,* 25–32.

Balanza-Martinez, V., Tabares-Seisdedos, R., Selva-Vera, G., Martinez-Aran, A., Torrent, C., Salazar-Fraile, J., et al. (2005). Persistent cognitive dysfunctions in bipolar I disorder and schizophrenic patients: A 3-year follow-up study. *Psychotherapy and Psychosomatics, 74,* 113–119.

Bartoshuk, L. M., Fast, K., & Snyder, D. J. (2005). Differences in our sensory worlds: Invalid comparisons with labeled scales. *Current Directions in Psychological Science, 14,* 122–125.

Berns, G. S., Martin, M., & Proper, S. M. (2002). Limbic hyperreactivity in bipolar II disorder. *American Journal of Psychiatry, 159,* 304–306.

Blumberg, H. P., Stern, E., Martinez, D., Ricketts, S., de Asis, J., White, T., et al. (2000). Increased anterior cingulate and caudate activity in bipolar mania. *Biological Psychiatry, 48,* 1045–1052.

Caliguiri, M. P., Brown, G. G., Meloy, M. J., Eberson, S. C., Kindermann, S. S., Frank, L. R., et al. (2003). An fMRI study of affective state and medication on cortical and subcortical regions during motor performance in bipolar disorder. *Psychiatry Research: Neuroimaging, 123,* 171–182.

Carver, C. S., & Scheier, M. F. (1998). *On the self-regulation of behavior.* New York: Cambridge University Press.

Chang, K., Adleman, N. E., Dienes, K., Simeonova, D. J., Menon, V., & Reiss, A. (2004). Anomalous prefrontal–subcortical activation in familial pediatric bipolar disorder: A functional magnetic resonance imaging investigation. *Archives of General Psychiatry, 61,* 781–792.

Chen, B. K., Sassi, R., Axelson, D., Hatch, J. P., Sanches, M., Nicoletti, M., et al. (2004). Cross-sectional study of abnormal amygdala development in adolescents and young adults with bipolar disorder. *Biological Psychiatry, 56,* 399–405.

Clark, L., Iversen, S. D., & Goodwin, G. M. (2001). A neuropsychological investigation of prefrontal cortex involvement in acute mania. *American Journal of Psychiatry, 158,* 1605–1611.

Cuellar, A. (2005). *Responses to interpersonal threat in bipolar disorder.* Unpublished doctoral dissertation, University of Miami, Miami, FL.

Cuellar, A., Johnson, S. L., & Winters, R. (2005). Distinctions between bipolar and unipolar depression. *Clinical Psychology Review, 25,* 307–339.

Depue, R. A., Kleiman, R. M., Davis, P., Hutchinson, M., & Krauss, S. P. (1985). The behavioral high-risk paradigm and bipolar affective disorder: VIII. Serum free cortisol in nonpatient cyclothymic subjects selected by the General Behavior Inventory. *American Journal of Psychiatry, 142,* 175–181.

Depue, R. A., Krauss, S., Spoont, M. R., & Arbisi, P. (1989). General Behavior Inventory identification of unipolar and bipolar affective conditions in a nonclinical university population. *Journal of Abnormal Psychology, 98,* 117–126.

Depue, R. A., & Zald, D. H. (1993). Biological and environmental processes in nonpsychotic psychopathology: A neurobehavioral perspective. In C. G. Costello (Ed.), *Basic issues in psychopathology* (pp. 127–237). New York: Guilford Press.

Dickerson, S. S., & Kemeny, M. E. (2004). Acute stressors and cortisol responses: A theoretical integration and synthesis of laboratory research. *Psychological Bulletin, 130,* 355–391.

Eckblad, M., & Chapman, L. J. (1986). Development and validation of a scale for hypomanic personality. *Journal of Abnormal Psychology, 95,* 214–222.

Ekman, P. (1994). Moods, emotions, and traits. In P. Ekman & R. Davidson (Eds.), *The nature of basic emotions* (pp. 56–67). New York: Oxford University Press.

Elliott, R., Ogilvie, A., Rubinsztein, J. S., Calderon, G., Dolan, R. J., & Sahakian, B. J. (2004). Abnormal ventral frontal response during performance of an affective go/no go task in patients with mania. *Biological Psychiatry, 55,* 1163–1170.

Ernst, M., Dickstein, D. P., Munson, S., Eshel, N., Pradella, A., Jazbec, S., et al. (2004). Reward-related processes in pediatric bipolar disorder: A pilot study. *Journal of Affective Disorders, 82*(Suppl. 1), S89–S101.

Feldman, G. C., Joormann, J., & Johnson, S. L. (in press). Responses to positive affect: A self-report measure of rumination and dampening. *Cognitive Therapy and Research.*

Forbes, E. E., Miller, A., Cohn, J. C., Fox, N. A., & Kovacs, M. (2005). Affect-modulated startle in adults with childhood-onset depression: Relations to bipolar course and number of lifetime depressive episodes. *Psychiatry Research, 134,* 11–25.

George, M. S., & Ketter, T. A. (1994). Activation studies in mood disorders. *Psychiatric Annals, 24,* 648–652.

Gotlib, I. H., Traill, S. K., Montoya, R. L., Joormann, J., & Chang, K. (2005). Attention and memory biases in the offspring of parents with bipolar disorder: Indications from a pilot study. *Journal of Child Psychology and Psychiatry, 46,* 84–93.

Gross, J. J. (2002). Emotion regulation: Affective, cognitive, and social consequences. *Psychophysiology, 39*, 281–291.

Gross, J. J., & John, O. P. (2003). Individual differences in two emotion regulation processes: Implications for affect, relationships, and well-being. *Journal of Personality and Social Psychology, 85*, 348–362.

Gruber, J., & Johnson, S. L. (2006). *Positive emotional traits and goal regulation and among people at risk for mania.* Manuscript in preparation.

Gruber, J., Johnson, S. L., Oveis, C., & Keltner, D. (2006). *Mania vulnerability and dysfunctional positive emotion.* Manuscript in preparation.

Harmon-Jones, E., Abramson, L. Y., Sigelman, J., Bohlig, A., Hogan, M. E., & Harmon-Jones, C. (2002). Proneness to hypomania/mania and asymmetrical frontal cortical responses to an anger-evoking event. *Journal of Personality and Social Psychology, 82*, 610–618.

Heerlein, A., Richter, P., Gonzalez, M., & Santander, J. (1998). Personality patterns and outcome in depressive and bipolar disorders. *Psychopathology, 31*, 15–22.

Hofmann, B. U., & Meyer, T. D. (2006). Mood fluctuations in people putatively at risk for bipolar disorders. *British Journal of Clinical Psychology, 45*, 105–110.

Jamison, K. R. (2004). *An unquiet mind: A memoir of moods and madness.* New York: Knopf.

Johnson, S. L. (2005). Mania and dysregulation in goal pursuit. *Clinical Psychology Review, 25*, 241–262.

Johnson, S. L., Greenhouse, W., McMurrich, S., & Ruggero, C. (2005). *The Goals Program.* Unpublished manuscript.

Johnson, S. L., Ruggero, C. J., & Carver, C. S. (2005). Cognitive, behavioral, and affective responses to reward: Links with hypomanic symptoms. *Journal of Social and Clinical Psychology, 24*, 894–906.

Johnson, S. L., Sandrow, D., Meyer, B., Winters, R., Miller, I., Solomon, D., & Keitner, G. (2000). Increases in manic symptoms following life events involving goal-attainment. *Journal of Abnormal Psychology, 109*, 721–727.

Johnson, S. L., Winett, C., Meyer, B., Greenhouse, W., & Miller, I. (1999). Social support and the course of bipolar disorder. *Journal of Abnormal Psychology, 108*, 558–566.

Johnson, S. L., Ruggero, C., & Laurenceau, J. P. (2006). *Cognitive responses to reward in bipolar I disorder.* Manuscript submitted for publication.

Klein, D. N., Durbin, C. E., Shankman, S. A., & Santiago, N. J. (2002). Depression and personality. In C. L. Hammen & I. H. Gotlib (Eds.), *Handbook of depression* (pp. 115–140). New York: Guilford Press.

Kruger, S., Seminowicz, S., Goldapple, K., Kennedy, S. H., & Mayberg, H. S. (2003). State and trait influences on mood regulation in bipolar disorder: Blood flow differences with an acute mood challenge. *Biological Psychiatry, 54*, 1274–1283.

Lam, D., Wong, G., & Sham, P. (2001). Prodromes, coping strategies and course of illness in bipolar affective disorder—A naturalistic study. *Psychological Medicine, 31*, 1397–1402.

Lawrence, N. S., Williams, A. M., Surguladze, S., Giampietro, V., Brammer, M. J., Andrew, C., et al. (2004). Subcortical and ventral prefrontal cortical neural responses to facial expressions distinguish patients with bipolar disorder and major depression. *Biological Psychiatry, 55*, 578–587.

Leibenluft, E., Charney, D. S., & Pine, D. S. (2003). Researching the pathophysiology of pediatric bipolar disorder. *Biological Psychiatry, 53*, 1009–1020.

Lembke, A., & Ketter, T. (2002). Impaired recognition of facial emotion in mania. *American Journal of Psychiatry, 159*, 302–304.

Lennox, B. R., Jacob, R., Calder, A. J., Lupson, V., & Bullmore, E. T. (2004). Behavioural and neurocognitive responses to sad facial affect are attenuated in patients with mania. *Psychological Medicine, 34*, 795–802.

Lovejoy, M. C., & Steuerwald, B. L. (1995). Subsyndromal unipolar and bipolar disorders: Comparisons on positive and negative affect. *Journal Abnormal Psychology, 104*, 381–384.

Lozano, B. L., & Johnson, S. L. (2001). Can personality traits predict increases in manic and depressive symptoms? *Journal of Affective Disorders, 63*, 103–111.

Lyon, H. M., Startup, M., & Bentall, R. P. (1999). Social cognition and the manic defense: Attributions, selective attention, and self-schema in bipolar affective disorder. *Journal of Abnormal Psychology, 108*, 273–282.

Malhi, G. S., Lagopoulos, J., Sachdev, P., Mitchell, P. B., Ivanovski, B., & Parker, G. B. (2004). Cognitive generation of affect in hypomania: An fMRI study. *Bipolar Disorders, 6*, 271–285.

Malhi, G. S., Lagopoulos, J., Ward, P. B., Kumari, V., Mitchell, P. B., Parker, G. B., et al. (2004). Cognitive generation of affect in bipolar depression: An fMRI study. *European Journal of Neuroscience, 19*, 741–745.

Meyer, B., Johnson, S. L., & Carver, C. S. (1999). Exploring behavioral activation and inhibition sensitivities among college students at risk for mood disorders. *Journal of Psychopathology and Behavioral Assessment, 21*, 275–292.

Meyer, B., Johnson, S. L., & Winters, R. (2001). Responsiveness to threat and incentive in bipolar disorder: Relations of the BIS/BAS scales with symptoms. *Journal of Psychopathology and Behavioral Assessment, 23*, 133–143.

Miklowitz, D. J., & Johnson, S. L. (2006). The psychopathology and treatment of bipolar disorder. *Annual Review of Clinical Psychology, 2*, 199–235.

Mitchell, P. B., Slade, T., & Andrews, G. (2004). Twelve-month prevalence and disability of *DSM–IV* bipolar disorder in an Australian general population survey. *Psychological Medicine, 34*, 777–785.

Murphy, F. C., Sahakian, B. J., Rubinsztein, J. S., Michael, A., Rogers, R. D., Robbins, T. W., & Paykel, E. S. (1999). Emotional bias and inhibitory control processes in mania and depression. *Psychological Medicine, 29*, 1307–1321.

Phillips, M. L., Drevets, W. C., Rauch, S. L., & Lane, R. (2003). Neurobiology of emotion perception II: Implications for major psychiatric disorders. *Biological Psychiatry, 54*, 515–528.

Rosenberg, E. (1998). Levels of analysis and the organization of affect. *Review of General Psychology, 2,* 247–270.

Ruggero, C., & Johnson, S. L. (2006). Reactivity to a laboratory stressor among individuals with bipolar I disorder in full or partial remission. *Journal of Abnormal Psychology, 115,* 539–544.

Stern, G. S., & Berrenberg, J. L. (1979). Skill-set, success outcome, and mania as determinants of the illusion of control. *Journal of Research in Personality, 13,* 206–220.

Strakowski, S. M., DelBello, M. P., Sax, K. W., Zimmerman, M. E., Shear, P. K., Hawkins, J. M., & Larson, E. R. (1999). Brain magnetic resonance imaging of structural abnormalities in bipolar disorder. *Archives of General Psychiatry, 56,* 254–260.

Strakowski, S. M., Stoll, A. L., Tohen, M., Faedda, G. L., & Goodwin, D. C. (1993). The Tridimensional Personality Questionnaire as a predictor of six-month outcome in first episode mania. *Psychiatric Research, 48,* 1–8.

Swann, A. C., Dougherty, D. M., Pazzaglia, P. J., Pham, M., & Moeller, F. G. (2004). Impulsivity: A link between bipolar disorder and substance abuse. *Bipolar Disorders, 6,* 204–212.

Sutton, S. K., & Johnson, S. J. (2002). Hypomanic tendencies predict lower startle magnitudes during pleasant pictures. *Psychophysiology, 39*(Suppl.), 80.

Yurgelun-Todd, D. A., Gruber, S. A., Kanayama, G., Killgore, W. D., Baird, A. A., & Young, A. D. (2000). Functional magnetic resonance imaging during affect discrimination in bipolar affective disorder. *Bipolar Disorders, 2,* 237–248.

7

MAJOR DEPRESSIVE DISORDER: EMERGING EVIDENCE FOR EMOTION CONTEXT INSENSITIVITY

JONATHAN ROTTENBERG

Major depressive disorder (MDD) is a devastating, disabling, and often deeply painful, psychiatric condition that affects the lives of nearly one in six people (Kessler, 2002). Reflecting the profound disturbance of affective function in depression, MDD is classified as a mood disorder by *The Diagnostic and Statistical Manual of Mental Disorders* (4th edition, text revision [*DSM–IV–TR*]; American Psychiatric Association, 2000). Consistent with this classification, *DSM–IV–TR* symptoms of MDD indicate disturbances in mood that encompass deficient positive affect (e.g., anhedonia) and/or excessive negative affect (e.g., sadness and guilt) that last for a minimum of 2 weeks. Patients who have been diagnosed with depression reliably report low positive affect and elevated negative affect on a variety of questionnaire and interview measures (Clark, Watson, & Mineka, 1994). Durable disturbance of mood is thus one of the most salient features of MDD.

Given the potent affective disturbances typically seen in depression, it is not surprising that MDD has been a ready subject for the application of affective science. Indeed, interest in affective functioning in MDD has led to advances in several research areas, including dysfunctions in affect-related neural circuitry (Davidson, Pizzagalli, Nitschke, & Putman, 2002), affect perception (Gotlib, Kraspnoperova, Neubauer Yue, & Joormann, 2004), and the affective consequences of antidepressant medications (chap. 12, this volume). This chapter considers what is being learned about the effects of depression on emotional reactivity.

The rate of progress toward understanding emotion in MDD has been uneven. Although there are likely several reasons for this, one obstacle to cumulative science has been a consistent lack of clarity on the core terminology that defines the subject. In particular, major constructs such as *mood* and *emotion* are notoriously slippery and have historically been used by investigators in confusing and often contradictory ways. In the context of MDD, researchers have used labels such as *affective disorder*, *mood disorder*, and *emotional disorder* casually and without proper explication. The fuzziness on these core terms has doubtlessly served to obscure a basic issue: What exactly is it that is disordered in MDD?

Fortunately, contemporary practices in affective science have increasingly moved toward consensual definitions of major terms (Rottenberg & Gross, 2003; Watson, 2000), allowing for more consistent use when characterizing depression and other forms of psychopathology. The term *affect* is increasingly used as the superordinate term, or category, to refer to all valenced states (Gross, 1998; Scherer, 1984). *Moods*, one class of affect, are generally seen as diffuse, slow-moving feeling states that are weakly tied to specific objects or elicitors (Watson, 2000). By contrast, *emotions* are affects that refer to quick-moving reactions that occur when an organism processes a meaningful stimulus that poses an opportunity or challenge for adaptation (e.g., Keltner & Gross, 1999). Emotional reactions typically involve coordinated changes in feelings, behavior, and physiology and last seconds or minutes (e.g., Ekman, 1992). Again by contrast, moods exert their clearest effects on feelings and cognitions (as opposed to behavior and physiology) and last hours or days.

Distinguishing between these related constructs is important for getting inquiry into emotions in MDD off on the right foot. When mood and emotion are so distinguished, it becomes apparent that the various diagnostic criteria for depression, such as pervasive sadness or anhedonia, indicate alterations in mood, but do not indicate alterations in emotion with corresponding specificity. Thus, the diagnostic criteria do not tell us how depression alters emotional reactivity. Empirical work is needed to determine this.

These conceptual distinctions are also useful for organizing hypotheses about depression: Given that MDD is essentially a disorder of mood, how does a major mood disturbance influence emotion? Using theory from affective science, in this chapter I first outline two initial hypotheses about how mood disturbance might influence depressed persons' responses to positive and negative emotional stimuli. Second, I review the empirical record, which includes a number of discrepancies that cannot be easily accommodated by these initial hypotheses. To better assimilate these discrepant findings, I out-line an alternative theory-based hypothesis concerning emotions in MDD, which I call the *emotion context-insensitivity* (ECI) hypothesis. I consider possible benefits of characterizing depression in terms of ECI and outline remaining areas of ambiguity concerning the ECI hypothesis. Finally, I outline several focal areas for future work designed to increase our under-standing of emotional reactivity in MDD and the role that emotion plays in this disorder.

GENERATING HYPOTHESES ABOUT
EMOTIONS IN MAJOR DEPRESSIVE DISORDER

Contemporary affective science has generally seen moods and emotions as interconnected constructs, with moods altering the probability of having specific emotions (e.g., Rosenberg, 1998). More specifically, moods are gen-erally thought to potentiate like-valenced or matching emotions (e.g., irri-table mood facilitates angry reactions, an anxious mood facilitates panic, etc.). This view that moods should enhance related emotional responses is doubtlessly intuitive and logical, but it should also be noted that empirical work to test this idea has lagged; thus, clear empirical demonstrations of mood facilitation, in clinical or nonclinical populations, would be useful.

The idea of mood facilitation suggests two initial hypotheses about emotions in MDD: (a) lack of positive mood will attenuate positive emo-tional reactivity, and (b) excessive negative mood will potentiate negative emotional reactivity. I now turn to a review of empirical evidence bearing on these predictions, with a focus on the stronger studies, defined as studies that have (a) enrolled individuals with diagnosed MDD (rather than indi-viduals with a more diffuse dysphoria) and (b) included measures of one or more of the major emotional response systems (i.e., self-reported emotional experience, expressive behavior, and emotion-relevant central and periph-eral physiology).

Does Depression Attenuate Positive Emotion?

The positive attenuation hypothesis predicts that MDD will be associ-ated with diminished emotional reactivity to positive emotional stimuli. The starting point for this hypothesis is depressed persons' strong tendency to exhibit low positive mood. Indeed, anhedonia (a reduced ability to experi-ence pleasure) is one of the cardinal symptoms of this disorder, and depressed individuals exhibit several other signs that are also indicative of deficient positive, or appetitive, motivation (e.g., psychomotor retardation, fatigue, anorexia). Not surprisingly, theorists have centered their accounts of emo-tion dysregulation in MDD around this constellation of motivational deficits (e.g., Clark et al., 1994; Depue & Iacono, 1989; Henriques & Davidson, 1991).

Empirical support for the positive attenuation hypothesis is relatively robust. For example, compared with nondepressed control participants, depressed individuals have been shown to be characterized by attenuated reactivity with respect to reports of affective experience when responding to slides depicting pleasant scenes (e.g., Allen, Trinder, & Brennan, 1999; Dunn, Dalgleish, Lawrence, Cusack, & Ogilvie, 2004; Sloan, Strauss, Quirk, & Sajatovic, 1997; Sloan, Strauss, & Wisner, 2001) and to an amusing film clip (Rottenberg, Kasch, Gross, & Gotlib, 2002). Depressed individuals have been found to exhibit less positive emotion-expressive behavior in response to pleasant films and beverages (Berenbaum & Oltmanns, 1992) and pleasant slides (Sloan et al., 2001) and to be less behaviorally responsive to reward contingencies (Henriques & Davidson, 2000). In sum, fairly consistent findings indicate that MDD involves deficits in reactivity to positive, approach-related emotion cues.

Does Depression Potentiate Negative Emotion?

The negative potentiation hypothesis predicts that depressed persons will exhibit potentiated emotional reactivity to negative emotional cues. Depressed persons' high negative mood is the starting point for this hypothesis. Perhaps most relevant to this prediction, cognitive theorists have advanced a view of depression in which negative moods and negative emotions are mutually reinforcing (e.g., Beck, 1976; Beck, Rush, Shaw, & Emery, 1979). Beck's schema model and related theories of depression (e.g., Bower, 1981) conceptualize the disorder in terms of cognitive structures, or schemas, that serve to negatively distort the processing of emotional stimuli. It is important to note that according to these theories, negative mood states prime, or activate, these cognitive structures (Scher, Ingram, & Segal, 2005). Once activated, these structures precipitate depressotypic emotional responses (e.g., acute feelings of sadness) whenever schema-matching negative emotion stimuli are encountered, presumably potentiating reactivity to negative emotional stimuli in MDD.

Some uncontrolled observations of depressed persons are consistent with the negative potentation prediction. For example, depressed persons often exhibit strong negative emotional behaviors such as crying when they are seen in therapeutic contexts (American Psychiatric Association, 2000). Such evidence is an ambiguous indicator of enhanced emotional reactivity, however, because observations such as notable crying to a therapist could as easily reflect changes in depressed persons' social behavior (e.g., increased reassurance seeking; Coyne, 1976) or more simply be explained by depressed persons' encountering more (or more potent) negative emotional stimuli than do healthy individuals (e.g., frequent attacks by a critical spouse). From this perspective, it is unclear whether the differences that emerge in naturalistic studies are telling us about depression-related changes to the emotion system or about the operation of situational factors. For these reasons, it is important to assess the negative-potentiation hypothesis under laboratory conditions by measuring responses to standardized negative stimuli (Rottenberg, 2005).

Where experiments have been performed, support for the negative potentiation hypothesis remains surprisingly limited. Supportive data have been obtained from analog studies of dysphoric persons (Golin, Hartman, Klatt, Munz, & Wolfgang, 1977; Lewinsohn, Lobitz, & Wilson, 1973), However, because findings using analog and subsyndromal samples may not generalize to diagnosed and syndromal depression persons, this is not strong evidence (e.g., Gotlib, 1984). Indeed, as I discuss later, it is possible that the effects of depression on emotion are different at different levels of depression symptom severity.

If we limit consideration to diagnosed samples, one study found that clinically depressed persons exhibited greater electrodermal reactivity to negative social scenarios than did healthy control participants (Sigmon & Nelson-Gray, 1992). In another study, people with major depression displayed greater blood flow to the amygdala (an important limbic structure implicated in emotional responding) to pictures of faces displaying negative emotion, a paradigm that likely elicits low levels of negative emotion in the viewer (e.g., Fu et al., 2004). Thus, there are two studies with data supportive of the negative potentiation hypothesis.

On the other hand, considerable data contradict the negative potentiation hypothesis. For example, studies have found depressed persons exhibit diminished electrodermal and startle reactivity to loud noise (e.g., Allen et al., 1999; Lader & Wing, 1969), diminished amygdala response to fearful faces (Thomas et al., 2001), and a diminished pain report to a range of noiceptive stimuli (reviewed in Dickens, McGowan, & Dale, 2003). Possibly mitigating these findings, one might argue that the negative stimuli used in these experiments do not provoke responses from people who are depressed because they are irrelevant to their compelling concerns (e.g., loud sounds, faces of strangers). Cognitive theories of MDD, for example, have suggested that idiographic, person-specific themes are particularly important triggers for emotional reactivity. One influential typology, for example, has identified two clusters of cognitive schemas that are activated differentially by person-specific content regarding either social relationships or achievement (e.g., Beck, 1983). This logic suggests that more support for the negative potentiation hypothesis might be obtained if personally relevant stimuli were used.

Although the relevant database on this question is small, we recently investigated the importance of the personal concern dimension in depression-related emotional reactivity. In this study, we examined healthy and depressed individuals' responses to traditional, standardized emotion films and to personally tailored emotion films. The tailored films were drawn from a videotaped interview in which each participant had described the saddest and happiest events from his or her own life (segments of videotape of participants answering demographic questions about themselves were used as a neutral reference). Results indicated that even when carefully constructed personally relevant sad emotion stimuli are used, depressed individuals do not exhibit enhanced responding (Rottenberg, Gross, & Gotlib, 2005).

Additional Discrepancies in the Data Suggest a Third View of Emotions in Major Depressive Disorder

Considered together, the data presented thus far support the positive attenuation hypothesis and either contradict, or are equivocal for, the negative potentiation hypothesis. One reading of this overall pattern is that individuals with MDD simply exhibit diminished reactivity to emotional stimuli, irrespective of valence, as part of a global deficit in emotional reactivity. This global deficit reading is strengthened considerably when one examines a number of studies that have employed within-subjects designs that expose the same participants to both positive and negative emotional stimuli. We turn now to these studies.

An impressive range of within-subject paradigms find that persons with depression exhibit nonspecific deficits in emotional responding. For example, compared with nondepressed control participants, depressed persons have been found to exhibit less affective modulation of startle during affective picture viewing (Allen et al., 1999; Dichter, Tomarken, Shelton, & Sutton, 2004), less electromyogram (EMG) modulation during the imagination of positive and negative scenarios (Gehricke & Shapiro, 2000; Greden, Genero, Price, Feinberg, & Levine, 1986; Schwartz, Fair, Salt, Mandel, & Klerman, 1976), less EMG modulation in response to expressive facial stimuli (Wexler, Levenson, Warrenburg, & Price, 1994), less reactivity of expressive behavior to positive and negative films (Renneberg, Heyn, Gebhard, & Bachmann, 2005), less valence-related modulation of event-related brain potentials (Deldin, Keller, Gergen, & Miller, 2001), less differential neural responding to valenced emotion face stimuli (Canli et al., 2004), less reported sadness reactivity to sad films and lower levels of amusement to amusing films (Rottenberg et al., 2002), and blunted autonomic responding to a range of stimuli (e.g., noise; Dawson, Schell, & Catania, 1977).

A New View of Emotions in Major Depressive Disorder: The Emotion Context-Insensitivity Hypothesis

Experimental data thus present a number of discrepancies that cannot be easily accommodated by the positive attenuation and negative potentiation hypotheses. My colleagues and I have recently been led to a third hypothesis that assimilates this evidence of valence-independent deficits in emotional reactivity in MDD. This hypothesis theorizes that severe depressive mood states might have general inhibitory effects on emotion. We label this third perspective the *emotion context-insensitivity* (ECI) hypothesis (Rottenberg, 2005; Rottenberg, Gross, & Gotlib, 2005).

The ECI hypothesis is derived from evolutionary accounts of depression that view this syndrome as strongly characterized by disengagement (Klinger, 1975; Nesse, 2000). In particular, the ECI hypothesis assumes that depressed mood states powerfully influence ongoing responses to the environment. Nesse (2000) has suggested that depressed mood states evolved as an internal signal designed to bias an organism against action. That is, depressed mood evolved originally as a defensive response to adverse situations in which continued activity might prove to be futile or dangerous (e.g., famine), but in modern times it is a response often set in motion by interpersonal triggers (e.g., loss of social rank; Gilbert et al., 2001). Pessimism, self-absorption, and loss of interest in the environment are all features of depression that hold a person in place and prevent ill-considered actions. Depressed mood states are thus postulated to prompt withdrawal and broad reductions in motivated activity, which encompass reduced reactivity to novel positive or negative emotional stimuli. In sum, the ECI hypothesis suggests that severe depressed mood states actually have an inhibitory effect on emotion and that this inhibitory effect is observed across a variety of stimuli that ordinarily generate emotional reactions.

Precedents for Emotion Context Insensitivity

ECI is a new term within experimental psychopathology. At the same time, ECI also has unmistakable precedents within the broader clinical literature. For example, ECI accords with several aspects of the phenomenology of depression: depressed people often use words such as *flat*, *dull*, and *empty* to describe their world and remark that "everything is the same" (Healy, 1993). ECI is also consistent with naturalistic observations of depressed persons as being behaviorally inexpressive across a range of environmental events (see Rottenberg & Gotlib, 2004). In fact, among depressed inpatients, a lack of behavioral expressivity can take extreme forms, even catatonia (Moskowitz, 2004). In sum, the picture that is emerging from contemporary emotion experiments is in keeping with older clinical observations of depressed patients as characterized by flat emotional reactivity simultaneous with sustained sad mood and guilt.

The Adaptive Significance of Emotion Context Insensitivity

In addition to further documenting the conditions under which ECI holds, it is important to consider the broader adaptive significance of this pattern of emotional response. Functionalist theories of emotion have argued that the capacity to react to changing stimuli with appropriate emotions is critical for guiding successful adjustment to the environment (e.g., Carver & Scheier, 1990; Keltner & Gross, 1999). By this logic, a relative absence of appropriate emotional reactivity (ECI) would presumably be associated with poorer adaptation in MDD. One might then expect, for example, that the more a depressed person exhibits ECI, the more severe and more long lasting his or her depressive episodes would tend to be.

Consistent with this expectation, the small body of data collected thus far indicates that an absence of appropriate emotional reactivity is associated with greater MDD episode severity and a more pernicious course of disorder. For example, in cross-sectional work Rottenberg et al. (2002) found that depressed persons who reported reduced reactivity to sad stimuli evidenced more severe depression and poorer overall psychosocial functioning. It is also interesting to note that blunted startle modulation has been associated with more severe depression (Allen et al., 1999) as well as a greater number of retrospectively reported depression episodes in a sample with childhood-onset depression (Forbes, Miller, Cohn, Fox, & Kovacs, 2005). Prospective studies in our laboratory have also consistently found associations between diminished emotional reactivity and poorer MDD outcome: blunted behavioral and heart rate reactions to amusing material predicted MDD nonrecovery 6 months later (Rottenberg et al., 2002); blunted vagal reactivity to sad material also predicted nonrecovery from disorder (Rottenberg, Salomon, Gross, & Gotlib, 2005), and low disclosure of sad emotion during discussion of past sad life events predicted greater depressive symptoms 1 year later (Rottenberg, Joormann, Brozovich, & Gotlib, 2005). In sum, data thus far accord with functionalist theories of emotion in suggesting that ECI in MDD is associated with more severe and long-lasting disorder.

Does Emotion Context Insensitivity Reflect a State or a Trait?

I suggested earlier that ECI may be a consequence of severe depressed mood states. This suggests that ECI may be a correlate of the depressed state rather than an enduring traitlike vulnerability characteristic. It would make good sense if ECI were statelike in light of three clusters of indirect evidence: (a) Depression-vulnerable individuals tend to report high levels of neuroticism, a major personality trait associated with a high degree of negative emotional reactivity (Gross, Sutton, & Ketelaar, 1998); high neuroticism predicts the onset of first-episode depression (e.g., Kendler, Neale, Kessler, Heath, & Eaves, 1993), and it is also observable in formerly depressed individuals (Bagby, Joffe, Parker, Kalemba, & Harkness, 1995). (b) Depression-vulnerable individuals are more cognitively dysregulated by bouts of dysphoria when they are tested in remission (e.g., greater number of dysfunctional attitudes; Scher et al., 2005); these cognitive dysfunctions presumably drive stronger emotional reactivity and increased vulnerability to new episodes of depression. (c) Criticism by a close relative is a robust predictor of relapse among remitted depression-vulnerable persons (Butzlaff & Hooley, 1998); this psychosocial process, too, is presumably mediated by enhanced negative emotional reactivity to criticism (Hooley, Gruber, Scott, Hiller, & Yurgelun-Todd, 2005). Taken together, these are suggestive hints that depression-vulnerable individuals might exhibit robust emotional volatility at times when they are not acutely ill. These data also raise an intriguing question: Do depression-vulnerable individuals oscillate between periods of reduced emotional reactivity and periods of heightened emotional reactivity, perhaps as a function of waxing and waning depressive symptoms?

Unfortunately, as yet few strong data confirm that ECI is a transient pattern of response. Determining decisively whether ECI is a trait or a state will require repeated testing of depression-vulnerable persons, ideally with longitudinal designs that comprehensively assess emotional reactivity at different phases of depressive illness (i.e., subsyndromal symptoms, syndromal symptoms, full recovery, relapse, etc). Because intensive longitudinal investigations of this kind present such formidable resource and logistical challenges, most available data on the trait–state issue are cross-sectional in nature. Further clouding the picture, extant cross-sectional data are equivocal. For example, we recently found that currently, but not formerly, depressed, participants were characterized by ECI, consistent with the idea that ECI is statelike (Rottenberg et al., 2005). However, other investigations suggest ECI might be traitlike: Iacono et al. (1984) found that currently and formerly depressed participants both exhibited similarly attenuated electrodermal responding across both emotional and nonemotional stimuli relative to control participants. Dichter et al. (2004) additionally found that even after a course of antidepressant treatment, which reduced symptoms, depressed persons' emotion-startle modulation continued to remain attenuated relative to control participants. Further complicating the picture, Sigmon and Nelson-Gray (1992) found results consistent with the trait position but opposite in direction: Formerly depressed and currently depressed persons were both characterized by potentiated electrodermal responding to negative stimuli relative to healthy control participants. Thus, despite the theoretical attractions of viewing ECI as a state, the small number of studies that demonstrate state effects, and the existence of several findings suggesting stable patterns of emotional reactivity in depression, vulnerable populations currently preclude any firm conclusions in this area of research.

DIRECTIONS FOR FUTURE RESEARCH ON EMOTIONAL REACTIVITY IN MAJOR DEPRESSIVE DISORDER

Although the progress toward understanding emotions in MDD has been uneven, this chapter has documented that considerable progress has in fact occurred. The field, aided by continuing improvements in emotion theory and method, is well positioned to consolidate these gains. This final section concludes with a brief consideration of three areas that will be critical in the future investigation of emotional reactivity in MDD.

Proximal Mechanisms for Abnormal Emotional Responding in Major Depressive Disorder

This chapter has, by design, taken a largely descriptive approach to emotion in MDD. I have considered the ways that depression alters emotional reactivity. Once a thorough depiction of emotional reactivity in MDD is achieved, the next stage of work must isolate the proximal mechanisms that are responsible for depression-related abnormalities. Indeed, our goal must be to develop a causal analysis of the underlying dysfunctional processes. Although challenging, causal, mechanistic accounts are ultimately needed if we are to identify specific points in the emotion generative–emotion regulatory process to target for novel treatment interventions for MDD.

With respect to ECI, the theory (that severe mood states have functional significance in reducing motivated activity) is relatively silent concerning proximal mechanisms (Rottenberg, 2005). My colleagues and I have speculated that ECI may reflect impairments in the capacity to offset or remove negative emotions (Rottenberg & Gross, 2003), which may operate via faulty emotion regulation strategies (e.g., rumination; Nolen-Hoesksema, 1991) and/or deficiencies in homeostatic mechanisms in MDD (e.g., vagal tone; Rottenberg et al., 2005). Clearly, a variety of psychobiological mechanisms may explain why severe mood states might have an inhibitory effect on emotion. In sum, one of the highest priorities for future work is to develop accounts of responsible proximal mechanisms for dysfunctional emotional reactivity in MDD, including possible neural substrates (Davidson et al., 2002).

Distinctions Between Affective Pathology in Major Depressive Disorder and Other Forms of Psychopathology

The complexity of emotion as a construct, paired with the demands of conducting clinical research, explains why understanding emotion dysfunction in even a single disorder is a daunting task. Nevertheless, a deeper understanding of how psychopathology influences emotion will require a more frankly comparative perspective. For example, it is not yet clear whether ECI is a biobehavioral marker for MDD or whether it is a pattern common in many forms of psychopathology. For example, some prior comparisons of depressed patients and patients with schizophrenia suggest that there are similar diminutions in expressive behavioral reactivity across the two disorders (Berenbaum & Oltmanns, 1992; Gaebel & Wölwer, 2004; Trémeau et al., 2005). The common co-occurrence of depression with anxiety disorders (Clark et al., 1994) makes comparative work on emotional reactivity in depression and anxiety disorders particularly important. One key question is whether clearer evidence of mood facilitation will be present in anxiety disorders relative to MDD. Barlow (2002) has suggested that several anxiety disorders are characterized by both prevailing anxious mood and by stronger emotional reactions to mood-relevant stimuli (i.e., panic attacks, phobic reactions). If comparative work can establish that clinically anxious and clinically depressed mood states have divergent effects on emotion, this may help to sharpen the often blurry clinical boundaries between anxiety and depressive syndromes (Watson, 2000).

Clinical Implications

One recurrent theme of this volume is the increasing recognition among clinicians of the importance of emotions in the generation and maintenance of psychopathology (e.g., Greenberg & Safran, 1987; Gross & Muñoz, 1995). In the case of MDD, there is increasing awareness among clinicians that emotion is central to the disorder, and the explicit use of emotion theory and methods to develop more effective treatments is now at an early, but important, phase. As a first step, continued dissemination of laboratory-based findings to clinicians is needed. I hope this chapter and others in this volume (see chap. 13) provide empirical guidance to the considerable enthusiasm for emotion-based treatments of MDD.

More concretely, I have presented findings suggesting that MDD impedes the normal ebb and flow of emotion, a process that ordinarily facilitates adaptive transactions with the environment (Keltner & Gross, 1999). These findings raise a question as to whether psychotherapeutic techniques that enhance patients' emotional reactivity could be developed as a potential treatment for syndromal MDD. The role of emotion and therapeutic potential of procedures explicitly designed to enhance emotional processing have been pursued vigorously in the anxiety disorders, perhaps most notably in posttraumatic stress disorder (Foa, Riggs, Massie, & Yarczower, 1995) and generalized anxiety disorder (chap. 11, this volume). Thus, both developments in related disorders and the MDD emotion data I have reviewed justify further exploration of the payoffs of explicit formulations of emotional reactivity into MDD treatment and the value of regular assessments of emotion experience and expression during the course of MDD therapy.

REFERENCES

Allen, N. B., Trinder, J., & Brennan, C. (1999). Affective startle modulation in clinical depression: Preliminary findings. *Biological Psychiatry, 46,* 542–550.

American Psychiatric Association. (2000). *Diagnostic and statistical manual of mental disorders* (4th ed., text revision). Washington, DC: Author.

Bagby, R. M., Joffe, R. T., Parker, J. D. A., Kalemba, V., & Harkness, K. L. (1995). Major depression and the five-factor model of personality. *Journal of Personality Disorders, 9,* 224–234.

Barlow, D. H. (2002). *Anxiety and its disorders.* New York: Guilford Press.

Beck, A. T. (1976). *Cognitive therapy and the emotional disorders.* Madison, CT: International Universities Press.

Beck, A. T. (1983). Cognitive therapy of depression: New perspectives. In P. J. Clayton & J. E. Barrett (Eds.), *Treatment of depression: Old controversies and new approaches* (pp. 265–290). New York: Raven.

Beck, A. T., Rush, A. J., Shaw, B. F., & Emery, G. (1979). *Cognitive therapy of depression.* New York: Guilford Press.

Berenbaum, H., & Oltmanns, T. F. (1992). Emotional experience and expression in schizophrenia and depression. *Journal of Abnormal Psychology, 101,* 37–44.

Bower, G. H. (1981). Mood and memory. *American Psychologist, 36,* 129–148.

Butzlaff, R. L., & Hooley, J. M. (1998). Expressed emotion and psychiatric relapse. *Archives of General Psychiatry, 55,* 547–552.

Canli, T., Sivers, H., Thomason, M., Whitfield, S., Gabrieli, J. D. E., & Gotlib, I. H. (2004). Brain activation to emotional words in depressed versus healthy subjects. *NeuroReport, 15,* 2585–2588.

Carver, C. S., & Scheier, M. F. (1990). Origins and functions of positive and negative affect: A control-process view. *Psychological Review, 97,* 19–35.

Clark, L. A., Watson, D., & Mineka, S. (1994). Temperament, personality, and the mood and anxiety disorders. *Journal of Abnormal Psychology, 103,* 103–116.

Coyne, J. C. (1976). Toward an interactional description of depression. *Psychiatry, 39,* 28–40.

Davidson R. J., Pizzagalli, D., Nitschke, J. B., & Putman, K. (2002). Depression: Perspectives from affective neuroscience. *Annual Review of Psychology, 53,* 545–574.

Dawson, M. E., Schell, A. M., & Catania, J. J. (1977). Autonomic correlates of depression and clinical improvement following electroconvulsive shock therapy. *Psychophysiology, 14,* 569–578.

Deldin, P. J., Keller, J., Gergen, J. A., & Miller, G. A. (2001). Cognitive bias and emotion in neuropsychological models of depression. *Cognition and Emotion, 15,* 787–802.

Depue R. A., & Iacono, W. G. (1989). Neurobehavioral aspects of affective disorders. *Annual Review of Psychology, 40,* 457–492.

Dichter, G. S., Tomarken, A. J., Shelton, R. C., & Sutton, S. K. (2004). Early- and late-onset startle modulation in unipolar depression. *Psychophysiology, 41,* 433–440.

Dickens, C., McGowan, L., & Dale, S. (2003). Impact of depression on experimental pain perception: A systematic review of the literature with meta-analysis. *Psychosomatic Medicine, 65,* 369–375.

Dunn, B. D., Dalgleish, T., Lawrence, A. D., Cusack, R., & Ogilvie, A. D. (2004). Categorical and dimensional reports of experienced affect to emotion-inducing pictures in depression. *Journal of Abnormal Psychology, 113,* 654–660.

Ekman, P. (1992). An argument for basic emotions. *Cognition and Emotion, 6,* 169–200.

Foa, E. B., Riggs, D. S., Massie, E. D., & Yarczower, M. (1995). The impact of fear activation and anger on the efficacy of exposure treatment for posttraumatic stress disorder. *Behavior Therapy, 26,* 487–499.

Forbes, E. E., Miller, A., Cohn, J. F., Fox, N. A., & Kovacs, M. (2005). Affect modulated startle in adults with childhood-onset depression: Relations to bipolar course and number of lifetime depressive episodes. *Psychiatry Research, 134,* 11–25.

Fu, C. H. Y., Williams, S. C. R., Cleare, A. J., Brammer, M. J., Walsh, N. D., Kim, J., et al. (2004). Attenuation of the neural response to sad faces in major depression by antidepressant treatment: A prospective, event-related functional magnetic resonance imaging study. *Archives of General Psychiatry, 61,* 877–889.

Gaebel, W., & Wölwer, W. (2004). Facial expressivity in the course of schizophrenia and depression. *European Archives of Psychiatry & Clinical Neuroscience, 254,* 335–342.

Gehricke, J. G., & Shapiro, D. (2000) Reduced facial expression and social context in major depression: Discrepancies between facial muscle activity and self-reported emotion. *Psychiatry Research, 95,* 157–167.

Gilbert, P., Birchwood, M., Gilbert, J., Trower, P., Hay, J., Murray, B., et al. (2001). An exploration of evolved mental mechanisms for dominant and subordinate behaviour in relation to auditory hallucinations in schizophrenia and critical thoughts in depression. *Psychological Medicine, 31,* 1117–1127.

Golin, S., Hartman, S. A., Klatt, E. N., Munz, K., & Wolfgang, G. L. (1977). Effects of self-esteem manipulation on arousal and reactions to sad models in depressed and nondepressed college students. *Journal of Abnormal Psychology, 86,* 435–439.

Gotlib, I. H. (1984). Depression and general psychopathology in university students. *Journal of Abnormal Psychology, 93,* 19–30.

Gotlib, I. H., Kraspnoperova, E., Neubauer Yue, D., & Joormann, J. (2004). Attentional biases for negative interpersonal stimuli in clinical depression. *Journal of Abnormal Psychology, 113,* 127–135.

Greden, J. F., Genero, N., Price, H. L., Feinberg, M., & Levine, S. (1986). Facial electromyography in depression. *Archives of General Psychiatry, 43,* 269–274.

Greenberg, L. S., & Safran, J. D. (1987). *Emotions in psychotherapy.* New York: Guilford Press.

Gross, J. J. (1998). The emerging field of emotion regulation: An integrative review. *Review of General Psychology, 2,* 271–299.

Gross, J. J., & Muñoz, R. F. (1995). Emotion regulation and mental health. *Clinical Psychology: Science and Practice, 2,* 151–164.

Gross, J. J., Sutton, S. K., & Ketelaar, T. (1998). Relations between affect and personality: Support for the affect-level and affective reactivity views. *Personality and Social Psychology Bulletin, 24,* 279–288.

Healy, D. (1993). Dysphoria. In C. G. Costello (Ed.), *Symptoms of depression* (pp. 23–42). New York: Wiley.

Henriques J. B., & Davidson, R. (1991). Left frontal hypoactivation in depression. *Journal of Abnormal Psychology, 100*, 535–545.

Henriques, J. B., & Davidson R. J. (2000). Decreased responsiveness to reward in depression. *Cognition and Emotion, 14*, 711–724.

Hooley, J. H., Gruber, S. A., Scott, L. A., Hiller, J. B., & Yurgelun-Todd, D. A. (2005). Activation in dorsolateral prefrontal cortex in response to maternal criticism and praise in recovered depressed and healthy control participants. *Biological Psychiatry, 57*, 809–812.

Iacono, W. G., Lykken, D. T., Haroian, K. P., Peloquin, L. H., Valentine, R. H., & Tuason, V. B. (1984). Electrodermal activity in euthymic patients with affective disorders: One-year retest stability and the effects of stimulus intensity and significance. *Journal of Abnormal Psychology, 93*, 304–311.

Keltner, D., & Gross, J. J. (1999). Functional accounts of emotions. *Cognition and Emotion, 13*, 467–480.

Kendler, K. S., Neale, M. C., Kessler, R. C., Heath, A. C., & Eaves, L. J. (1993). A longitudinal twin study of personality and major depression in women. *Archives of General Psychiatry, 50*, 853–862.

Kessler, R. C. (2002). Epidemiology of depression. In I. H Gotlib & C. L. Hammen (Eds.), *Handbook of depression* (pp. 23–42). New York: Guilford Press.

Klinger, E. (1975). Consequences of commitment to and disengagement from incentives. *Psychological Review, 82*, 1–25.

Lader, M. H., & Wing, L. W. (1969). Physiological measures in agitated and retarded depressed patients. *Journal of Psychiatry Research, 7*, 89–100.

Lewinsohn, P. M., Lobitz, W. C., & Wilson, S. (1973). "Sensitivity" of depressed individuals to aversive stimuli. *Journal of Abnormal Psychology, 81*, 259–263.

Moskowitz, A. K. (2004). "Scared stiff": Catatonia as an evolutionary-based fear response, *Psychological Review, 111*, 984–1002.

Nesse, R. M. (2000). Is depression an adaptation? *Archives of General Psychiatry, 57*, 14–20.

Nolen-Hoesksema, S. (1991). Responses to depression and their effects on the duration of depressive episodes. *Journal of Abnormal Psychology, 97*, 569–582.

Renneberg, B., Heyn, K., Gebhard, R., & Bachmann, S. (2005). Facial expression of emotions in borderline personality disorder and depression. *Journal of Behavior Therapy and Experimental Psychiatry, 36*, 183–196.

Rosenberg, E. L. (1998). Levels of analysis and the organization of affect. *Review of General Psychology, 2*, 247–270.

Rottenberg, J. (2005). Mood and emotion in major depression. *Current Directions in Psychological Science, 14*, 167–170.

Rottenberg, J., & Gotlib, I. H. (2004). Socioemotional functioning in depression. In M. Power (Ed.), *Mood disorders: A handbook of science and practice* (pp. 61–77). New York: Wiley.

Rottenberg, J., & Gross, J. J. (2003). When emotion goes wrong: Realizing the promise of affective science. *Clinical Psychology: Science and Practice, 10*, 227–232.

Rottenberg, J., Gross, J. J., & Gotlib, I. H. (2005). Emotion context insensitivity in major depressive disorder. *Journal of Abnormal Psychology, 114*, 627–639.

Rottenberg, J., Joormann, J., Brozovich, F., & Gotlib, I. H. (2005). Emotional intensity of idiographic sad memories in depression predicts symptom levels one year later. *Emotion, 5*, 238–242.

Rottenberg, J., Kasch, K. L., Gross, J. J., & Gotlib, I. H. (2002). Sadness and amusement reactivity differentially predict concurrent and prospective functioning in major depressive disorder. *Emotion, 2*, 135–146.

Rottenberg, J., Salomon, K., Gross, J. J., & Gotlib, I. H. (2005). Vagal withdrawal to a sad film predicts recovery from depression. *Psychophysiology, 42*, 277–281.

Scher, C. D., Ingram, R. E., & Segal, Z. V. (2005). Cognitive reactivity and vulnerability: Empirical evaluation of construct activation and cognitive diatheses in unipolar depression. *Clinical Psychology Review, 25*, 487–510.

Scherer, K. R. (1984). On the nature and function of emotion: A component process approach. In K. R. Scherer & P. Ekman (Eds.), *Approaches to emotion* (pp. 293–317). Hillsdale, NJ: Erlbaum.

Schwartz, G. E., Fair, P. L., Salt, P., Mandel, M. R., & Klerman, G. L. (1976, April 30). Facial muscle patterning to affective imagery in depressed and nondepressed subjects. *Science, 192*, 489–491.

Sigmon, S. T., & Nelson-Gray, R. O. (1992). Sensitivity to aversive events in depression: Antecedent, concomitant, or consequent? *Journal of Psychopathology and Behavioral Assessment, 14*, 225–246.

Sloan, D. M., Strauss, M. E., Quirk, S. W., & Sajatovic, M. (1997). Subjective and expressive emotional responses in depression. *Journal of Affective Disorders, 46*, 135–141.

Sloan, D. M., Strauss, M. E., & Wisner, K. L. (2001). Diminished response to pleasant stimuli by depressed women. *Journal of Abnormal Psychology, 110*, 488–493.

Thomas, K. M., Drevets, W. C., Dahl, R. E, Ryan, N. D., Birmaher, B., Eccard, C. H., et al. (2001). Amygdala response to fearful faces in anxious and depressed children. *Archives of General Psychiatry, 58*, 1057–1063.

Trémeau, F., Malaspina, D., Duval, F., Corrêa, H., Hager-Budny, M., Coin-Bariou, L., et al. (2005). Facial expressiveness in patients with schizophrenia compared to depressed patients and nonpatient comparison subjects. *American Journal of Psychiatry, 162*, 92–101.

Watson, D. (2000). *Mood and temperament.* New York: Guilford Press.

Wexler, B. E., Levenson, L., Warrenburg, S., & Price, L. H. (1994). Decreased perceptual sensitive to emotion-evoking stimuli in depression. *Psychiatry Research, 51*, 127–138.

8

FOUR PRINCIPLES OF FEAR AND THEIR IMPLICATIONS FOR PHOBIAS

ARNE ÖHMAN AND CHRISTIAN RÜCK

Fear is an activated, aversive emotional state that serves to motivate organisms to cope with threatening events (Öhman, 2000b). Subjectively, fear denotes dread of impending disaster and an intense urge to leave the situation. The body is activated, and the behavioral output may include facial expressions of fear and actions related to avoidance or flight.

Fear promotes escape and avoidance of circumstances with potentially deadly outcomes. Because staying alive is a prerequisite for the central goal of biological evolution—the transfer of genes across generations—fear has been a favored target for natural selection. Its evolutionary origin makes fear a normal human emotion. But fear is also a central component in many psychopathologies, which may seem hard to reconcile with its nature as an evolved trait. How can something that has evolved because of its functionality often undermine human adjustment? Basically, the answer relates to cost and benefit. The maximal benefit promoted by fear is substantial: the deferral of death. This benefit outweighs cost in terms of potential impediment to function for emotional reasons. In essence, evolution cares less for how we feel than for what we do.

Research during the past decades has generated important strides in our understanding of fear at the psychological and neural levels. Öhman and Mineka (2001) reviewed an extensive literature on fear and fear learning, which they summarized in the concept of the *fear module*. The fear module is a relatively independent behavioral, mental, and neural system, which is intimately linked to the evolution of mammalian defense systems and which determines important characteristics of fear.

The purpose of this chapter is to elucidate fear-related psychopathology by means of principles derived from the field of emotion. In particular, the four principles of fear that we discuss in the main sections of the chapter are derived from the fear module. They include the following: (a) Fear mobilizes the body, (b) fear can be conditioned and extinguished, (c) an effective fear stimulus needs not be consciously perceived, and (d) fear stimuli guide attention. In the concluding discussion, we analyze how far our understanding of normal fear brings us to understanding phobias and, to some extent, other anxiety disorders. Before we discuss these four principles of fear and their biological bases, it is useful to provide brief overviews of the anxiety disorders, emphasizing the phobias.

FEAR AND THE ANXIETY DISORDERS

Fear and its close ally, anxiety, are the central problem in the anxiety disorders. For example, crippling fear may force avoidance of situations that are critical to normal adjustment, such as encounters with superiors. As a background for our discussion, we first provide a brief description of the anxiety disorders (see Barlow, 2002, for in-depth coverage).

Specific Phobia

Specific phobia involves an excessive, uncontrollable fear of specific objects or events. The fear is excessive in the sense that it is out of proportion to the real danger of the situation. Excessive fear promotes excessive avoidance that restricts normal life by interfering with the fulfillment of important life goals. For example, flight phobia may lead a person to decline an attractive job offer that requires frequent flying. The *Diagnostic and Statistical Manual of Mental Disorders* (4th ed.; American Psychiatric Association, 1994) defines five types of specific phobias: animal (e.g., spiders and snakes), situational (e.g., airplanes, elevators), natural environment (e.g., heights), blood–injection–injury, and other (e.g., vomiting).

Social Phobia

Social phobia concerns extreme fear of situations in which the anxious individual is the center of social attention or the object of social evaluation.

As a result, public speaking, social gatherings, confronting superiors, or contacts with potential sexual partners are either avoided or endured only with fear or panic. Because social encounters are critical to human adjustment, fear that forces their avoidance has more serious consequences than the avoidance of the typically more isolated situations avoided in specific phobia.

Agoraphobia

Agoraphobia involves a still more diffuse set of avoided situations than those in social phobia; they are most economically described as lacking an escape route to a safe base. For example, people diagnosed with agoraphobia fear public transportation, particularly those forms of transportation, such as airplanes and underground trains, in which individuals are confined once they enter until travel is completed. Other feared situations include crowded places (e.g., shopping malls, sport events), tunnels, bridges, and so on. Diagnostically, agoraphobia is closely related to *panic disorder*, a state characterized by panic attacks defined by sudden surges of physiological symptoms (heart palpitation, sweating, difficulties breathing, shakiness, dizziness, etc.) and feelings (e.g., derealization, fear of losing control, fear of dying) that may come suddenly and without provocation, then subside. Fear of panic is considered a central component of the agoraphobia, and the avoidance is driven by attempts to minimize the perceived risk for panic attacks by staying away from situations that are perceived as panic inducing.

Other Anxiety Disorders

Life-threatening traumatic events such as wartime atrocities, rape, assault, natural disasters, and severe accidents elicit intense acute fright, but they may also lead to the lasting emotional problems that define *posttraumatic stress disorder* (PTSD). PTSD is characterized by reexperiencing the trauma in emotionally painful flashbacks as well as avoidance of situations and events reminding of the trauma. *Generalized anxiety disorder* (GAD) lacks the distinct fear that is evident in other anxiety syndromes. Instead, it is characterized by an always-present anxiety that is driven by excessive, chronic, and uncontrollable worry about various life circumstances. In *obsessive–compulsive disorder* (OCD), the conspicuous symptoms are not manifest fear or anxiety but obsessions (i.e., mental preoccupations, uncontrollable thoughts) and compulsions (i.e., involuntary actions). Their function is to reduce anxiety, but they are often so intrusive that they undermine a normal life.

THE NEURAL MACHINERY OF FEAR

Fear is controlled by a specific neural circuit that has been evolutionarily shaped to mediate functional relationships between threats to survival or well-being and defensive behavior. The circuit is organized around the *amygdala,* a collection of nuclei in the anterior medial temporal lobe, which is strategically placed to mediate emotional input and output (Davis & Whalen, 2001). Its lateral nucleus receives input from all sensory modalities. It is interesting to note that sensory information may access the amygdala via two routes: a high road and a low road (LeDoux, 1996). The high road is the well-known pathway from the sensory receptors via sensory thalamic nuclei to the primary sensory cortices and associated areas of the cortex. However, lesion studies demonstrated that cortical processing is not necessary for auditory or visual information to reach the amygdala and activate fear responses (Doron & LeDoux, 1999; Shi & Davis, 2001). This direct route to the amygdala via thalamic nuclei provides a low road of crudely processed information that may alert the amygdala to deal with potentially significant stimuli (for a concise review of human studies evaluating the low road concept, see Öhman, 2005).

Further processed information then reaches the amygdala from a series of cortical sites, including the frontal lobes. These sites have recurrent connections from the lateral amygdala, which suggests that cortical processing may be tuned by the amygdala (Emery & Amaral, 2000). After a quick assessment for threat potential in the lateral and basolateral nuclei of the amygdala, information is conveyed to the central nucleus, which has efferent connections to nuclei in the diencephalon and brain stem that mediate emotional output. For example, emotional behavior (flight, fight, "freezing") is controlled from the periaqueductal gray substance in the upper midbrain. Autonomic responses are activated through connections between the central nucleus and the lateral hypothalamus for sympathetic activation and to brain-stem nuclei (dorsal nucleus of the vagus and nucleus ambiguus) for parasympathetic effects. Defensive reflexes (e.g., the startle reflex; see section titled Four Principles of Fear, this chapter) are controlled by connections from the central nucleus to the nucleus reticularis pontis caudalis in the brain stem. Further, fibers to the bed nucleus of the stria terminalis are an important link in activation of stress hormones by the corticotropin releasing factor (CRF) that activates the hypothalamic–pituitary hormonal axis. Finally, via connections to the basal nucleus of the forebrain and the locus coeruleus, the central nucleus may produce widespread activation of the cortex through activation of cholinergic and noradrenergic pathways, respectively. The ancient origin and location in the brain of this fear network makes it automatic and relatively impenetrable to cognition (LeDoux, 1996; Öhman & Mineka, 2001).

DISTINGUISHING FEAR FROM ANXIETY

Fear and anxiety are both aversive activated emotional states that mobilize body responses. However, there are obvious differences between the two states. Fear is typically episodic and tied to an eliciting stimulus, whereas anxiety is more lasting and less clearly related to an identifiable stimulus. Therefore, a common distinction between them is that fear, but not anxiety, is stimulus driven.

Epstein (1972) argued that the defining feature of fear is its role as an escape and avoidance motive (cf. Öhman, 2000b), which, in effect, makes it a coping emotion. Anxiety, however, takes over when the coping attempts fail (Öhman, 2000a), the roads to safety are blocked, and there is not much one can do but helplessly wait for bad things to happen. Thus, whereas fear is related to attempts to cope with an acutely unfolding threat, anxiety is directed toward uncertain future threats, which may be something to worry and ruminate about rather than to run away from. This distinction preserves the notion that fear is more stimulus driven than anxiety but makes the states two branches of a common evolutionary route for which situational contingencies determine which one will be activated. Furthermore, it recognizes that anxiety also may be tied to an aversive context, albeit one that cannot be behaviorally controlled.

Davis (1998; Walker, Toufexis, & Davis, 2003) proposed that both fear and anxiety are related to the extended amygdala complex, which reaches from the medial temporal lobe to the nearby ventral striatum. The central nucleus of the amygdala mediates acute fear responses to specific stimuli, whereas the anatomically closely related bed nucleus of the stria terminalis mediates anxiety, that is, more long-lasting, tonic responses without an obvious, discrete eliciting stimulus. Therefore, although fear and anxiety are overlapping responses, they can be distinguished in terms of stimuli (i.e., presence vs. absence of a discrete eliciting stimulus), behavior (i.e., coping vs. noncoping), and neuroanatomy (i.e., central nucleus of the amygdala vs. bed nucleus of the stria terminalis).

FOUR PRINCIPLES OF FEAR

In this section, we summarize the extensive research on fear in terms of four empirical generalizations. They concern the role of bodily activation in fear, fear learning and unlearning, the role of awareness in fear, and the role of fear in attention.

Principle 1: Fear Mobilizes the Body

Experiencing the activated body has been regarded as a central component in emotion. Feeling the heart beat hard and fast, shortness of breath, and a dry mouth are central to the fear experience.

Bodily and Behavioral Responses to Fear Stimuli

The basic function of fear is to mobilize defense behavior (Öhman & Wiens, 2003). An important component of this function is to tune the autonomic nervous system to ensure metabolic resources for vigorous action. The autonomic nervous system is composed of the sympathetic and parasympathetic branches, the former generally functioning to mobilize and the latter to restore metabolic resources.

Defensive behavior includes defensive reflexes as well as more strategically controlled avoidance behavior. The startle reflex is a primary example of the former. It is elicited by any abrupt, unexpected stimulus that makes us jump. In humans it is commonly measured by the eyeblink response (see chap. 3, this volume). Fear potentiates the startle reflex; for example, the reflex is larger to startle probes presented when research participants look at aversive than neutral pictures (Lang, Bradley, & Cuthbert, 1997). This effect is mediated by the central nucleus of the amygdala (e.g., Lang, Davis, & Öhman, 2000).

Defensive behavior can be functionally organized into two broad output classes: (a) defensive immobility (i.e., freezing) in which the organism is behaviorally passive but primed to respond actively to further stimulation and (b) defensive action (i.e., variations of fight or flight; Lang et al., 2000). These response patterns can be seen as stages, with immobility dominant when threat is more remote and active defenses, such as fight or flight, emerging as the threat becomes imminent (Fanselow, 1994; Lang, Bradley, & Cuthbert, 1997).

Freezing is an evolved defense response that should not be misunderstood as the mere absence of active responses. It involves active scanning of the environment and a readiness to act. Immobility may help to prevent discovery by predators. A freezing animal is primarily focused on the discovered, distant threat, and exhibits psychophysiological responses that are associated with orienting, that is, the taking in of information from the surroundings (e.g., Öhman & Wiens, 2003). These orienting responses include, for example, skin conductance responses (SCRs), heart rate deceleration, and startle inhibition (Öhman, Hamm, & Hugdahl, 2000). As the threat becomes imminent, there is a shift to active defense (e.g., flight or fight), with an associated shift in heart rate from deceleration to acceleration and a shift in the startle reflex from inhibition to facilitation (fear-potentiated startle; Lang et al., 1997; Öhman & Wiens, 2003).

Bodily Responses to Feared and Phobic Stimuli

To examine the activation of responses to feared stimuli, Globisch, Hamm, Esteves, and Öhman (1999) exposed student volunteers with a phobic-level fear of snakes or spiders as well as nonfearful control participants to pictures of snakes or spiders, household objects, erotica, and cute animals. The fearful participants rated snake or spider pictures as much more unpleasant and arousing than neutral and positive pictures and much more so than did control participants. In terms of autonomic responses, fearful participants showed larger SCRs to animal pictures than did control participants, and their responses to animals were larger than their responses to neutral or positive pictures. Further, fearful participants showed a strong heart rate acceleration to snake or spider pictures, which was in marked contrast to the deceleration control participants showed and to the small and indistinguishable response shown by both groups to neutral stimuli. The startle data showed a rapid relative startle potentiation to feared compared with neutral stimuli that was obvious to probes presented as early as 300 milliseconds after picture onset and then remained (or even increased) for at least 4 seconds of picture viewing. Control participants, in contrast, showed a rapid relative startle inhibition to animal stimuli that lasted for more than a second. Together these data show that enhanced (phobic) fear to animal stimuli is associated with a distinct psychophysiological response suggesting activation of fight-or-flight behavior, which stands in stark contrast to the orienting pattern elicited by these stimuli in nonfearful participants.

Brain Responses to Phobic Stimuli

Carlsson et al. (2004) recruited participants who were phobic of either snakes or spiders (but not of both) for a brain-imaging study. Some positron emission tomography (PET) scans were done while participants were exposed to repeated brief (but clearly perceivable) presentations of pictures of snakes, spiders, or mushrooms. Confirming the notion of the amygdala as the hub in the fear network of the brain, the results showed strong bilateral amygdala activation to the feared stimulus (e.g., a snake for a participant with snake phobia) compared with the neutral stimulus (mushroom) and the fear-relevant but nonfeared stimulus (e.g., spiders for a participant with snake phobia). Furthermore, the enhanced amygdala response to the feared stimulus was associated with activation of a cortical affective processing network that included the anterior cingulate cortex, the anterior insula, the orbitofrontal cortex, and the midbrain periaqueductal gray. Bilateral amygdala activations to snakes in participants with snake phobia were also reported by Sabatinelli, Bradley, Fitzsimmons, and Lang (2005) and Dilger et al. (2003). The latter study also reported, as did Carlsson et al. (2004), reliable activations of the anterior insula and the orbitofrontal cortex, whereas Sabatinelli et al. (2005) and Dilger et al. (2003) both found significant activations of the inferotemporal cortex–fusiform gyrus. Thus, several studies have shown amygdala activation in response to phobic stimulation as well as activation of both frontal and posterior cortical networks.

Fear Activation in Anxiety Patients

Cuthbert et al. (2003) measured psychophysiological responses in patients diagnosed with different anxiety disorders while they were engaged in imagery of different fear scenes. On the basis of previously learned sentences, patients were instructed to imagine fear scenes based on previously learned sentences briefly describing personal fear experiences (referring to "the worst fear you ever experienced"), standard danger scenes ("Taking a shower, alone in the house, I hear the sound of someone forcing open the door, and I panic"), social fear scenes ("My heart pounds in the suddenly silent room; everyone is watching me"), or neutral control scenes ("Soft music is playing on the stereo as I snooze lazily on my favorite chair").

Even though the group did not differ in ratings of vividness of imagery and fear, Cuthbert et al. (2003) found that heart rate increases when imagining the fear scenes were larger in the specific and social phobia groups than in the PTSD, panic disorder, and control groups, which did not differ among each other. The participants with specific phobias showed considerably more startle potentiation than the other diagnostic groups when imagining both their personal and other fear scenes.

These results are consistent with previous data showing larger heart rate responses under exposure to fear imagery for individuals with specific compared with social phobia, both of whom showed larger responses than did participants with agorapnobia (E. W. Cook, Melamed, Cuthbert, McNeil, & Lang, 1988). Similarly, Lang, McTeague, and Cuthbert (in press) observed larger fear-potentiated startle to fear imagery in patients with specific and social phobia than in patients with panic disorder or GAD.

Keane et al. (1998) reported that a large group of Vietnam War veterans with a current PTSD diagnosis showed larger heart rate, skin conductance, and systolic and diastolic blood pressure responses to both standard combat and imagined personal combat scenes than veterans never diagnosed with PTSD. Veterans with a lifetime but not a current PTSD diagnosis were generally intermediate to the other two groups. In addition, the group with a current diagnosis showed higher resting heart rate and skin conductance but lower heart rate and diastolic blood pressure responses to standard stress than the other two groups.

In contrast to patients diagnosed with other anxiety disorders, those with specific phobia did not differ from control participants, in self-reported anxiety and depression (Cuthbert et al., 2003; Lang et al., in press). Likewise, in agreement with other data (Brown, Campbell, Lehman, Grisham, & Mancill, 2001), patients with specific phobias had less comorbidity with other anxiety disorders than patients diagnosed with PTSD, panic disorder, and GAD.

Principle 2: Fear Can Be Conditioned and Extinguished

Fear can be evoked in a bewildering multitude of situations, which suggests that learning is an important determinant of which situations acquire power to elicit fear. However, this should not be taken to suggest that there is no role for genes in deciding what people fear. Genes indeed may constrain or enhance fear learning.

Human Fear Conditioning

Danger may be heralded by subtle cues. For example, a predator may provide clues to its presence by faint sounds or odor. When organisms learn that a stimulus that is by itself innocuous (e.g., a sound) signals the occurrence of a threatening stimulus (e.g., an attacking predator), fear and defense elicited by the predator (the unconditioned stimulus [US]) are transferred to the sound (the conditioned stimulus [CS]; e.g., Domjan, 2005). Such Pavlovian fear conditioning is a powerful mechanism for extending the range of events that can elicit fear, and it provides a critical functional advantage because it promotes early escape from predators (e.g., Hollis, 1982).

In a human example, Hamm and Vaitl (1996) exposed participants to two pictures, one of which was presented alone (the CS–) and another (the CS+) that was followed by the US (a mild electric shock). Startle responses to probes presented during the shock-associated CS+, but not to those presented during the CS–, were clearly enhanced compared with responses to probes presented during the intertrial interval. Furthermore, there was no relationship between conditioned startle potentiation and the participants' ability to report correctly the CS–US relationship. Participants who evidenced conditioned HR accelerations also showed conditioned startle potentiation, whereas those evidencing conditioned HR decelerations did not show any enhanced startle to probes presented during the CS+. Thus, together startle potentiation and heart rate acceleration indexed the conditioning of a genuine fear response, much like the one displayed to the feared animal in the animal-fearful participants reported in the previously discussed study by Globisch et al. (1999).

There is now strong evidence that fear conditioning occurs in the lateral amygdala (Fanselow & Poulos, 2005; LeDoux, 2000). This is consistent with human brain imaging studies showing that both the learning (e.g., Morris, Buchel, & Dolan, 2001) and the expression (e.g., Morris, Öhman, & Dolan, 1998) of human fear-conditioned responses involve the amygdala.

Evolutionary Preparedness and Conditioning

In the natural environment, the US and CS tend to be nonrandomly connected (Domjan, 2005). It is not just any sound or smell that is likely to warn a potential prey of a lurking predator, but sounds or smells emitted by the predator. The associative apparatus of animals is likely to have been biased by evolution to pick up readily such systematic ecological relationships (Seligman, 1971). This hypothesis, known as the *preparedness hypothesis*, explains why phobias are seen to a large but still limited set of objects and events that tend to cluster on situations that in themselves involve some degree of danger, particularly in an evolutionary perspective (Öhman, Dimberg, & Öst, 1985). For example, common phobic objects and events, such as snakes, enclosed spaces, and heights, have been related to recurrent survival threats in mammalian evolution, which has placed a premium on learning to fear and avoid them. Öhman et al. (1985) argued that dominant social threat (e.g., an angry face) has also served a similar function in evolution within the context of dominance conflicts, thus incorporating social phobia in the preparedness argument. Consistent with this hypothesis, Öhman and Mineka (2001) reviewed reports from many laboratories that evolutionary fear-relevant stimuli (e.g., pictures of snakes, spiders, angry faces) result in more persistent conditioned responses (CRs) when paired with aversive events than do neutral stimuli (e.g., pictures of flowers, mushrooms, happy faces; for a recent example of such a report, see Olsson, Ebert, Banaji, & Phelps, 2005). Furthermore, when presented with pictures that are randomly related to mild electric shock stimulations, participants perceive illusory correlations between snakes or angry faces and shock, whereas they detect the random relationship between shocks and neutral pictures (see review by Öhman & Mineka, 2001).

The preparedness hypothesis is also strongly supported by research on fear learning in monkeys. For example, when nonfearful, lab-reared monkeys were given the opportunity to observe a "model" wild-reared monkey exhibiting fear of a snake or snakelike stimulus, they rapidly acquired a strong fear of snakes (Mineka & Cook, 1993; Mineka, Davidson, Cook, & Keir, 1984). Furthermore, identical fear responses exhibited by a model monkey resulted in strong fear conditioning to a snake but no conditioning to a flower displayed in manipulated video clips (M. Cook & Mineka, 1989, 1990). Furthermore, snakes and flowers served equally well as discriminative stimuli for food, thus showing that the superior conditioning to snakes was specific to the aversive context.

Using behavior genetics methods, Hettema, Annas, Neale, Kendler, and Fredrikson (2003) provided a direct test of the hypothesized genetic basis of the prepared conditioning effect. Their data favored the hypothesis by suggesting a stronger genetic component for conditioning to evolutionarily prepared (snakes vs. spiders) compared with neutral (circles vs. triangles) stimuli.

Extinction of Conditioned Fear

Pavlovian conditioned responses wane if the CS is repeatedly presented in the absence of the US. This phenomenon (and procedure) is referred to as *extinction*. Conditioning and extinction of CRs are separate processes. Indeed, the effect of prepared stimuli such as snakes or angry faces in humans typically is more evident in elevated resistance to extinction than in rapid conditioning (McNally, 1987; Öhman & Mineka, 2001). From this perspective, what makes phobias pathological is the persistence of the resulting conditioned fear.

Empirical findings on extinction and conditioning warrant a strong conclusion: Extinction is more context-dependent than conditioning (Bouton, 2005). A fear-conditioned CS to a particular cue is typically elicited by that cue even if the context is changed. However, if a CR is conditioned in a particular context (Context A) and is extinguished in a different context (e.g., a distinctly different chamber used in an animal experiment; e.g., Context B), the CR disappears. If the experimental animal is brought back to Context A and exposed to the CS, it shows a full-strength CR compared with a control animal extinguished in Context A. This is referred to as *renewal* of the CR (see reviews by Bouton, 2005; Davis, Walker, & Myers, 2003). It is as if the animal extinguished in Context B learns that the CS–US contingency is not valid in this new situation (i.e., Context B) rather than learning a general rule that the US no longer follows the CS (e.g., in Context A). Indeed, renewal is also observed after extinction in Context B if the CS is introduced in a completely new context (C) or even if the new context (C) is presented after extinction in the original conditioning context (A; see Bouton, 2005).

Renewal after extinction has been demonstrated in human Pavlovian conditioning (Milad, Orr, Pitman, & Rauch, 2005; Vansteenwegen et al., 2005). For example, Milad et al. (2005) presented participants with pictures on a computer screen of two rooms. Lamps embedded in the room could be turned on and off and served as CSs, one of which was followed by shock (CS+) and the other not (CS–). Reliable SCR conditioning in one room context and extinction in the other were demonstrated in one experimental session. On the following day, participants were tested for recall of extinction in the extinction context from the previous day, and extinction remained complete. However, when the context was changed back to that of conditioning from the previous day, there was rather complete renewal with significantly larger responses to the CS+ than the CS–.

Consistent with the concept of renewal, return of fear after successful therapy is considered a problem for exposure treatments of phobias (Rachman, 1989). Experimental tests demonstrate a significant (albeit small) renewal of self-reported fear after intense exposure therapy with change of treatment room and therapist (Mineka, Mystkowsky, Hladek, & Rodriguez, 1999) or a change from an inside to outside context (Mystkowski, Craske, & Echiverri, 2002).

Evidence suggests that the amygdala is a site of fear extinction and that it uses similar molecular mechanisms to those that mediate fear conditioning (e.g., Davis & Myers, 2002). Indeed, pharmacological manipulation of these mechanisms to enhance extinction has been demonstrated to facilitate exposure treatment of specific phobia (Ressler et al., 2004). However, there are also animal (see review by Sotres-Bayon, Bush, & LeDoux, 2004) as well as human (Phelps, Delgado, Nearing, & LeDoux, 2004) data that strongly implicate a role for the ventromedial prefrontal cortex in extinction, presumably by inhibiting expression of conditioning via the amygdala.

Fear Conditioning and Anxiety Disorders

Principles of conditioning have a long precedence as explanations for anxiety disorders in general and phobias in particular (see, e.g., Mineka, 1985). There is an appealing simplicity to the argument that excessive fear of particular situations results from learned associations between these events and strong fear produced for other reasons, such as a panic-stricken companion (e.g., Mineka et al., 1984). Indeed, many people with phobias seem to recall such events as the start of their phobia (e.g., Öst & Hugdahl, 1981). Furthermore, conditioning to masked, potentially phobic stimuli that were neither recognized nor recalled has been demonstrated (Esteves, Parra, Dimberg, & Öhman, 1994; Öhman & Soares, 1998) and provides an explanation for why not all people with phobias recall a traumatic conditioning incident as the start of their fear. The principle of preparedness explains why only some types of stimuli come to elicit phobic fear and why these stimuli are dangerous in an evolutionary rather than a contemporary perspective (Seligman, 1971).

Conditioning principles may also be useful for understanding facets of PTSD, when stimuli present at the trauma subsequently elicit fear. Similarly, new knowledge about the extinction of fear responses is highly relevant for understanding the behavioral and neural principles behind treatment of phobia (e.g., Bouton, 2005; Davis & Myers, 2002; Ressler et al., 2004).

Principle 3: Effective Fear Stimuli Need Not Be Consciously Perceived

The concept of a low road that mediates information about threatening events sent to the amygdala without involving the cortex (LeDoux, 1996, 2000; Öhman, 2005) implies that it should be possible to elicit fear from stimuli that have been subjected to only a rudimentary perceptual analysis. The low-road concept therefore provides a neural underpinning for a role of automatic cognition in anxiety (Öhman, 2000c).

Autonomic Responses to Masked Stimuli

Conscious access of stimuli for processing can be controlled by masking techniques. For example, if a target picture is presented very briefly and immediately followed by another picture—this time a masking picture—research participants may report that they see only the masking picture (see Wiens & Öhman, in press).

Examining participants with an intense fear of snakes but not of spiders, or vice versa, Öhman and Soares (1994) reported that snake-fearful participants showed larger SCRs to masked pictures of snakes than to masked pictures of spiders, and vice versa for the spider-fearful participants. The fearful participants did not respond more to the fear-relevant but nonfeared stimulus (e.g., spiders for snake-fearful participants) than to neutral stimuli (e.g., flowers and mushrooms), nor did their responses to nonfeared stimuli exceed the levels of responses to any of the masked stimuli for a nonfearful control group. These results show that conscious recognition of a fear stimulus is not necessary for activating fear responses.

Ruiz-Padial, Mata, Rodriguez, Fernandez, and Vila (2005) extended this finding by demonstrating that masked presentation of feared stimuli (i.e., spiders) were as effective as nonmasked presentations in priming the cardiac defense response to an intense (105-decibel) noise. The cardiac defense response is a large, rapid heart rate acceleration (by 10–15 beats per minute) that may last for more than a minute after the presentation of an intense auditory stimulus (see Vila, 2002). This defense response was enhanced when it was preceded by a few (nonmasked or masked) presentations of a picture of a spider as opposed to a flower in spider-fearful female students, who also rated the noise as more intense after the feared pictures. These data support that masked pictures prime emotional responding to ensuing highly aversive stimuli.

Similar results to those reported by Öhman and Soares (1994) have been reported from studies of nonfearful participants who were exposed to masked pictures of snakes or spiders (Öhman & Soares, 1993) or masked angry faces (Esteves, Dimberg, & Öhman, 1994) after Pavlovian conditioning to unmasked presentations of the stimuli. Furthermore, another series of studies demonstrated reliable conditioning of SCRs to masked presentations of evolutionary fear-relevant (e.g., snakes, spiders, angry faces) but not of fear-irrelevant (e.g., flowers, mushrooms, happy faces) stimuli that were followed by an electric shock US (faces: Esteves, Dimberg, & Öhman, 1994; snakes and spiders: Öhman & Soares, 1998).

Brain Responses to Masked Stimuli

Carlsson et al. (2004) examined PET responses to masked pictures of snakes, spiders, and mushrooms in participants with specific fear. Compared with the mushroom control condition, the left amygdala was activated both by the feared (e.g., snakes) and the fear-relevant but nonfeared (e.g., spiders) pictures with no difference between the two types of fear-relevant stimuli, which suggests that that the left amygdala provided an initial assessment of the stimuli as potentially dangerous. With more processing time, amygdala activation was augmented to the feared stimulus and attenuated to the fear-relevant but nonfeared stimulus, eventually resulting in the clearly enhanced amygdala response to the former and the disappearance of the amygdala response to latter, with full conscious processing of the stimuli (Carlsson et al., 2004; see also section titled Brain Responses to Phobic Stimuli, this chapter).

Nonconscious Fear Activation and Anxiety Disorder

The fact that both the expression and learning of fear responses can be evoked by masked stimuli shows that fear responses can be automatically elicited after only a preliminary, preattentive processing of the stimuli, which bypasses higher cognition. This nonconscious, automatic nature of fear activation explains a core feature of anxiety disorders, namely, the involuntary, irrational nature of anxiety symptoms. Individuals with anxiety problems often experience themselves as helpless victims of their fear or panic. For example, because the fear response may be well on its way to full activation when people with phobias consciously realize that they are about to confront their feared object, there is little time for deliberation, leaving few options but avoidance or flight. Similarly, it provides an interesting perspective on the presumed spontaneous nature of panic attacks, which in effect may be triggered by subtle stimuli that elude conscious recognition, for example, because of their origin in obscure bodily sensations (Öhman, 2000c).

Principle 4: Fear Stimuli Guide Attention

Even though nonconscious stimuli may elicit emotions, the general principle is that emotional stimuli are focally attended, that is, they are felt in conscious awareness. An important role of the amygdala may indeed be to prioritize emotional stimuli for focal attention.

Attention Guidance by Frightening Stimuli

The masking data suggest that some fear stimuli can be preattentively, and thus very quickly, identified. Öhman, Flykt, and Esteves (2001) demonstrated fast detection of evolutionarily fear-relevant stimuli (i.e., pictures of snakes and spiders) in a complex array of stimuli (i.e., pictures of flowers and mushrooms). They used a visual search paradigm in which research participants selected for being nonfearful or specifically fearful of snakes or spiders searched for a discrepant target stimulus among different exemplars of a background category of stimuli. For example, the target could be a snake picture presented among distractor pictures of flowers. Nonfearful participants were faster to locate snakes and spiders among flowers and mushrooms than vice versa, and the detection of fear-relevant, but not of fear-irrelevant, targets was independent of the number of distractors in the display, which suggests that the detection of snakes and spiders had a preattentive origin (see, e.g., Eastwood et al., 2005). The basic finding that threatening animals are more quickly detected than plants in complex displays has been replicated in several laboratories (e.g., Flykt, 2005; Lipp, Derakshan, Waters, & Logies, 2004). Finally, there is evidence that although snake-fearful participants are as quick as the control participants in detecting spiders, they are still faster in detecting snakes, and vice versa for spider-fearful participants (Öhman, Flykt, & Esteves, 2001). In sum, not only are people generally sensitive to evolutionarily relevant fear stimuli, these detection abilities are further enhanced among participants for whom the stimuli actually elicit fear.

Research using visual search paradigms has shown that fear stimuli are automatically detected and guide attention under both a condition of top-down attentional control (Öhman, Flykt, & Esteves, 2001; Rinck, Reinecke, Ellwart, Heuer, & Becker, 2005) and in a stimulus-driven mode when unexpectedly presented among distractors while participants searched for neutral targets (Miltner, Kriechel, Hecht, Trippe, & Weiss, 2004). In addition, fear stimuli interfered with the detection of neutral targets when they served as a class of distractors to be ignored (Rinck et al., 2005). Whereas the former two effects suggest that feared stimuli are effective in *shifting* and *engaging* attention, the latter suggests, in addition, that it is more difficult to *disengage* attention from a feared stimulus (see Posner & Peterson, 1990).

Attention to Social Threat

Visual search studies that compare detection of schematic faces showing different emotions among distractor faces consistently report faster detection of threatening (angry) than friendly (happy) targets (Eastwood, Smilek, & Merikle, 2001; Fox et al., 2000; Öhman, Lundqvist, & Esteves, 2001; Tipples, Atkinson, & Young, 2002). This advantage of angry over happy face targets was obvious both with neutral and emotional distractors, and it was specific for threatening rather than negative faces (Öhman, Lundqvist, & Esteves, 2001). Furthermore, it is closely related to ratings of negative valence and high arousal of the stimuli, and the threat advantage is primarily conveyed by the upper part of the face (Lundqvist & Öhman, 2005; Tipples et al., 2002).

Examining participants who were high and low in social anxiety, Juth, Lundqvist, Karlsson, and Öhman (2005) found that those high in social anxiety detected threatening targets more accurately than friendly targets, particularly when social anxiety was elevated by an observer in the room and when the distractors were emotional (i.e., happy for angry targets, angry for happy targets). This effect, however, rather was due to poor performance with friendly targets and threatening distractors than to good performance with angry targets and happy distractors, which suggests difficulties in disengaging from threat rather than more effective shift–engagement with threatening stimuli. Eastwood et al. (2005) compared individuals diagnosed with social phobia, panic disorder, and OCD with healthy control individuals in a visual search task with schematic faces. They reported that participants with social phobia and panic disorder were unaffected by the number of distractor stimuli (varying from 7–19) to negative but not to positive faces, which suggest that the negative targets automatically "popped out" from the display. Those with OCD and the control participants did not differentiate the negative and positive targets. These findings were taken to strongly support the hypothesis that the attention of people with social phobia and with panic disorder was engaged by threatening stimuli before they were represented in awareness. Taken together, the research by Eastwood et al. (2005) and Juth et al. (2005) suggests that stimuli signifying social threat may affect both the shift–engagement and the disengagement of the attention by socially fearful individuals.

Biased Attention for Threat and the Anxiety Disorders

The research reviewed in this section shows that fear stimuli facilitate and interfere with attention depending on whether they serve as targets or distractors for a search task. This means that the attention of fearful individuals tends to be focused on fear-related stimuli in their surroundings. It is typically the person with spider phobia who detects the inconspicuous spider on the ceiling. For people preferentially attending to threatening objects in the environment, the world will appear a more dangerous and risky place than for those oblivious of such stimuli. If the bias for attending to threat is of a more general nature, it may be an important factor in the maintenance of anxiety over time, creating a vicious circle in which anxiety promotes a bias for threat, which results in more anxiety, promoting further threat bias, and so on. Furthermore, people who have difficulty disengaging attention from threatening information will be preoccupied by threat. If the threatening event that holds attention in this way is mental (i.e., a memory, a thought, or an image), this is tantamount to getting stuck on ruminative worry. Indeed, an extensive literature documents both specific and more generalized attention biases in patients with anxiety disorders (see reviews of different attentional paradigms by Mogg & Bradley, 1998, and Mathews & MacLeod, 1994; see also chap. 4, this volume).

CLINICAL IMPLICATIONS

The common thread running through our review is that contemporary knowledge of fear helps to explain several important aspects of phobias. Thus, individuals with specific phobias (or selected as highly fearful of phobic objects), and to some extent those with social phobias, show elevated autonomic responses to pictorial representation as well as to mental imagery of relevant fear scenes (e.g., Cuthbert et al., 2003; Globisch et al., 1999) when compared with both healthy control participants and individuals diagnosed with panic disorder or GAD (E. W. Cook et al., 1988; Lang et al., in press). However, individuals with PTSD show psychophysiological mobilization when imagining trauma-relevant scenes or with exposure to combat-related sights and sounds (Keane et al., 1998).

Conditioning principles, including the preparedness theory and social conditioning to a fearful model (e.g., Mineka & Cook, 1993), provide viable accounts of the etiology of specific phobia and for some aspects of social phobia as well as a convincing framework for the treatment of phobia in terms of extinction principles. An intriguing feature of the preparedness theory is that it explains the selectivity of phobias, that is, the fact that phobic stimuli tend to cluster in a meaningful way by being threatening in an evolutionary rather than a contemporary perspective. Some of the prominent symptoms of PTSD, such as flashbacks and the frightening effects of anything associated with the trauma, may also be accountable for in terms of conditioning.

Rapid recruitment of fear responses on the basis of a crude, nonconscious stimulus analysis is an important component of specific phobia, and data point in a similar direction for aspects of social phobia. Less direct evidence is available for nonconscious activation of fear physiology to discrete fear stimuli in the other anxiety disorders.

With regard to attentional function there are convincing data to suggest that individuals with specific fears or phobias for small animals (snakes, spiders) show enhanced shift and engagement of attention to the feared stimulus as well as difficulties in disengaging attention from such stimuli (e.g., Rinck et al., 2005). Individuals with social phobia may show a similar pattern even though this conclusion is supported by fewer data.

From this summary, it is clear that specific phobia is the primary fear-related disorder, which implies that phobias are controlled by the fear network of the brain. Accordingly, functional magnetic resonance imaging experiments on people with specific phobias who were exposed to pictures of the phobic object show activation of the hub of this network, the amygdala (Carlsson et al., 2004; Dilger et al., 2003; Sabatinelli et al., 2005). The data are less compelling for social phobia, partly because fewer data are available and partly because social phobia has a less distinct symptomatology than specific phobia. However, Tillfors et al. (2001) showed more amygdala activations in social phobia than in control participants when the participants were required to present a short speech for a small audience standing in front of the PET scanner. For PTSD, some studies report amygdala activation to combat-related sounds or script-driven imagery of combat (Pissiota et al., 2002; Shin et al., 2004), but taken together the results are mixed (see review by Rauch, 2003). Fredrikson and Furmark (2003) reanalyzed several PET studies from their group for relationships between self-rated fear and brain activation to fear-relevant stimuli and reported reliable relationships to right amygdala activation for individuals diagnosed with specific phobia ($r = .62$), social phobia ($r = .52$), and PTSD ($r = .78$).

As a final note, the data reviewed in this chapter document that a considerable proportion of the processing of fear stimuli can occur outside of awareness. Not only do humans unconsciously detect, recognize, and respond physiologically to fear stimuli, but our attention is also automatically shifted to and held by fearful information. Furthermore, we can even learn to fear stimuli that have been prevented from reaching conscious representation. The unconscious mechanisms we have discussed are consequences of how fear is organized and produced in the brain. This brain circuitry, furthermore, was shaped by evolutionary contingencies reflecting the ecology of early mammals, which had to survive in a world ruled by reptiles. Compared with our brains, theirs were very primitive with virtually no cortex and were thus limited foundation for cognition. But they had the motivational circuits that allowed them to navigate their world to find mates and food and avoid deadly threats. The reptilian shape of the latter may be one reason for the preponderance of reptiles in our images of evil (and the use of snakes as the prototypical fear stimulus in emotion research).

REFERENCES

American Psychiatric Association. (1994). *Diagnostic and statistical manual of mental disorders* (4th ed.). Washington, DC: Author.

Barlow, D. H. (2002). *Anxiety and its disorders: The nature and treatment of anxiety and panic* (2nd ed.). New York: Basic Books.

Bouton, M. (2005). Behavior systems and the contextual control of anxiety, fear, and panic. In L. Feldman Barrett, P. M. Niedenthal, & P. Winkielman (Eds.), *Emotion and consciousness* (pp. 205–227). New York: Guilford Press.

Brown, T. A., Campbell, L. A., Lehman, C. L., Grisham, J. R., & Mancill, R. B. (2001). Current and lifetime comorbidity of the *DSM–IV* anxiety and mood disorders in a large clinical sample. *Journal of Abnormal Psychology, 110,* 585–599.

Carlsson, K., Petersson, K. M., Lundqvist, D., Karlsson, A., Ingvar, M., & Öhman, A. (2004). Fear and the amygdala: Manipulation of awareness generates differential cerebral responses to phobic and fear-relevant (but non-feared) stimuli. *Emotion, 4,* 340–353.

Cook, E. W., III, Melamed, B. G., Cuthbert, B. N., McNeil, D. W., & Lang, P. J. (1988). Emotional imagery and the differential diagnosis of anxiety. *Journal of Consulting and Clinical Psychology, 56,* 734–740.

Cook, M., & Mineka, S. (1989). Observational conditioning of fear to fear-relevant versus fear-irrelevant stimuli in rhesus monkey. *Journal of Abnormal Psychology, 98,* 448–459.

Cook, M., & Mineka, S. (1990). Selective associations in the observational conditioning of fear in rhesus monkeys. *Journal of Experimental Psychology: Animal Behavior Processes, 16,* 372–389.

Cuthbert, B. N., Lang, P. J., Strauss, C., Drobes, D., Patrick, C. J., & Bradley, M. M. (2003). The psychophysiology of anxiety disorder: Fear memory imagery. *Psychophysiology, 40,* 407–422.

Davis, M. (1998). Are different parts of the extended amygdala involved in fear versus anxiety? *Biological Psychiatry, 44,* 1239–1247.

Davis, M., Walker, D. L., & Myers, K. M. (2002). The role of the amygdala measured with potential startle. In P. Shinnick-Gallagher, A. Pitkänen, A. Shekar, & L. Cahill (Eds.), *Annals of the New York Academy of Sciences: Vol. 985. The amygdala in brain function: Basic and clinical approaches* (pp. 218–232). New York: New York Academy of Sciences.

Davis, M., & Whalen, P. (2001). The amygdala: Vigilance and emotion. *Molecular Psychiatry, 6,* 13–34.

Dilger, S., Straube, T., Mentzel, H.-J., Fitzek, C., Reichenbach, J. R., Hecht, H., et al. (2003). Brain activation to phobia-related pictures in spider phobic humans: An event-related functional magnetic resonance imaging study. *Neuroscience Letters, 348,* 29–32.

Domjan, M. (2005). Pavlovian conditioning: A functional perspective. *Annual Review of Psychology, 56,* 179–206.

Doron, N. N., & LeDoux, J. E. (1999). Organization of projections to the lateral amygdala from auditory and visual areas of the thalamus in the rat. *Journal of Comparative Neurology, 412,* 383–409.

Eastwood, J. D., Smilek, D., & Merikle, P. M. (2001). Differential attentional guidance by unattended faces expressing positive and negative emotion. *Perception and Psychophysics, 63,* 1004–1013.

Eastwood, J. D., Smilek, D., Oakman, J. M., Farvolden, P., van Ameringen, M., Mancini, C., & Merikle, P. M. (2005). Individuals with social phobia are biased to become aware of negative faces. *Visual Cognition, 12,* 159–179.

Emery, N. J., & Amaral, D. G. (2000). The role of the amygdala in primate social cognition. In R. Lane & L. Nadel (Eds.), *The cognitive neuroscience of emotion* (pp. 156–191). New York: Oxford University Press.

Epstein, S. (1972). The nature of anxiety with emphasis upon its relationship to expectancy. In C. D. Spielberger (Ed.), *Anxiety: Current trends in theory and research* (Vol. II, pp. 292–338). New York: Academic Press.

Esteves, F., Dimberg, U., & Öhman, A. (1994). Automatically elicited fear: Conditioned skin conductance responses to masked facial expressions. *Cognition and Emotion, 8,* 393–413.

Esteves, F., Parra, C., Dimberg, U., & Öhman, A. (1994). Nonconscious associative learning: Pavlovian conditioning of skin conductance responses to masked fear-relevant facial stimuli. *Psychophysiology, 31,* 375–385.

Fanselow, M. S. (1994). Neural organization of the defensive behavior system responsible for fear. *Psychonomic Bulletin and Review, 1,* 429–438.

Fanselow, M. S., & Poulos, A. M. (2005). The neuroscience of mammalian associative learning. *Annual Review of Psychology, 56,* 207–234.

Flykt, A. (2005). Visual search with biological threat stimuli: Accuracy, reaction times, and heart rate changes. *Emotion, 5,* 349–353.

Fox, E., Lester, V., Russo, R., Bowles, R. J., Pichler, A., & Dutton, K. (2000). Facial expressions of emotion: Are angry faces detected more efficiently? *Cognition and Emotion, 14,* 61–92.

Fredrikson, M., & Furmark, T. (2003). Amygdaloid regional cerebral blood flow and subjective fear during symptom provocation in anxiety disorders. In P. Shinnick-Gallagher, A. Pitkänen, A. Shekar, & L. Cahill (Eds.), *Annals of the New York*

Academy of Sciences: Vol. 985. *The amygdala in brain function: Basic and clinical approaches* (pp. 341–347). New York: New York Academy of Sciences.

Globisch, J., Hamm, A. O., Esteves, F., & Öhman, A. (1999). Fear appears fast: Temporal course of startle reflex potentiation in animal fearful subjects. *Psychophysiology, 36,* 66–75.

Hamm, A. O., & Vaitl, D. (1996). Affective learning: Awareness and aversion. *Psychophysiology, 33,* 698–710.

Hettema, J. M., Annas, P., Neale, M. C., Kendler, K. S., & Fredrikson, M. (2003). A twin study of the genetics of fear conditioning. *Archives of General Psychiatry, 60,* 702–708.

Hollis, K. L. (1982). Pavlovian conditioning of signal-centered action patterns and autonomic behavior: A biological analysis of function. *Advances in the Study of Behavior, 12,* 1–64.

Juth, P., Lundqvist, D., Karlsson, A., & Öhman, A. (2005). Looking for foes and friends: Perceptual and emotional factors when finding a face in the crowd. *Emotion, 5,* 379–395.

Keane, T. M., Kolb, L. C., Kaloupek, D. G., Orr, S. P., Blanchard, E. B., Thomas, R. G., et al. (1998). Utility of psychophysiological measurement in the diagnosis of posttraumatic stress disorder: Results from the Department of Veterans Affairs Cooperative Study. *Journal of Consulting and Clinical Psychology, 66,* 914–923.

Lang, P. J., Bradley, M. M., & Cuthbert, B. N. (1997). Motivated attention: Affect, activation, and action. In P. J. Lang, R. F. Simons, & M. T. Balaban (Eds.), *Attention and orienting: Sensory and motivational processes* (pp. 97–136). Hillsdale, NJ: Erlbaum.

Lang, P. J., Davis, M., & Öhman, A. (2000). Fear and anxiety: Animal models and human cognitive psychophysiology. *Journal of Affective Disorders, 61,* 137–159.

Lang, P. J., McTeague, L. M., & Cuthbert, B. N. (in press). Fear startle, and the anxiety disorder spectrum. In B. Rothbaum (Ed.), *The nature and treatment of pathological anxiety: Essays in honor of Edna B. Foa.* New York: Guilford Press.

LeDoux, J. E. (1996). *The emotional brain.* New York: Simon & Schuster.

LeDoux, J. E. (2000). Emotion circuits in the brain. *Annual Review of Neuroscience, 23,* 155–184.

Lipp, O. V., Derakshan, N., Waters, A., & Logies, S. (2004). Snakes and cats in the flower bed: Fast detection is not specific to pictures of fear-relevant stimuli. *Emotion, 4,* 233–250.

Lundqvist, D., & Öhman, A. (2005). Emotion regulates attention: The relation between facial configuration, facial emotion, and visual attention. *Visual Cognition, 12,* 51–84.

Mathews, A., & MacLeod, C. (1994). Cognitive approaches to emotion and emotional disorders. *Annual Review of Psychology, 45,* 25–50.

McNally, R. J. (1987). Preparedness and phobias: A review. *Psychological Bulletin, 101,* 283–303.

Milad, M. R., Orr, S. P., Pitman, R. K., & Rauch, S. L. (2005). Context modulation of memory for fear extinction in humans. *Psychophysiology, 42,* 456–464.

Miltner, W. H. R., Kriechel, S., Hecht, H., Trippe, R., & Weiss, T. (2004). Eye movements and behavioral responses to threatening and nonthreatening stimuli during visual search in phobic and nonphobic subjects. *Emotion, 4,* 323–339.

Mineka, S. (1985). Animal models of anxiety-based disorders: Their usefulness and limitations. In A. H. Tuma & J. Maser (Eds.), *Anxiety and the anxiety disorders* (pp. 199–244). Hillsdale, NJ: Erlbaum.

Mineka, S., & Cook, M. (1993). Mechanisms involved in the observational conditioning of fear. *Journal of Experimental Psychology: General, 122,* 23–38.

Mineka, S., Davidson, M., Cook, M., & Keir, R. (1984). Observational conditioning of snake fear in rhesus monkeys. *Journal of Abnormal Psychology, 93,* 355–372.

Mineka, S., Mystkowski, J. L., Hladek, D., & Rodriguez, B. I. (1999). The effects of changing contexts on return of fear following exposure treatment for spider fear. *Journal of Consulting and Clinical Psychology, 67,* 599–604.

Mogg, K., & Bradley, B. P. (1998). A cognitive–motivational analysis of anxiety. *Behaviour Research and Therapy, 36,* 809–848.

Morris, J. S., Buchel, C., & Dolan, R. J. (2001). Parallel neural responses in amygdala subregions and sensory cortex during implicit fear learning. *NeuroImage, 13,* 1044–1052.

Morris, J. S., Öhman, A., & Dolan, R. J. (1998, June 4). Conscious and unconscious emotional learning in the human amygdala. *Nature, 393,* 467–470.

Mystkowski, J. L., Craske, M. G., & Echiverri, A. M. (2002). Treatment context and return of fear in spider phobia. *Behavior Therapy, 33,* 399–416.

Öhman, A. (2000a). Anxiety. In G. Fink (Ed.), *Encyclopedia of stress* (Vol. 1, pp. 226–231). San Diego: Academic Press.

Öhman, A. (2000b). Fear. In G. Fink (Ed.), *Encyclopedia of stress* (Vol. 2, pp. 111–116). San Diego: Academic Press.

Öhman, A. (2000c). Fear and anxiety: Clinical, evolutionary, and cognitive perspectives. In M. Lewis & J. M. Haviland (Eds.), *Handbook of emotions* (2nd ed., pp. 573–593). New York: Guilford Press.

Öhman, A. (2005). The role of the amygdala in human fear: Automatic detection of threat. *Psychoneuroendocrinology, 30,* 953–958.

Öhman, A., Dimberg, U., & Öst, L.-G. (1985). Animal and social phobias: Biological constraints on learned fear responses. In S. Reiss & R. R. Bootzin (Eds.), *Theoretical issues in behavior therapy* (pp. 123–178). New York: Academic Press.

Öhman, A., Flykt, A., & Esteves, F. (2001). Emotion drives attention: Detecting the snake in the grass. *Journal of Experimental Psychology: General, 130,* 466–478.

Öhman, A., Fredrikson, M., Hugdahl, K., & Rimmö, P. A. (1976). The premise of equipotentiality in human classical conditioning: Conditioned electrodermal responses to potentially phobic stimuli. *Journal of Experimental Psychology: General, 103,* 313–337.

Öhman, A., Hamm, A., & Hugdahl, K. (2000). Cognition and the autonomic nervous system: Orienting, anticipation, and conditioning. In J. T. Cacioppo, L. G.

Tassinary, & G. G. Berntson (Eds.), *Handbook of psychophysiology* (pp. 522–575). New York: Cambridge University Press.

Öhman, A., Lundqvist, D., & Esteves, F. (2001). The face in the crowd revisited: An anger superiority effect with schematic stimuli. *Journal of Personality and Social Psychology, 80,* 381–396.

Öhman, A., & Mineka, S. (2001). Fears, phobias, and preparedness: Toward and evolved module of fear and fear learning. *Psychological Review, 108,* 483–522.

Öhman, A., & Soares, J. J. F. (1993). On the automatic nature of phobic fear: Conditioned electrodermal responses to masked fear-relevant stimuli. *Journal of Abnormal Psychology, 102,* 1221–1132.

Öhman, A., & Soares, J. J. F. (1994). "Unconscious anxiety": Phobic responses to masked stimuli. *Journal of Abnormal Psychology, 103,* 231–240.

Öhman, A., & Soares, J. J. F. (1998). Emotional conditioning to masked stimuli: Expectancies for aversive outcomes following nonrecognized fear-relevant stimuli. *Journal of Experimental Psychology: General, 127,* 69–82.

Öhman, A., & Wiens, S. (2003). On the automaticity of autonomic responses in emotion: An evolutionary perspective. In R. J. Davidson, K. R. Scherer, & H. H. Goldsmith (Eds.), *Handbook of affective sciences* (pp. 256–275). New York: Oxford University Press.

Olsson, A., Ebert, J. P., Banaji, M. R., & Phelps, E. A. (2005, July 29). The role of social groups in the persistence of learned fear. *Science, 309,* 785–787.

Öst, L.-G., & Hugdahl, K. (1981). Acquisition of phobias and anxiety response patterns in clinical patients. *Behaviour Research and Therapy, 19,* 439–447.

Phelps, E. A., Delgado, M. R., Nearing, K. I., & LeDoux, J. E. (2004). Extinction learning in humans: Role of the amygdala and vmPFC. *Neuron, 43,* 897–905.

Pissiota, A., Frans, O., Fernandez, M., von Knorring, L., Fischer, H., & Fredrikson, M. (2002). Neurofunctional correlates of posttraumatic stress disorder: A PET symptom provocation study. *European Archives of Psychiatry and Clinical Neuroscience, 252,* 68–75.

Posner, M. I., & Peterson, S. E. (1990). The attention system of the human brain. *Annual Review of Neuroscience, 13,* 25–42.

Rachman, S. (1989). The return of fear: Review and prospect. *Clinical Psychology Review, 9,* 147–168.

Rauch, S. L. (2003). Neuroimaging and the neurobiology of anxiety disorders. In R. J. Davidson, K. R. Scherer, & H. H. Goldsmith (Eds.), *Handbook of affective sciences* (pp. 963–975). New York: Oxford University Press.

Ressler, K. J., Rothbaum, B. O., Tannenbaum, L., Anderson, P., Zimand, E., Hodges, L., & Davis, M. (2004). Cognitive enhancers as adjuncts to psychotherapy: Use of D-cycloserine in phobics to facilitate extinction of fear. *Archives of General Psychiatry, 61,* 1136–1144.

Rinck, M., Reinecke, A., Ellwart, T., Heuer, K., & Becker, E. S. (2005). Speeded detection and increased distraction in fear of spiders: Evidence from eye movements. *Journal of Abnormal Psychology, 114,* 235–248.

Ruiz-Padial, E., Mata, J. L., Rodriguez, S., Fernandez, M. C., & Vila, J. (2005). Nonconscious modulation of cardiac defense by masked phobic pictures. *International Journal of Psychophysiology, 56*, 271–281.

Sabatinelli, D., Bradley, M. M., Fitzsimmons, J. R., & Lang, P. J. (2005). Parallel amygdala and inferotemporal activation reflect emotional intensity and fear relevance. *NeuroImage, 24*, 1265–1270.

Seligman, M. E. P. (1971). Phobias and preparedness. *Behavior Therapy, 2*, 307–320.

Shi, C.-J., & Davis, M. (2001). Visual pathways involved in fear conditioning measured with fear-potentiated startle: Behavior and anatomical studies. *Journal of Neuroscience, 21*, 9844–9855.

Shin, L. M., Orr, S. P., Carson, M. A., Rauch, S. L., Macklin, M. L., Lasko, N. B., et al. (2004). Regional cerebral blood flow in the amygdala and medial prefrontal cortex during traumatic imagery in male and female Vietnam veterans with PTSD. *Archives of General Psychiatry, 61*, 168–176.

Sotres-Bayon, F., Bush, D. E. A., & LeDoux, J. E. (2004). Emotional perseveration: An update on prefrontal–amygdala interactions in fear extinction. *Learning & Memory, 11*, 525–535.

Tillfors, M., Furmark, T., Marteinsdottir, I., Fischer, H., Pissiota, A., Langstrom, B., & Fredrikson, M. (2001). Cerebral blood flow in subjects with social phobia during stressful speaking tasks: A PET study. *American Journal of Psychiatry, 158*, 1220–1226.

Tipples, J., Atkinson, A. P., & Young, A. E. (2002). The eyebrow frown: A salient social signal. *Emotion, 2*, 288–296.

Vansteenwegen, D., Hermans, D., Vervliet, B., Francken, G., Beckers, T., Baeyens, F., & Eelen, P. (2005). Return of fear in a human differential conditioning paradigm caused by a return to the original acquisition context. *Behaviour Research and Therapy, 43*, 323–336.

Vila, J. (2002). Cardiac defense and emotion: Psychophysiological and clinical implications. In L. Bäckman & C. von Hofsten (Eds.), *Psychology at the turn of the millennium* (Vol. 1, pp. 413–439). Hove, England: Psychology Press.

Walker, D. L., Toufexis, D. J., & Davis, M. (2003). Role of the bed nucleus of the stria terminalis versus the amygdala in fear, stress, and anxiety. *European Journal of Pharmacology, 463*, 199–216.

Wiens, S., & Öhman, A. (in press). Probing unconscious emotional processes: On becoming a successful masketeer. In J. Allen & J. Coan (Eds.), *Handbook of emotion elicitation and assessment*. New York: Oxford.

9

ALCOHOL AND EMOTION: INSIGHTS AND DIRECTIVES FROM AFFECTIVE SCIENCE

JOHN J. CURTIN AND ALAN R. LANG

Among the properties of alcohol that define it as a psychoactive substance are its ability to alter psychological processes that include emotion and cognition. More specifically, mood lability and affect-linked responses such as sexual and aggressive behavior figure prominently in the *Diagnostic and Statistical Manual of Mental Disorders* (4th ed., text revision; American Psychiatric Association, 2000) description of alcohol intoxication; "clinically significant . . . distress" (pp. 181–182) is a primary dimension on which individuals are expected to be high when they meet diagnostic criteria for alcohol abuse or dependence. Not surprisingly then, virtually all major theories of drinking behavior and its problems include an important role for emotional factors and affect regulation. In this connection, Goldman, Brown, and Christiansen (1987) asserted, "If any characteristic has been seen as a central, defining aspect of alcohol use, it is the presumed capacity of alcohol to alter anxiety, depression, and other moods" (p. 200). Given the pivotal position assigned to emotion in most conceptualizations of drinking behavior and alcohol use disorders, it is useful to examine how modifications of emotional response associated with alcohol intoxication

191

operate at the different levels of analysis featured in major theories of drinking-related phenomena.

Influential biological models of drinking incorporate stimulant properties of alcohol that are evident while blood-alcohol level (BAL) is low and ascending shortly after consumption begins. For example, early in an episode of intoxication, humans exhibit increased cortical activity that often correlates with self-reported experience of positive emotions such as elation and euphoria as well as increased arousal described as energy and vigor (Lukas, Mendelson, Benedikt, & Jones, 1986; Martin, Earleywine, Musty, Perrine, & Swift, 1993). Such stimulation is also apparent in the initially increased spontaneous motor activity of lower animals exposed to alcohol (Lewis & June, 1990). Furthermore, alcohol-induced psychomotor activation is associated with stimulation of brain reward systems, an effect that is important because alcohol and many other psychoactive drugs are thought to exert their addictive power through actions on dopaminergic fibers projecting into areas of the brain that mediate reinforcement, emotional state, and approach behavior (e.g., Robinson & Berridge, 2003; Wise & Bozarth, 1987). In another vein, several theorists (e.g., Baker et al., 2004; Koob & Le Moal, 2001; Solomon, 1977) have noted that certain neuroendocrine and central nervous systems are organized to oppose or suppress the unconditioned, hedonic effects of alcohol and other addictive drugs. Accordingly, with repeated alcohol or other drug use, neuroplastic adaptations in affect systems designed to support homeostasis may lead to persistent dysphoria and/or other problems with negative affect in the absence of the drug. As a result, drinking or other drug use may eventually come to be motivated more by a desire to relieve dysphoria than by a desire to attain euphoria. In any case, it is clear that modulation of emotional state is a major force driving the indulgence.

At a cognitive level of analysis, Goldman et al. (1987) concluded from their early work on alcohol expectancies that beliefs about the drug's ability to alter mood and affective reaction are both prevalent and pivotal, with arousal (activation–sedation) and affective–social valence (positive–negative) as the primary dimensions organizing alcohol expectancies (for a review, see Goldman, Del Boca, & Darkes, 1999). Furthermore, Cooper, Frone, Russell, and Mudar (1995) have demonstrated that such expectancies and the memory networks presumed to underlie them map onto important motives for drinking, with drinkers reporting that enhancement of positive emotions and/or coping with negative ones are central motives for alcohol use.

The key role of emotion in drinking and drinking problems is also suggested by the high rate of comorbidity of alcohol use disorders with other mental disorders (e.g., anxiety, mood, and antisocial personality disorders) that involve abnormalities in affective response (e.g., Regier et al., 1990) as well as in the observation that negative emotional traits and states are often associated with alcoholic relapse (e.g., Hodgins, el-Guebaly, & Armstrong, 1995). The myriad of such connections suggests that study of the alcohol–

emotion nexus is critical for understanding drinking and its attendant problems. Integration of the diverse and complex array of variables and mechanisms that comprise this connection is a challenging task. In attempting to tackle it, we maintain that psychology is the discipline perhaps best equipped to make such a contribution because of its potential to overcome artificial boundaries between biological, psychological, and social levels of analysis.

We begin with a brief review of prominent contemporary theories that specifically address alcohol–emotion relationships. We then survey the theoretical and basic research literature in affective science to develop a multidimensional, multilevel model of emotion and identify research directives that derive from this model. With this framework in mind, we turn to examination of emerging evidence regarding alcohol's effects on affective response. Because experimental analog investigations of these phenomena afford the greatest opportunity for elucidation of the mechanisms that might underlie connections between alcohol and emotion across different levels of analysis, we place our emphasis there, with special attention to one particular aspect of the relationship: the impact of acute alcohol intoxication on precisely measurable human psychophysiological response to emotional stimuli. We view a better understanding of the interplay between acute intoxication and emotional response as an essential foundation for enlightened application of affective science to the more clinical domain of chronic alcohol use disorders within which experimental administration of alcohol is proscribed for ethical reasons. Accordingly, in the concluding section, we not only seek to integrate research findings within the basic research framework of affective science to plot future research directions there but also to suggest their possible relevance to clinical science applications.

CONTEMPORARY THEORIES OF ALCOHOL–EMOTION RELATIONSHIPS: THE ROLE OF COGNITION

Although it continues to hold a central position in key theories of drinking and alcoholism, the thesis that alcohol reliably reduces stress or dampens response to threatening stimuli (e.g., Sher, 1987) is without convincing empirical support, despite more than 50 years of intense scrutiny. Even greater doubt surrounds the purported mechanism(s) that might underlie purported stress response dampening (SRD) effects (Greeley & Oei, 1999). Equivocal evidence pertinent to the SRD thesis has been interpreted to indicate that alcohol intoxication does not invariably reduce distress but rather that it does so only under certain circumstances and that it may involve mechanisms other than direct cause alone (Stritzke, Lang, & Patrick, 1996). Specifically, it has been proposed that alcohol can function as an anxiolytic through its disruption of attention to stressors and/or by altering evaluation of the aversiveness of threatening events. At least two important models consistent with this broad cognitive disruption perspective have emerged:

the attention allocation model (Steele & Josephs, 1988, 1990) and the appraisal disruption model (Sayette, 1993). Although to date the predictive scope of these cognitive mediational models has been limited to the effects of alcohol on negative affect, Sayette (1993) allowed that alcohol may differentially affect response to benign or positive information and suggested that future theorizing and research might profitably consider both phenomena. In any case, a brief overview and evaluation of the basic tenets and status of attention allocation and appraisal disruption approaches is in order.

Attention Allocation

The attention allocation model (Steele & Josephs, 1988, 1990) posits that alcohol intoxication modulates affective experience through its effects on information processing. Alcohol's pharmacological action on the brain is thought to impair cognitive activity that requires controlled, effortful processing and restrict attention to the most salient stimuli impinging on the drinker. Although near-ataxic doses of alcohol could obviously prevent concern about any stressor by disrupting all processing of it (Steele & Josephs, 1990), the means by which lower doses might reduce anxious response is not as clear. Attention allocation theory proposes that at more modest doses, psychological distress can be reduced by a complex interaction between alcohol-modified information processing and certain contextual conditions. More specifically, this interaction is thought to involve the combined effects of intoxication in reducing attentional capacity and the presence and nature of stimuli and task demands that compete for available attentional resources. To the extent that attentional resources are captured by nonaversive distractions, there is enhanced potential for anxiety reduction. In fact, if distracting activities are highly demanding, worry over an impending or concurrent negative event can be diminished even without alcohol intoxication (Josephs & Steele, 1990). Nonetheless, alcohol-induced reduction of attentional capacity is regarded as essential to the effects of intoxication on emotion, and moderate doses of alcohol are not predicted to attenuate stress responding in the absence of concurrent distractions. Indeed, proponents of this approach have speculated that drinking in the absence of stimuli that compete with a stressor for attentional resources may even increase the impact of a stressor by intensifying attention to it. Although Steele and his colleagues have provided some support for their model, unfortunately the data have generally been limited to self-reports of anxiety that do not exactly coincide with the presence of distractors (cf. Josephs & Steele, 1990; Steele, Southwick, & Pagano, 1986).

Appraisal Disruption

The appraisal disruption model shares many of the tenets of the attention allocation model, but concurrent distraction during processing of emotional information is viewed merely as one way in which appraisal of that information can be disrupted (Sayette, 1993). The appraisal disruption model more generally holds that alcohol acts pharmacologically to interfere with the initial appraisal of emotional information by constraining the spread of activation of associated information previously established in long-term memory. A central prediction of this model is that individuals who consume alcohol before they are made aware of an imminent stressor are more likely to show SRD than those already aware of the stressor at the time of drinking. In support of this hypothesis, Sayette's (1993) review of the relevant literature noted that none of the psychophysiological studies providing details of a stressor to participants before they drank found SRD effects and that several such studies actually reported an increase in physiological stress responses. However, he also acknowledged that SRD effects were not observed consistently even when participants gained detailed knowledge of the stressor after drinking. Thus, the explanation that alcohol's anxiolytic effects are mediated by disrupted appraisal of stressors remains tentative.

Despite their differences, these two recently developed cognitive models of alcohol–emotion relations converge on the view that alcohol's influence on affective reactivity, at least at the moderate BALs typically tested, probably does not occur directly at the level of subcortical motivational systems but rather through its effect on higher information processing centers that participate in "top-down" regulation of emotional response (cf. LeDoux, 1995). We believe that that adequate evaluation of this thesis depends on more sophisticated conceptual approaches to the construct of emotion and on research methods that permit exploration of the impact of alcohol on higher associative processes concurrent with refined measurement of affective response. Fortunately, recent advances in theory and methodology guiding basic affective science, including neuroscience, offer just such an opportunity to enhance our understanding of how alterations in emotional reactivity might relate to alcohol use and its associated disorders. Reference to the same literature should also ensure that neurobiologically plausible models of the mechanisms underlying alcohol's actions on emotion response are developed. Following this tack, we now move to an overview of current conceptualizations of emotion, their biological substrates, and issues critical to clarification of the alcohol–emotion nexus.

AFFECTIVE SCIENCE: THEORY, METHODS, AND DIRECTIVES FOR ALCOHOL RESEARCH

There is now considerable agreement in affective science that emotion or affective state involves central activation of "action dispositions" or response tendencies that prepare an organism to act (Davidson, Jackson, & Kalin, 2000; Izard, 1993; Lang, 1995). Theorists (e.g., Lang, 1995; Larsen &

Diener, 1992) suggest that these action dispositions are organized within a two-factor framework, defined by the primary, or what some (Lang, Bradley, & Cuthbert, 1990) have called the "strategic," affective dimensions of arousal (degree of activation) and valence (pleasant or unpleasant). Moreover, emotional response within this two-factor framework is believed to represent activity in two primary brain motivational systems: an aversive system that governs defensive reactions and an appetitive system that governs consummatory and other approach behaviors (Davidson et al., 2000; Lang, 1995).[1] Substantial evidence from both animal and human studies indicates that the amygdala is critically involved in the operations of the aversive motivation system (for a review, see Ledoux, 1996), whereas activation of the ventral striatum (including the caudate, putamen, and the nucleus accumbens) has been observed in studies that involved manipulation of positive affect or administration of primary reinforcers (for a review, see Davidson et al., 2000). Meanwhile, the ventral striatum, which is richly innervated by dopaminergic neurons from the mesolimbic dopamine system, has been implicated in incentive motivation (Berridge & Robinson, 1998) and likely plays an important role in pregoal attainment of positive affect (Davidson, 1994). Substantial evidence from lesioning, neuroimaging, and electrophysiological studies also points to various sectors of prefrontal cortex as critical to both positive and negative affect, with important distinctions between these sectors and left versus right hemispheres for processes related to emotion regulation and goal-directed behavior (Davidson et al., 2000; Harmon-Jones, 2003).

A second important theme evident in contemporary affective science is that emotional reactivity involves the interplay of primitive action mobilization systems and higher cortical processes. In other words, subcortical motivational systems can both influence and be influenced by more complex cognitive processes such as attention, perception, declarative memory, and imagery, through reciprocal connections between subcortical and cortical regions. Thus, the processes involved in emotion cannot be fully understood without reference to potentially interactive cognitive processes. In fact, there is mounting evidence to suggest that emotional phenomena involve a hierarchy of neural, sensorimotor, motivational, and cognitive processes (Izard, 1993; LeDoux, 1996). For example, information-processing theories of emotion (e.g., Bower, 1981) maintain that emotional episodes are represented in associative networks that differ from other memory structures in that they include links between cortical processing regions and the subcortical systems that govern primitive defensive and appetitive reactions (Lang, 1995).

---

[1]An alternative perspective is that positive affect (PA) and negative affect (NA) dimensions represent the primary axes of emotional space (Tellegen, 1985). This viewpoint derives from a somewhat different database involving primarily mood reports, but many contemporary theorists (Lang, 1995; Larsen & Diener, 1992) have been inclined to view it as complementary to rather than incompatible with the arousal–valence model. This view also can be reconciled with Gray's (1987) model, which includes a nonspecific arousal system that is driven by both appetitive and aversive motive systems.

In other research, interesting dissociations have been observed between the fear-conditioning capacities of animals, such that selective reductions in fear responses evoked by complex multimodal, contextual cues—but not simpler unimodal, punctuate cues—can be observed after surgical ablations of the hippocampus (Kim, Rison, & Fanselow, 1993; Phillips & LeDoux, 1992). These findings have been interpreted to mean that connections between sensory processing regions (thalamus, auditory cortex) and the amygdala are sufficient to mediate fear conditioning to simple or explicit cues but that pathways from the hippocampus to the amygdala are required for fear to be elicited by more elaborate or diffuse contextual cues that require information processing. In general, more complex emotion-eliciting stimuli or situations are more likely to entail higher order processing and top-down connections to subcortical emotion centers. Provocative data from emerging research now challenge the assumption that anxiolytic effects of alcohol are exclusively or even typically attributable to direct actions of the drug on the primary, subcortical motivational (i.e., approach or defensive) systems. Instead, evidence points to alcohol's impact on higher level cognitive functions—including attention, appraisal, and declarative memory—that normally participate in and mediate affective processing and expression (Sayette, 1993; Steele & Josephs, 1990; Stritzke et al., 1996).

A third theme highlighted by contemporary affective science concerns the need to consider the temporal nature of emotional processes. Emotions in general, and their psychophysiological manifestations in particular, are dynamic events, and thus the time frame in which they are considered is important. Davidson and his colleagues (Davidson, 1998; Davidson et al., 2000) have been influential in directing attention to the chronometry of emotional response in the study of affective contributions to psychopathology. More specifically, they argued that emotional response is a dynamic phenomenon and that it can be characterized by possibly independent components including tonic level, threshold to respond, initial peak amplitude, risk time to peak, and recovery time (for more detail, see Davidson, 1998). Each of these components of emotional response may represent the action of different underlying neurobiological mechanisms, with variations in some, but perhaps not others, particularly important to understanding acute alcohol challenge effects as well as their relevance to alcohol use disorders. In this connection, Levenson (1987) noted that the grain of physiological measurement in alcohol studies has often been too coarse (20-second to 30-second averages) to allow precise tracking of the effects of alcohol on emotional processes as they unfold over time, a shortcoming that still characterizes much of the alcohol challenge research addressing emotional response.

Finally, affective scientists have highlighted the need to differentiate initial emotional response from the processes involved in subsequent regulation of emotion (Davidson, 1998; Gross, 1999). The latter includes a broad array of both automatic and volitional processes that are designed to enhance, suppress, or maintain the strength of an initial emotional response. Influences of these regulatory processes may be observed in one or more temporal components of emotional response (e.g., duration–recovery, but not initial response intensity). Given that affect regulation is held by many addiction theorists (e.g., Baker et al., 2004; Cooper et al., 1995; Koob & Le Moal, 2001) to be a primary motive for the use of drugs, including alcohol, measurement with sufficient temporal resolution to parse these components is important.

In sum, affective science directs us to (a) examine the entire range of the emotional valence dimension (i.e., both negative and positive emotions) as well as emotional arousal, with explicit reference to their neurological substrates; (b) consider the dynamic interplay between cognitive and affective processes; and (c) use measures with adequate precision and temporal resolution to parse emotional response into its constituent components and effectively separate emotional response from processes that regulate emotion. The following section reviews an emerging database that shows promising signs of progress toward embracing these directives.

ALCOHOL AND THE MULTIDIMENSIONAL–MULTILEVEL FRAMEWORK OF EMOTION

Alcohol and Arousal

Almost a century ago, Smith (1922) used the "psychogalvanic reflex" to measure the intensity of emotional arousal in the investigation of the effects of alcohol on reactions to emotional stimuli. He reported that alcohol diminished electrodermal response to affect-laden words in an association test but hastened to add that this observation revealed little about the specific valence of emotion involved. In other words, the observed changes were understood to reflect primarily the intensity of nonspecific arousal that might be associated with any kind of emotional excitement, positive or negative. In the ensuing decades, Smith's finding of alcohol-attenuated electrodermal response to affective stimuli was often replicated, using both verbal (e.g., Lienert & Traxel, 1959) and sensory (e.g., Carpenter, 1957) stimuli, but his cautions about their interpretation have gone largely unheeded.

The classic critique of activation theory by Lacey (1967) was important in further exposing the liabilities of heavy reliance on the arousal construct in descriptions of complex physiological response patterns, including those pertinent to emotion. He derived this conclusion from evidence that (a) somatic and behavioral arousal do not necessarily covary, particularly after pharmacological manipulations; (b) different physiological indices of activation are dissociable; and (c) specific situations prompt unique patterns of physiological response, depending on the nature of the stimuli, their context, and task requirements. The implications of Lacey's theoretical advances for the study of alcohol–emotion relationships were recognized by Naitoh (1972), who urged researchers to move beyond simplistic, activation-based studies of stress reduction, toward development of a perspective permitting exploration of possible connections between alcohol-induced physiological arousal and the experience of "pleasant drunkenness." Naitoh proposed that interpretation of alcohol-mediated changes in the relatively ambiguous, altered state of arousal occasioned by intoxication may be either pleasant or unpleasant depending on the context.

The best alcohol–emotion experiments of the 1980s (e.g., Levenson, Sher, Grossman, Newman, & Newlin, 1980) advanced the assessment of the arousal dimension of emotion through the simultaneous and continuous psychophysiological measurement of multiple aspects of autonomic reactivity (e.g., heart rate, blood pressure, and skin conductance), thereby allowing for control of baseline differences and finer grained analyses of response patterns and changes over time. Although the initial enthusiasm these experiments generated by suggesting the possibility that systematic individual variation in alcohol-induced SRD represented a risk factor for problem drinking (e.g., Levenson, Oyama, & Meek, 1987; Peterson & Pihl, 1990; Sher & Levenson, 1982) was later tempered by failures to replicate (e.g., Sayette, Breslin, Wilson, & Rosenblum, 1994; Sher & Walitzer, 1986), they left their mark on measurement strategy.

Despite these methodological improvements, however, alcohol–emotion research stagnated in its maintenance of a relatively narrow focus on the conditions under which alcohol intoxication influences the impact of anxiety-provoking stimuli or stressful situations on nonspecific psychophysiological measures of autonomic arousal and self-reports (cf. Sayette, 1993; Sher, 1987). Persistence in this approach precluded capitalization on important advances in the conceptualization of emotion, including recognition and measurement of its valence dimension and attention to how alcohol effects may be mediated by cortical–subcortical interactions and/or cognitive processes that change as a function of acute intoxication. Fortunately, recent work illustrates the potential benefits of application of more sophisticated conceptualization and measurement of emotion for understanding how alcohol affects it.

Alcohol and Emotional Valence

Although self-report measures of emotional valence have been a staple of emotion research for years, these measures are suboptimal because they are subject to distortion by experimental demand and intentional dissimulation. Such limitations provided a major impetus for the development of psychophysiological indices of emotional valence tied closely to underlying action dispositions and having limited vulnerability to spontaneous efforts at volitional control (see chap. 3, this volume). In particular, alcohol research has begun to profit from the application of such methods that include evaluation of facial expression via assessment of electromyographic activity and inference of affective disposition from startle response patterns. Increases in electromyogram (EMG) activity over the corrugator supercilium muscle that produces frowning and increases over the zygomaticus major muscle involved in smiling have consistently covaried with the unpleasantness and pleasantness of emotions, respectively (for a review, see Tassinary & Cacioppo, 1992). In addition, the magnitude of the startle response to a sudden, intense stimulus "probe" (e.g., a burst of white noise) has been shown reliably to reflect the valence of emotional state in that startle reactivity is augmented if the probe occurs in the context of an unpleasant stimulus and attenuated if the probe coincides with a pleasant stimulus (Lang, 1995; Lang et al., 1990).

Direct Effects of Alcohol on Emotional Valence

Capitalizing on these developments in the measurement of emotional valence, Stritzke, Patrick, and Lang (1995) conducted the first alcohol challenge experiment to manipulate positive as well as negative affect in a design based explicitly on a multidimensional (arousal–valence) model of emotion. Participants received either a moderate dose of alcohol or no alcohol before viewing pleasant, neutral, and unpleasant pictures, with the affect-laden images matched for arousal. Eyeblink startle response was used to index the valence of the emotional response evoked by the slides. Changes in emotional valence were also assessed using EMG recording of corrugator ("frown") activity, and skin conductance responses were assessed to index of physiological arousal. Results indicated that although alcohol diminished the overall magnitude of both startle and phasic skin conductance response—regardless of the valence of the foreground images—it did not disturb the normal affective modulation of startle. In other words, regardless of the general reduction in startle magnitude observed in the alcohol group during picture viewing, intoxicated subjects and no-alcohol control participants showed similar, higher magnitude startle blinks to probes delivered during aversive images and lower magnitude blink reactions to probes during pleasant images, both relative to neutral.[2] A comparable valence effect (i.e., unpleasant > neutral

___

[2]It is worth noting in this context that the general suppressant effect of alcohol on overall startle response reactivity has been known for some time (e.g., Greenberg & Carpenter, 1957). In addition to the recent human eyeblink studies cited in the following sections (Curtin, Lang, Patrick, & Stritzke, 1998; Curtin, Patrick, Lang, Cacioppo, & Birbaumer, 2001; Donohue et al., in press; Stritzke et al., 1995), alcohol challenge has also been shown to substantially reduce general startle reactivity, as indexed by whole-body motor reactions, in lower animals (e.g., Pohorecky, Cagan, Brick, & Jaffe, 1976; Rassnick, Koob, & Geyer, 1992). However, the startle response is a reflex, and care must be taken not to confuse this effect on overall startle response reactivity with either the affective modulation of startle or traditional sympathetic nervous system indices (e.g., skin conductance response) typically linked to the arousal component of emotional state. Although it is possible that a general decrease in startle associated with rising BAL reflects a reduction in activity at the level of the

> pleasant) was also observed for corrugator EMG reactions in both beverage groups. These results run counter to the SRD perspective (Sher, 1987), which would predict that alcohol should selectively block negative reactions to aversive images.

The startle response was also used in two more recent studies (Curtin et al., 1998, 2001) examining the effect of moderate doses of alcohol on negative affective reactions during exposure to explicit threat. In Curtin et al. (1998), sober and moderately intoxicated participants were presented with a series of 2-minute light cues denoting either (a) the possibility that an electric shock could be delivered at any instant (red light = threat), or (b) that no shock would be administered (green light = safe). Startle response was assessed intermittently during these cueing periods. In addition, autonomic activity (skin conductance and heart rate), and corrugator EMG were monitored throughout the experiment. Results indicated that the presence (vs. absence) of shock threat evoked predictable increases in autonomic arousal, in EMG indices of facial frowning, and in startle response magnitude. However, there was no main effect of alcohol on magnitude of negative affective response across these various indices of affective valence. Similarly, in a conceptual replication that included numerous brief (approximately 2-second) exposures to periods of electric shock threat, Curtin et al. (2001) demonstrated that *fear-potentiated startle* (FPS; i.e., the elevation of startle responses observed during the presence of a fear or threat cue vs. during its absence) was not altered by a moderate dose of alcohol when the threat cue was the only focus of attention.

Taken together, these three well-controlled experiments failed to support the notion that alcohol has a direct, suppressive effect on negative affective response. However, one potentially important limitation of this series of studies was neglect of possible dose–response effects. In each of the studies (Curtin et al., 1998, 2001; Stritzke et al., 1995), all participants in the alcohol condition attained only a single, moderate BAL. This was unfortunate because some evidence (e.g., Sher & Walitzer, 1986; Stewart, Finn, & Pihl, 1992) suggests that SRD effects may be more reliably observed at higher alcohol doses.

To address this limitation, Donohue, Curtin, Patrick, and Lang (in press) examined emotional reactivity to the same pleasant, unpleasant, and neutral pictures used in Stritzke et al. (1995) but presented them to participants for whom beverage conditions resulted in zero, low, moderate, or high BALs. The illuminating result emerging from this study was that, as predicted by the SRD model, alcohol selectively diminished the startle response index of negative affective responding to unpleasant images but only when responses

---

nucleus reticularis pontis caudalis, which, in turn, could reflect an overall reduction in arousal state—that is, nucleus reticularis pontis caudalis activity may indeed covary with general brainstem reticular activation—but this has yet to be confirmed.

in the moderate- and high-BAL groups were contrasted with those in the zero- and low-BAL groups. Startle response inhibition to pleasant images was unaffected by any BAL. To our knowledge, this was the first experiment to demonstrate a selective SRD effect—albeit one confined to higher BALs—using psychophysiological methods specifically designed to index the valence of emotional response.

Possible Cognitive Mediation of Alcohol–Emotion Relationships

Our earlier summary of contemporary models of alcohol–emotion relations (i.e., attention allocation and appraisal disruption) indicates a growing consensus that at least under certain circumstances and/or at certain BALs, alcohol might exert its effect on emotional responding indirectly through its alteration of cognitive function. Two of the experiments described earlier (Curtin et al., 1998, 2001) incorporated design features to evaluate this potential role of cognitive mechanisms in the effects of alcohol on emotional response. They provided converging evidence in support of this thesis. Recall that in Curtin et al. (1998) participants were exposed to alternating 2-minute periods involving the presence or absence of a shock threat, with red or green lights, respectively, serving as cues for the two types of blocks. In addition to this threat manipulation, during half of the cue periods of each type, intermittent presentations of pleasant pictures were made via a large monitor positioned immediately in front of participants. These presentations were intended to compete with the threat-cue signal lights for participants' attention. Comparative analysis of the FPS index of emotional response across all possible combinations of beverage, threat, and pleasant picture conditions revealed that FPS was attenuated by alcohol only when pleasant picture presentations competed with threat signals for participant attention. When there were no pleasant pictures distractors, intoxicated participants showed the same level of FPS as sober participants, whose FPS reactions were unaffected by picture presentations. The fact that FPS was significantly reduced only among intoxicated participants distracted from their threatened state by pleasant pictures is consistent with the notion that alcohol's effect on negative emotional response can be mediated by its effect on cognitive functioning because it was the divided attention occasioned by the combination threat–picture condition that involved the greatest cognitive demand, particularly in terms of simultaneous allocation of attention to the processing of competing stimuli. However, without an online measure of alcohol-induced changes in the processing of threat cues, one cannot be altogether confident of just what it was that captured participants' attention. To clarify this, a direct measure the cognitive processing of threat cues concurrent with the measurement of emotional response to them would be needed.

To address this issue, the Curtin et al. (2001) experiment incorporated simultaneous measurement of threat-cue processing, using event-related potentials (ERPs), and of fear responding, using FPS. Sober and moderately intoxicated participants viewed compound stimuli that varied across two dimensions (color and semantic category) in two task conditions. In a threat-focused condition, participants attended only to the semantic category of the word (words came from two semantic categories: animals and body parts), which indicated the threat of administration of electric shock (electric shocks followed a subset of words from one semantic category). Alternatively, in a divided-attention condition, participants were aware of the threat associated with the semantic category of each word but were instructed to attend to the color of the word (red or green) and make a speeded button-press response when words appeared in green type but withhold this response when the word appeared in red. Thus, in the divided-attention condition, the semantic category indicating shock threat was made peripheral or task irrelevant. Results of this study replicated the pattern of affective responding observed in Curtin et al. (1998), with alcohol selectively reducing FPS only in the divided-attention condition in which attention to both the threat parameters and task demands apparently exceeded the cognitive capacity of intoxicated participants. However, the most novel and compelling aspect of this study resided in its online measurement of cognitive processing.

The use of ERPs in the Curtin et al. (2001) experiment afforded an opportunity to evaluate directly the impact of alcohol intoxication on threat-cue processing. In general, the magnitude of the P3 component of the ERP is larger in connection with important stimuli, that is, stimuli that capture or focus attention. Consistent with this principle, P3 was comparably enhanced by the presentation of threat words in the threat-focused condition for both sober and intoxicated participants. Sober participants also displayed comparably enhanced P3 to threat words in the divided-attention condition. However, P3 enhancement to threat words was significantly reduced for intoxicated participants in the divided-attention condition. This last outcome indicates that intoxicated individuals exhibited decrements in threat-cue processing and that the level of FPS associated with threat cues was diminished when participants' alcohol-impaired cognitive capacity was stretched beyond its limits by a task that divided their attention and rendered them less able to process threat cues. In contrast, the responses of sober subjects were not significantly affected by cognitive demands; they apparently had sufficient cognitive capacity to process threat while also performing the assigned reaction-time task. These results are consistent with higher cortical mediation of alcohol's effects on fear and illustrate more broadly how disruption of a cognitive process can lead to alterations in emotional reactivity and adaptive behavior. They also encourage use of the general strategy of simultaneous measurement of cognitive and emotional processes as a promising approach applicable to the broader study of alcohol effects on both positive and negative emotion.

THEORETICAL INTEGRATION, FUTURE RESEARCH, AND POSSIBLE APPLICATIONS

Affective Science Revisited

Our thesis throughout this chapter has been that research on alcohol and emotional response can profit from a conceptualization of emotion that recognizes its multidimensional, multilevel nature. In this connection, we have argued that until recently the valence dimension of emotion has been largely ignored or inadequately represented in alcohol–affect research and noted that this limitation manifests itself in two ways. First, much of the relevant literature has failed to address the possible impact of alcohol on positive emotion altogether, let alone examine its effects across the entire range of valence within the same study. Second, only the rare experiment has moved beyond self-report measures of emotional valence to include specific psychophysiological indices such as startle response, facial EMG, or frontal cortical electroencephalographic (EEG) asymmetries to tap this critical dimension. In addition, although a number of contemporary theories hold that alcohol's effect on emotion, particularly at low to moderate BALs, may depend on its compromise of cognitive capacity and concurrent demands on it, this hypothesis has yet to be subjected to much rigorous study using appropriate designs and measures.

Mechanisms of Action for Alcohol

Application of a multidimensional, multilevel conceptualization of emotion provides a useful framework for interpretation of the extant literature on alcohol and affective response and for generation and evaluation of further hypotheses. Our review of available evidence suggests that for intoxication within the range normally experienced by humans, the influence that alcohol exerts on emotional response might involve at least two mechanisms, depending on BAL. When BALs are relatively high, alcohol appears to selectively dampen defensive responding to unpleasant stimuli via a rather direct and specific mechanism, regardless of context (Donohue et al., in press; Sher & Walitzer, 1986; Stewart et al., 1992). Donohue et al. (in press) offered perhaps the most convincing demonstration of this by using affect-modulated startle as a key measure of emotional response, thereby providing an arguably more direct index of activation of the subcortical components of the defensive motivational system, including the amygdala, than is available in the typical SRD study. This is important, considering evidence reviewed by McBride (2002) indicating that intermediate to high doses of ethanol (but not low doses) produce selective activation of GABAergic neurons in the central nucleus of the amygdala (CeA) in rats, as indexed by changes in levels of c-fos, a biochemical marker of neuronal activity (Morales, Criado, Sanna, Henriksen, & Bloom, 1998). Because gamma-aminobutyric acid (GABA) is the major inhibitory neurotransmitter in the central nervous system, this suggests that increased GABA activity in the CeA, occasioned by higher doses of alcohol, constitutes a plausible mechanism underlying the decreased negative emotional response observed for startle and accounts for the depressant and anxiolytic effects associated with elevated BALs (cf. Fromme & D'Amico, 1999). This interpretation also resonates with results from studies showing that animals exposed to classic approach–avoidance conflict manipulations tend to exhibit reduced inhibition by fear and hence resolve conflicts in the approach direction (cf. Gray, 1987).

In contrast to the apparently direct effect of alcohol on negative emotions observed at BALs above a certain threshold, the anxiolytic effects of alcohol at low to moderate BALs appear to depend on cognitive mediation. Curtin et al. (1998, 2001) provided convincing evidence that the ability of modest alcohol intoxication to attenuate FPS was confined to contexts in which attention to threat faced competition from other salient stimuli or prioritized task demands within individuals whose cognitive processing capacity had been compromised by intoxication. In these same studies, a significant level of FPS—equivalent to that observed in sober participants—was evident among intoxicated participants when the context was devoid of stimuli that might compete for attention to threat.

Also relevant here is the work of Melia, Ryabinin, Corodimas, Wilson, and LeDoux (1996) showing "dissociations" in the fear conditioning of animals as a function of alcohol administration. These investigators examined explicit cue versus contextual cue fear conditioning in rats that were administered low and moderate doses of ethanol, with behavioral freezing used as an index of fear. They reported that alcohol did not affect conditioning to tone cues explicitly paired with the shock, but it blocked acquisition of the association between the situational context (novel cage) and aversive stimulation (shock). These findings by Melia et al. (1996) are consistent with the hypothesis that low to moderate doses of alcohol can reduce sensitivity to fear cues by interfering with higher order processing. As described earlier, disruption of hippocampal functioning is one potential mechanism by which alcohol might produce such effects. Although apparently not essential to explicit fear learning, input from the hippocampus to the amygdala is clearly critical for contextual fear learning (LeDoux, 1995). Because alcohol has well-documented effects on a variety of cognitive functions, including vigilance and attention (Casbon, Curtin, Lang, & Patrick, 2003; Curtin & Fairchild, 2003; Holloway, 1994), that reflect its impact on neural systems probably not intimately involved with the hippocampus, it seems likely that other systems are involved as well. For instance, Davis, Walker, and Lee (1999) suggested that the bed nucleus of the stria terminalis comprises the basic substrate of an anxiety system analogous to, but functionally distinct from, the amygdaloid fear system. This could represent another avenue by which alcohol exerts its effects on emotional response.

Promising Avenues for Further Research

The approach to alcohol–emotion research we have promoted encourages consideration of dimensions, variables, and measures often neglected in prior studies of these phenomena: the joint consideration of the valence and intensity of emotion-eliciting cues, the context of affective stimulation, the brain systems and cognitive processes required to register and process cues of different sorts, and the dynamic nature of affective responding. A few of the particularly salient research questions and promising directions that emanate from a strategy that addresses this neglect are outlined here, together with some brief suggestions about what can be learned from the affective science of alcohol and emotion and how it might be applied to clinical science problems.

Specification of the positive emotional concomitants of drinking has remained an elusive goal, probably in part because of the inadequacies of methods applied to the study of such effects so far. Thus, one high-priority starting point should be development and/or utilization of alternative means to phasically manipulate positive affect. In particular, manipulations of pregoal-attainment positive affect (Davidson et al., 2000) that occurs simultaneously with strong approach motivation have yet to be used in alcohol research and may yield interesting results, especially given observed effects of alcohol on pregoal states surrounding, for example, sexual and aggressive behavior. EEG asymmetry measures that represent affective valence may prove to be particularly useful indices in such studies (for a review, see Harmon-Jones, 2003).

Further tests of the cognitive mediation of alcohol effects on both positive and negative emotion should be conducted. Such tests can follow from two independent methodological approaches. First, additional studies that simultaneously measure both affective and cognitive processing of emotionally evocative stimuli are clearly warranted, given the strong evidence for cognitive–emotional interactions. Curtin et al. (2001) can serve as a model for how to operationalize simultaneous, online assessment of both constructs to test critical predictions for cognitive models of alcohol effects. Second, there is a need to develop manipulations specifically designed to dissociate various emotion processing pathways, both direct and indirect (LeDoux, 1995). For example, comparisons of explicit versus contextual fear conditioning in humans as a function of alcohol intoxication are of interest, particularly given that surgical ablation of the hippocampus in lower animals reduced fear response to complex multimodal, contextual cues but not to simpler explicit cues (Kim et al., 1993; Phillips & LeDoux, 1992). Such results have obvious implications for the work of Melia et al. (1996), which revealed that contextual, but not explicit, fear responding in animals was reduced by low to moderate doses of alcohol. Grillon and Davis (1997) developed an experimental paradigm to examine contextual fear responding in humans using FPS. In applying it to alcohol research, a strong prediction would be that moderate doses of alcohol should eliminate the context-related enhancement of startle but should have no effect on startle potentiation associated with simpler explicit threat cues. Such a result would provide convincing evidence of a differential impact of alcohol as a function of the complex cognitive processes involved in context cueing.

Still another promising avenue would be systematic examination of alcohol effects on the constituent components of emotional response (e.g., response threshold, peak intensity, duration, subsequent regulatory processes). To this end, measures with precise temporal resolution, such as the startle response, could be combined with innovative manipulations to probe the dynamic nature of emotional response. For example, in research on the affective concomitants of tobacco withdrawal, Hogle and Curtin (in press) used FPS to examine both the initial intensity of affective responding and the duration of the affective response to stressors in nicotine-deprived smokers. Of special interest here was the fact that tobacco withdrawal did not appear to alter the initial intensity of response but did delay recovery from the stress, suggesting that a disruption of homeostatic processes related to emotion regulation was at work. In other research, Jackson et al. (2003) combined EEG asymmetry and startle response measures to demonstrate that individual differences in frontal cortical asymmetries predict the persistence but not the initial intensity of affective response to emotionally evocative images. Jackson, Malmstadt, Larson, and Davidson (2000) have also developed an experimental task that dissociates emotional response from volitional emotion regulatory processes using the startle response (for application of this task to study emotion regulation during tobacco withdrawal, see Piper & Curtin, 2006). Similar methods could be fruitfully applied to the study of alcohol challenge effects. Moreover, attention to constituent components of emotion might help reduce the equivocation so often associated with the findings from less refined research approaches and thus better inform us of the mechanisms underlying alcohol effects.

Clinical Implications

At first glance, it might not appear that research addressing the acute effects of alcohol on emotional response in relatively normal drinkers could do much to inform clinical science. However, several insights that can be derived from the foregoing review seem worthy of mention. First, there can be little doubt that alcohol expectancies and motives, the psychiatric disorders comorbid with alcohol use disorders, and the antecedents and consequences of nonproblem and problem drinking alike are intimately related to emotion. This fact alone should make understanding of the nature and mechanisms of alcohol–emotion relationships of interest to clinicians. Appreciation of the role of cognitive processes in the dynamic interplay between drinking and affect seems particularly important. Consider, for example, the forces at work in decision making about initiation and continuation of a drinking episode for the typical alcoholic. Often such individuals start with ambivalence: They are aware from experience that drinking can have immediate and simple reinforcing (euphoric, anxiolytic, etc.) emotional effects, but they also know that drinking often has more delayed and complex punishing effects (impaired role performance, conflicts, illness or injury, etc.) with attendant aversive emotions. Particularly in the absence of alternative coping responses, ongoing or anticipated distress can create pressure to resolve such ambivalence by indulgence in the immediate gratification expected from drinking. As we have seen, however, even modest intoxication compromises cognitive capacity, leading to its association with shallower and more simplistic thinking and a tendency to confine focus to only the most salient aspects of the immediate situation. This concurrently serves to decrease access to more distal concerns about adverse consequences that might otherwise restrain further drinking, hence precipitating an elevated risk for just the sorts of outcomes that define alcohol use disorders. Greater awareness of such processes could facilitate refinement of relapse prevention (Marlatt & Donovan, 2005) and other interventions designed to address drinking problems.

CONCLUSION

The first wave of empirical evidence yielded by psychophysiological studies designed to be sensitive to emotional valence suggests that alcohol can act both directly on subcortical affect systems and indirectly via acute impairment of cognitive functioning. Further, the relative contribution of each of these effects on the emotional experience of the individual is likely interwoven with variations related to BAL, contextual factors, and individual differences. These results and their implications provide ample reason to continue to develop and use a multidimensional, multilevel framework for conceptualizing the alcohol–emotion nexus and pursuing its implications for drinking and alcohol-related problems.

REFERENCES

American Psychiatric Association. (2000). *Diagnostic and statistical manual of mental disorders* (4th ed., text revision). Washington, DC: Author.

Baker, T. B., Piper, M. E., McCarthy, D. E., Majeskie, M. R., & Fiore, M. C. (2004). Addiction motivation reformulated: An affective processing model of negative reinforcement. *Psychology Review, 111,* 33–51.

Berridge, K. C., & Robinson, T. E. (1998). What is the role of dopamine in reward: Hedonic impact, reward learning, or incentive salience? *Brain Research Reviews*, *29*, 309–369.

Bower, G. H. (1981). Mood and memory. *American Psychologist*, *36*, 129–148.

Carpenter, J. A. (1957). Effects of alcoholic beverages on skin conductance. *Quarterly Journal of Studies on Alcohol*, *18*, 1–18.

Casbon, T. S., Curtin, J. J., Lang, A. R., & Patrick, C. J. (2003). Deleterious effects of alcohol intoxication: Diminished cognitive control and its behavioral consequences. *Journal of Abnormal Psychology*, *112*, 476–487.

Cooper, M. L., Frone, M. R., Russell, M., & Mudar, P. (1995). Drinking to regulate positive and negative moods: A motivational model of alcohol use. *Journal of Personality and Social Psychology*, *69*, 990–1005.

Curtin, J. J., & Fairchild, B. A. (2003). Alcohol and cognitive control: Implications for regulation of behavior during response conflict. *Journal of Abnormal Psychology*, *112*, 424–436.

Curtin, J. J., Lang, A. R., Patrick, C. J., & Stritzke, W. G. K. (1998). Alcohol and fear-potentiated startle: The role of competing cognitive demands in the stress-reducing effects of intoxication. *Journal of Abnormal Psychology*, *107*, 547–565.

Curtin, J. J., Patrick, C. J., Lang, A. R., Cacioppo, J. T., & Birbaumer, N. (2001). Alcohol affects emotion through cognition. *Psychological Science*, *12*, 527–531.

Davidson, R. J. (1994). Asymmetric brain function, affective style and psychopathology: The role of early experience and plasticity. *Development and Psychopathology*, *6*, 741–758.

Davidson, R. J. (1998). Affective style and affective disorders: Perspectives from affective neuroscience. *Cognition and Emotion*, *12*, 307–330.

Davidson, R. J., Jackson, D. C., & Kalin, N. H. (2000). Emotion, plasticity, context, and regulation: Perspectives from affective neuroscience. *Psychological Bulletin*, *126*, 890–909.

Davis, M., Walker, D. L., & Lee, Y. (1999). Neurophysiology and neuropharmacology of startle and its affective modification. In M. E. Dawson & A. M. Schell (Eds.), *Startle modification: Implications for neuroscience, cognitive science, and clinical science* (pp. 95–113). New York: Cambridge University Press.

Donohue, K. F., Curtin, J. J., Patrick, C. J., & Lang, A. R. (in press). Alcohol and emotion: Potential dose effects. *Emotion*.

Fromme, K., & D'Amico, E. J. (1999). In K. E. Leonard & H. T. Blane (Eds.), *Psychological theories of drinking and alcoholism* (2nd ed.). New York: Guilford Press.

Goldman, M. S., Brown, S. A., & Christiansen, B. A. (1987). Expectancy theory: Thinking about drinking. In H. Blane & K. Leonard (Eds.), *Psychological theories of drinking and alcoholism* (pp. 181–226). New York: Guilford Press.

Goldman, M. S., Del Boca, F. K., & Darkes, J. (1999). Alcohol expectancy theory: The application of cognitive neuroscience. In K. Leonard & H. Blane (Eds.), *Psychological theories of drinking and alcoholism* (2nd ed., pp. 203–246). New York: Guilford Press.

Gray, J. (1987). *The psychology of fear and stress* (2nd ed.). Cambridge, England: Cambridge University Press.

Greeley, J., & Oei, T. (1999). Alcohol and tension reduction. In K. Leonard & H. Blane (Eds.), *Psychological theories of drinking and alcoholism* (2nd ed., pp. 14–53). New York: Guilford Press.

Greenberg, L., & Carpenter, J. (1957). The effect of alcoholic beverages on skin conductance and emotional tension: I. Wine, whiskey and alcohol. *Quarterly Journal of Studies on Alcohol, 18*, 190–204.

Grillon, C., & Davis, M. (1997). Fear-potentiated startle conditioning in humans: Explicit and contextual cue conditioning following paired versus unpaired training. *Psychophysiology, 34*, 451–458.

Gross, J. J. (1999). Emotion regulation: Past, present, future. *Cognition and Emotion, 13*, 551–573.

Harmon-Jones, E. (2003). Clarifying the emotive functions of asymmetrical frontal cortical activity. *Psychophysiology, 40*, 838–848.

Hodgins, D., el-Guebaly, N., & Armstrong, S. (1995). Prospective and retrospective reports of mood states before relapse to substance use. *Journal of Consulting and Clinical Psychology, 63*, 400–407.

Hogle, J., & Curtin, J. (in press). Tobacco withdrawal and negative affect: Sex differences in psychophysiological measures of affective response. *Psychophysiology.*

Holloway, F. (1994). *Low-dose alcohol effects on human behavior and performance: A review of post-1984 research* (Technical Report No. DOT/FAA/AM-94/24). Washington, DC: Office of Aviation Medicine.

Izard, C. E. (1993). Four systems for emotion activation: Cognitive and noncognitive processes. *Psychological Review, 100*, 68–90.

Jackson, D. C., Malmstadt, J. R., Larson, C. L., & Davidson, R. J. (2000). Suppression and enhancement of emotional responses to unpleasant pictures. *Psychophysiology, 37*, 515–522.

Jackson, D. C., Mueller, C. J., Dolski, I., Dalton, K. M., Nitschke, J. B., Urry, H. L., et al. (2003). Now you feel it, now you don't: Frontal brain electrical asymmetry and individual differences in emotion regulation. *Psychological Science, 14*, 612–617.

Josephs, R. A., & Steele, C. M. (1990). The two faces of alcohol myopia: Attentional mediation of psychological stress. *Journal of Abnormal Psychology, 99*, 115–126.

Kim, J., Rison, R., & Fanselow, M. (1993). Effects of amygdala, hippocampus, and peri-aqueductal gray lesions on short- and long-term contextual fear. *Behavioral Neuroscience, 107*, 1093–1098.

Koob, G. F., & Le Moal, M. (2001). Drug addiction, dysregulation of reward, and allostasis. *Neuropsychopharmacology, 24*, 97–129.

Lacey, J. (1967). Somatic response patterning and stress: Some revisions of activation theory. In M. Appley & R. Turnbull (Eds.), *Psychological stress: Issues in research* (pp. 14–37). New York: Appleton.

Lang, P. J. (1995). The emotion probe: Studies of motivation and attention. *American Psychologist, 50*, 372–385.

Lang, P. J., Bradley, M. M., & Cuthbert, B. N. (1990). Emotion, attention, and the startle reflex. *Psychological Review, 97,* 377–395.

Larsen, R. J., & Diener, E. (1992). Promises and problems with the circumplex model of emotion. In M. S. Clark (Ed.), *Review of personality and social psychology* (Vol. 13). Newbury Park, CA: Sage.

LeDoux, J. (1995). Emotion: Clues from the brain. *Annual Review of Psychology, 46,* 209–235.

LeDoux, J. (1996). *The emotional brain: The mysterious underpinnings of emotional life.* New York: Touchstone.

Levenson, R. W. (1987). Alcohol, affect, and physiology: Positive effects in the early stages of drinking. In E. Gottheil, K. Druley, S. Pasko, & S. Weinstein (Eds.), *Stress and addiction* (pp. 173–196). New York: Brunner/Mazel.

Levenson, R. W., Oyama, O. N., & Meek, P. S. (1987). Greater reinforcement from alcohol for those at risk: Parental risk, personality risk, and sex. *Journal of Abnormal Psychology, 96,* 242–253.

Levenson, R. W., Sher, K. J., Grossman, L. M., Newman, J., & Newlin, D. B. (1980). Alcohol and stress response dampening: Pharmacological effects, expectancy, and tension reduction. *Journal of Abnormal Psychology, 89,* 528–538.

Lewis, M. J., & June, H. J. (1990). Neurobehavioral studies of ethanol reward and activation. *Alcohol, 7,* 213–219.

Lienert, G. A., & Traxel W. (1959). The effects of meprobamate and alcohol on galvanic skin response. *Journal of Psychology, 48,* 329–334.

Lukas, S., Mendelson, J., Benedikt, R., & Jones, B. (1986). EEG alpha activity increases during transient episodes of ethanol-induced euphoria. *Pharmacology, Biochemistry, and Behavior, 25,* 889–895.

Marlatt, G. A., & Donovan, D. M. (Eds.). (2005). *Relapse prevention: Maintenance strategies in the treatment of addictive behaviors* (2nd ed.). New York: Guilford Press.

Martin, C., Earleywine, M., Musty, R., Perrine, M., & Swift, R. (1993). Development and validation of the Biphasic Effects of Alcohol Scale (BEAS). *Alcoholism: Clinical and Experimental Research, 17,* 140–146.

McBride, W. J. (2002). Central nucleus of the amygdala and the effects of alcohol and alcohol-drinking behavior in rodents. *Pharmacology, Biochemistry, and Behavior, 71,* 509–515.

Melia, K. R., Ryabinin, A. E., Corodimas, K. P., Wilson, M. C., & Ledoux, J. E. (1996). Hippocampal-dependent learning and experience-dependent activation of the hippocampus are preferentially disrupted by ethanol. *Neuroscience, 74,* 313–322.

Morales, M., Criado, J. R., Sanna, P. P., Henriksen, S. J., & Bloom, F. E. (1998). Acute ethanol induces c-fos immunoreactivity in GABAergic neurons of the central nucleus of the amygdala. *Brain Research, 798,* 333–336.

Naitoh, P. (1972). The effect of alcohol on the autonomic nervous system of humans: Psychophysiological approach. In B. Kissin & H. Begleiter (Eds.), *The biology of alcoholism,* (Vol. 2, pp. 367–433). New York: Plenum Press.

Peterson, J., & Pihl, R. O. (1990). Information processing, neuropsychological function, and the inherited predisposition to alcoholism. *Neuropsychological Review, 1,* 343–369.

Phillips, R., & LeDoux, J. (1992). Differential contribution of the amygdala and hippocampus to cued and contextual fear conditioning. *Behavioral Neuroscience, 106,* 274–285.

Piper, M. E., & Curtin, J. J. (2006). Tobacco withdrawal and negative affect: An analysis of initial emotional response intensity and voluntary emotion regulation. *Journal of Abnormal Psychology, 115,* 96–102.

Pohorecky, L. A., Cagan, M., Brick, J., & Jaffe, L. S. (1976). The startle response in rats: Effect of ethanol. *Pharmacology Biochemistry & Behavior, 4,* 311–316.

Rassnick, S., Koob, G. F., & Geyer, M. A. (1992). Responding to acoustic startle during chronic ethanol intoxication and withdrawal. *Psychopharmacology, 106,* 351–358.

Regier, D. A., Farmer, M. E., Rae, D. S., Locke, B. Z., Keith, S. J., Judd, L. L., & Goodwin, F. K. (1990). Comorbidity of mental disorders with alcohol and other drug abuse. *JAMA, 264,* 2511–2518.

Robinson, T. E., & Berridge, K. C. (2003). Addiction. *Annual Review of Psychology, 54,* 25–53.

Sayette, M. A. (1993). An appraisal–disruption model of alcohol's effects on stress responses in social drinkers. *Psychological Bulletin, 114,* 459–476.

Sayette, M., Breslin, F. C., Wilson, G. T., & Rosenblum, G. (1994). Parental history of alcohol abuse and the effects of alcohol and expectations of intoxication on social stress. *Journal of Studies on Alcohol, 55,* 214–223.

Sher, K. J. (1987). Stress response dampening. In H. T. Blane & K. E. Leonard (Eds.), *Psychological theories of drinking and alcoholism* (pp. 227–271). New York: Guilford Press.

Sher, K. J., & Levenson, R. W. (1982). Risk for alcoholism and individual differences in the stress-response-dampening effect of alcohol. *Journal of Abnormal Psychology, 91,* 350–367.

Sher, K. J., & Walitzer, K. S. (1986). Individual differences in the stress-response-dampening effect of alcohol: A dose–response study. *Journal of Abnormal Psychology, 95,* 159–167.

Smith, W. W. (1922). *The measurement of emotion.* New York: Harcourt-Brace.

Solomon, R. L. (1977). An opponent-process theory of acquired motivation: The affective dynamics of addiction. In J. Maser & M. Seligman (Eds.), *Psychopathology: Experimental models* (pp. 66–103). San Francisco: Jossey-Bass.

Steele, C., & Josephs, R. (1988). Drinking your troubles away: II. An attention–allocation model of alcohol's effect on psychological stress. *Journal of Abnormal Psychology, 97,* 196–205.

Steele, C. M., & Josephs, R. A. (1990). Alcohol myopia: Its prized and dangerous effects. *American Psychologist, 45,* 921–933.

Steele, C., Southwick, L., & Pagano, R. (1986). Drinking your troubles away: The role of activity in mediating alcohol's reduction of psychological stress. *Journal of Abnormal Psychology*, 95, 173–180.

Stewart, S. H., Finn, P. R., & Pihl, R. O. (1992). The effects of alcohol on the cardiovascular stress response in men at high risk for alcoholism: A dose response study. *Journal of Studies on Alcohol*, 53, 499–506.

Stritzke, W. G. K., Lang, A. R., & Patrick, C. J. (1996). Beyond stress and arousal: A reconceptualization of alcohol–emotion relations with reference to psychophysiological methods. *Psychological Bulletin*, 120, 376–395.

Stritzke, W. G. K., Patrick, C. J., & Lang, A. R. (1995). Alcohol and human emotion: A multidimensional analysis incorporating startle-probe methodology. *Journal of Abnormal Psychology*, 104, 114–122.

Tassinary, L. G., & Cacioppo, J. T. (1992). Unobservable facial actions and emotion. *Psychological Science*, 3, 28–33.

Tellegen, A. (1985). Structures of mood and personality and their relevance to assessing anxiety, with an emphasis on self-report. In A. H. Tuma & J. D. Maser (Eds.), *Anxiety and the anxiety disorders* (pp. 681–706). Hillsdale, NJ: Erlbaum.

Wise, R., & Bozarth, M. (1987). A psychomotor stimulant theory of addiction. *Psychological Review*, 94, 469–492.

10

AFFECTIVE PROCESSES
IN PSYCHOPATHY

CHRISTOPHER J. PATRICK

Psychopathy is a severe personality syndrome that entails abnormalities in affective and interpersonal functioning accompanied by marked behavioral deviance. Psychopathic individuals appear charming and insouciant and exhibit a striking absence of guilt, remorse, or empathic concern for others. These characteristics have led theorists to postulate a core underlying affective deficit in psychopathy, and considerable effort has been devoted to exploring the nature of this underlying deficit. The goal of this chapter is to review evidence concerning distinctive components of the psychopathy construct and their relations with personality and neurobiological measures. Findings are discussed with reference to three influential conceptualizations of psychopathy: Cleckley's (1941/1976) classic clinical description, Hare's (1991, 2003) Psychopathy Checklist—Revised (PCL–R), and Lilienfeld's (1990) Psychopathic Personality Inventory (PPI). The major focus of the chapter is on the emotional–interpersonal component of psychopathy (and

Preparation of this chapter was supported by National Institute of Mental Health Grants MH52384, MH65137, and MH072850; National Institute on Alcohol Abuse and Alcoholism Grant R01 AA12164; and funds from the Hathaway endowment at the University of Minnesota, Minneapolis.

its affiliated positive adjustment features) and the associations this component of psychopathy shows with affect and temperament measures.

THE CLASSIC PORTRAIT OF THE PSYCHOPATH: CLECKLEY'S *MASK OF SANITY*

The conceptualization of psychopathy that served as the foundation for currently prominent methods of assessment was that presented by Hervey Cleckley in his book *The Mask of Sanity* (1941/1976). Drawing on his clinical experiences with psychopathic clients in a large psychiatric inpatient hospital, Cleckley presented a series of vivid case histories to illustrate the characteristic traits and behaviors of these individuals. Countering historic trends toward broadening of the construct to encompass various forms of delinquency, impulse control problems, addictions, and sexual deviations (as well as, in some cases, neurotic conditions and organic brain syndromes), Cleckley characterized psychopathy as a highly distinctive syndrome with a specific underlying etiology, involving a basic deficit in affective reactivity.

From the material presented in his case histories, Cleckley (1941/1976) distilled a list of 16 specific criteria for diagnosing psychopathic individuals. Central to Cleckley's conceptualization was the idea that psychopathy entails the presence of a severe underlying pathology masked by an external appearance of good psychological adjustment. In this regard, Cleckley's 16 diagnostic criteria can be grouped into three categories. The first category includes items reflecting positive psychological adjustment (i.e., superficial charm and good "intelligence"; absence of delusions and other signs of irrational thinking; absence of "nervousness" or psychoneurotic manifestations; suicide rarely carried out). Notably, Cleckley was referring not merely to the absence of typical signs of mental disturbance but to the presence of hardiness and positive adjustment:

> The surface of the psychopath . . . shows up as equal to or better than normal and gives no hint at all of a disorder within. Nothing about him suggests oddness, inadequacy, or moral frailty. His mask is that of robust mental health. (p. 383)

However, in contrast with this overt social demeanor, the psychopath exhibits obvious and severe maladjustment in his day-to-day behavior: "Yet he has a disorder that often manifests itself in conduct far more seriously abnormal than that of the schizophrenic" (p. 383).

> The psychopath, however perfectly he mimics man theoretically, that is to say, when he speaks for himself in words, fails altogether when he is put into the practice of actual living. His failure is so complete and so dramatic that it is difficult to see how such a failure could be achieved by anyone less defective than a downright madman . . . (p. 370)

This behavioral maladjustment component of the syndrome is captured by a second set of indicators, as follows: inadequately motivated antisocial behavior; poor judgment and failure to learn by experience; unreliability; fantastic and uninviting behavior with drink (and sometimes without); sex life impersonal, trivial, and poorly integrated; and failure to follow any life plan. Along with criteria reflecting positive psychological adjustment and overt behavioral maladjustment, Cleckley's diagnostic indicators of psychopathy also included items reflecting the affective impoverishment and absence of close interpersonal ties that Cleckley considered to be central to psychopathy (i.e., untruthfulness and insincerity; lack of remorse or shame; general poverty in major affective reactions; pathological egocentricity and incapacity for love; specific loss of insight; unresponsiveness in general interpersonal relations).

PSYCHOPATHY IN CRIMINAL OFFENDERS: THE PSYCHOPATHY CHECKLIST—REVISED

Hare's (1991, 2003) PCL–R was devised to identify individuals within prison or forensic settings who appear psychopathic according to Cleckley's (1941/1976) definition of the syndrome. The original PCL (Hare, 1980) developed out of an earlier global rating system in which raters familiar with the background and recent behavior of the participant assigned scores from 1 to 7 to indicate the degree of match to Cleckley's description of the prototypic psychopath (1 = *clearly non-psychopathic*; 7 = *definitely psychopathic*). Hare's strategy in developing the PCL was to identify items from among a large set of candidate indicators that discriminated between individuals assigned low versus high scores on the global rating system. The original version of the PCL consisted of 22 items. Two of these items ("previous diagnosis as a psychopath or similar" and "antisocial behavior not due to alcohol intoxication") were eliminated in the PCL–R (Hare, 1991, 2003), and the scoring criteria for the remaining 20 items were modified somewhat. The 20 items of the PCL–R are each rated on a 3-point scale (0 = *does not apply*; 1 = *applies somewhat, or evidence is mixed*; 2 = *definitely applies*) using relevant case facts gathered from a semistructured interview and from institutional file records. The PCL–R manual (Hare, 2003) provides scoring criteria for each item that indicate the types and sources of information to be used in scoring. Scores are summed across the 20 items to yield an overall score, and cut-offs are applied to total scores (Hare, 2003) to classify individuals as psychopathic (overall PCL–R score ≥ 30), nonpsychopathic (overall score ≤ 20), or intermediate (overall PCL–R score > 20 and < 30).

In comparing the 20 items of the PCL–R with Cleckley's 16 diagnostic criteria for psychopathy, it is apparent that the aforementioned behavioral deviance indicators and emotional–interpersonal features described by

Cleckley are well represented in the PCL–R. On the other hand, the indicators of positive psychological adjustment that Cleckley listed are not. Although an argument could be made that the "superficial charm" component of Cleckley's first criterion is tapped by Item 1 of the PCL–R ("glibness and superficial charm"), Cleckley's description of "superficial charm" is actually quite different from that associated with PCL–R Item 1. Item 1 of the PCL–R includes reference to excessive verbosity, slickness, and a lack of sincerity and believability in the demeanor of the target participant. The scoring instructions for this item indicate that an intermediate rating of "1" should be assigned in cases where the participant presents with a "macho" or "tough guy" image, whereas a rating of "0" should be assigned if the participant presents as sincere and straightforward. Thus, the scoring criteria for PCL–R Item 1 emphasize a somewhat deviant ("too good to be true") or hypermasculine interpersonal style. In contrast with this, the description of Cleckley's "superficial charm" item indicates that

> there is nothing at all odd or queer about him, and in every respect he tends to embody the concept of a well-adjusted, happy person. Nor does he, on the other hand, seem to be artificially exerting himself like one who is covering up or who wants to sell you a bill of goods. . . . Signs of affectation or excessive affability are not characteristic. He looks like the real thing. (Cleckley, 1941/1976, p. 338)

Furthermore, the fact that Cleckley included "good intelligence" (i.e., rationality and above-average intellect) as a component of this item makes it clear that he intended it to be an indicator of positive psychological adjustment.

What might account for the lack of pure indicators of adjustment among the items of the PCL–R? Although complete details regarding the statistical methods used to develop the original PCL are lacking from the article on its initial development, the main elements of the item selection strategy are possible to infer with reasonable confidence. According to Hare (1991), from amongst an initial pool of 100 candidate items, the items that were retained were those that best discriminated between individuals assigned high versus low scores on the Cleckley global rating system and had the "best psychometric properties" (Hare, 1991, p. 3). The latter phrase suggests that indicators were chosen if they contributed to the reliability (internal consistency) of the overall instrument as well as helping to discriminate extreme groups. This selection strategy would have operated to homogenize the final PCL item set: good–discriminating indicators that correlated with many other discriminating indicators would be retained, whereas good–discriminating indicators that correlated with fewer other discriminating indicators would be dropped. Because the majority of Cleckley's diagnostic criteria (12 of 16) reflect inclinations toward deviance as opposed to positive adjustment, it seems likely that the initial candidate pool would have included more indicators of deviance. Positive adjustment indicators that failed to coalesce with the larger proportion of (pathologic) indicators would have been selected out. The end result would be an item set more uniformly indicative of deviance and psychological maladjustment than Cleckley's original criterion set (for further discussion of this issue, see Patrick, 2006).

Distinctive Factors of the Psychopathy Checklist—Revised

Although the strategy that was used to select items for the PCL and PCL–R favored the measurement of a unitary construct, this instrument nevertheless contains distinctive subgroups of items (i.e., factors) that exhibit discriminant validity in their associations with external criterion variables. The dominant structural model of the PCL–R for many years has been the two-factor model (Hare, 1991; Harpur, Hakstian, & Hare, 1988). Within this model, Factor 1 is marked by items reflecting the interpersonal (charm, grandiosity, and deceitfulness or conning behavior) and affective features of psychopathy (absence of remorse, empathy, and emotional depth; blame externalization). Factor 2 is marked by items describing a chronic antisocial lifestyle, including child behavior problems, impulsivity, irresponsibility, and a lack of long-term goals. Scores on these two PCL–R factors are typically correlated around .5 (Hare, 1991, 2003). Cooke and Michie (2001) proposed an alternative three-factor model of the PCL–R in which the items of Factor 1 were parsed into two separate (but correlated) factors: "arrogant and deceitful personality style," marked by charm, grandiosity, deceitfulness, and manipulation, and "deficient affective experience," consisting of absence of remorse or empathy, shallow affect, and failure to accept responsibility. The third "impulsive–irresponsible behavioral style" factor consisted of a truncated version of Factor 2, comprising the five items considered to be most traitlike. More recently, Hare (2003) has advanced a four-factor model.

Most of the available data concerning the discriminant validity of these PCL–R item subsets pertains to the factors of the original two-factor model. PCL–R Factors 1 and 2 show markedly different associations with various criterion measures of personality and behavior, particularly when their shared variance is controlled for using partial correlation or hierarchical regression methods. One consistent finding is that the unique variance in PCL–R Factor 1 (affective–interpersonal features) is negatively correlated with measures of trait anxiety, whereas Factor 2 (behavioral deviance) is positively related to such measures (Hicks & Patrick, in press; Patrick, 1994; Verona, Patrick, & Joiner, 2001). The unique variance in Factor 1 is also positively associated with measures of social dominance (Verona et al., 2001; see also Hare, 1991; Harpur, Hare, & Hakstian, 1989) and, in some work, with achievement (Verona et al., 2001) and trait positive affect (Patrick, 1994). These results suggest that the positive adjustment features included in Cleckley's concept of psychopathy may be tapped to some extent by the unique variance in Factor 1 (i.e., the variance in Factor 1 that is unrelated to behavioral deviance). In particular, it appears that the unique variance in the interpersonal component of Factor 1 is positively associated with indices of adjustment and resiliency (Hall, Benning, & Patrick, 2004). On the other hand, scores on PCL–R Factor 1 also show negative associations with measures of empathy (Hare, 2003) and positive associations with constructs reflecting self-centeredness and exploitativeness, such as narcissistic personality and Machiavellianism (Hare, 1991; Harpur et al., 1989; Verona et al., 2001). Factor 1 also shows selective positive correlations with measures of instrumental (proactive) aggression (Patrick & Zempolich, 1998; Porter & Woodworth, 2006).

In comparison with Factor 1, Factor 2 of the PCL–R shows selective positive associations with child symptoms of antisocial personality disorder (APD) and markedly stronger associations with adult APD symptoms (Hare, 2003; Verona et al., 2001). Factor 2 also shows much stronger associations with criminal history measures such as onset and frequency of criminal offending (Hare, 2003). In addition, this factor of the PCL–R shows robust positive associations with measures of alcohol and drug dependence, whereas Factor 1 of the PCL–R is negligibly related to substance abuse measures (Hare, 2003). Other research has demonstrated selective positive relations between scores on PCL–R Factor 2 and measures of reactive aggression (Patrick & Zempolich, 1998; Porter & Woodworth, 2006). PCL–R Factor 2 also shows positive relations with measures of suicidal behavior, whereas the unique variance in PCL–R Factor 1 tends to be negatively related to suicidal thoughts and attempts (Verona et al., 2001; Verona, Hicks, & Patrick, 2006). With regard to personality traits, scores on PCL–R Factor 2 show robust positive correlations with measures of aggression, impulsivity, and general sensation seeking (Hare, 1991; Harpur et al., 1989).

These diverging associations for the two factors of the PCL–R are striking for two variables considered to be facets of a single higher order construct (e.g., Hare, 1991, 2003). Particularly notable are instances of *cooperative suppression* (Paulhus, Robins, Trzesniewski, & Tracy, 2004) in which opposing associations for the two PCL–R factors with criterion measures become stronger once their overlap (covariance) is removed. For example, Hicks and Patrick (in press) reported evidence of suppressor effects in the associations of the two PCL–R factors with varying facets of negative emotionality—including distress (or general anxiousness), fearfulness, and anger—along with depression. For three of these four criterion variables (emotional distress, fear, depression), cooperative suppressor effects were evident—that is, correlations for both PCL–R factors increased, in opposing directions, when the two were included simultaneously in a prediction model. For the fourth variable, anger, a crossover suppression effect was found—that is, when the two PCL–R factors were included together in a prediction model, a reversal occurred in the direction of association for Factor 1 (i.e., from significantly positive to nonsignificantly negative), whereas the association for Factor 2 became somewhat more positive. Moreover, for all four criterion variables, prediction based on the two PCL–R factors together was superior to that based on PCL–R total scores alone.

The occurrence of suppressor effects, and in particular instances of cooperative suppression, strongly suggests that the items of a measurement instrument presumed to index a single broad construct are actually tapping separable, distinctive underlying constructs (Paulhus et al., 2004). The presence of suppressor effects for the two factors of the PCL–R, in particular, fits with Cleckley's original idea that the syndrome of psychopathy reflects the unusual co-occurrence within the same person of tendencies toward psychological resiliency on one hand and behavioral maladjustment on the other. Despite the fact that PCL items were intended to index a unitary construct, the instrument nevertheless contains distinctive subgroups of items that show markedly different (and in some cases opposing) relations with external criterion measures. As discussed in the following sections, there is also evidence that these separable components of psychopathy have distinctive etiological underpinnings.

Emotional Reactivity Deficits Associated With Factor 1 of the Psychopathy Checklist—Revised

A good deal of research has been conducted on emotional response differences in psychopathic individuals, using peripheral physiologic measures (skin conductance, heart rate, and facial muscle activity); electrocortical response; and, more recently, brain imaging methods. One of the most consistent findings—beginning with Lykken's (1957) early study of anxiety in psychopathy and continuing with Hare's studies of autonomic reactivity though the 1960s and 1970s—has been that individuals high in overall psychopathy show reduced skin conductance (SC) reactivity to stressors of various kinds, particularly cues signaling an impending noxious event. This has been interpreted as reflecting a basic deficiency in anxiety or fear. However, a limitation of this work is that SC response is a general index of sympathetic activation rather than a specific index of fear reactivity (Lang, Bradley, & Cuthbert, 1990), so that response differences in this system may reflect differences in arousability rather than fear. However, subsequent research examining startle blink modulation as an index of defensive activation has provided more direct evidence of fear reactivity deficits in PCL–R psychopaths.

Background: Startle Response Modulation as a Measure of Emotional Valence

Vrana, Spence, and Lang (1988) presented evidence that the eyeblink component of the startle reflex can be used to index the valence (pleasantness) component of affective responding in humans. Vrana et al. found that the blink response to a brief loud noise probe was enhanced (potentiated) during viewing of unpleasant scenes (e.g., snakes, mutilations, aimed guns) compared with neutral scenes and reduced (inhibited) during viewing of pleasant scenes (e.g., smiling babies, nudes, adventure scenes). This finding, which has been replicated in many subsequent studies (see chap. 3, this volume), can be understood from the behavioral perspective of fear as defensive action readiness (Lang et al., 1990). Unpleasant pictures evoke a state of defensive readiness that is synchronous with the reaction to the aversive noise probe, resulting in potentiation of the startle reflex; this effect has been termed *fear-potentiated startle*. Pleasant stimuli evoke an incipient approach state that is antagonistic to the defensive startle response, resulting in reflex inhibition.

Affective modulation of startle can also be understood in terms of the neuroanatomy of the basic startle circuit and its connections with brain motivational systems. For example, Davis and his colleagues (see Davis, 1989) established that potentiation of the acoustic startle reflex by fear cues in rodents is mediated by a pathway from the central nucleus of the amygdala to the nucleus reticularis pontis caudalis, a component of the basic startle circuit. Lesions of this pathway selectively abolish fear-potentiated startle, leaving the primary reflex intact. There is evidence that parallel inputs from the appetitive motivational system (in particular, the nucleus accumbens) mediate inhibition of the startle reflex during processing of pleasurable stimulus cues. In conjunction with this, Lang, Bradley, and Cuthbert (1997) theorized that foreground attentional engagement (perceptual orienting) may be important to this startle inhibition effect. This position is supported by at least three lines of evidence.

One is that startle reflex inhibition occurs most reliably during perceptual processing of positively valent stimuli (Witvliet & Vrana, 1995). Second, control subjects show attenuated startle reactivity for both pleasurable and aversive pictures during the first few hundred milliseconds after a picture is presented (Bradley, Cuthbert, & Lang, 1993). Specifically, blinks are generally smaller to probes presented at 300 milliseconds and 800 milliseconds after picture onset than later, implying enhanced processing protection early in the viewing interval. Also, startle reactions to probes presented at 300 milliseconds tend to be smaller for both pleasant and unpleasant pictures than for neutral pictures, indicating rapid discrimination and enhanced processing protection for motivationally relevant stimuli. By 800 milliseconds, startle reflex potentiation becomes evident for unpleasant pictures, signifying the emergence of defensive priming, with the magnitude of this effect increasing at later points in the viewing interval. These findings indicate that startle reactivity is inhibited for both pleasant and unpleasant pictures at early attentional stages of perceptual processing, giving way to emotional modulation at subsequent stages.

A third source of evidence indicating that foreground attention contributes to startle inhibition is a study by Cuthbert, Bradley, and Lang (1996), in which startle blink and SC reactions were assessed during viewing of pleasant and unpleasant pictures that varied in rated arousal. For both pleasant and unpleasant scenes, SC response (a nonspecific measure of arousal) increased monotonically with picture intensity. For pleasant pictures, startle blink magnitude decreased monotonically with increasing stimulus arousal. For unpleasant pictures, startle magnitude also showed a decreasing trend up to an intermediate level of picture intensity. Beyond this point, the direction of startle reflex modulation was reversed, with blinks showing increasing potentiation across higher levels of aversive picture intensity. This was interpreted as indicating that less intense aversive pictures engage attention and thereby reduce processing of noise probes, whereas highly evocative aversive scenes prompt activation of the defensive motivational system, which overrides the inhibitory effect of attention on the startle reflex.

Lang et al. (1997) postulated that attention is engaged more readily by pleasant or unpleasant cues in the environment than by neutral or routine events because affective cues have survival significance. For aversive cues, perceptual orienting gives way automatically to defensive activation as cue intensity increases. Lang et al. (1997) theorized that this transition occurs in stages, with orienting and defense dispositions coexisting at intermediate levels of affective stimulus intensity but shifting to pure defense (active fight or flight) when danger becomes imminent. This transition from orienting to defense reflects an adaptive trade-off between two basic survival tendencies, appetitive approach and defensive withdrawal or attack. Evidence reviewed in the next subsection indicates that the threshold of transition from orienting to defense is higher in psychopathic individuals (particularly those who score high on the core affective–interpersonal features of psychopathy) than in healthy control participants.

Psychopathy Checklist—Revised Psychopathy and Emotion-Modulated Startle

Patrick, Bradley, and Lang (1993) examined startle blink responses to unsignaled noise probes during viewing of affective and neutral pictures in groups assessed using the PCL–R. Three groups ($n = 18$ each) were tested: nonpsychopathic individuals (PCL–R total score ≤ 20), psychopathic individuals (PCL–R ≥ 30), and an intermediate group (PCL–R > 20 and < 30). Pleasant picture scenes included appetizing food, babies, action–adventure, and erotica. Unpleasant picture scenes included snakes, physical attack, injury, and aimed weapons. No group differences in overall startle reactivity were found. Participants in both the nonpsychopathic and intermediate groups showed a normal, linear pattern of startle modulation, with blinks larger during unpleasant pictures and smaller during pleasant slides, relative to neutral. In contrast, psychopathic participants showed no evidence of startle potentiation for aversive pictures in relation to neutral. Instead, they showed a deviant quadratic startle pattern, with blinks attenuated during both pleasant and unpleasant pictures in relation to neutral pictures.

This finding of deficient fear-potentiated startle in PCL–R-defined psychopathic individuals has been replicated in several subsequent studies (Herpertz et al., 2001; Levenston, Patrick, Bradley, & Lang, 2000; Patrick, 1994; Sutton, Vitale, & Newman, 2002; Vanman, Mejia, Dawson, Schell, & Raine, 2003). This effect suggests a weakness in the capacity of an aversive stimulus to prime defensive actions—in this context, to amplify a protective reflex, but perhaps more broadly to interrupt goal seeking and to promote avoidance of danger. Consistent with this hypothesis, Blair and his colleagues have reported deficits among psychopathic individuals on behavioral tasks believed to be sensitive to amygdala function (for a review of this work, see Blair, 2006), and recent neuroimaging research has demonstrated reduced amygdala activity during aversive conditioning in high PCL–R scorers (Veit et al., 2002).

A post hoc reanalysis of offender groups in the Patrick et al. (1993) study revealed that abnormal startle modulation was especially evident among participants who scored highest on Factor 1 of the PCL–R. When participants with high "antisocial deviance" scores (i.e., at least two thirds of the maximum on PCL–R Factor 2) were subgrouped into those low and high on Factor 1 ("affective–interpersonal"), only the High Factor 1–High Factor 2 group showed a deviant startle pattern (see Figure 10.1). Participants with high scores on the antisocial deviance factor only showed a normal pattern of startle potentiation during viewing of aversive scenes.

Patrick (1994) replicated and extended these findings using a procedure involving anticipation of a stressor. Four prisoner groups were selected a priori on the basis of scores on the two PCL–R factors: (a) nonpsychopaths, rated low on both factors (n = 18); (b) high Factor 1 offenders, with high scores on Factor 1 but low scores on Factor 2 (n = 14); (c) high Factor 2 offenders, scoring high on Factor 1 but low on Factor 2 (n = 8); and (d) psychopaths, with high scores on both factors (n = 18). In the first (baseline) phase of the test procedure, participants viewed a monitor on which a simple cue was displayed intermittently for 6 seconds. Acoustic probes were presented at varying times during cue intervals and intertrial intervals to elicit startle blink reactions. In the second (anticipation) phase, the procedure was identical, except that a loud (110-dB) aversive noise blast occurred following the offset of the visual cue. Startle probes were again presented at varying times during warning cue intervals and intertrial intervals. No group differences in overall startle magnitude were found, and within the baseline phase, startle magnitude during cue intervals did not differ from magnitude during intertrial intervals in any of the participant groups. Within the anticipation phase, in which the cue signaled an upcoming noxious event, startle reactions during cue intervals generally exceeded reactions during intertrial intervals. However, the psychopathic and high Factor 1 groups both showed reduced startle potentiation during noise anticipation compared with the nonpsychopathic and high Factor 2 groups.

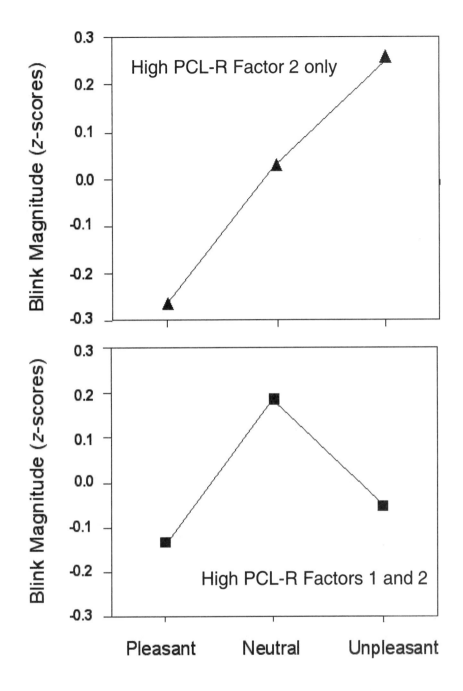

Figure 10.1. Mean magnitude of startle blink responses to noise probes presented during viewing of pleasant, neutral, and unpleasant picture stimuli in two male prisoner groups: prisoners high on Psychopathy Checklist—Revised (PCL–R) Factor 2 only (*n* = 18; top), and prisoners high on both factors of the PCL–R (*n* = 17; bottom). Blink magnitude means are presented in *z* score units (*M* = 0, *SD* = 1) based on standardization of raw blink magnitude scores across trials for each individual subject. The data are from a study by Patrick et al. (1993).

These results provide further evidence that psychopathy is associated with diminished fear reactivity. In addition, the findings indicate that this fear deficit is linked specifically to the core affective-interpersonal features. An interesting divergence from Patrick et al.'s (1993) findings was that psychopaths and high Factor 1 offenders in the noise anticipation study did not show inhibition of the startle reflex during aversive (warning cue) periods relative to neutral (intertrial) intervals. A potential explanation is that the aversive foreground in the noise anticipation procedure, which consisted of a simple character string, was not inherently interesting: The warning cue engaged attention only because it signaled an upcoming aversive event. Thus, psychopaths showed lesser defensive activation in relation to the impending stressor, as evidenced by reduced blink potentiation, but startle inhibition did not occur because attention was not sufficiently engaged. Similar to this, Levenston et al. (2000; discussed subsequently) reported group differences in the degree of startle potentiation, as opposed to differences in the direction of modulation, for scenes of direct threat stimuli (i.e., aimed weapons, attackers).

Psychopathic offenders in the Patrick et al. (1993) study did not differ from nonpsychopathic or mixed participants in their reactions to pleasant picture stimuli: All groups showed normal inhibition of the startle reflex during viewing of pleasant compared with neutral pictures. The observed pattern of deficient startle potentiation for aversive pictures but normal inhibition for pleasant pictures is consistent with the hypothesis that "primary" psychopathy is characterized by weak defensive responsivity but by at least normal reactivity to appetitive stimuli (Fowles, 1980). However, an intriguing question is why psychopathic individuals showed comparative inhibition of startle during aversive picture viewing, a pattern that might be interpreted as reflecting appetitive activation (Lang et al., 1990). According to evidence reviewed in the preceding section, this pattern could instead reflect a predominance of foreground attention over defensive reactivity. In normal individuals, the startle reflex is inhibited for both pleasant and aversive pictures during the earliest stages of picture processing, reflecting immediate prioritization of attention to stimuli with motivational significance (Bradley et al., 1993). As perceptual processing continues, pictures with strong aversive connotations prime the defensive system, producing startle potentiation (Cuthbert et al., 1996). During subsequent stages of processing, this potentiation effect becomes maximal for potent, directly threatening pictures.

From this perspective, blink inhibition during aversive picture viewing in psychopaths could reflect a predominance of attentional modulation of startle in the absence of the defensive activation that normally emerges across time and with increasing picture intensity. Data relevant to this hypothesis come from a study by Levenston et al. (2000). This study examined startle modulation in psychopathic and nonpsychopathic offender groups for discrete categories of aversive and pleasant pictures. Nonpsychopathic offenders were selected to be low on both factors of the PCL–R, and psychopathic offenders were selected to be high on both. Aversive pictures included scenes of direct threat (aimed weapons, menacing attackers) and victimization (assaults on other people, physical injury). The pleasant categories consisted of erotic (nudes, intimate couples) and adventure scenes (e.g., roller-coaster, cliff diving). Noise probes were presented at early (300-millisecond, 800-millisecond) and late (1,800-millisecond, 3,000-millisecond, 4,500-millisecond) time points during the picture-viewing interval. Replicating Patrick et al. (1993), different startle patterns were observed for high versus low PCL–R scorers: Nonpsychopathic offenders showed blink potentiation for unpleasant pictures beginning at 800 milliseconds, whereas psychopathic offenders showed blink inhibition for both pleasant and unpleasant pictures compared with neutral. For specific picture contents, nonpsychopathic offenders showed moderate potentiation for victim scenes, strong potentiation for threat, and inhibition for erotic but not adventure scenes (the latter produced modest potentiation in this group). For psychopathic offenders, startle was inhibited during viewing of victim scenes and potentiated only weakly during threat scenes. Psychopathic offenders showed reliable blink reflex inhibition for both erotic and action–adventure scenes.

The authors interpreted these group differences as indicating a higher threshold for activation of the defense system in psychopaths. The fact that psychopathic offenders showed blink inhibition during viewing of victim scenes implies that attentive engagement (orienting) predominated during viewing of these scenes. The weak potentiation shown by psychopathic participants to threat scenes suggests that attentional orienting began to give way to defensive reactivity at a level of aversive cue intensity at which nonpsychopathic participants were already exhibiting strong defensive mobilization. The group differences for adventure scenes compared with erotic scenes were interpreted in a similar way. Both groups showed startle inhibition for erotic pictures, which were engaging and purely pleasurable. In contrast, for the adventure scenes, which included elements of danger as well as fun, nonpsychopathic participants showed modest defensive potentiation, whereas psychopathic participants showed significant blink inhibition—again indicating a heightened threshold for shifting from orienting to defense in psychopaths.

However, a further group difference at the 300-millisecond probe time suggested a somewhat different interpretation of the findings. Nonpsychopathic participants (like control participants; Bradley et al., 1993) showed enhanced blink inhibition for both pleasant and unpleasant pictures compared with neutral pictures at this early probe time, whereas psychopathic participants showed this pattern only at the next (800-millisecond) probe time, implying delayed detection of the motivational significance of these stimuli. In light of other data suggesting that psychopathic individuals may process affective stimuli in a weak, undifferentiated fashion (e.g., Verona, Patrick, Curtin, Bradley, & Lang, 2004; Williamson, Harpur, & Hare, 1991), this difference at 300 milliseconds could indicate an impairment in the early, automatic detection of affect-relevant stimuli. From this perspective, the deviant startle pattern shown by psychopathic individuals late in the viewing interval could reflect the persistence of purely attentional processing following this initial delay in affective differentiation. This interpretation is compatible with the low-fear hypothesis, but it is also potentially broader, in that it extends to appetitive as well as defensive cues (cf. Cleckley, 1976). One way to test this alternative hypothesis would be to measure brain potential responses to determine whether the cortical differentiation that is normally evident for affective versus neutral pictures by 300 milliseconds (e.g., Cuthbert et al., 2000) is absent or reduced in psychopathic participants.

A final point is that the Levenston et al. (2000) study focused on psychopathic individuals who scored high on both factors of the PCL–R. In view of other work tying late-interval startle modulation effects specifically to PCL–R Factor 1 (Patrick, 1994; Patrick et al., 1993; Vanman et al., 2003), it is possible that different facets of psychopathy may have accounted for early- versus late-interval group differences in the Levenston et al. (2000) study. For example, it is possible that deficient late startle potentiation for aversive scenes was associated mainly with the affective–interpersonal (Factor 1) features of psychopathy, whereas separate processing deviations associated with overall psychopathy or with the antisocial deviance (Factor 2) component accounted for the early attentional differences. Further research using groups selected for elevations on one or the other PCL–R factor are needed to resolve this issue.

Psychopathy Checklist—Revised Factor 2, Antisocial Personality, and the Externalizing Spectrum

As noted earlier, the two PCL–R factors show an asymmetric association with APD: The social deviance (Factor 2) component of the PCL–R is related selectively to the child component of APD and is also related more substantially to the adult component than PCL–R Factor 1. A recently emerging perspective on the comorbidity between APD and substance abuse problems and their common association with Factor 2 of the PCL–R is that these disorders are manifestations of a shared underlying vulnerability factor—with which PCL–R Factor 2 is also strongly associated.

Krueger et al. (2002) presented behavior genetic evidence for a shared vulnerability factor underlying antisocial behavior and substance use disorders. These investigators conducted a factor analysis of symptom scores for four externalizing syndromes (child conduct disorder, adult antisocial behavior, alcohol dependence, and drug dependence) and an index of disinhibitory personality (the Constraint factor of the Multidimensional Personality Questionnaire [MPQ]; Tellegen, in press) obtained from a sample of male and female twins recruited from the community ($N = 1,048$). The analysis yielded evidence of a general Externalizing factor on which all of these diagnostic variables loaded substantially (.58–.78). The twin nature of the sample permitted a decomposition of causal influences on this Externalizing factor into genetic and environmental sources of variance; more than 80% of the variance in this general factor was found to be attributable to additive genetic influence. The residual variance in each distinctive indicator not accounted for by the broad Externalizing factor was attributable mainly to nonshared environmental influence, although for conduct disorder, a significant contribution of shared environment was also found. On the basis of these findings, Krueger et al. (2002) postulated that a broad constitutional factor contributes to the genesis of various disorders within the externalizing spectrum but that the precise expression of this underlying vulnerability (i.e., as antisocial deviance, alcohol or drug problems, or other forms of disinhibition) is determined by specific causal influences.

Patrick, Hicks, Krueger, and Lang (2005) examined associations between the two components of psychopathy indexed by Factors 1 and 2 of the PCL–R and the broad externalizing factor that links various impulse control disorders. In this study, scores on the latent externalizing factor were estimated from child and adult symptoms of APD, measures of alcohol and drug abuse or dependence, and scores on the higher order Constraint dimension of the MPQ (cf. Krueger et al., 2002). Simple correlations between the latent externalizing factor and the two psychopathy factors modeled as latent variables were $r = .44$ for Factor 1 and $r = .84$ for Factor 2, respectively. Moreover, when associations between the unique variance in each psychopathy factor and the externalizing factor (i.e., the association between each psychopathy factor and externalizing after controlling for variance in the other psychopathy factor) were examined within a structural equation model, the partial association between Factor 2 and externalizing approached 1.0, whereas the relationship between the unique variance in Factor 1 and externalizing was negligible. When the model was reparameterized with Factor 1 separated into its Interpersonal and Affective components, neither component showed a significant relationship with externalizing independently of Factor 2. This pattern of findings confirms that Factor 2 of the PCL–R taps the broad externalizing factor of general psychopathology, of which APD represents one indicator.

PSYCHOPATHY IN CRIMINAL OFFENDERS: THE PSYCHOPATHIC PERSONALITY INVENTORY

Limitations of the PCL–R include the fact that it neglects coverage of the positive adjustment features emphasized by Cleckley (1941/1976), that it is time-consuming to administer, and that a number of its items (those scored with reference to criminal offense behaviors) are not applicable to individuals outside correctional or forensic settings. For these reasons, other strategies for assessing psychopathy have been sought, a number of them based on self-report. Most self-report psychopathy inventories show much stronger associations with the antisocial deviance component of the disorder indexed by PCL–R Factor 2 than with the emotional–interpersonal (Factor 1) component (Hare, 1991, 2003). However, a self-report instrument that indexes the two components of psychopathy more equally is the Psychopathic Personality Inventory (PPI; Lilienfeld, 1990; Lilienfeld & Andrews, 1996).

The PPI was developed using a personality-based approach in which the aim was to comprehensively index trait constructs relevant to Cleckley's (1941/1976) concept of psychopathy. A detailed survey of the literature was undertaken to identify all constructs with potential relevance, and questionnaire items were written to index these various constructs. Through successive rounds of data collection and analysis, the initial item set was refined, and the target constructs were clarified using item analytic techniques. This process resulted in a final set of 187 items for the PPI. Scores derived from the PPI include an overall (total) psychopathy score and scores on eight subscales: Social Potency (reflecting dominance and persuasiveness), Stress Immunity (diminished capacity for anxiety), Fearlessness (proneness to take risks and seek thrills through danger), Impulsive Nonconformity (recklessness, rebelliousness, and unconventionality), Blame Externalization (proneness to blame others and perceive oneself as a victim), Machiavellianism Egocentricity (aggressive, selfish, and exploitative), Carefree Nonplanfulness (present oriented and lacking in forethought and planning), and Coldheartedness (lacking in sentimentality, sensitivity, and imaginative capacity).

The process used to develop items and subscales for the PPI was not guided by preconceptions about the underlying structure of the psychopathy construct. However, recent research indicates that the PPI subscales tap distinctive higher order factors. Benning et al. (2003) reported evidence of two general factors accounting for a sizable portion of the covariance (51%) among seven of the eight scales. The Social Potency, Stress Immunity, and Fearlessness subscales defined one factor (PPI–I), and the Impulsive Nonconformity, Blame Externalization, Machiavellian Egocentricity, and Carefree Nonplanfulness subscales defined the other (PPI–II). In contrast with PCL–R Factors 1 and 2, which are moderately correlated, the two factors of the PPI were essentially uncorrelated ($r = -.07$). The eighth subscale of the PPI, Coldheartedness, did not load appreciably on either of these factors. The two-factor structure of the PPI was replicated by Benning, Patrick, Salekin, and Leistico (2005) in mixed-gender college sample ($N = 326$).

Correlates of the Psychopathic Personality Inventory Factors: Personality and Behavioral Measures

Recent research indicates that the two orthogonal factors of the PPI show conceptually meaningful and, in many cases, diverging patterns of associations with a wide variety of external criterion variables. Benning et al. (2003) found opposing associations for PPI–I and II with measures of adaptive functioning, including verbal IQ, educational achievement, and occupational attainment and income level: PPI–II showed a significant negative correlation with each of these variables, whereas in each case the direction of association for PPI–I was positive (i.e., higher scores on PPI–I were associated with higher functioning). However, in accordance with the notion that these factors represent facets of an overarching psychopathy construct, both PPI–I and PPI–II showed significant positive correlations with adult symptoms of antisocial personality disorder. On the other hand, PPI–II alone showed a significant relationship with child symptoms of APD. PPI–II also showed selective associations with measures of alcohol and drug problems (i.e., scores on PPI–I did not correlate significantly with these variables). Consistent with these findings, Patrick, Edens, Poythress, and Lilienfeld (2006) reported positive correlations for PPI–II but not PPI–I with the Alcohol Problems and Drug Problems scales of the Personality Assessment Inventory (PAI; Morey, 1991). PPI–II also showed strong positive associations with the Antisocial Features, Aggression, Borderline Features, and Suicidal Ideation scales of the PAI, whereas associations for PPI–I with these variables were negligible. Moreover, the two PPI factors showed marked divergence in their associations with the Anxiety Disorders and Somatization scales of the PAI: Correlations with these scales were significantly positive for PPI–II and significantly negative for PPI–I. In addition to this, scores on PPI–I were associated uniquely and positively with scores on the Dominance scale of the PAI. As a whole, these results indicate that PPI–I indexes a component of psychopathy that reflects elements of psychological and social adaptation as well as some tendencies toward deviance, whereas scores on PPI–II are more generally reflective of psychological and behavioral maladjustment—including tendencies toward child and adult antisociality, alcohol and drug problems, heightened anxiousness and somatic complaints, and suicidal ideation.

Another approach to investigating the two components of psychopathy indexed by the PPI has been to estimate scores on the two PPI factors from omnibus personality inventories in large existing data sets that also include relevant criterion measures. For example, Benning et al. (2003) reported that scores on PPI–I and II could be predicted quite accurately (Rs = .70 and .67, respectively) from the lower order trait scales of the MPQ (Tellegen, in press). Benning, Patrick, Blonigen, Hicks, and Iacono (2005) used the regression weights reported by Benning et al. (2003) to estimate scores on the two PPI factors in three independent samples for which scores on the MPQ were available in conjunction with criterion measures relevant to the construct of psychopathy: a sample of male and female undergraduates recruited from psychology classes (n = 346); a sample of male and female twins recruited from the community (n = 1,122); and a sample of male prisoners assessed within a federal correctional facility (n = 218).

Analyses of associations between MPQ-estimated PPI scores and available criterion measures in these three participant samples yielded meaningful patterns of discriminant relations. In both the undergraduate and the prisoner samples, higher scores on PPI–I (as estimated by the MPQ) were associated with lower scores on temperament traits of fearfulness and distress and higher scores on traits of activity and sociability, higher scores on the thrill- and adventure-seeking facet of sensation seeking, and higher levels of narcissism. Within these same samples, higher PPI–II scores were associated with higher scores on temperament traits of anger and impulsivity; higher scores on the boredom susceptibility facet of sensation seeking; and lower levels of socialization as indexed by the Socialization scale (Gough, 1960). Within the community and prisoner samples, higher scores on PPI–I were associated with lower symptoms of phobic disorders (social phobia, in particular) and lower symptoms of depression, whereas higher PPI–II scores were associated with higher depressive symptoms as well as higher symptoms of alcohol and drug dependence. In the prisoner sample, scores on both PPI–I and II showed significant negative correlations with a self-report index of emotional empathy.

In addition, the availability of PCL–R scores in the prisoner sample permitted an assessment of relations between the two factors of the PPI (as estimated by the MPQ) and the two factors of the PCL–R. Using simple (zero-order) correlations, a significant association was found between PPI–I and PCL–R Factor 1 only, whereas significant associations were found between PPI–II and both PCL–R factors. However, when the overlap between the two PCL–R factors was controlled for using partial correlations, PPI–I exhibited a significant positive relationship with PCL–R Factor 1 only ($r = .28$), and PPI–II showed a significant positive relationship with PCL–R Factor 2 exclusively ($r = .31$). A further analysis examining relations between PPI–I and the two components of Factor 1 described in Cooke and Michie's (2001) three-factor model revealed that the association was stronger for the Interpersonal component than the Affective component. As noted earlier, the unique variance in the Interpersonal component of the PCL–R (i.e., that unrelated to the affective and antisocial deviance components) accounts for most of the association between Factor 1 and measures of positive adjustment (Hall et al., 2004). Taken together, these results indicate that the variance in PCL–R Factor 1 that is most related to PPI–I taps something of the positive adjustment features of psychopathy included in Cleckley's (1941/1976) description of the syndrome.

Correlates of the Psychopathic Personality Inventory Factors: Affective–Physiological Response

Benning, Patrick, and Iacono (2005) investigated relations between PPI factor scores and startle reflex modulation during affective picture viewing in a sample of 307 male participants recruited from the community. Scores on PPI–I and PPI–II were estimated using the trait scales of the MPQ (cf. Benning, Patrick, Blonigen, et al., 2005). Participants with high scores on PPI–I showed an abnormal pattern of startle response modulation similar to that of incarcerated offenders with high scores on PCL–R Factor 1 (i.e., a lack of fear-potentiated startle; see Figure 10.2). In contrast, participants with high scores on PPI–II showed a normal linear pattern of affective startle modulation. These findings suggest that PPI–I taps to some degree the same blunted emotional reactivity (i.e., diminished defensive reactivity to aversive cues) that has been reported in connection with PCL–R Factor 1. An additional finding of this study was that participants selected to be high on PPI–II showed generally reduced electrodermal responses to picture stimuli, whether affective or neutral, compared with participants low on PPI–II. This result is consistent with other data indicating reduced overall arousability in individuals high in impulsive–antisocial tendencies (cf. Raine, 1997).

Gordon, Baird, and End (2004) used functional magnetic resonance imaging to assess the brain responses of low and high PPI scorers during performance of a face recognition task in which attention was directed on some trials to the identity of a target face and on other trials to the category of affective expression appearing on the target face. On affect-processing trials, participants with high scores on PPI–I showed reduced activation in the right amygdala and affiliated regions of frontal cortex (i.e., right inferior frontal cortex, medial prefrontal cortex) compared with participants scoring low on PPI–I, along with enhanced activation in visual cortex and right dorsolateral prefrontal cortex. In contrast, high and low PPI–I groups did not differ in brain activation during identity-processing trials. Gordon et al. interpreted these findings as indicating that high PPI–I scorers relied on cognitive and perceptual processing regions of the brain to perform the affect recognition task, whereas low PPI–I scorers relied on brain regions known to be involved in affective evaluation and reactivity. Statistical comparisons of participants scoring high versus low on PPI–II revealed, if anything, evidence of enhanced amygdala activation during affect-processing trials among high PPI–II scorers. This result is consistent with prior evidence indicating that individuals who are highly antisocial but lack the core affective–interpersonal features of psychopathy show normal or heightened physiological reactivity to aversive stimuli (cf. Patrick & Lang, 1999).

SUMMARY AND CLINICAL IMPLICATIONS

Psychopathy as assessed by Hare's (1991, 2003) PCL–R includes Factor 1 items that capture, to some degree, the combination of positive adjustment and interpersonal–affective features that Cleckley (1941/1976) described as the "mask" component of psychopathy. The items of PCL–R Factor 2, on the other hand, tap the broad externalizing factor of psychopathology that encompasses APD and substance use disorders. Recent data suggest that the

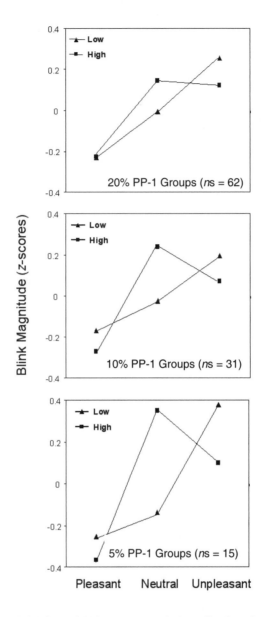

Pleasant   Neutral   Unpleasant

Figure 10.2. Startle blink modulation patterns during affective picture viewing for subgroups of nonincarcerated men (overall *n* = 307) selected to be low or high on the first factor of the Psychopathic Personality Inventory (PPI–I) according to various distributional cutoffs: lowest 20% of sample versus highest 20% (*n*s = 62; top panel); lowest 10% versus highest 10% (*n*s = 31; center panel); (c) lowest 5% versus highest 5% (*n*s = 15; bottom panel). Blink magnitude means are presented in *z*-score units (*M* = 0, *SD* = 1) based on standardization of raw blink magnitude scores across trials for each individual subject. Differences in startle patterns become stronger as groupings become more extreme: *F* values for the Group × Quadratic Valence interaction (reflecting group differences in comparative reactivity to affective vs. neutral pictures; cf. Patrick et al., 1993) are 4.3 (*p* < .05), 8.6 (*p* < .01), and 11.8 (*p* < .005) for the 20%, 10%, and 5% groups, respectively. The data are from a study by Benning, Patrick, and Iacono (2005).

first factor of Lilienfeld's (1990) PPI may index the mask component of psychopathy in a purer fashion than Factor 1 of the PCL–R. Findings from affective processing studies, including studies of emotion-modulated startle, indicate that this mask component of the disorder reflects a different underlying biological mechanism (i.e., low trait fear) than the externalizing component. The idea that different etiologic mechanisms underlie these two distinctive components of psychopathy has been discussed in terms of a "dual process" model of psychopathy (for a more detailed presentation of this model, see Patrick, 2001, in press; see also Fowles & Dindo, 2006).

The idea that the syndrome of psychopathy reflects separable underlying processes that can occur either separately or conjointly in specific individuals has important clinical implications. One is that distinct subtypes of psychopathic individuals exist, reflecting the predominance of one underlying process or the other. For example, Hicks et al. (2004) reported evidence of two subtypes of psychopathic individuals, an aggressive–externalizing type and an emotionally stable–agentic type, on the basis of a model-based cluster analysis of the personality profiles of PCL–R psychopathic criminal offenders.

Another implication is that rather than continuing to rely on assessment instruments that emphasize psychopathy as a unitary entity, it may prove more useful to devise new inventories that assess the components of psychopathy as separate entities. There is evidence that this approach may improve the predictive power of psychopathy in relation to important criterion variables. For example, Hicks and Patrick (in press) reported that various facets of negative emotionality (i.e., distress, fear, anger, and depression) were predicted better by the two factors of the PCL–R in combination than by scores on either factor alone or by overall scores on the PCL–R. Likewise, Verona et al. (2006) reported improved prediction of suicidal behavior when scores on the two factors of the PCL–R were entered concurrently as predictors in a regression model.

These distinctive components of psychopathy are also important to consider in relation to the issue of treatment. It seems likely that the two major components of psychopathy indexed by the PCL–R and the PPI would be associated differently with the psychological distress that is a crucial motivator for therapeutic change because they show differential relations with measures of emotional reactivity. Related to this, the dual-process perspective on psychopathy encourages a multifaceted approach to treatment that includes various methods of intervention aimed at altering the separable processes that contribute to distinctive features of the disorder.

REFERENCES

Benning, S. D., Patrick, C. J., Blonigen, D. M., Hicks, B. M., & Iacono, W. G. (2005). Estimating facets of psychopathy from normal personality traits: A step toward community-epidemiological investigations. *Assessment, 12,* 3–18.

Benning, S. D., Patrick, C. J., Hicks, B. M., Blonigen, D. M., & Krueger, R. F. (2003). Factor structure of the Psychopathic Personality Inventory: Validity and implications for clinical assessment. *Psychological Assessment, 15*, 340–350.

Benning, S. D., Patrick, C. J., & Iacono, W. G. (2005). Psychopathy, startle blink modulation, and electrodermal reactivity in twin men. *Psychophysiology, 42*, 753–762.

Benning, S. D., Patrick, C. J., Salekin, R. T., & Leistico, A. R. (2005). Convergent and discriminant validity of psychopathy factors assessed via self-report: A comparison of three instruments. *Assessment, 12*, 270–289.

Blair, R. J. R. (2006). Subcortical brain systems in psychopathy: The amygdala and associated structures. In C. J. Patrick (Ed.), *Handbook of psychopathy* (pp. 296–312). New York: Guilford Press.

Bradley, M. M., Cuthbert, B. N., & Lang, P. J. (1993). Pictures as prepulse: Attention and emotion in startle modification. *Psychophysiology, 30*, 541–545.

Cleckley, H. (1976). *The mask of sanity* (5th ed.). St. Louis, MO: Mosby. (Original work published 1941)

Cooke, D. J., & Michie, C. (2001). Refining the construct of psychopathy: Towards a hierarchical model. *Psychological Assessment, 13*, 171–188.

Cuthbert, B. N., Bradley, M. M., & Lang, P. J. (1996). Probing picture perception: Activation and emotion. *Psychophysiology, 33*, 103–111.

Cuthbert, B. N., Schupp, H., McManis, M., Hillman, C., Bradley, M. M., & Lang, P. J. (2000). Brain potentials in affective picture processing: Covariation with autonomic arousal and affective report. *Biological Psychology, 52*, 95–111.

Davis, M. (1989). Neural systems involved in fear-potentiated startle. In M. Davis, B. L. Jacobs, & R. I. Schoenfeld (Eds.), *Annals of the New York Academy of Sciences, Vol. 563. Modulation of defined neural vertebrate circuits* (pp. 165–183). New York: Author.

Fowles, D.C. (1980). The three arousal model: Implications of Gray's two-factor learning theory for heart rate, electrodermal activity, and psychopathy. *Psychophysiology, 17*, 87–104.

Fowles, D. C., & Dindo, L. (2006). A dual deficit model of psychopathy. In C. J. Patrick (Ed.), *Handbook of psychopathy* (pp. 14–34). New York: Guilford Press.

Gordon, H. L., Baird, A. A., & End, A. (2004). Functional differences among those high and low on a trait measure of psychopathy. *Biological Psychiatry, 56*, 516–521.

Gough, H. G. (1960). Theory and measurement of socialization. *Journal of Consulting and Clinical Psychology, 24*, 23–30.

Hall, J., Benning, S., & Patrick, C. J. (2004). Criterion-related validity of the three-factor model of psychopathy: Personality, behavior, and adaptive functioning. *Assessment, 11*, 4–16.

Hare, R. D. (1980). A research scale for the assessment of psychopathy in criminal populations. *Personality and Individual Differences, 1*, 111–119.

Hare, R. D. (1991). *The Hare Psychopathy Checklist—Revised*. Toronto, Ontario, Canada: Multi-Health Systems.

Hare, R. D. (2003). *The Hare Psychopathy Checklist—Revised* (2nd ed.). Toronto, Ontario, Canada: Multi-Health Systems.

Harpur, T. J., Hakstian, A. R., & Hare, R. D. (1988). Factor structure of the psychopathy checklist. *Journal of Consulting and Clinical Psychology, 56*, 741–747.

Harpur, T. J., Hare, R. D., & Hakstian, A. R. (1989). Two-factor conceptualization of psychopathy: Construct validity and assessment implications. *Psychological Assessment, 1*, 6–17.

Herpertz, S. C., Werth, U., Lukas, G., Qunaibi, M., Schuerkens, A., Kunert, H., et al. (2001). Emotion in criminal offenders with psychopathy and borderline personality disorder. *Archives of General Psychiatry, 58*, 737–744.

Hicks, B. M., Markon, K. E., Patrick, C. J., Krueger, R. F., & Newman, J. P. (2004). Identifying psychopathy subtypes on the basis of personality structure. *Psychological Assessment, 16*, 276–288.

Hicks, B. M., & Patrick, C. J. (in press). Psychopathy and negative affectivity: Analyses of suppressor effects reveal distinct relations with trait anxiety, depression, fearfulness, and anger-hostility. *Journal of Abnormal Psychology.*

Krueger, R. F., Hicks, B., Patrick, C. J., Carlson, S., Iacono, W. G., & McGue, M. (2002). Etiologic connections among substance dependence, antisocial behavior, and personality: Modeling the externalizing spectrum. *Journal of Abnormal Psychology, 111*, 411–424.

Lang, P. J., Bradley, M. M., & Cuthbert, B. N. (1990). Emotion, attention, and the startle reflex. *Psychological Review, 97*, 377–398.

Lang, P. J., Bradley, M. M., & Cuthbert, B. N. (1997). Motivated attention: Affect, activation, and action. In P. J. Lang, R. F. Simons, & M. T. Balaban (Eds.), *Attention and orienting: Sensory and motivational processes* (pp. 97–135). Hillsdale, NJ: Erlbaum.

Levenston, G. K., Patrick, C. J., Bradley, M. M., & Lang, P. J. (2000). The psychopath as observer: Emotion and attention in picture processing. *Journal of Abnormal Psychology, 109*, 373–385.

Lilienfeld, S. O. (1990). *Development and preliminary validation of a self-report measure of psychopathic personality.* Unpublished doctoral dissertation, University of Minnesota, Minneapolis.

Lilienfeld, S. O., & Andrews, B. P. (1996). Development and preliminary validation of a self-report measure of psychopathic personality traits in noncriminal populations. *Journal of Personality Assessment, 66*, 488–524.

Lykken, D. T. (1957). A study of anxiety in the sociopathic personality. *Journal of Abnormal and Clinical Psychology, 55*, 6–10.

Morey, L. (1991). *The Personality Assessment Inventory professional manual.* Odessa, FL: PAR.

Patrick, C. J. (1994). Emotion and psychopathy: Startling new insights. *Psychophysiology, 31*, 319–330.

Patrick, C. J. (2001). Emotions and psychopathy. In A. Raine & J. Sanmartin (Eds.), *Violence and psychopathy* (pp. 57–77). New York: Kluwer Academic.

Patrick, C. J. (2006). Back to the future: Cleckley as a guide to the next generation of psychopathy research. In C. J. Patrick (Ed.), *Handbook of psychopathy* (pp. 605–617). New York: Guilford Press.

Patrick, C. J. (in press). Antisocial personality disorder and psychopathy. In W. O'Donohue, K. A. Fowler, & S. O. Lilienfeld (Eds.), *Handbook of personality disorders*. New York: Sage.

Patrick, C. J., Bradley, M. M., & Lang, P. J. (1993). Emotion in the criminal psychopath: Startle reflex modulation. *Journal of Abnormal Psychology, 102,* 82–92.

Patrick, C. J., Edens, J. F., Poythress, N., & Lilienfeld, S. O. (2006). Construct validity of the PPI two-factor model with offenders. *Psychological Assessment, 18,* 204–208.

Patrick, C. J., Hicks, B. M., Krueger, R. F., & Lang, A. R. (2005). Relations between psychopathy facets and externalizing in a criminal offender sample. *Journal of Personality Disorders, 19,* 339–356.

Patrick, C. J., & Lang, A. R. (1999). Psychopathic traits and intoxicated states: Affective concomitants and conceptual links. In M. E. Dawson, A. M. Schell, & A. H. Boehmelt (Eds.), *Startle modification: Implications for clinical science, cognitive science, and neuroscience* (pp. 209–230). New York: Cambridge University Press.

Patrick, C. J., & Zempolich, K. A. (1998). Emotion and aggression in the psychopathic personality. *Aggression and Violent Behavior, 3,* 303–338.

Paulhus, D. L., Robins, R. W., Trzesniewski, K. H., & Tracy, J. L. (2004). Two replicable suppressor situations in personality research. *Multivariate Behavioral Research, 39,* 303–328.

Porter, S., & Woodworth, M. (2006). Psychopathy and aggression. In C. J. Patrick (Ed.), *Handbook of psychopathy* (pp. 481–494). New York: Guilford Press.

Poythress, N. G., Edens, J. F., & Lilienfeld, S. O. (1998). Criterion-related validity of the Psychopathic Personality Inventory in a prison sample. *Psychological Assessment, 10,* 426–430.

Raine, A. (1997). Antisocial behavior and psychophysiology: A biosocial perspective and a prefrontal dysfunction hypothesis. In D. M. Stoff, J. Breiling, & J. D. Maser (Eds.), *Handbook of antisocial behavior* (pp. 289–303). New York: Wiley.

Sutton, S. K., Vitale, J. E., & Newman, J. P. (2002). Emotion among females with psychopathy during picture perception. *Journal of Abnormal Psychology, 111,* 610–619.

Tellegen, A. (in press). *Manual for the Multidimensional Personality Questionnaire.* Minneapolis: University of Minnesota Press.

Vanman, E. J., Mejia, V. Y., Dawson, M. E., Schell, A. M., & Raine, A. (2003). Modification of the startle reflex in a community sample: Do one or two dimensions of psychopathy underlie emotional processing? *Personality and Individual Differences, 35,* 2007–2021.

Veit, R., Flor, H., Erb, M., Lotze, M., Grodd, W., & Birbaumer, N. (2002). Brain circuits involved in emotional learning in antisocial behavior and social phobia in humans. *Neuroscience Letters, 328*, 233–236.

Verona, E., Hicks, B. M., & Patrick, C. J. (2006). Psychopathy and suicidal behavior in female offenders: Effects of personality and abuse history. *Journal of Consulting and Clinical Psychology, 73*, 1065–1073.

Verona, E., Patrick, C. J., Curtin, J. J., Bradley, M. M., & Lang, P. J. (2004). Psychopathy and physiological response to emotionally evocative sounds. *Journal of Abnormal Psychology, 113*, 99–108.

Verona, E., Patrick, C. J., & Joiner, T. E. (2001). Psychopathy, antisocial personality, and suicide risk. *Journal of Abnormal Psychology, 110*, 462–470.

Vrana, S. R., Spence, E. L., & Lang, P. J. (1988). The startle probe response: A new measure of emotion? *Journal of Abnormal Psychology, 97*, 487–491.

Williamson, S. E., Harpur, T. J., & Hare, R. D. (1991). Abnormal processing of affective words by psychopaths. *Psychophysiology, 28*, 260–273.

Witvliet, C. V., & Vrana, S. R. (1995). Psychophysiologial responses as indices of affective dimensions. *Psychophysiology, 32*, 436–443.

III

TREATMENT APPLICATIONS AND FUTURE DIRECTIONS

11

EMOTION-BASED APPROACHES TO THE ANXIETY DISORDERS

FRANK J. FARACH AND DOUGLAS S. MENNIN

In this chapter, we review the profound influence of affective science research on the anxiety disorders field. Research on emotion, motivation, and emotion regulation has played a critical role in the development of unifying theories of anxiety disorders (e.g., Barlow, 2002; Barlow, Allen, & Choate, 2004) and novel clinical approaches to their treatment (e.g., Mennin, 2004; Newman, Castonguay, Borkovec, & Molnar, 2004; Orsillo, Roemer, Block-Lerner, LeJeune, & Herbert, 2005). Our aims in this chapter are (a) to review concepts from basic research in different areas of affective science (e.g., emotion, motivation, and emotion regulation) pertinent to emotion-focused clinical issues; (b) to illustrate how these areas of research have advanced understanding of the nature of anxiety disorders; (c) to describe how emotion research can be applied to the development of anxiety disorder treatments, using an example drawn from our own research program, emotion regulation therapy (ERT; Mennin, 2004) for generalized anxiety disorder (GAD); and (d) to highlight challenges and suggest future directions for emotion-based translational research agenda and treatment development for the anxiety disorders.

EMOTIONS MATTER:
THE ROLE OF AFFECTIVE SCIENCE IN ANXIETY

Emotion in behavioral and cognitive theory has been brought increasingly to the forefront. The last 2 decades have witnessed a number of persuasive calls for greater attention to the role of emotion in anxiety (e.g., Barlow, 2002) and in mental disorders more broadly (e.g., Gross & Muñoz, 1995). For example, Barlow (2002) synthesized research on cognition, behavior, and emotion to develop an overarching theoretical perspective on anxiety and mood disorders. He explained that these disorders are primarily emotional disorders involving dysfunction in emotional processes such as anxiety and fear. Citing a number of empirical investigations that examined the hierarchical structure of anxiety and mood pathology (e.g., Brown, Chorpita, & Barlow, 1998), he concluded that anxiety and mood symptoms share a higher order factor of negative affect. Further, behavioral accounts of anxiety disorders have begun to assert the importance of emotional responses as automatic, interoceptive cues for fear (Bouton, Mineka, & Barlow, 2001). S. C. Hayes and colleagues have maintained that radical behavior analysts should not avoid anxiety and emotions as concepts solely because they are difficult to operationalize (Friman, Hayes, & Wilson, 1998). Rather, they have argued, behavior analysts can study functional relationships among one's attempts to master, control, or accentuate emotions and the contexts in which they occur (Friman et al., 1998). Finally, investigators in social– and clinical–cognitive science increasingly have studied emotional and motivational processes in the anxiety disorders (e.g., Mogg & Bradley, 2004).

Although clinical psychology regarded emotion as a disruptive and empirically intractable phenomenon throughout much of the 20th century (see Samoilov & Goldfried, 2000), contemporary approaches to understanding emotion emphasize its adaptive value (Berenbaum, Raghavan, Le, Vernon, & Gomez, 2003; Greenberg, 2002; Samoilov & Goldfried, 2000). It is now generally agreed that emotions represent more than idiosyncratic reactions to environmental stimuli—they serve various biological, psychological, and social functions that increased the probability of reproductive success among our distant ancestors (for a review, see Ekman & Davidson, 1994). Emotions are complex responses characterized by rapid and often discordant change across multiple response domains, including physiology, behavior, and subjective experience (Bradley, Codispoti, Cuthbert, & Lang, 2001). Further, current theorists have argued that emotions are cues for readiness for action that work to establish, maintain, or disrupt relationships with personally relevant internal and external environmental stimuli (Frijda, 1986). In addition, emotion is seen by many as serving an information function, notifying individuals of the relevance of their concerns, needs, or goals in a given moment (Schwarz & Clore, 2003).

Functional accounts of emotions have affected clinical psychology in several important ways. First, they have fostered greater interest in the role of emotion both in psychological science and in clinical subdisciplines of psychopathology (Kring & Werner, 2004) and psychotherapy (Samoilov & Goldfried, 2000). Second, functional accounts of emotion have spawned interest in the ways in which emotional dysfunction may occur. For example, much is known about how emotion may disrupt cognitive processes, but less is known about the conditions and skills sets under which individuals are able to utilize emotional information. Finally, a functional view of emotions suggests that they do not exist in a vacuum; emotions have an "aboutness" to them. As we will see next, motivational research provides a deeper perspective on just what emotions—especially anxiety—may be about.

MOTIVATIONAL PERSPECTIVE ON ANXIETY DISORDERS

Emotional responding may be seen as organized by opposing motivational systems that respond differentially to punishment and reward (Bradley et al., 2001). Important for our purposes is the fact that several investigators have applied a motivational perspective to the anxiety disorders. J. A. Gray and McNaughton (2000), synthesizing decades of ethological, pharmacological, and neuropsychological animal research, developed a neuropsychological trait theory of anxiety. The theory holds that three neurobiological systems coordinate appetitive and aversive responses to motivationally relevant stimuli. The behavioral inhibition system (BIS) inhibits behavior in response to stimuli that signal punishment or nonreward (e.g., aversive or novel stimuli), increases cognitive vigilance and analysis of potential threat, and increases arousal in preparation for possible action. Accordingly, J. A. Gray and McNaughton (2000) have called the BIS the "stop, look, and listen" system and have proposed that it is the biological seat of anxiety. In contrast to the BIS, the behavioral activation system (BAS) activates behavior in response to stimuli that signal reward or relief from punishment (i.e., appetitive stimuli). Finally, a fight–flight system (FFS) mediates active defense and escape behavior in response to unconditioned stimuli (e.g., being attacked) through massive physiological arousal.

Several commentators (e.g., Fowles, 1992) have noted the strong convergence between J. A. Gray and McNaughton's (2000) animal-based theory of anxiety and Barlow's (2002) theoretical account of human anxiety disorders. Barlow distinguished sharply between fear and anxiety. Fear is a high-intensity, alarmlike bodily response to an immediate and imminent threat, resembling the functions of J. A. Gray and McNaughton's FFS. In contrast, anxiety is characterized by the process of anxious apprehension—a combination of negative affect, physiological arousal, and hypervigilance in response to interoceptive or environmental cues (Barlow, 2002). The perception that one cannot control or predict personally relevant events is one of the hallmarks of anxious apprehension. These features appear to be analogous to J. A. Gray and McNaughton's description of the BIS as the "stop, look, and listen" system. Both theorists emphasized that strong activation of the BIS or anxious apprehension is part of normal anxiety; it is the chronicity of these processes that characterizes pathological anxiety.

J. A. Gray and McNaughton (2000) theorized that individual differences in activity in the BIS and BAS should be linked to anxiety-relevant differences in personality and temperament. For example, individuals with chronic overactivation of the BIS should be high on the personality dimensions of introversion and neuroticism, whereas individuals with chronic BAS hyperactivation should be high on extraversion and emotional stability. Individuals high on neuroticism tend to have high tonic levels of sympathetic arousal and to habituate slowly to stimuli (Eysenck, 1967). In addition, individuals with chronically high activation of the BIS tend to be socially withdrawn and reticent, temperamental factors that appear to be relatively stable during early development (Kagan, Reznick, & Snidman, 1988) and that predict development of social anxiety disorder (SAD; Biederman et al., 1993).

EMOTION REGULATION

Frijda (1986) commented that "people not only have emotions, they also handle them" (p. 401). Although the idea that emotions can be regulated has a long intellectual history (e.g., Aristotle's *Nicomachean Ethics*), empirical research on emotion regulation has accelerated since the mid-1990s, leading to its declaration as a new field of study (Gross, 1998b). However, emotion regulation has been conceptualized and operationalized in many ways, reflecting a wide variety of research questions across subdisciplines, populations, and levels of analysis. For example, some researchers have discussed emotion regulation primarily in terms of cognitive processes that up-regulate (i.e., enhance) or down-regulate (i.e., dampen) emotion (e.g., Ochsner & Gross, 2005). In this vein, a recent and popular description is that emotion regulation, as a field of study, examines how individuals influence, control, experience, and express their emotions (Gross, 1998a). Others (e.g., Dodge & Garber, 1991), however, have argued that emotion regulation encompasses not only the regulation *of* emotion by cognition, but also the regulation *by* emotion of other emotional, cognitive, and behavioral processes in oneself and others. Yet another approach studies emotion regulation from a functional systems perspective in which emotion regulation is characterized as a collection of highly interdependent cognitive, emotional, behavioral, and physiological processes. Indeed, basic research on cognition–

emotion interaction has begun to blur traditional boundaries between these systems (see J. R. Gray, 2004). A functional systems approach to the study of emotion regulation seeks to explain how these systems work together to maintain dynamic homeostasis between bodily systems and internal and external stimuli in a context-appropriate manner (Bonanno, 2001). The three perspectives on emotion regulation described earlier are neither mutually exclusive nor exhaustive (for a review, see Gross, 1998a). It is important for the field to continue to work toward building larger frameworks that encompass these definitions and to demonstrate how their components interrelate.

Fortunately, as the field of emotion regulation has progressed, research in several different traditions has begun to be applied to similar questions. For example, there has been increasing attention to individual differences both in the operation of component subsystems and in their interaction. A richer appreciation of how individual differences in emotion regulation relate to well-being, adaptive functioning, and dysfunction may bolster our understanding of anxiety disorders and inform their treatment.

Models of Emotion Regulatory Ability and Dysfunction

Considerable evidence suggests that individuals differ widely in their ability to attend to, process, and act on their emotions effectively. Salovey, Mayer, and colleagues (Mayer & Salovey, 1997; Mayer, Salovey, Caruso, & Sitarenios, 2001) have stressed the value of these abilities for emotional, physical, and societal success, coining the term *emotional intelligence* (Salovey & Mayer, 1990). Emotional intelligence may be demonstrated at four levels: (a) perception, appraisal, and expression of emotion; (b) emotion's facilitative effect on thinking; (c) understanding and analyzing emotions and employing emotional knowledge; and (d) reflective regulation of emotions to promote emotional and intellectual growth. Accordingly, individuals who are able to recognize emotional experiences, understand their meaning, use their informational value, and manage their experience in a context-appropriate manner would be expected to respond more effectively to life's demands. Research supports the benefits of emotional intelligence and implicates the emotional management factor as being central to functional outcome (e.g., Lopes et al., 2004).

Researchers have devised a number of taxonomies, distinctions, and heuristics to provide guidance in delineating adaptive and maladaptive emotion regulation (Berenbaum et al., 2003; Cicchetti, Ackerman, & Izard, 1995; Rottenberg & Gross, 2003). For example, Cicchetti et al. (1995) divided emotional regulation problems into two categories: The first involves difficulties in modulation of emotional experience or expression; the second involves frequent or automatic attempts to control or suppress emotional experience or expression. In the first scenario, the person experiences emotions with great intensity but is unable to modulate the experience adequately (e.g., by self-soothing, by inhibiting emotional expression). In the second scenario, the person engages in excessive control strategies (e.g., behavioral or cognitive avoidance) that prevent emotion from being experienced, making it difficult to act on desired goals. Similarly, Kring and Werner (2004) noted that emotion dysregulation can arise from deficits in regulatory components themselves (e.g., attention, working memory, limbic reactivity) as well as from poor implementation of intact emotion regulatory abilities. Although this distinction is not often addressed in psychopathology research, it is important because the difference between emotion regulatory deficits versus problems in emotion regulation suggests fundamentally different kinds of intervention (Kring & Werner, 2004).

Emotion Dysregulation Perspective on Anxiety Disorders

Despite the increasingly sophisticated use of emotion theory to address psychopathology (Berenbaum et al., 2003; Gross & Muñoz, 1995; Kring & Bachorowski, 1999) and the delineation of abnormal emotion reactivity in emotional disorders, such as posttraumatic stress disorder (e.g., Miller & Litz, 2004) and unipolar depression (e.g., Rottenberg, Gross, Wilhelm, Najmi, & Gotlib, 2002), surprisingly little psychopathology research has explicitly focused on emotion (dys)regulation. We have recently developed an emotion dysregulation model of anxiety and mood disorders (for an introduction, see Mennin, 2005). In this model, emotion disruption and dysregulation may be reflected in (a) heightened intensity of emotions (i.e., emotional reactions occur intensely, easily, and quickly), (b) poor understanding of emotions (i.e., difficulty in identifying emotions such as anger, sadness, fear, disgust, and joy and instead experiencing emotions as undifferentiated, confusing, and overwhelming), (c) negative reactivity to one's emotional state (i.e., emotions are experienced as aversive and anxiety provoking, as reflected in rigid attentional processes, lack of acceptance, and the activation of negative beliefs about emotions), and (d) maladaptive emotional management responses (e.g., difficulty knowing when or how to enhance or diminish emotional experience in a manner that is appropriate to the environmental context and personal goals).

Mennin (2005) argued that these components may interact and interrelate temporally. Given both intense emotional responses and poor understanding of these responses, anxious individuals may react to emotions with rigid attentional processes and a negative cognitive set, which might beget a need to manage this experience. Without such management skills, however, a person with an anxiety disorder may choose poor or ineffective strategies or lose the ability to regulate altogether. Indeed, heightened emotional intensity and reactivity have been found to decrease one's ability to regulate emotions successfully (Eisenberg, Cumberland, & Spinrad, 1998; Linehan, 1993; Thompson & Calkins, 1996). Further, individuals are more likely to regulate their intense emotional experiences effectively when they can differentiate the emotions being experienced (an indicator of emotional understanding; Feldman Barrett, Gross, Christensen, & Benvenuto, 2001).

A number of studies have demonstrated relationships between deficits in each of these components and a number of emotional disorders. Heightened intensity of emotions has been found to characterize individuals with GAD, in particular. Heightened intensity has been demonstrated in GAD relative to nonanxious control participants (Mennin, Heimberg, Fresco, & Turk, 2005, Studies 1 and 2), SAD (Mennin, Holaway, Fresco, & Heimberg, in press; Turk, Heimberg, Luterek, Mennin, & Fresco, 2005), eating disorders (Fresco, Wolfson, Crowther, & Moore, 2005), and depression (Mennin et al., in press). Consistent with the notion in the Mennin (2005) model that individuals with anxiety disorders have poor understanding of their emotions, individuals with GAD (Mennin et al., 2005, Studies 1 and 2; Mennin et al., in press; Turk et al., 2005), SAD (Mennin et al., in press; Turk et al., 2005), panic disorder (Baker, Holloway, Thomas, Thomas, & Owens, 2004; Parker, Taylor, Bagby, & Acklin, 1993; Tull & Roemer, 2006), and childhood sexual abuse–related posttraumatic stress disorder (Cloitre, Koenen, Cohen, & Han, 2002) have reported more difficulty than nonanxious control participants in identifying, describing, and clarifying the motivational content of their emotions.

The third component of this emotion regulation model—that individuals with anxiety disorders may react negatively to their emotions with fear and anxiety—has been demonstrated repeatedly. Leahy (2002) found that both depression and anxiety were characterized by guilt and were associated with viewing one's own emotions as incomprehensible, uncontrollable, and different from others' emotions. However, whereas depression was more closely associated with expectations of long mood duration, anxiety was more likely to be associated with lack of acceptance of emotions. Chambless and colleagues found that individuals who feared emotions were more likely to be reactive to induced bodily sensations (Williams, Chambless, & Ahrens, 1997), even beyond the effects of state and trait anxiety (Berg, Shapiro, Chambless, & Ahrens, 1998). Individuals with GAD (Mennin et al., 2005, Studies 1 and 2; Roemer, Salters, Raffa, & Orsillo, 2005; Turk et al., 2005) and SAD (Turk et al., 2005) also have reported greater fear of negative and positive emotions than control participants. Further, negative reactivity to one's emotions, measured 4 months after the terrorist attacks on September 11, 2001, mediated the relationship between analogue GAD (measured September 10, 2001) and increases in anxiety and mood symptoms and functional impairment 12 months after the attacks in young adults directly exposed to the World Trade Center collapse (Farach, Mennin, Smith, & Mandelbaum, 2006). Another aspect of negative reactivity is an inability to accept experienced emotions, which has been demonstrated in GAD (state level: Mennin et al., 2005, Study 3; trait level: Farach et al., 2006; Roemer et al., 2005; Salters-Pedneault,

Roemer, Tull, Rucker, & Mennin, in press) and panic disorder (Tull & Roemer, 2006).

Individuals with anxiety disorders have demonstrated difficulty managing emotions (i.e., maladaptive management of emotions). Difficulty repairing a negative mood has been found to be associated with trait levels of GAD (Mennin et al., 2005, Studies 1 and 2; Turk et al., 2005) and SAD (Salovey, Stroud, Woolery, & Epel, 2002; Turk et al., 2005), as well as state responses to an induced negative mood in GAD (Mennin et al., 2005, Study 3). GAD and worry have also been found to be associated with deficits in the ability to engage in goal-directed behavior when distressed, to display impulse control, and to access effective regulation strategies (Salters-Pedneault et al., in press). In a recent study, Tull and Roemer (2006, Study 2) found that individuals with uncued panic reported greater use of emotionally avoidant emotion regulation strategies in response to both negative and positive film clips despite comparable levels of self-reported distress and physiological arousal. Baker et al. (2004) found that patients with panic disorder were more likely to be controlling of negative emotions, using maladaptive strategies such as "smothering" or "bottling up" emotions and expressive inhibition. These findings appeared to be independent of anxiety or depressive symptoms, intensity and frequency of emotion, phobic avoidance, agoraphobic cognitions, or bodily sensations. In addition, Cloitre and colleagues have shown that the inability to regulate negative moods in women with posttraumatic stress disorder and a history of child abuse is associated with functional impairment beyond the effects of posttraumatic symptoms (Cloitre, Miranda, Stovall-McClough, & Han, 2005) and with poor treatment response (Cloitre et al., 2002; Cloitre, Stovall-McClough, Miranda, & Chemtob, 2004).

INTEGRATING AFFECTIVE AND CLINICAL APPROACHES TO TREATING ANXIETY DISORDERS

In addition to expanding the knowledge base and unifying theories of psychopathology in the anxiety disorders, a research focus on emotion's function as well as dysfunction may have implications for treatment. For example, exposure to fear-provoking cues is at the core of behavioral treatments for anxiety disorders. Since its original formulation by Wolpe (1958) and refinement by other researchers (e.g., Foa & Kozak, 1986), exposure therapy has been demonstrated repeatedly to be efficacious for the treatment of anxiety disorders (see Whelton, 2004). Mowrer's (1947) two-factor theory holds that fear is acquired through classical conditioning and maintained operantly through avoidance of fear-conditioned stimuli. Traditional exposure therapy elegantly addresses both factors by having clients repeatedly access cognitive–affective representations of their fear in the presence of incompatible contextual information (e.g., safety cues, habituation of fear; Foa & Kozak,

1986). Successful emotional processing of fear is inferred from initial increases in physiological and verbal self-report of fear followed by steady decreases in these emotional response domains within and across exposure sessions (Foa & Kozak, 1986).

Despite robust empirical support for the efficacy of exposure therapy in the anxiety disorders, a number of challenges to treatment remain that can limit efficacy. One major challenge is that traditional exposure therapy may not work well for all anxiety disorders. The mechanisms believed to underlie emotional processing—fear structure activation and habituation—may operate best when the fear stimulus is focal and difficult to avoid. Exposure therapy for anxiety disorders that best meet these criteria, such as specific phobia, tends to be highly efficient, effective, and robust (e.g., Öst, 1989). Yet some investigators have noted that traditional exposure therapy may be less efficacious in anxiety disorders characterized by less-circumscribed fear, diffuse anxiety, and high levels of covert avoidance (Mennin, Heimberg, Turk, & Fresco, 2002; Roemer & Orsillo, 2002). Recent meta-analyses of randomized, controlled trials of cognitive and behavioral treatments for GAD found that purely behavioral treatments have demonstrated modest efficacy in GAD (Borkovec & Ruscio, 2001; Gould, Otto, Pollack, & Yap, 1997). Further, despite statistically significant change at posttreatment and follow-up observed across cognitive and behavioral treatment studies included in the analyses by Borkovec and Ruscio (2001), only 50% to 60% of patients achieved high end-state functioning. End-state functioning was not substantially improved with a doubling of therapeutic contact (Borkovec, Newman, Pincus, & Lytle, 2002). These findings are not an indictment of traditional exposure therapy, but they suggest the need for new approaches to extending its efficacy and improving end-state functioning in the treatment of this impairing disorder. A promising line of research would attempt to ameliorate or work around factors (e.g., cognitive avoidance, slow habituation) that may obstruct or dampen emotional processing during psychotherapy in individuals with more diffuse anxiety. A broader, integrative perspective on emotional processing may suggest ways to accomplish this.

Expanding the Construct of Emotional Processing

The basic research just reviewed on emotion, motivation, and emotion regulation, which focuses on the adaptive value of these processes, suggests an expanded view of emotional processing in the anxiety disorders. *Emotional processing* was originally defined as "a process whereby emotional disturbances are absorbed and decline to the extent that other experiences and behaviour can proceed without disruption" (Rachman, 1980, p. 51). This view informed the evaluation of emotional processing and the focus on symptom reduction in traditional exposure therapy. However, emotional processing can also be considered as an active attending to emotion such that motivational information can be used to accomplish important goals. The ability to process emotion effectively, in this manner, is viewed as an indicator of positive emotion regulation or emotional intelligence. Furthermore, this ability can be cultivated and improved through active intervention and skill development.

Functional views of emotion and emotion-regulation skills have been foundational for a number of recently developed interventions for the anxiety disorders. Newman et al. (2004) have developed an intervention that focuses on improving emotional processing through associations with the interpersonal context. Acceptance- and mindfulness-based approaches increasingly have been developed as stand-alone, supplemental, or integrated interventions with cognitive–behavioral therapy for anxiety disorders (Eifert & Forsyth, 2005; Orsillo & Batten, 2005; Roemer & Orsillo, 2005; Singh, Wahler, Winton, & Adkins, 2004). These interventions view the allowance of emotional experiences as essential to breaking maladaptive intrapersonal and interpersonal patterns. Linehan (1993) developed dialectical behavior therapy, an empirically supported mindfulness-based and emotion regulatory skills-based intervention for individuals with borderline personality disorder, that has served as a resource for individuals developing mindfulness-based approaches to the treatment of anxiety disorders (Gratz, Tull, & Wagner, 2005). In acceptance and commitment therapy (ACT; S. C. Hayes, Strosahl, & Wilson, 1999), clients are given extensive training in attending to and examining their internal experiences (e.g., emotions, thoughts, sensations) without avoiding them. Elements of this intervention have been combined with mindfulness techniques and integrated with cognitive–behavioral therapy for GAD to help clients increase awareness of their emotional state and to allow them to use this information to set, prioritize, and achieve adaptive personal goals (Roemer & Orsillo, 2005).

Experiential therapists have also developed conceptualizations of emotional processing consistent with a functional view of emotion processing. These individuals have discussed interventions intended to increase clients' ability to tolerate and embrace emotional experience (e.g., Greenberg, 2002; Greenberg & Safran, 1987). In particular, emotion-focused therapy (Greenberg, 2002) targets factors similar to the components of emotional intelligence described earlier (Mayer & Salovey, 1997). Goals of this treatment include acceptance of emotional experiences, adaptive use of this experience to create meaning, and the transformation of maladaptive emotional states to more productive emotional states that aid in effective decision making and adaptive action engagement (Greenberg, 2002).

Although it has incorporated functional views of emotion since its inception, the experiential tradition has historically not been committed to an empirical approach to understanding the relationship between emotion and psychopathology and psychotherapeutic process. However, contemporary experiential therapy has improved this state of affairs in several ways. First,

Greenberg has developed his approach largely from basic findings concerning the functional role of emotions and their putative neurobiological substrates. Investigators have shown through a number of studies that depth of emotional experiencing in session is related to positive therapeutic outcome (see Whelton, 2004). Recently, in line with current trends in emotion research, Greenberg (2002) has begun to stress not only the experience of emotions but also the need for their management and regulation. Finally, although experiential traditions originally eschewed the concept of disorder, experiential therapists have begun to delineate their approaches to specific populations, such as people with depression (Pos, Greenberg, Goldman, & Korman, 2003). This may eventually allow experiential therapeutic processes to be specified for different forms of psychopathological conditions.

Emotion Regulation Therapy for Generalized Anxiety Disorder

An alternative approach to incorporating affective sciences into treatment for anxiety disorders is ERT for GAD (for other approaches that incorporate emotion elements in treating GAD, see also Huppert & Alley, 2004; Newman et al., 2004; Roemer & Orsillo, 2005). ERT is based on a model of emotion dysregulation in psychopathology developed by Mennin and colleagues (Mennin, 2005; Mennin et al., 2005) and integrates conceptualizations of functional emotions, motivation, emotion regulation, and emotional intelligence into an intervention for GAD, a condition that is often resistant to traditional treatments (Borkovec & Ruscio, 2001). ERT draws from both traditional and acceptance-based behavioral and cognitive treatments but also integrates experiential interventions from emotion-focused approaches. Given the findings concerning emotion deficits in GAD reviewed earlier, treatment for this disorder may benefit from the incorporation of these emotion-based approaches.

The goals of ERT are for individuals to become better able to (a) identify, differentiate, and describe their emotions, even in their most intense forms; (b) increase acceptance of affective experience and ability to manage emotions adaptively when necessary; (c) decrease use of emotional avoidance strategies (e.g., worry); and (d) increase ability to use emotional information in identifying needs, making decisions, guiding thinking, motivating behavior, and managing interpersonal relationships and other contextual demands. Achievement of these therapeutic goals should equip clients with the ability to increase or decrease their attention to emotional experience as is necessary to attain desired outcomes, tolerate distress, and properly adapt to life's inevitable challenges.

Initial sessions of ERT (Phase I) focus on psychoeducation about GAD, functional patterns of worry and emotions in past and current situations, and self-monitoring of worry or anxiety episodes. The sessions next focus on the development of somatic awareness and emotion-regulation skills (Phase II).

Phase III is composed of the most essential and intensive sessions of the treatment, because they focus on the application of skills during exposure to emotionally evocative themes. The final sessions focus on terminating the therapeutic relationship, relapse prevention, and future goals (Phase IV).

Skills-training elements related to awareness of bodily reactions, acceptance, and adaptive regulation of emotions are included in ERT. Berenbaum et al. (2003) recommended the use of skills training for individuals with deficits in emotional understanding, especially before the use of exposure techniques with anxious individuals. Indeed, other treatments have demonstrated the efficacy and utility of providing skills training in emotion regulation to increase patients' ability to engage in a later exposure component (Cloitre et al., 2002; Linehan, 1993).

The regulation skills taught in ERT correspond to the deficits outlined in the emotion dysregulation model. In particular, patients learn about identifying intense emotional reactions, understanding their motivational meaning, using this affective information (rather than reacting in a constraining and negative manner), and regulating these emotions appropriately to the given context. As part of learning to understand the motivational values of their emotional reactions, patients explore the balance of prevention and promotion goals (Higgins, 1997; Rodebaugh & Heimberg, in press), which in session are termed *security needs* and *fulfillment needs*, respectively (Mennin, 2004). Patients also learn to attend to situational demands to help determine which motivational goals will be most productive in a given situation.

Following skills training, emotion-focused techniques from the experiential tradition (Greenberg, 2002) are used for the purpose of in-session emotion evocation to generate experiential learning of the skills that have been developed. In-session exposure exercises (referred to as *thematic experiential exposure* exercises) are used to help clients actively engage emotions, attenuate the anxiety engendered by these emotions, and use increased understanding of their emotional reactions to inform needs, goals, and plans for action. If treatment focused solely on learning new skills to tolerate and regulate emotions, clients could continue to avoid aversive emotions by thinking about problems and needs intellectually without exposing themselves to feared emotional experiences (and their associated core thematic meaning) or practicing using the adaptive information these emotional experiences provide.

Thematic experiential exposure exercises are aimed at raising awareness of emotions, encouraging acceptance of emotional experience, and fostering regulatory strategies to generate adaptive courses of action related to core thematic issues. Each of these exercises is used to induce emotional arousal, increase understanding about the nature of these conflicts, and develop adaptive plans of action. By the end of this phase, clients will have had multiple opportunities to actively test their beliefs about emotional arousal; use their skills of somatic awareness and emotion regulation to address these concerns; and generate new courses of action based on the integration of cognitive, emotional, and contextual sources of information. A number of techniques are used to help clients experience feared emotional themes ranging from more experientially focused exercises aimed at increasing attention to emotions to cognitive and behavioral exercises aimed at addressing defensive and avoidant behavior.

Formal outcome data for ERT are not yet available. Given that ERT is currently under development and will likely be altered from its present form as lessons are learned from its ongoing implementation, it is unclear how this type of integrative approach will fare for GAD or other anxiety disorders. Some evidence is available that an integrative, acceptance-based behavioral approach that incorporates acceptance and experiential techniques within an emotion regulation framework is effective for treating depression (A. M. Hayes, Beevers, Feldman, Laurenceau, & Perlman, 2005). However, further research is clearly necessary to determine whether an explicit emotion focus and integration of emotion-focused interventions is beneficial.

CONCLUSION

In this chapter, we have highlighted the importance of emotion-based research for the conceptualization and treatment of anxiety disorders. However, much challenging work lies ahead in translating affective science research to psychotherapy for anxiety disorders. Progress in translational research agendas will depend critically on creative and integrative synthesis by investigators across basic and applied research contexts. For example, experimental psychopathology is well equipped to extend research from basic affective science to a range of clinical phenomena (Zvolensky, Lejuez, Stuart, & Curtin, 2001), as it has done many times in the area of anxiety disorders. However, much of this research has focused on emotion in the intrapersonal domain; there is a clear need for more translational research on interpersonal aspects of emotion in anxiety and other disorders. Emotional, motivational, and emotion-regulatory processes are ripe for further exploration in the laboratory as well as in more naturalistic settings via advances in multimethod assessment. As theory and experimental research grow more complex, however, it becomes increasingly important for researchers to clarify and agree on what emotion regulation is; how it should be measured; and how clinical approaches, such as those for anxiety disorders, may benefit from the research. In addition, researchers and clinicians have begun to apply findings from the translational research spectrum to treatment development (e.g., Roemer & Orsillo, 2005). Major challenges in this area are to determine the incremental validity of integrating emotion-based approaches into existing cognitive–behavioral treatment packages as well as to explore potential moderators (e.g., diagnosis) and mediators (e.g., changes in emotion regulatory skills) of therapeutic change in these integrated packages. It is our hope that basic affective science and clinical science will continue to build partnerships for translational research on anxiety disorders as exemplified by the perspectives and research programs presented in this book.

REFERENCES

Baker, R., Holloway, J., Thomas, P. W., Thomas, S., & Owens, M. (2004). Emotional processing and panic. *Behaviour Research and Therapy, 42,* 1271–1287.

Barlow, D. H. (2002). Fear, anxiety, and theories of emotion. In D. H. Barlow (Ed.), *Anxiety and its disorders: The nature and treatment of anxiety and panic* (2nd ed., pp. 37–63). New York: Guilford Press.

Barlow, D. H., Allen, L. B., & Choate, M. L. (2004). Toward a unified treatment for emotional disorders. *Behavior Therapy, 35,* 205–230.

Berenbaum, H., Raghavan, C., Le, H.-N., Vernon, L. L., & Gomez, J. J. (2003). A taxonomy of emotional disturbances. *Clinical Psychology: Science and Practice, 10,* 206–226.

Berg, C. Z., Shapiro, N., Chambless, D., & Ahrens, A. (1998). Are emotions frightening? II: An analogue study of fear of emotion, interpersonal conflict, and panic onset. *Behaviour Research and Therapy, 36,* 3–15.

Biederman, J., Rosenbaum, J. F., Bolduc, E. A., Faraone, S. V., Chaloff, J., Hirshfeld, D. R., et al. (1993). A three-year follow-up of children with and without behavioral inhibition. *Journal of the American Academy of Child and Adolescent Psychiatry, 32,* 814–821.

Bonanno, G. A. (2001). Self-regulation of emotions. In T. J. Mayne & G. A. Bonanno (Eds.), *Emotions: Current issues and future directions* (pp. 251–285). New York: Guilford Press.

Borkovec, T. D., Newman, M. G., Pincus, A. L., & Lytle, R. (2002). A component analysis of cognitive–behavioral therapy for generalized anxiety disorder and the role of interpersonal problems. *Journal of Consulting and Clinical Psychology, 70,* 288–298.

Borkovec, T. D., & Ruscio, A. M. (2001). Psychotherapy for generalized anxiety disorder. *Journal of Clinical Psychiatry, 62,* 37–42.

Bouton, M. E., Mineka, S., & Barlow, D. H. (2001). A modern learning theory perspective on the etiology of panic disorder. *Psychological Review, 108,* 4–32.

Bradley, M. M., Codispoti, M., Cuthbert, B. N., & Lang, P. J. (2001). Emotion and motivation I: Defensive and appetitive reactions in picture processing. *Emotion, 1,* 276–298.

Brown, T. A., Chorpita, B. F., & Barlow, D. H. (1998). Structural relationships among dimensions of the *DSM–IV* anxiety and mood disorders and dimensions of negative affect, positive affect, and autonomic arousal. *Journal of Abnormal Psychology, 107,* 179–192.

Cicchetti, D., Ackerman, B. P., & Izard, C. E. (1995). Emotions and emotion regulation in developmental psychopathology. *Development and Psychopathology, 7,* 1–10.

Cloitre, M., Koenen, K. C., Cohen, L. R., & Han, H. (2002). Skills training in affective and interpersonal regulation followed by exposure: A phase-based treatment for PTSD related to child abuse. *Journal of Consulting and Clinical Psychology, 70,* 1067–1074.

Cloitre, M., Miranda, R., Stovall-McClough, K. C., & Han, H. (2005). Beyond PTSD: Emotion regulation and interpersonal problems as predictors of functional impairment in survivors of childhood abuse. *Behavior Therapy, 36,* 119–124.

Cloitre, M., Stovall-McClough, K. C., Miranda, R., & Chemtob, C. M. (2004). Therapeutic alliance, negative mood regulation, and treatment outcome in child abuse–related posttraumatic stress disorder. *Journal of Consulting and Clinical Psychology, 72,* 411–416.

Dodge, K. A., & Garber, J. (1991). Domains of emotion regulation. In J. Garber & K. A. Dodge (Eds.), *The development of emotion regulation and dysregulation* (pp. 3–14). Cambridge, England: Cambridge University Press.

Eifert, G. H., & Forsyth, J. P. (2005). *Acceptance and commitment therapy for anxiety disorders: A practitioner's treatment guide to using mindfulness, acceptance, and values-based behavior change strategies.* Oakland, CA: New Harbinger.

Eisenberg, N., Cumberland, A., & Spinrad, T. L. (1998). Parental socialization of emotion. *Psychological Inquiry, 9,* 241–273.

Ekman, P., & Davidson, R. J. (Eds.). (1994). *The nature of emotion: Fundamental questions.* New York: Oxford University Press.

Eysenck, H. J. (1967). *The biological basis of personality.* Springfield, IL: Springer-Verlag.

Farach, F. J., Mennin, D. S., Smith, R. L., & Mandelbaum, M. G. (2006). *The impact of pretrauma GAD and posttraumatic emotional reactivity following exposure to the September 11 terrorist attacks: A longitudinal study.* Manuscript submitted for publication.

Feldman Barrett, L., Gross, J. J., Christensen, T. C., & Benvenuto, M. (2001). Knowing what you're feeling and knowing what to do about it: Mapping the relation between emotion differentiation and emotion regulation. *Cognition and Emotion, 15,* 713–724.

Foa, E. B., & Kozak, M. J. (1986). Emotional processing of fear: Exposure to corrective information. *Psychological Bulletin, 99,* 20–35.

Fowles, D. C. (1992). Motivational approach to anxiety disorders. In D. G. Forgays, T. Sosnowski, & K. Wrzesniewski (Eds.), *Anxiety: Recent developments in cognitive, psychophysiological, and health research* (pp. 181–192). Washington, DC: Hemisphere.

Fresco, D. M., Wolfson, S. L., Crowther, J. H., & Moore, M. T. (2005, November). *Distinct and overlapping patterns of emotion regulation in the comorbidity of GAD and binge/purge eating disorders.* Paper presented at the Annual Meeting of the Association for Behavioral and Cognitive Therapies, Washington, DC.

Frijda, N. H. (1986). *The emotions.* Cambridge, England: Cambridge University Press.

Friman, P. C., Hayes, S. C., & Wilson, K. G. (1998). Why behavior analysts should study emotion: The example of anxiety. *Journal of Applied Behavior Analysis, 31,* 137–156.

Gould, R. A., Otto, M. W., Pollack, M. H., & Yap, L. (1997). Cognitive behavioral and pharmacological treatment of generalized anxiety disorder: A preliminary meta-analysis. *Behavior Therapy, 28*, 285–305.

Gratz, K. L., Tull, M. T., & Wagner, A. W. (2005). Applying DBT mindfulness skills to the treatment of clients with anxiety disorders. In S. M. Orsillo & L. Roemer (Eds.), *Acceptance and mindfulness-based approaches to anxiety: Conceptualization and treatment* (pp. 147–164). New York: Springer Science & Business Media.

Gray, J. A., & McNaughton, N. (2000). *The neuropsychology of anxiety: An enquiry into the functions of the septo-hippocampal system* (2nd ed.). New York: Oxford University Press.

Gray, J. R. (2004). Integration of emotion and cognitive control. *Current Directions in Psychological Science, 13*, 46–48.

Greenberg, L. S. (2002). *Emotion-focused therapy: Coaching clients to work through their feelings.* Washington, DC: American Psychological Association.

Greenberg, L. S., & Safran, J. D. (1987). *Emotion in psychotherapy: Affect, cognition, and the process of change.* New York: Guilford Press.

Gross, J. J. (1998a). Antecedent- and response-focused emotion regulation: Divergent consequences for experience, expression, and physiology. *Journal of Personality and Social Psychology, 74*, 224–237.

Gross, J. J. (1998b). The emerging field of emotion regulation: An integrative review. *Review of General Psychology, 2*, 271–299.

Gross, J. J., & Muñoz, R. F. (1995). Emotion regulation and mental health. *Clinical Psychology: Science and Practice, 2*, 151–164.

Hayes, A. M., Beevers, C., Feldman, G., Laurenceau, J. P., & Perlman, C. (2005). Preliminary outcome of an integrated depression treatment and wellness promotion program. *International Journal of Behavioral Medicine, 12*, 111–122.

Hayes, S. C., Strosahl, K., & Wilson, K. G. (1999). *Acceptance and commitment therapy: An experiential approach to behavior change.* New York: Guilford Press.

Higgins, E. T. (1997). Beyond pleasure and pain. *American Psychologist, 52*, 1280–1300.

Huppert, J. D., & Alley, A. C. (2004). The clinical application of emotion research in generalized anxiety disorder: Some proposed procedures. *Cognitive and Behavioral Practice, 11*, 387–392.

Kagan, J., Reznick, J. S., & Snidman, N. (1988, April 8). Biological bases of childhood shyness. *Science, 240*, 167–171.

Kring, A. M., & Bachorowski, J.-A. (1999). Emotions and psychopathology. *Cognition and Emotion, 13*, 575–599.

Kring, A. M., & Werner, K. H. (2004). Emotion regulation and psychopathology. In P. Philippot & R. S. Feldman (Eds.), *The regulation of emotion* (pp. 359–385). Mahwah, NJ: Erlbaum.

Leahy, R. L. (2002). A model of emotional schemas. *Cognitive and Behavioral Practice, 9*, 177–190.

Linehan, M. M. (1993). *Cognitive–behavioral treatment of borderline personality disorder*. New York: Guilford Press.

Lopes, P. N., Brackett, M. A., Nezlek, J. B., Schutz, A., Sellin, I., & Salovey, P. (2004). Emotional intelligence and social interaction. *Personality and Social Psychology Bulletin, 30*, 1018–1034.

Mayer, J. D., & Salovey, P. (1997). What is emotional intelligence? In P. Salovey & D. J. Sluyter (Eds.), *Emotional development and emotional intelligence: Educational implications* (pp. 3–34). New York: Basic Books.

Mayer, J. D., Salovey, P., Caruso, D. R., & Sitarenios, G. (2001). Emotional intelligence as a standard intelligence. *Emotion, 1*, 232–242.

Mennin, D. S. (2004). An emotion regulation treatment for generalized anxiety disorder. *Clinical Psychology and Psychotherapy, 11*, 17–29.

Mennin, D. S. (2005). Emotion and the acceptance-based approaches to the anxiety disorders. In S. M. Orsillo & L. Roemer (Eds.), *Acceptance and mindfulness-based approaches to anxiety: Conceptualization and treatment* (pp. 37–58). New York: Springer Science & Business Media.

Mennin, D. S., Heimberg, R. G., Fresco, D. M., & Turk, C. L. (2005). Preliminary evidence for an emotion dysregulation model of generalized anxiety disorder. *Behaviour Research and Therapy, 43*, 1281–1310.

Mennin, D. S., Heimberg, R. G., Turk, C. L., & Fresco, D. M. (2002). Applying an emotion regulation framework to integrative approaches to generalized anxiety disorder. *Clinical Psychology: Science and Practice, 9*, 85–90.

Mennin, D. S., Holaway, R., Fresco, D. M., & Heimberg, R. G. (in press). Delineating components of emotion dysregulation in anxiety and mood psychopathology. *Behavior Therapy*.

Miller, M. W., & Litz, B. T. (2004). Emotional-processing in posttraumatic stress disorder II: Startle reflex modulation during picture processing. *Journal of Abnormal Psychology, 113*, 451–463.

Mogg, K., & Bradley, B. P. (2004). A cognitive–motivational perspective on the processing of threat information and anxiety. In J. Yiend (Ed.), *Cognition, emotion and psychopathology: Theoretical, empirical and clinical directions* (pp. 68–85). New York: Cambridge University Press.

Mowrer, O. H. (1947). On the dual nature of learning: A re-interpretation of "conditioning" and "problem-solving." *Harvard Educational Review, 17*, 102–148.

Newman, M. G., Castonguay, L. G., Borkovec, T. D., & Molnar, C. (2004). Integrative psychotherapy. In R. G. Heimberg, C. L. Turk, & D. S. Mennin (Eds.), *Generalized anxiety disorder: Advances in research and practice* (pp. 320–350). New York: Guilford Press.

Ochsner, K. N., & Gross, J. J. (2005). The cognitive control of emotion. *Trends in Cognitive Sciences, 9*, 242–249.

Orsillo, S. M., & Batten, S. V. (2005). Acceptance and commitment therapy in the treatment of posttraumatic stress disorder. *Behavior Modification, 29*, 95–129.

Orsillo, S. M., Roemer, L., Block-Lerner, J., LeJeune, C., & Herbert, J. D. (2005). ACT with anxiety disorders. In S. C. Hayes & K. D. Strosahl (Eds.), *A practical guide to acceptance and commitment therapy* (pp. 103–132). New York: Springer Science & Business Media.

Öst, L.-G. (1989). One-session treatment for specific phobias. *Behaviour Research and Therapy, 27*, 1–7.

Parker, J. D., Taylor, G. J., Bagby, R. M., & Acklin, M. W. (1993). Alexithymia in panic disorder and simple phobia: A comparative study. *American Journal of Psychiatry, 150*, 1105–1107.

Pos, A. E., Greenberg, L. S., Goldman, R., & Korman, L. (2003). Emotional processing during experiential treatment. *Journal of Consulting and Clinical Psychology, 71*, 1007–1016.

Rachman, S. (1980). Emotional processing. *Behaviour Research and Therapy, 18*, 51–60.

Reiss, S. (1991). Expectancy model of fear, anxiety, and panic. *Clinical Psychology Review, 11*, 141–153.

Rodebaugh, T. L., & Heimberg, R. G. (in press). Emotion regulation and the anxiety disorders: Adopting a self-regulation perspective. In J. Denollet, I. Nyklicek, & A. Vingerhoets (Eds.), *Emotion, emotion regulation, and health*. New York: Springer Science & Business Media.

Roemer, L., & Orsillo, S. M. (2002). Expanding our conceptualization of and treatment for generalized anxiety disorder: Integrating mindfulness/acceptance-based approaches with existing cognitive–behavioral models. *Clinical Psychology: Science and Practice, 9*, 54–68.

Roemer, L., & Orsillo, S. M. (2005). An acceptance-based behavior therapy for generalized anxiety disorder. In S. M. Orsillo & L. Roemer (Eds.), *Acceptance and mindfulness-based approaches to anxiety: Conceptualization and treatment* (pp. 213–240). New York: Springer Science & Business Media.

Roemer, L., Salters, K., Raffa, S. D., & Orsillo, S. M. (2005). Fear and avoidance of internal experiences in GAD: Preliminary tests of a conceptual model. *Cognitive Therapy and Research, 29*, 71–88.

Rottenberg, J., & Gross, J. J. (2003). When emotion goes wrong: Realizing the promise of affective science. *Clinical Psychology: Science and Practice, 10*, 227–232.

Rottenberg, J., Gross, J. J., Wilhelm, F. H., Najmi, S., & Gotlib, I. H. (2002). Crying threshold and intensity in major depressive disorder. *Journal of Abnormal Psychology, 111*, 302–312.

Salovey, P., & Mayer, J. D. (1990). Emotional intelligence. *Imagination, Cognition and Personality, 9*, 185–211.

Salovey, P., Stroud, L. R., Woolery, A., & Epel, E. S. (2002). Perceived emotional intelligence, stress reactivity, and symptom reports: Further explorations using the Trait Meta-Mood Scale. *Psychology and Health, 17*, 611–627.

Salters-Pedneault, K., Roemer, L., Tull, M. T., Rucker, L., & Mennin, D. S. (in press). Evidence of broad deficits in emotion regulation associated with chronic worry and generalized anxiety disorder. *Cognitive Therapy and Research*.

Samoilov, A., & Goldfried, M. R. (2000). Role of emotion in cognitive–behavior therapy. *Clinical Psychology: Science and Practice, 7*, 373–385.

Schwarz, N., & Clore, G. L. (2003). Mood as information: 20 years later. *Psychological Inquiry, 14*, 296–303.

Singh, N. N., Wahler, R. G., Winton, A. S. W., & Adkins, A. D. (2004). A mindfulness-based treatment of obsessive–compulsive disorder. *Clinical Case Studies, 3*, 275–287.

Thompson, R. A., & Calkins, S. D. (1996). The double-edged sword: Emotional regulation for children at risk. *Development and Psychopathology, 8*, 163–182.

Tull, M. T., & Roemer, L. (2006). *Emotion regulation deficits among a non-treatment seeking sample of individuals with uncued panic attacks: Evidence of emotional avoidance, non-acceptance, and decreased emotional clarity.* Manuscript submitted for publication.

Turk, C. L., Heimberg, R. G., Luterek, J. A., Mennin, D. S., & Fresco, D. M. (2005). Emotion dysregulation in generalized anxiety disorder: A comparison with social anxiety disorder. *Cognitive Therapy and Research, 29*, 89–106.

Whelton, W. J. (2004). Emotional processes in psychotherapy: Evidence across therapeutic modalities. *Clinical Psychology and Psychotherapy, 11*, 58–71.

Williams, K. E., Chambless, D. L., & Ahrens, A. (1997). Are emotions frightening? An extension of the fear of fear construct. *Behaviour Research and Therapy, 35*, 239–248.

Wolpe, J. (1958). *Psychotherapy by reciprocal inhibition.* Stanford, CA: Stanford University Press.

Zvolensky, M. J., Lejuez, C., Stuart, G. L., & Curtin, J. J. (2001). Experimental psychopathology in psychological science. *Review of General Psychology, 5*, 371–381.

12

AFFECTIVE SCIENCE AS A FRAMEWORK FOR UNDERSTANDING THE MECHANISMS AND EFFECTS OF ANTIDEPRESSANT MEDICATIONS

ANDREW J. TOMARKEN, RICHARD C. SHELTON, AND STEVEN D. HOLLON

It has become evident in recent years that basic research in the area of affective science is relevant to many—and perhaps all—forms of psychopathology (e.g., Kring & Bachorowski, 1999; Mohanty et al., 2005; Newman, MacCoon, Vaughn, & Sadeh, 2005). Of particular importance in the present context is the evidence that affective science can inform treatment approaches to various types of psychopathology (e.g., Davis & Myers, 2002; Ressler et al., 2004). In this chapter, our primary goal is to highlight how the concepts and methods of affective science can promote greater understanding of the mechanisms and effects of pharmacological treatments for unipolar depression (i.e., major depressive disorder). We focus on the treatment of depression for the following reasons: (a) Of all manifestations of psychopathology, it is arguably the case that the depressive disorders have the strongest links to basic research on the psychobiology of emotion and motivation, (b) the neural systems that are modulated by antidepressant medications have been a major focus of research in affective neuroscience, and (c) unipolar depression has been the focus of our own research.

PHARMACOLOGICAL TREATMENT OF DEPRESSION

Types and Efficacy of Antidepressants

Over the past 40 years, pharmacotherapy has been the most widely used and best-studied therapeutic approach for the treatment of depression. The majority of commonly prescribed antidepressants fall into one of several classes (e.g., Thase & Kupfer, 1996): monamine oxidase inhibitors (MAOIs; e.g., phenelzine, tranylcypromine), tricyclic antidepressants (TCAs; e.g., imipramine, amitriptyline, nortriptyline), and selective serotonin reuptake inhibitors (SSRIs; e.g., fluoxetine, sertraline, paroxetine). In the 1960s and 1970s, the TCAs were generally the first-line class of antidepressants prescribed for treatment. Currently, most U.S. physicians favor the SSRIs as the first-line choice. In recent years, several new antidepressants (e.g., bupropion, venlafaxine) have also appeared with different apparent mechanisms of action that may be linked to advantages relative to the older agents.

Response rates for all of the major medication classes just noted are greater than those for pill placebo (Hollon, Thase, & Markowitz, 2002; Thase & Kupfer, 1996). Across medication classes, 45% to 65% of patients are responders, whereas 20% to 40% of patients respond to placebo. A closer examination of the data, however, reveals that the benefits due to the active pharmacological effects of medications are not large. If such benefits are quantified as the difference in response rates between medication and placebo conditions, it appears that only about 20% to 25% of the patients administered a given antidepressant benefit from its active pharmacological properties (Depression Guideline Panel, 1993; Hollon et al., 2002). Similarly, when outcome is quantified on a continuous metric, average effect sizes for drug–placebo differences are typically in the small to medium range (Kirsch, Moore, Scoboria, & Nicholls, 2002).

Different classes of antidepressants generally produce equivalent outcomes (e.g., Anderson, 2000; Hollon et al., 2002). This conclusion might seem surprising in light of the fact that SSRIs have replaced TCAs as the first-line choice. In actuality, the major empirical justification for this change is the more benign side-effect profile of SSRIs and their markedly greater safety from overdose. Indeed, TCAs may be more effective than SSRIs for patients with more severe and melancholic features (e.g., Shelton, 2004).

Most outcome studies have focused on the acute (i.e., initial) phase of treatment. Successful treatment during the acute phase should always be followed by at least 6 months of continuation treatment to prevent relapse (e.g., Prien & Kupfer, 1986). Longer term maintenance treatment is also recommended for the prevention of future episodes. Such preventive effects last only as long as patients continue taking medication (Keller & Boland, 1998). In contrast, cognitive therapy may have enduring effects that extend beyond the end of treatment and that lower vulnerability for relapse and recurrence (Hollon et al., 2002). In this respect, it appears to have genuine advantages relative to antidepressant medications.

Why Do Antidepressants Work? Mechanisms of Action

After more than 40 years of study, it is still unclear exactly how antidepressants work. The main focus of research on mechanisms of action has been on the monoaminergic neurotransmitters (norepinephrine, serotonin, and dopamine) that are involved in the regulation of mood and other processes implicated in depression. Because the immediate effect of many antidepressants is blockade of reuptake of neurotransmitters at presynaptic sites, this effect was the initial focus of research and theorizing about mechanisms of action during the 1960s and 1970s. In time, however, it became evident that the inhibition of reuptake per se did not account for the temporal course of therapeutic effects. Although such inhibition occurs almost immediately, several weeks of antidepressant treatment are typically necessary for a measurable change in depressive symptoms beyond those that would be attributable to placebo effects. The focus of interest soon shifted to the longer term effects of medications on pre- and postsynaptic receptors. Currently, the most seminal models of drug action have moved "beyond the synapse" and from extracellular to intracellular processes within the postsynaptic cell. Emphasized are the effects of antidepressants on second messenger systems and gene transcription processes (the turning on and off of genes) and the subsequent effects of such gene expression on neural and hormonal systems (see, e.g., Nestler, 1998).

Although our understanding of mechanisms of action has clearly progressed, a precise delineation of the latter is still lacking. A major reason is the large number of hurdles that make research in this area quite difficult. Among the difficulties are (a) limited understanding of how molecular and cellular events summate to mediate complex behaviors (Nestler, 1998), (b) unresolved diagnostic issues that increase the possibility that individuals nested within the same diagnostic category are biologically heterogeneous, (c) the likelihood that the neurobiological dysfunction linked to depression reflects subtle problems in the dynamic properties of neural systems rather than levels of molecular compounds that are simply "too high" or "too low" (e.g., Hyman & Nestler, 1996; Siever & Davis, 1985), and (d) the failure of many treatment studies to parse depression into its constituent components and test more fine-grained hypotheses concerning the links between particular classes of medications and particular components. We believe that contemporary research on affective science can address several of these limitations of contemporary research on antidepressants.

POTENTIAL CONTRIBUTIONS FROM AFFECTIVE SCIENCE

Dimensional Structure of Emotion, Motivation, and Psychopathology

The field of affective science can inform research on the effects and mechanisms of antidepressant treatment in several respects. One particular area of synergism is research on the psychobiological correlates of fundamental dimensions of emotion and motivation. Although the identification and validation of a limited number of primary dimensions of emotion has been a long-standing area of interest, it has grown tremendously in recent years. Several of the most influential models posit two higher order dimensions that reflect the operation of biologically based systems that organize and activate responses to rewarding, appetitive, or otherwise positive hedonic stimuli and to aversive, threatening, or otherwise negative hedonic stimuli, respectively (e.g., Carver & White, 1994; Higgins, 1997; Watson, Wiese, Vaidya, & Tellgen, 1999; see also chap. 1, this volume). Although there are clearly commonalities among various models, there are also important differences (cf. Higgins, 1997; Watson et al., 1999), and additional questions have been raised about the primacy of specific emotion dimensions and the nature of their relations (e.g., Russell & Carroll, 1999). Unfortunately, space constraints preclude an extensive discussion of these issues. In the present context, we focus on the commonalities among models and, in particular, their relevance to depression.

Positive Affect, Negative Affect, and Depression

Evidence from various sources supports the proposal (e.g., Fowles, 1988) that unipolar depression is a disorder characterized by a combination of hypoactivation in a biologically based positive affect (PA) system and hyperactivation in a negative affect (NA) system. As noted in chapter 7, this volume, when assessing the relation between depression and the PA and NA constructs, it is important to distinguish between disturbances in mood and in emotional reactivity (e.g., chap. 1, this volume). Moods are defined as diffuse, slow-moving states that are only weakly linked to emotion elicitors and may have a long duration. In contrast, emotional reactions typically are short-term, coordinated responses to specific elicitors (although see our later discussion concerning the issue of long-term reactivity among depressed individuals). On measures of mood states, depressed individuals consistently demonstrate a pattern of heightened NA and lowered PA. For example, on self-report measures, depressed individuals report less PA and behavioral activation and more anhedonia, NA, behavioral inhibition, and generalized distress than nondepressed individuals (e.g., Kasch, Rottenberg, Arnow, & Gotlib, 2002; Watson et al., 1995). Indeed, the two primary diagnostic criteria for the *Diagnostic and Statistical Manual of Mental Disorders* (4th ed.; American Psychiatric Association, 1994) major depressive disorder separately specify the presence of negative states (e.g., "irritable mood") and the absence of positive states (e.g., "markedly diminished interest or pleasure").

As reviewed in chapter 7, this volume, depressed individuals also demonstrate deficits in processing of and responses to positive hedonic stimuli on self-report (e.g., Sloan, Strauss, & Wisner, 2001), behavioral (e.g., Henriques & Davidson, 2000), and psychophysiological (e.g., Dichter, Tomarken, Shelton, & Sutton, 2004) measures. In contrast, the evidence concerning hyperreactivity to negative affective stimuli in depressed individuals is more equivocal. Although some studies have found exaggerated responses to aversive or otherwise negative stimuli, a number of others have not, and within-subject comparisons often indicate that depressed individuals are less responsive to variations in affective valence than nondepressed individuals (for a more detailed review, see chap. 7, this volume). Consistent with the latter conclusion, we have found that the startle-blink responses of depressed individuals are generally unresponsive to variations in the valence and arousal dimensions of emotional stimuli assessed either during the anticipation of or exposure to such stimuli (Dichter et al., 2004; Dichter, Tomarken, Shelton, & Hollon, 2006). Rottenberg and his collaborators (e.g., chap. 7, this volume) have argued that such evidence is consistent with the view that depression is associated with a broad emotion context-insensitivity. It may also be the case that depressed individuals do demonstrate hyperreactivity to negative affective stimuli in at least some contexts, but this effect is not well captured by the stimuli or by paradigms used in many laboratory studies. We elaborate on this point later when offering recommendations for future studies.

Relevance to Treatment

To our knowledge, no studies have examined the effects of treatment interventions on either the mood or emotional reactivity components of PA and NA among depressed individuals. Such assessments would be especially important if PA and NA are in fact separable components of depression. If so, then certain interventions might well have greater effects on PA than NA, whereas other interventions might have the reverse effect. Of course, such assessments would require that treatment studies include measures of the PA and NA constructs. Unfortunately, such measures have not typically been used in treatment studies. Assessing the effects of treatments on PA and NA also clearly has implications for understanding mechanisms of action. Indeed, Shelton and Tomarken (2001) have proposed that because of differing mechanisms of action, specific antidepressants and other biological interventions may have relatively selective effects on the NA and PA dimensions of depression. Specifically, we have proposed that drugs having a more substantial and primary effect on serotonergic (5-HT) systems will promote stronger reductions in NA than increases in PA. Conversely, drugs that primarily modulate dopaminergic (DA) systems will have more substantial effects on PA or other indicators of behavioral activation. We now review the evidence supporting these hypotheses.

Links Between Serotonergic Systems and Dimensions of Emotion and Personality

A review of the literature indicates two distinct behavioral correlates of 5-HT activation. One body of evidence indicates a link between the 5-HT system and the NA dimension of emotion. For example, SSRIs and serotonin receptor modulators such as mirtazapine and nefazodone are often effective in the treatment of anxiety disorders (e.g., Gorman & Kent, 1999) and inhibit behaviors that are linked to anxiety in animals (e.g., Petty, Kramer, & Wu, 1997). These findings are significant given the well-known link between NA and anxiety. In addition it has been shown that among healthy volunteers, paroxetine (a commonly used SSRI), relative to placebo, elicited declines in NA over the course of 4 weeks, but there were no significant changes in PA (Knutson et al., 1998). Finally, Bodkin, Lasser, Wines, Gardner, and Baldessarini (1997) showed that SSRIs reduced a variety of symptoms of anxiety and panic in 18 of 20 depressed patients. No patients treated with SSRIs alone reported increases in indicators of PA.

Additional evidence comes from genetic studies of functional polymorphisms in the promoter region of the gene coding for the human serotonin transporter. The latter regulates reuptake of serotonin at synaptic sites. The short allele of the serotonin transporter promoter polymorphism has been associated with reduced transporter expression and function. Studies by Hariri and colleagues have shown that individuals characterized by the short allele demonstrate increased amygdaloid activation in response to threatening stimuli (e.g., Hariri et al., 2005). This result is noteworthy given the evidence that (a) heightened self-reported NA predicts increased amygdaloid activation among depressed individuals (Abercrombie et al., 1998) and (b) individuals characterized by the short allele are more likely to become depressed when exposed to stressful events (Caspi et al., 2003).

As reviewed by Depue and Spoont (1986) and Carver and Miller (2005), other evidence suggests a more fundamental link between 5-HT and a temperamental dimension of constraint versus impulsivity. For example, a number of infrahuman and human studies have indicated that low levels of 5-HT metabolites or other indicators of lowered functional serotongergic activity are associated with impulsive aggression and other indicators of behavioral disinhibition (e.g., alcohol and drug use; see, e.g., Higley et al., 1992; for a review, see Carver & Miller, 2005). In addition, initial findings indicating a link between the short allele of the serotonin transporter gene and neuroticism (e.g., Lesch et al., 1996) have proved difficult to replicate. Instead, a case can be made that measures that assess a dimension of constraint versus impulsivity are more strongly linked to this genetic marker (e.g., Carver & Miller, 2005; Munafò, Clark, & Flint, 2005). Of particular relevance to depression, it is likely that serotonergic dysfunction contributes to the association between impulsive aggression and heightened risk for suicide (Mann, Waternaux, Haas, & Malone, 1999).

Considered as a whole, this evidence raises an important question: What are the precise components of depression that are mediated by serotonergic dysfunction? Unfortunately, space constraints preclude extensive treatment of this issue. As Shelton and Tomarken (2001) pointed out, perhaps the most important point in the present context is that available evidence indicates that SSRIs produce larger reductions in NA than increases in PA (e.g., Bodkin et al., 1997; Knutson et al., 1998; see also Zald & Depue, 2001).

Links Between Positive Affect and Dopaminergic Activity

In contrast to the findings summarized in the previous section indicating the correlates of functional 5-HT activity, several sources of evidence indicate a link between heightened functional DA activity (particularly in the mesocorticolimbic branch of the DA system) and a higher order approach motivational system that is responsive to cues of reward or other positive outcomes. A number of infrahuman studies have indicated a link between heightened activation in neural structures subserved by the mesocorticolimbic branch of the DA system and reward-oriented behaviors (for a review, see, e.g., Berridge & Robinson, 1998). This system appears particularly important for mediating preparatory and appetitive behaviors that occur in anticipation of responses for rewards (e.g., Berridge & Robinson, 1998). Recent human studies also have indicated links between DA and the behavioral approach system, which has been described elsewhere with the broad term *positive affect* (e.g., Depue & Collins, 1999; Depue, Luciana, Arbisi, Collins, & Leon, 1994; Knutson, Adams, Fong, & Hommer, 2001).

On the basis of evidence indicating a link between DA and PA, Shelton and Tomarken (2001) hypothesized that the effects of antidepressant medications or other biological interventions on PA are mediated by changes induced in the mesocorticolimbic branch of the DA system. We have further argued that medications or other interventions that preferentially target DA systems will produce greater effects on PA. Consistent with this proposal is animal research indicating (a) that various antidepressants can reverse the effects of stress-induced anhedonia and (b) that such effects appear mediated by the effects of antidepressants on the DA system (e.g., Willner, Muscat, Papp, & Sampson, 1991).

Initial Studies Assessing Effects of Antidepressant Treatments on Positive Affect

To date, Tomarken and Shelton and their collaborators (Tomarken, Dichter, Freid, Addington, & Shelton, 2004; Tomarken, Shelton, Elkins, & Anderson, 2006) have conducted two studies testing these hypotheses concerning the effects of biological interventions on PA. These studies were exploratory in nature and do not constitute an optimal test of hypotheses in certain respects. Even given these limitations, we believe that they are noteworthy given the paucity of research studies that have assessed interventions on measures of PA or related constructs.

Joint Effects of Sleep Deprivation and Antidepressant Treatment

One study assessed the interactive effects of sleep deprivation (SD) and antidepressant treatment with the TCA nortriptyline (Tomarken et al., 2006). Approximately 60% of depressed patients benefit from one night of SD. Unfortunately, such effects are typically transient. The results of several studies indicate, however, that 1 or more nights of SD may potentiate responses to antidepressants (Leibenluft & Wehr, 1992). Of particular interest in the present context is the evidence from infrahuman studies indicating that SD might selectively enhance PA and other signs of behavioral facilitation via effects on the DA system (Ebert & Berger, 1998). For example, several infrahuman studies have shown (a) that SD lowers thresholds for responding to positive hedonic stimuli (e.g., Steiner & Ellman, 1972), (b) that such behavioral changes may be mediated by the effects of SD on the mesolimbic or nigrostriatal DA systems (Ebert & Berger, 1998), and (c) that SD is a potential animal model of mania (Gessa, Pani, Fadda, & Fratta, 1995). These results converge with evidence from human studies indicating (a) that a positive response to SD is correlated with biological indicators of enhanced DA activity (e.g., Ebert, Feistel, Barocka, Kaschka, & Pirner, 1994) and (b) that SD can induce manic episodes (e.g., Wehr, Goodwin, Wirz-Justice, Breitmaier, & Craig, 1982). Although SD induces changes in multiple physiological systems, this evidence offers support for the notion that it would selectively enhance various indicators of PA among depressed patients.

Because 1 night of SD alone has transient effects on mood, Tomarken et al. (2006) were interested in the effects of SD on potentiating the effects of nortriptyline across the first 2 weeks of treatment. They randomly assigned 95 depressed individuals to one of three treatment conditions: sleep deprivation plus nortriptyline (SLMED), sleep deprivation plus pill placebo (PLAC), and no sleep deprivation plus nortriptyline (MED). Participants in the first two groups were sleep-deprived for 1 night, after which all three groups received either medication or placebo initiated on the following day. Because of the interest in the effects of SD on rapid responding to antidepressants, focus was the first 2 weeks of treatment. The primary outcome measures included self-report measures of PA and NA, as assessed by the Positive and Negative Affect Schedule (PANAS; Watson, Clark, & Tellegen, 1988). Participants completed these mood measures presented in a diary format three times per day. In addition, once per day they were administered the Beck Depression Inventory (BDI; Beck, Steer, & Brown, 1996) and the Sleep Deprivation Depression Rating Scale (SDDRS), a revised version of the Hamilton Rating Scale for Depression (Hamilton, 1960) appropriate for SD studies.

Tomarken et al. (2006) hypothesized that SD would prime the DA system for the subsequent effects of nortriptyline. On this basis, they predicted that the combination of SD and nortriptyline treatment would selectively enhance self-reported PA. The results of analyses supported predictions. Figure 12.1 depicts changes relative to pretreatment baseline assessments on NA and PA across the first 2 weeks of treatment. To facilitate examination of effects, half-week means averaged across daily observation are shown. Although there were overall declines on NA scores, there were no significant between-groups differences on this measure. An identical pattern of effects was observed on the BDI and the SDDRS. In contrast, the SLMED group demonstrated significantly greater increases on PA than both of the other groups. Indeed, as indicated by Figure 12.1, the SLMED group was the only one to demonstrate a significant increase in PA relative to pretreatment levels. Thus, although nortriptyline treatment was sufficient to induce declines in NA, BDI, and SDDRS scores over the 2-week interval, the addition of SD to nortriptyline was necessary to produce enhancements in PA. These findings support the notion that specific components of interventions can have separable effects on PA and NA.

Effects of Bupropion on Symptom Dimensions

The results of the sleep deprivation study raised the issue of whether there might be specific antidepressant medications that would similarly enhance PA among depressed patients in the absence of sleep deprivation. To test this hypothesis, Tomarken et al. (2004) evaluated the effects of the atypical antidepressant bupropion. They chose to assess the effects of bupropion for two reasons. First, although its precise mechanisms of action are unclear, it enhances the extracellular availability of DA and norepinephrine in selected brain regions (e.g., Gobbi, Slater, Boucher, Debonnel, & Blier, 2003). In addition, Bodkin et al.'s (1997) results suggest that bupropion has stronger effects on depressive symptoms linked to anhedonia than anxiety (Shelton & Tomarken, 2001). However, the measures that they used were neither well validated nor comprehensive.

In the Tomarken et al. (2004) study, the primary outcome measure was the Mood and Anxiety Symptom Questionnaire (MASQ; e.g., Watson et

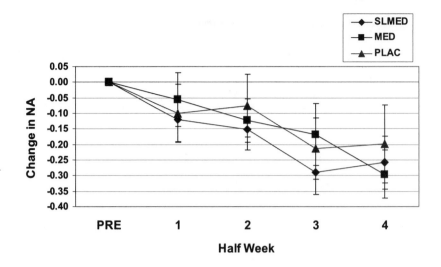

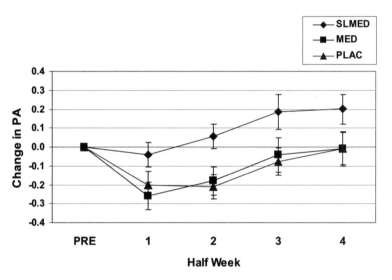

Figure 12.1. Changes in Positive and Negative Affect Schedule Negative Affect (NA; top) and Positive Affect (PA; bottom) scores over the first 2 weeks (i.e., 4 half weeks) of treatment. SLMED = sleep deprivation plus medication, MED = medication alone, PLAC = sleep deprivation plus placebo.

al., 1995). This measure is derived from the tripartite model of mood disorders (e.g., Clark & Watson, 1991) that posits three higher order dimensions of symptoms: general distress, anhedonia–PA, and somatic anxiety. According to this model, symptoms of general distress are common to both affective and anxiety disorders. In contrast, symptoms of anhedonia are relatively specific to depression, whereas somatic anxiety appears primarily linked to panic disorder and perhaps other types of anxiety disorders.

Nineteen participants were randomly assigned to either bupropion (BUP) or placebo (PLAC) groups. Primary interest was on the first 6-week phase of treatment, because PLAC patients initiated BUP treatment in an open-label format during the second 6-week phase. To assess effects, the MASQ, the 17-item version of the Hamilton Depression Scale (HAM–D) and the Hamilton Anxiety Scale (HAM–A; Hamilton, 1959) were administered weekly. The results indicated that relative to placebo, bupropion produced a steeper decline in anhedonic symptoms during Phase 1 than placebo. Effects of a similar nature were also found on the MASQ General Distress Depressive Symptoms subscale and the HAM–D. In contrast, groups failed to differ on three measures of anxiety (MASQ General Distress Anxiety Symptoms subscale, MASQ Anxious Arousal scale, and the HAM–A) despite the fact that there were significant overall declines on these indices.

Thus, although effects were not as selective as had been predicted, the results of this study did indicate that bupropion tends to produce stronger effects on a dimension of anhedonia–PA than on a dimension of NA–anxiety. The pattern of change within the placebo group also merits comment. This group demonstrated significant linear declines on all measures of anxiety. In contrast, the pattern of change on the MASQ anhedonia scale was curvilinear in nature: Participants reported an initial decline in anhedonic symptoms over the first several weeks of treatment but a return to pretreatment baseline levels over the final weeks. These findings are broadly consistent with those of the sleep deprivation study. In that context, the placebo group demonstrated significant declines on NA but not significant increases in PA. The results of these two studies suggest that (a) placebo might primarily reduce distress and anxiety rather than reduce anhedonia and (b) measures of PA, anhedonia, or related constructs might yield more robust differences between medication and placebo.

Limitations

It is important to note several limitations of our initial studies: (a) the small sample size used in the bupropion study, (b) the failure to assess directly whether DA changes mediated treatment effects, (c) the reliance on self-report measures of these constructs, and (d) the failure to assess separately the mood and reactivity components of daily emotion. In our subsequent recommendations for future studies, we discuss several of these issues at greater length.

In addition, there is an important psychometric issue to consider that is particularly relevant to the sleep deprivation study. One limitation of the original version of the PANAS is that it assesses only the high activation poles of each construct. For example, the PA scale includes adjectives such as *enthusiastic* and *determined* but not adjectives such as *tired* or *bored*. The NA scale includes adjectives such as *distressed* and *afraid* but not adjectives such as *relaxed* or *calm*. We agree with several commentators (e.g., Russell & Carroll, 1999) that a compelling case can be made that the PA and NA dimensions are bipolar rather than unipolar. For example, one can conceivably think about PA as spanning a broad dimension that ranges from highly activated PA on one end to states resembling anhedonia on the other end. Although space constraints preclude an extensive discussion of the ramifications of this point, we should note that sole assessment of the high-activation poles introduces a potential psychometric confound: Any differences in results might reflect the differential sensitivity of the specific measures used rather than differential treatment effects on the PA and NA latent constructs (for a related argument, see, e.g., Russell & Carroll, 1999). Indeed, in the sleep deprivation study, exploratory analyses indicated some treatment effects on measures of the low-activation pole of NA. Clearly, it is important to address this issue in future studies by more comprehensively assessing affective space.

A final limitation of work conducted to date is the failure to assess comprehensively whether medications that primarily modulate serotonergic systems selectively inhibit NA among depressed patients. A recent study found that venlafaxine and paroxetine produced equivalent effects on all the MASQ dimensions (Dichter, Tomarken, Freid, Addington, & Shelton, 2005). However, this study was limited by the fact that the drugs assessed both modulate 5-HT functioning. In our view, the optimal study to test hypotheses would be one that compared an SSRI with both placebo and a medication with stronger effects on DA systems, such as bupropion.

Implications

Even given the noted limitations, the initial findings of the studies described suggest several implications for future research. At a broad level, these results indicate the potential value of an approach that parses depressive symptoms into constituent dimensions or subtypes and specifies testable links between particular treatment components and such dimensions or subtypes. Clearly, these findings also have important implications for assessment. For example, if the SD study had included only the "typical" treatment outcome measures (HAM–D, BDI), there would have been no compelling evidence for the potentiating effects of SD on any measures. These results suggest the potential importance of measuring PA and NA in treatment protocols.

Methodological Recommendations for Future Studies

Although we could offer a number of possible recommendations for future studies in this area, we concentrate on one primary issue: the benefits that would accrue from the broader inclusion into treatment studies of the methods and paradigms used in affective science. This addition would allow researchers to (a) better parse the complex constructs and nosological entities involved, (b) assess more comprehensively multiple components of emotional reactivity, and (c) better assess potential biological mediators of the effects of treatments.

For example, as noted earlier, neither of the studies described here assessed the hypothesized mediator of the effects on PA or anhedonia—that is, changes in functional activation in the DA system. Several approaches to the assessment of DA activity have appeared recently in human studies conducted by affective neuroscientists. For example, researchers have assessed the effects of DA agonists (e.g., Depue et al., 1994) and drugs (e.g., d-amphetamine) that stimulate dopamine release (e.g., Tremblay, Naranjo, Cardenas, Herrmann, & Busto, 2002). An especially promising approach is the use of neuroimaging techniques (positron emission tomography, functional magnetic resonance imaging) to image neural structures that are innervated by DA (e.g., nucleus accumbens) or the binding of radioligands to DA receptors (an indirect measure of the release of endogenous dopamine; e.g., Zald et al., 2004).

To link such neurobiological changes to relevant psychological constructs, such assessments would ideally occur in conjunction with experimental paradigms that have been developed by affective neuroscientists to assess responses to emotional or motivational stimuli. For example, Knutson and his colleagues have found increased activation in the nucleus accumbens and several other components of the ventral striatum "motivational circuit" during the anticipation of responding for monetary rewards (e.g., Knutson et al., 2001; see also, e.g., Zald et al., 2004). These findings are significant given the evidence that DA modulates postsynaptic excitability in the nucleus accumbens and more generally increases activation in the ventral striatum. It would be valuable to assess whether biological interventions that increase self-reported PA among depressed patients (e.g., SD, bupropion) also potentiate neural responses to the anticipation of reward.

A similar point could be made about the use of neuroimaging paradigms to assess treatment-induced changes in NA responses to threatening stimuli. Although such paradigms are increasingly applied to psychopathology research (e.g., Hariri et al., 2005), they are still only rarely used to assess the effects of treatment. Conversely, although recent studies have demonstrated changes in functional brain activity after antidepressant treatment (e.g., Mayberg et al., 1999), such investigations have typically not assessed the effects of treatment on neural responses to affective challenges. We believe that such assessments are critical to forge links among treatments, specific dimensions of emotion and motivation, and specific neural circuits. For example, several imaging studies have indicated medication-induced increases in cortical (e.g., prefrontal) activation and decreases in limbic and paralimbic (e.g., subgenual cingulate) activation (e.g., Mayberg et al., 1999). It would be interesting to assess whether, in turn, these changes in tonic activation predict a corresponding inhibition in the amplitude or duration of phasic neural and behavioral responses to NA stimuli.

We believe that such assessments are particularly important given the evidence reviewed earlier indicating a discrepancy between depressed individuals' heightened NA on self-reports of mood and their general lack of responsivity to positive or negative emotion elicitors in experimental contexts. Consistent with this evidence, it recently has been shown that depressed patients' anomalous startle-blink responses during exposure to affective stimuli (pictures that are either pleasant, unpleasant, or neutral in tone) fail to normalize after antidepressant treatment with bupropion—despite the fact that self-report measures and other clinical indices (e.g., HAM–D scores) indicate dramatic declines in depressive symptoms (Dichter et al., 2004). These results suggest a subtle yet chronic deficit in responding to affective stimuli that may persist despite an acute phase of treatment that would be deemed otherwise successful. Several neuroimaging findings also indicate that remission is not always accompanied by a normalization of activation in regions hypothesized to be important components of vulnerability to depression (e.g., Drevets et al., 1997).

There is a related respect in which the incorporation of the experimental paradigms used by emotion researchers would benefit treatment studies. Psychopathologists routinely use extremely global constructs that have multiple components. Given the detailed specialization of function of the human brain, however, the establishment of links between such constructs and brain function requires that the former be parsed. For example, consider anhedonia, a construct central to theories of depression. Among the potential causes or components of anhedonia are deficits in the ability to (a) experience pleasure, (b) express pleasure, (c) make preparatory adjustments in anticipation of pleasurable stimuli, (d) engage in effortful responses to attain rewards, and (e) sustain or amplify pleasant states over time. In addition, in naturalistic contexts, an individual could be anhedonic simply because he or she is not exposed to pleasurable stimuli. A number of animal studies have documented that several of these features of reward-oriented behavior have unique neural substrates (e.g., Salamone, Cousins, & Snyder, 1997). The results of recent human studies point toward the same conclusion (e.g., Elliott, Friston, & Dolan, 2000; Knutson et al., 2001). By parsing complex constructs into their constituent components, the behavioral paradigms increasingly used by affective neuroscientists can help researchers assess which particular motivational or behavioral parameters are linked to psychopathology and its treatment. By this means, for example, one could address such intriguing questions as whether treatment modulates the anticipation of rewards, actual responses to rewards, or both.

Although we have emphasized the laboratory paradigms used in contemporary affective neuroscience, it would also be extremely valuable to incorporate methods used for the assessment of responses to naturalistic stimuli.

As reviewed above, a number of studies have failed to find increased responsivity to negative affective stimuli among depressed individuals. Possible reasons are (a) that depressed individuals have particular difficulty regulating long-term responses to stressors or other negative affective stimuli and (b) that such deficits are not well captured by laboratory studies that typically assess short-term responses to affective stimuli. Indeed, one of the notable commonalities between psychological (e.g., Nolen-Hoeksema, 2000) and biological (e.g., Siever & Davis, 1985) perspectives on depression is the notion that a hallmark feature is deficits in counterregulatory processes designed to "turn off" longer term responses to stressors and promote a return to prestress levels.

To assess such deficits, we highly recommend the use of daily mood diaries or other methods for intensive assessment of naturalistic mood states (for a review and summary of recent methodological developments, see Bolger, Davis, & Rafaeli, 2003). Although daily mood assessments are associated with their own methodological problems (e.g., the presence of missing data), two clear advantages are greater freedom from retrospective biases and a greater ability to reveal the temporal course of naturalistic changes in emotions or symptoms over time. When mood diaries are combined with assessments of daily stressors or other events, critical features of affective responses to naturalistic stimuli can be revealed. A classic demonstration of this point was provided by Goplerud and Depue (1985), who found that dysthymic and cyclothymic participants failed to differ from normal control participants in their immediate responses to significant daily stressors but did differ greatly in the number of days required for mood to return to prestress levels. This finding underscores the importance of considering the temporal course of affective responding. In the context of treatment, one wonders, for example, whether specific interventions serve to (a) marshal negative feedback processes and produce a more rapid return to baseline after a daily stressor and (b) amplify and sustain responses to positive events. Based on the reasoning summarized here, one might hypothesize that treatments enhancing functional 5-HT activation have the former effect, whereas treatments enhancing functional DA activation have the latter effect. In our view, these are fundamental questions that typical treatment studies are not well suited to address.

SUMMARY AND CONCLUSION

We have described several respects in which the incorporation of constructs and methods from affective neuroscience can benefit research on the effects of antidepressants and their mechanisms of action. The inclusion of multimodal measures that assess the broad constructs of positive and negative affectivity can capture important effects of treatment that may differentiate specific classes of medication. In addition, the incorporation into treatment studies of several laboratory paradigms and naturalistic methods used by affective scientists can shed greater light on mechanisms of action and the temporal course of affective changes and help researchers parse complex global constructs. It is our hope that such a synthesis of the concepts and methods of affective science and intervention research will contribute to the development of more effective treatments and more sensitive assessments of their effects and mechanisms of action.

REFERENCES

Abercrombie, H. C., Schaefer, S. M., Larson, C. L., Oakes, T. R., Lindgren, K. A., Holden, J. E., et al. (1998). Metabolic rate in the right amygdala predicts negative affect in depressed patients. *Neuroreport, 9,* 3301–3307.

American Psychiatric Association. (1994). *Diagnostic and statistical manual of mental disorders* (4th ed.). Washington, DC: Author.

Anderson, I. M. (2000). Selective serotonin reuptake inhibitors versus tricycle antidepressants: A meta-analysis of efficacy and tolerability. *Journal of Affective Disorders, 58,* 19–36.

Beck, A. T., Steer, R. A., & Brown, G. K. (1996). *Manual for Beck Depression Inventory—II.* San Antonio, TX: Psychological Corporation.

Berridge, K. C., & Robinson, T. E. (1998). What is the role of dopamine in reward: Hedonic impact, reward learning, or incentive salience? *Brain Research. Brain Research Reviews, 28,* 309–369.

Bodkin, J. A., Lasser, R. A., Wines, J. D., Jr., Gardner, D. M., & Baldessarini, R. J. (1997). Combining serotonin reuptake inhibitors and bupropion in partial responders to antidepressant monotherapy. *Journal of Clinical Psychiatry, 58,* 137–145.

Bolger, N., Davis, A., & Rafaeli, E. (2003). Diary methods: Capturing life as it is lived. *Annual Review of Psychology, 54,* 579–616.

Carver, C. S., & Miller, C. J. (2005). *How does serotonin function relate to personality? Current status and a methodological issue.* Manuscript submitted for publication.

Carver, C. S., & White, T. L. (1994). Behavioral inhibition, behavioral activation, and affective responses to impending reward and punishment: The BIS/BAS scales. *Journal of Personality and Social Psychology, 67,* 319–333.

Caspi, A., Sugden, K., Moffitt, T. E., Taylor, A., Craig, I. W., Harrington, H., et al. (2003, July 18). Influence of life stress on depression: Moderation by a polymorphism in the 5-HTT gene. *Science, 301,* 386–389.

Clark, L. A., & Watson, D. (1991). Tripartite model of anxiety and depression: Psychometric evidence and taxonomic implications. *Journal of Abnormal Psychology, 100,* 316–336.

Davis, M., & Myers, K. M. (2002). The role of glutamate and gamma-aminobutryic acid in fear extinction: Clinical implications for exposure therapy. *Biological Psychiatry, 52,* 998–1007.

Depression Guideline Panel. (1993). *Depression in primary care: Vol. 2. Treatment of major depression* (Clinical Practice Guideline No. 5, AHCPR Publication No. 93-0551). Rockville, MD: U.S. Department of Health and Human Services, Public Health Service, Agency for Health Care Policy and Research.

Depue, R. A., & Collins, P. F. (1999). Neurobiology of the structure of personality: Dopamine, facilitation of incentive motivation, and extraversion. *Behavioral and Brain Sciences, 22,* 491–569.

Depue, R. A., Luciana, M., Arbisi, P., Collins, P., & Leon, A. (1994). Dopamine and the structure of personality: Relation of agonist-induced dopamine activity to positive emotionality. *Journal of Personality and Social Psychology, 67,* 485–498.

Depue, R. A., & Spoont, M. R. (1986). Conceptualizing a serotonin trait: A behavioral dimension of constraint. In *Annals of the New York Academy of Sciences: Vol. 487. Psychobiology of suicidal behavior* (pp. 48–62). New York: New York Academy of Sciences.

Dichter, G. S., Tomarken, A. J., Freid, C. M., Addington, S., & Shelton, R. C. (2005). Do venlafaxine XR and paroxetine equally influence negative and positive affect? *Journal of Affective Disorders, 85,* 333–339.

Dichter, G. S., Tomarken, A. J., Shelton, R. C., & Hollon, S. D. (2006). *The time-course of affective startle modulation in unipolar depression.* Manuscript under review.

Dichter, G. S., Tomarken, A. J., Shelton, R. C., & Sutton, S. K. (2004). Early- and late-onset startle modulation in unipolar depression. *Psychophysiology, 41,* 433–440.

Drevets, W. C., Price, J. L., Simpson, J. R., Todd, R. D., Reich, T., Vannier, M., & Raichle, M. E. (1997, April 24). Subgenual prefrontal cortex abnormalities in mood disorders. *Nature, 386,* 824–827.

Ebert, D., & Berger, M. (1998). Neurobiological similarities in antidepressant sleep deprivation and psychostimulant use: A psychostimulant theory of antidepressant sleep deprivation. *Psychopharmacology, 140,* 1–10.

Ebert, D., Feistel, H., Barocka, A., Kaschka, W. P., & Pirner, A. (1994). SPECT assessment of cerebral dopamine D_2 receptor blockade in depression before and after sleep deprivation. *Biological Psychiatry, 35,* 880–885.

Elliott, R., Friston, K. J., & Dolan, R. J. (2000). Dissociable neural responses in human reward systems. *Journal of Neuroscience, 16,* 6159–6165.

Fowles, D. C. (1988). Psychophysiology and psychopathology: A motivational approach. *Psychophysiology, 25,* 373–391.

Gessa, G. L., Pani, L., Fadda, P., & Fratta, W. (1995). Sleep deprivation in the rat: An animal model of mania. *European Neuropsychopharmacology, 5*(Suppl.), 89–93.

Gobbi, G., Slater, S., Boucher, N., Debonnel, G., & Blier, P. (2003). Neurochemical and psychotropic effects of bupropion in healthy male subjects. *Journal of Clinical Psychopharmacology, 23,* 233–239.

Goplerud, E., & Depue, R. A. (1985). Behavioral responses to naturally occurring stress in cyclothymia and dysthymia. *Journal of Abnormal Psychology, 94,* 128–139.

Gorman, J. M., & Kent, J. M. (1999). SSRIs and SMRIs: Broad spectrum of efficacy beyond major depression. *Journal of Clinical Psychiatry, 60*(Suppl. 4), 33–38.

Hamilton, M. (1959). The assessment of anxiety states by rating. *British Journal of Medical Psychology, 32*, 50–55.

Hamilton, M. A. (1960). A rating scale for depression. *Journal of Neurology and Neurosurgery in Psychiatry, 23*, 56–62.

Hariri, A. R., Drabant, E. M., Munoz, K. E., Kolachana, B. S., Mattay, V. S., Egan, M. F., & Weinberger, D. R. (2005). A susceptibility gene for affective disorders and the response of the human amygdala. *Archives of General Psychiatry, 62*, 146–152.

Henriques, J. B., & Davidson, R. J. (2000). Decreased responsiveness to reward in depression. *Cognition and Emotion, 14*, 711–724.

Higgins, E. T. (1997). Beyond pleasure and pain. *American Psychologist, 52*, 1280–1300.

Higley, J. D., Mehlman, P. T., Taub, D. M., Higley, S. B., Suomi, S. J., Vickers, J. D., & Linnoila, M. (1992). Cerebrospinal fluid monamine and adrenal correlates of aggression in free-ranging rhesus monkeys. *Archives of General Psychiatry, 49*, 436–441.

Hollon, S. D., Thase, M. E., & Markowitz, J. C. (2002). Treatment and prevention of depression. *Psychological Science in the Public Interest, 3*, 39–77.

Hyman, S. E., & Nestler, E. J. (1996). Initiation and adaptation: A paradigm for understanding psychotropic drug action. *American Journal of Psychiatry, 153*, 151–162.

Kasch, K. L., Rottenberg, J., Arnow, B. A., & Gotlib, I. H. (2002). Behavioral activation and inhibition systems and the severity and course of depression. *Journal of Abnormal Psychology, 111*, 589–597.

Keller, M. B., & Boland, R. J. (1998). Implications of failing to achieve successful long-term maintenance treatment of recurrent unipolar depression. *Biological Psychiatry, 44*, 348–360.

Kirsch, I., Moore, T. J., Scoboria, A., & Nicholls, S. S. (2002). The emperor's new drugs: An analysis of antidepressant medication data submitted to the U.S. Food and Drug Administration. *Prevention and Treatment, 5*(5), 1–11.

Knutson, B., Adams, C. M., Fong, G. W., & Hommer, D. (2001). Anticipation of increasing monetary reward selectively recruits nucleus accumbens. *Journal of Neuroscience, 21*, 1–5.

Knutson, B., Wolkowitz, O. M., Cole, S. W., Chan, T., Moore, E. A., Johnson, R. C., et al. (1998). Selective alteration of personality and social behavior by serotonergic innervation. *American Journal of Psychiatry, 155*, 373–379.

Kring, A. M., & Bachorowski, J. B. (1999). Emotions and psychopathology. *Cognition and Emotion, 13*, 575–579.

Leibenluft, R., & Wehr, T. A. (1992). Is sleep deprivation useful in the treatment of depression? *American Journal of Psychiatry, 149*, 159–168.

Lesch, K. P., Bengel, D., Heils, A., Sabol, S. Z., Greenberg, B. D., Petri, S., et al. (1996, November 29). Association of anxiety-related traits with a polymorphism in the serotonin transporter gene regulatory region. *Science, 274,* 1527–1531.

Mann, J. J., Waternaux, C., Haas, G. L., & Malone, K. M. (1999). Toward a clinical model of suicidal behavior in psychiatric patients. *American Journal of Psychiatry, 156,* 181–189.

Mayberg, H. S., Liotti, M., Brannan, S. K., McGinnis, S., Mahurin, R. K., Jerabek, P. A., et al. (1999). Reciprocal limbic–cortical function and negative mood: Converging PET findings in depression and normal sadness. *American Journal of Psychiatry, 156,* 675–682.

Mohanty, A., Herrington, J. D., Koven, N. S., Fisher, J. E., Wenzel, E. A., Webb, A. G., et al. (2005). Neural mechanisms of affective interference in schizotypy. *Journal of Abnormal Psychology, 114,* 16–27.

Munafò, M. R., Clark, T., & Flint, J. (2005). Does measurement instrument moderate the association between the serotonin transporter gene and anxiety-related personality traits? A meta-analysis. *Molecular Psychiatry, 10,* 415–419.

Nestler, E. J. (1998). Antidepressant treatments in the 21st century. *Biological Psychiatry, 44,* 526–533.

Newman, J. P., MacCoon, D. G., Vaughn, L. J., & Sadeh, N. (2005). Validating a distinction between primary and secondary psychopathy with measures of Gray's BIS and BAS constructs. *Journal of Abnormal Psychology, 114,* 319–323.

Nolen-Hoeksema, S. (2000). The role of rumination in depressive disorders and mixed anxiety/depressive symptoms. *Journal of Abnormal Psychology, 109,* 514–511.

Petty, F., Kramer, G. L., & Wu, J. (1997). Serotonergic modulation of learned helplessness. In R. Yehuda & A. C. McFarlane (Eds.), *Annals of the New York Academy of Sciences: Vol. 821. Psychobiology of posttraumatic stress disorder* (pp. 538–541). New York: New York Academy of Sciences.

Prien, R. F., & Kupfer, D. (1986). Continuation drug therapy for major depressive episodes: How long should it be maintained? *American Journal of Psychiatry, 143,* 18–23.

Ressler, K. J., Rothbaum, B. O., Tannenbaum, L., Anderson, P., Graap, K., Zimand, E., et al. (2004). Cognitive enhancers as adjuncts to psychotherapy: Use of D-cycloserine in phobic individuals to facilitate extinction of fear. *Archives of General Psychiatry, 61,* 1136–1144.

Russell, J. A., & Carroll, J. M. (1999). On the bipolarity of positive and negative affect. *Psychological Bulletin, 125,* 3–30.

Salamone, J. D., Cousins, M. S., & Snyder, B. J. (1997). Behavioral functions of nucleus accumbens dopamine: Empirical and conceptual problems with the anhedonia hypothesis. *Neuroscience and Biobehavioral Reviews, 21,* 341–359.

Schwartz, G. E., Fair, P. L., Salt, P., Mandel, M. R., Klerman, G. L. (1976, April 30). Facial muscle patterning to affective imagery in depressed and nondepressed subjects. *Science, 192,* 489–491.

Shelton, R. C. (2004). The dual action hypothesis: Does pharmacology matter? *Journal of Clinical Psychiatry, 65*(Suppl. 17), 5–10.

Shelton, R. C., & Tomarken, A. J. (2001). Can recovery from depression be achieved? *Psychiatric Services, 52*, 1469–1478.

Siever, L. J., & Davis, K. L. (1985). Overview: Toward a dysregulation hypothesis of depression. *American Journal of Psychiatry, 142*, 1017–1031.

Sloan, D. M., Strauss, M. E., & Wisner, K. L. (2001). Diminished response to pleasant stimuli by depressed women. *Journal of Abnormal Psychology, 110*, 488–493.

Steiner, S. S., & Ellman, S. J. (1972, September 22). Relation between REM sleep and intracranial self-stimulation. *Science, 177*, 1122–1124.

Thase, M. E., & Kupfer, D. J. (1996). Recent developments in the pharmacotherapy of mood disorders. *Journal of Consulting and Clinical Psychology, 64*, 646–659.

Tomarken, A. J. (1999). Methodological issues in psychophysiological research. In P. C. Kendall, J. N. Butcher, & G. N. Holmbeck (Eds.), *Handbook of research methods in clinical psychology* (2nd ed., pp. 251–275). New York: Wiley.

Tomarken, A. J., Dichter, G. S., Freid, C., Addington, S., & Shelton, R. C. (2004). Assessing the effects of bupropion SR on mood dimensions of emotion. *Journal of Affective Disorders, 78*, 235–241.

Tomarken, A. J., Shelton, R. C., Elkins, L., & Anderson, T. (2006). *Effects of sleep deprivation and antidepressant medication on positive and negative affect.* Manuscript in preparation.

Tremblay, L. K., Naranjo, C. A., Cardenas, L., Herrmann, N., & Busto, U. E. (2002). Probing brain reward system function in major depressive disorder: Altered response to dextroamphetamine. *Archives of General Psychiatry, 59*, 409–416.

Watson, D., Clark, L. A., & Tellegen, A. (1988). Development and validation of brief measures of positive and negative affect: The PANAS scales. *Journal of Personality and Social Psychology, 54*, 1063–1070.

Watson, D., Clark, L. A., Weber, K., Assenheimer, J. S., Strauss, M. E., & McCormick, R. A. (1995). Testing a tripartite model II: Exploring the symptom structure of anxiety and depression in student, adult, and patient samples. *Journal of Abnormal Psychology, 104*, 15–25.

Watson, D., Wiese, D., Vaidya, J., & Tellegen, A. (1999). The two general activation systems of affect: Structural findings, evolutionary considerations, and psychobiological evidence. *Journal of Personality and Social Psychology, 76*, 820–838.

Wehr, T. A., Goodwin, F. K., Wirz-Justice, A., Breitmaier, J., & Craig, C. (1982). 48-hour sleep–wake cycles in manic–depressive illness: Naturalistic observations and sleep deprivation experiments. *Archives of General Psychiatry, 39*, 559–565.

Willner, P., Muscat, R., Papp, M., & Sampson, D. (1991). Dopamine, depression, and anti-depressant drugs. In P. Willner & J. Scheel-Kruger (Eds.), *The mesolimbic dopamine system: From motivation to action* (pp. 389–410). New York: Wiley.

Zald, D. H., Boileau, I., El-Dearedy, W., Gunn, R., McGlone, F., Dichter, G. S., & Dagher, A. (2004). Dopamine transmission in the human striatum during monetary reward tasks. *Journal of Neuroscience, 24*, 4105–4112.

Zald, D. H., & Depue, R. A. (2001). Serotonergic functioning correlates with positive and negative affect in psychiatrically healthy males. *Personality and Individual Differences, 30*, 71–86.

13

AFFECTIVE SCIENCE AND PSYCHOTHERAPY: IN SEARCH OF SYNERGY

TIMOTHY J. STRAUMAN, KARI MERRILL EDDINGTON, AND MEGAN C. McCRUDDEN

The outcome of any serious research can only be to make two questions grow where one question grew before.
    —Thorstein Veblen, *University of California Chronicle*

This chapter endeavors to respond to the following question: How can we apply affective science to understanding the processes and outcomes of psychotherapy? Our response to that question, as we elaborate here, involves turning it into not two but three distinct questions: First, how can affective science benefit psychotherapy research? Second, how can psychotherapy research benefit affective science? And finally, what might be the limits of convergence between the two fields?

Before addressing these questions, however, it is important to define the scope of the fields in question. As this entire volume demonstrates, *affective science* serves as a general label for the psychological and neurobiological study of emotion, the results of which have been substantially surveyed and summarized by the various chapters. For the purpose of this discussion, we view psychotherapy as a clinical science that applies psychological theory and data to the treatment of mental disorders (Barlow, 2004; Salkovskis, 2002; Strauman & Merrill, 2004). As these broad definitions suggest, there is an enormous range of affective science research with potential applicability to psychotherapy, and our goal in this discussion is to suggest cross-cutting issues and themes rather than to focus on individual trends or particular research findings.

In posing the three related questions just described, we are seeking to identify actual and possible synergies between the two fields. The term *synergy* can be defined as a mutually advantageous conjunction or compatibility of distinct elements or, similarly, as the interaction of two or more agents or forces so that their combined effect is greater than the sum of their individual effects. As this volume clearly documents, there are many potential avenues for attaining synergy between affective science and the study of mental disorders. We believe that additional synergies exist specifically between affective science and psychotherapy. We note as well, however, that there are also ways in which the two intellectual domains are unlikely to be synergistic, and we comment on some possible points of divergence in the final section of the chapter.

HOW CAN AFFECTIVE SCIENCE BENEFIT PSYCHOTHERAPY RESEARCH?

Affective science is a thriving research domain that draws on and contributes to a number of scientific disciplines. However, surprisingly little integration between affective science and psychotherapy research has been attained to date, at least in terms of explicit application of emotion theory and research to the treatment of mental disorders. In this section, we suggest several ways in which the scientific study of emotion can enhance our understanding of psychotherapy outcome (what works, and for whom) and process (what happens in psychotherapy that leads to good outcomes) and point out some recent studies in which progress toward integration has been made. It may be worth noting that a number of the applications of affective science to psychotherapy that we mention are probably best conceptualized as indirect, for example, targeting cognitive processes to influence affect and motivation. Clearly such applications have been both clinically and theoretically valuable, but they nonetheless support our assertion that there is much yet to be done in terms of applying affective science to the treatment and prevention of psychological disorders.

Affective Science Provides a Sound Basis for Understanding How Psychotherapy Works

Our first suggestion is broadly applicable to different types of affective science as well as different kinds of psychological therapies. Simply put, we believe that affective science can help guide theory and research that accounts for how psychological interventions alleviate and prevent mental disorders. Although from a clinical science perspective this assertion might seem obvious, the unfortunate reality is that even among PhD psychologists, the value of basic science for guiding (and understanding) intervention is not uniformly acknowledged (McFall, 2000) and has even been relegated to secondary status (Levant, 2004). We are convinced that affective science is not only compatible with effective psychotherapeutic practice but that many of the specific and nonspecific factors implicated in treatment efficacy have their basis in emotional processes.

The National Institutes of Health have been encouraging the development of collaborative partnerships between scientists who study basic behavioral and neurobiological processes and those who study the etiology, diagnosis, treatment, and prevention of mental and behavioral disorders (National Institute of Mental Health, 1999). Because most of those disorders involve disruptions of emotional processes and experience, affective science is highly relevant to both treatment and prevention (Whelton, 2004). Therefore, it is hardly a risky prediction to suggest that the study of emotion has much to offer psychotherapy research. A more useful contribution might be to make some specific suggestions about likely points of synergy (or at least intersection).

In what ways does affective science provide the theoretical and empirical foundations for understanding how treatments work? Among the most important developments in the psychological treatment literature over the past quarter century has been the emergence of brief focused therapies based on cognitive models of disordered affect (A. T. Beck, 2005; Samoilov & Goldfried, 2000). Psychosocial interventions based on cognitive models have a number of distinct advantages (Brewin, 1996): They are easily integrated within behaviorally focused treatments; they allow for the teaching of specific techniques for symptom control as well as relapse prevention; and they have broad applicability across disorders (such as major depression and generalized anxiety disorder), particularly those that are highly comorbid. It is interesting to note from a translational perspective that the development of cognitively focused interventions in psychotherapy has, in turn, contributed back to the continued development of basic science approaches to disordered affect (Ingram, 2003), although it bears repeating that much of the cognitive–behavioral tradition can be considered affective science only in an indirect sense.

The dynamic link between affective science and cognitive–behavioral therapy also brings into relief a challenge for contemporary psychotherapy research: whether to focus treatment development and training on theory-based models of intervention or on transtheoretical aspects of patient–therapist interaction—a dichotomy with "empirically supported treatments" on one side and "empirically supported relationships" on the other (Beutler, Machado, & Neufeldt, 2004). The past decade has seen both an increasing emphasis on the importance of randomized clinical trials in psychotherapy research (e.g., Chambless & Ollendick, 2001) as well as a reaction against this emphasis that has argued for the primacy of therapist and patient variables (e.g., Norcross, 2002). Given the evidence that many types of psychotherapy have reliable dose–response associations to symptom improvement and well-being (Howard, Leuger, Maling, & Martinovich, 1993; Lutz, Martinovich, & Howard, 1999), affective science may be able to provide a critical perspective to overcome this unfortunate polarization. In particular, theories of emotion and coping should be useful for identifying how a person's behavior, or mere presence, influences another person's emotional state—at both psychological (Levenson, 1999) and biological (Davidson, Jackson, & Kalin, 2000) levels. Several interesting applications of emotion theories addressing interpersonal influences on affect (including both the actual presence of the therapist as well as the imagined presence of past or current significant others) already can be found within the psychotherapy literature (e.g., Greenberg & Paivio, 1997), but greater integration is both feasible and desirable.

Other influential lines of emotion research likewise could be highly relevant to the study of when and how psychotherapy works, and psychotherapy outcome and process data can provide useful feedback for those theories. For example, dialectical behavior therapy (Linehan, 1993, 2000) is based in part on the assumption that individuals meeting criteria for borderline personality disorder have profound difficulties with affect regulation. Dialectical behavior therapy presumes that borderline personality disorder results from a pattern of parent–child socialization based on invalidation, that is, the failure of parental figures to accurately and genuinely reflect back to the child their understanding of and empathy toward the emotional states the child is experiencing. This assumption, in turn, has generated a growing body of laboratory and correlational research to determine the nature, origins, and consequences of such difficulties (for a review, see Mikulincer & Florian, 2004). Although in the case of dialectical behavior therapy, the treatment preceded the basic research on affect regulation, the potential for such translation is considerable, and new interventions based on this translational process are beginning to appear (e.g., Mennin, 2004).

As this cursory review implies, many conceptual models within affective science have yet to be applied to studying how psychological interventions work. We offer a suggestion in this regard, based on our own reading of the other chapters in this volume. That is, affective science provides a means to identify physiological aspects of mental disorders, which in turn can be incorporated into more comprehensive theories of etiology. Better theories lead to better treatments as well as to a broader range of effective treatment options (Barlow, 2004; Bouton, Mineka, & Barlow, 2001).

Affective Science Can Help to Improve the Outcomes From Current Psychotherapies

Current research on psychotherapy outcome and process has struggled to identify the mechanisms or active ingredients of therapy that mediate change (Doss, 2004), with the unfortunate result that in many disorders it is not yet possible to identify a priori which treatment will be most effective for a particular individual (Norcross, Beutler, & Caldwell, 2002). It may be fair to say that the field has yet to settle even on a dominant metaphor for change—hence the dual terminology of *mechanism of action* versus *active ingredient* and the preferences of different investigators to use different perspectives on how psychotherapy works (Kopta, Lueger, Saunders, & Howard, 1999). Much of the psychotherapy process literature stands in isolation from studies of the etiology of the disorders for which those interventions were designed (Brent & Kolko, 1998). Nonetheless, it is clear that affective science has an enormous amount to offer psychotherapy research in this regard, specifically regarding development of a more microanalytic understanding of how psychosocial interventions work. Both modality-specific (e.g., Brewin, 1996; DeRubeis & Feeley, 1990) and universal or transtheoretical (e.g., Orlinsky & Howard, 1975) models of psychotherapy process have potential parallels in theories of normal and disordered emotions, although many of those parallels have yet to be fully explored. How might such exploration proceed?

One possibility is to link the strategic and technical aspects of therapies to specific theories or models within affective science (Kazdin, 1999). Although a number of recent studies have made inroads in this direction, we were unable to identify systematic programs of research using affective science to "unpack" the mechanisms by which a particular intervention helps individuals with a particular disorder. However, an intriguing study that illustrates the potential for such unpacking research is the work of Goldapple et al. (2004), which applied Mayberg's systems model of the pathophysiology of depression to a clinical trial of cognitive therapy (CT) for depression. Goldapple et al. observed that CT was associated with specific cognitive and associated neurophysiological changes, consistent with its underlying rationale and with previous studies of its mechanisms of action. Such research could be particularly useful to the extent that it considers different types of interventions shown to be effective for the same disorder—for instance, CT (J. S. Beck, 1995) and interpersonal therapy (Klerman, Weissman, Rounsaville, & Chevron, 1984) for depression. Taking this approach to understanding how a particular treatment works would allow researchers to learn more about why many types of psychotherapy can be efficacious (including the universal–transtheoretical aspects of interventions) and to determine whether and how particular treatments also have particular mechanisms of action.

Following this general approach, the research group Strauman et al., (2001) applied self-discrepancy theory (Higgins, 1987), a model of the relation between self-evaluation and affect, to the study of cognitive change processes in treatment for depression. Strauman et al. found that across three distinct empirically supported treatments—Beck's CT (J. S. Beck, 1995), interpersonal psychotherapy (Klerman et al., 1984), and pharmacotherapy with selective serotonin reuptake inhibitors—depressed individuals with chronic actual–ideal discrepancy showed less improvement than other patients. From this perspective, if the depressive episodes experienced by those patients were at least in part a consequence of individual differences in self-regulation and self-evaluation, then focusing more directly on those processes might help such individuals benefit more fully from treatment. This hypothesis, in turn, led to the development of self-system therapy (SST; Vieth et al., 2003), a treatment for depression designed specifically for depressed patients with chronic difficulties attaining ideals (and, more broadly, what regulatory focus theory [Higgins, 1997] refers to as *promotion goals*). A recent clinical trial (Strauman et al., 2006) found that SST was more efficacious than CT for patients who reported not knowing how to pursue promotion goals effectively, whereas CT tended to be more effective for patients not characterized by difficulties pursuing promotion goals.

Another possibility is to apply theories and models within affective science to a dose–response curve analysis of psychotherapy (Hansen, Lambert, & Forman, 2002; Howard et al., 1993). Kolden and his colleagues (e.g., Kolden et al., 2006) used a statistical approach to model change processes in early sessions of generic psychotherapy based on the Howard et al. dose–response framework. They observed that improvement over early sessions of treatment was associated with increases in both positive and negative affect during the third session (a critical point in the establishment of an effective working relationship between therapist and patient). Specifically, Kolden et al. (2006) found that greater improvement early in treatment was associated independently with two types of change in patients' self-reported affect: positive affect based on a sense of remoralization that resulted from establishing a trusting attachment to the therapist and negative affect associated with the therapist beginning to ask challenging questions and "probe" the issues that led the patient to seek treatment. Those two affective changes were statistically independent, consistent with the research of Watson and colleagues exploring positive and negative affectivity (e.g., Watson, Wiese, Vaidya, & Tellegen, 1999).

In summary, affective science represents a largely untapped resource for improving the efficacy of existing treatments. How might psychotherapy researchers incorporate affective science? One possibility is to draw on affective scientists' expertise in measures that are independent of self-report to provide an essential complementary perspective on how people change during and after treatment. Another is to use affective science to assess directly whether people's emotional responses to everyday life are in fact altered substantially by psychological interventions—a deceptively simple task. Similarly, affective science provides techniques for determining the change processes that are shared by pharmacotherapy and psychotherapy as well as those that are likely to be distinct. We elaborate on these suggestions in the following paragraphs.

Affective Science Can Provide Theory-Based Targets for Change in Therapy

To the extent that theories in affective science are relevant to understanding how psychotherapy works, they also should be useful in developing and testing hypotheses regarding what psychological interventions should be trying to accomplish—that is, the development of theory-based targets for change. Across the psychotherapy process literature, there are at least two major conceptualizations of treatment-induced change: (a) adapting to or compensating for a presumably irreversible pathological process and (b) altering or reversing the pathology itself (Badgio, Halperin, & Barber, 1999). Both conceptualizations are amenable to theory-based approaches, and examples of theory-based hypotheses regarding both types of change can be found in the recent psychotherapy process literature.

One such example is the widespread use of the notion of a *schema* (a mental structure representing some aspect of the world) within cognitive–behavioral therapies (James, Southam, & Blackburn, 2004). Although there is substantial variability in the operationalizations of schema implicit (and occasionally explicit) within particular interventions, all can be traced back to classic work in cognitive psychology (e.g., Bartlett, 1932) as well as to large, if somewhat fragmented, research literatures (Singer & Salovey, 1991). The schema concept offers two particularly noteworthy advantages as a basis for psychotherapeutic intervention. First, it provides a parsimonious conceptual framework for teaching and acquisition of cognitive skills (such as practice in noticing and evaluating one's thoughts and feelings), so that the therapist and patient can use the concept to interpret the patient's difficulties and intervene at the source of those difficulties. Second, because of its basis in cognitive psychology, it allows for measurement at various points in treatment, so that change processes themselves can be assessed using methods that allow for disentanglement of symptomatic improvement from change in underlying affective processes.

Our own research has begun to explore the use of theoretically driven targets for therapeutic change in the treatment of depression. Because SST was derived from regulatory focus theory and a self-regulation model of depression (Strauman, 2002), it is possible to identify and measure aspects of the hypothesized self-regulatory system for pursuing promotion (ideal) goals that are likely to be dysfunctional during a depressive state and, in turn, that a self-regulation-based treatment such as SST should alter. For instance, previous research had shown that depressed individuals tend to respond with increased dysphoric affect when they are exposed incidentally to their own promotion (ideal) goals, presumably because they appraise themselves as failing to make progress toward them (e.g., Strauman, 1992). In a clinical trial comparing SST with CT, Strauman et al. (2006) asked patients to participate in an autobiographical memory task before and after their course of treatment in which they heard a series of words and then recalled events from childhood after each word. Unknown to the patients, some of the words were their own promotion goals, as assessed in a prior semistructured interview. At the start of treatment, the same increase in dysphoric affect following promotion goal exposure was observed; however, after treatment, patients who had received SST showed a significant decrease in dysphoric affect when exposed to their own promotion goals, whereas patients who received CT did not. This change in self-regulatory cognition (and resultant affect) predicted improvement in the SST condition but not in the CT condition.

In that study (as in much treatment research), treatment was deemed complete by agreement of the patient and therapist. However, given the availability of different techniques for assessing self-regulation (including the autobiographical memory technique), it might be possible to develop a "treat-to-criterion" strategy to ensure that patients receive a sufficient dose of SST. For example, the priming task could easily be modified for use within the treatment itself so that the patient and therapist could monitor the extent to which the process of self-regulation is changing as the treatment progresses.

Affective Science Provides Conceptually Sound and Empirically Supported Bases for Treatment Matching

Discussion of theory-based targets for therapy-induced change implies a pathology-focused perspective on psychological interventions, which some clinicians find comfortable but others reject. An alternative conceptualization that still allows for meaningful input from affective science is a person-focused approach (Ackerman et al., 2001). From this perspective, we assert that theory and research on emotion provide a sound basis for *treatment matching*, which we define as a systematic a priori process by which a treatment is selected as most likely to provide maximum benefit for a particular individual (Beutler & Martin, 2000).

The depression literature contains a number of interesting models regarding matching interventions and/or specific techniques to the characteristics of individual patients, such as cognitive styles, relationship status, and personality profiles (e.g., Beutler, Clarkin, & Bongar, 2000). In one recent study, Beevers and Miller (2005) used a longitudinal hierarchical linear modeling design to observe that cognitive therapy, relative to two other treatments (family therapy and pharmacotherapy), appeared to "unlink" negative cognitions and symptoms of depression. Their analysis suggested that patients receiving CT were better able to present the occurrence of negative thoughts from triggering symptoms than patients receiving the other treatments. Furthermore, interpersonal psychotherapy for depression (IPT) itself is organized around a matching principle, with the therapist encouraged to choose from among a set of foci (grief, transition, dispute, deficit) the emphasis that best fits the particular patient. However, there are as yet no systematic treatment-matching algorithms or guidelines derived from emotion theory or research. There is some evidence that SST is more effective than other treatments for depressed individuals who describe themselves as lacking the ability to pursue promotion goals and gain satisfaction from attaining them (Strauman et al., 2006), but we have yet to conduct a clinical trial in which patients are assigned a priori to particular treatments based on assessment of self-regulation.

As the following sections suggest, the difficulties inherent in identifying optimal treatments for particular patients reflect a more fundamental challenge to behavioral science: how to maintain scientific rigor while accounting for individuality and uniqueness of human experience (Rychlak, 2001). We wish to note, however, that psychologists engaged in the study of affect have long recognized that effective theories must balance the nomothetic and idiographic aspects of emotional experience. In this respect, constructivist theories of emotion, many of which can be traced to the influence of George Kelly's personal construct theory (e.g., Kelly, 1955), are particularly translatable into the theory as well as the actual work of psychotherapy—as Kelly modeled in his own theory-based intervention.

HOW CAN PSYCHOTHERAPY RESEARCH BENEFIT AFFECTIVE SCIENCE?

There are many more potential applications of affective science to psychotherapy than we can summarize in a single chapter. Our strategy has been to highlight ideas that we view as particularly promising, or at least reasonably instantiated, to serve as illustrations for translating theories of emotion into the domain of psychotherapy. Nonetheless, our review also revealed pathways by which psychotherapy research can influence affective science. We take a similar strategy here by looking for synergies, with a particular emphasis on translational principles in the dynamic tension between basic and applied behavioral science. The fact that this section of the chapter is shorter than the previous one is a reflection of the relative dearth of studies in which the implications of psychotherapy outcome or process for theories about emotion were examined but not of the potential for psychotherapy research to feed back valuable observations to the basic science of emotions.

Psychotherapy Research Provides a "Laboratory" in Which to Determine the Limitations of Current Theories in Affective Science

Just as most psychotherapy researchers are not also basic researchers (i.e., do not also conduct research on basic cognitive, motivational, or affective processes), few affective scientists are engaged in psychotherapy research. As a result, opportunities for testing models of disordered emotion through converting hypotheses into controlled interventions within treatment modalities are often lost.

The depression treatment literature provides numerous examples of this trend. Mayberg (2003) noted that current models of the neurophysiology of depression, including her own, do not map cleanly onto what is known about the effects of different treatment modalities on psychological and physiological functioning in episodes of depression. Although this apparent lack of parsimony could be due as much to limitations in our understanding of treatment mechanisms of action as to theories of etiology, at present there are no valid and reliable markers (biological or psychological) that provide improved diagnostic accuracy and treatment selection. Mayberg suggested that development of such markers will require a multitheory, multivariate approach in which hypotheses about intervention-specific functional associations (i.e., Treatment A leads to functional change in Brain Region X under particular conditions) are refined experimentally and then tested clinically.

Although the current focus at the National Institutes of Health on translational research is a welcome change in the way researchers obtain funding, the principles underlying that emphasis have not yet permeated either affective science or psychotherapy research. Nonetheless, if affective science is to advance in its understanding of both normal and disordered emotion, psychotherapy research will have to play a larger role (Lisanby & Sackeim, 2000). In particular, treatment research can provide invaluable data regarding etiologic hypotheses by measuring the impact of treatment on psychological or biological targets (such as schemas) and then determining whether altering the target processes leads to clinical change.

An example of the potential for two-way translational "cross talk" between psychotherapy research and affective science comes from the work of Siegle and colleagues (e.g., Siegle, Steinhauer, Thase, Stenger, & Carter, 2002). They observed that compared with nondepressed individuals, depressed individuals manifested sustained amygdala activation during a laboratory task requiring identification of the valence of a series of stimuli. This finding, which is consistent with prior research (Drevets, 1999), raises multiple questions regarding treatment selection. Is the sustained amygdalar activation indicative of a core aspect of the psychopathological process underlying depression, or is it epiphenomenal to some other pathology? Should the goal of treatment be to dampen activation (e.g., to minimize affective processing)? Alternatively, should treatment focus on helping the individual to process affective stimuli more effectively, assuming that such cognitive change would in turn normalize amygdalar function? Whereas the first question primarily implicates etiology, the remaining questions challenge both basic and applied researchers to consider the implications of treatment for our understanding of emotion per se.

Another example of the feedback potential between psychotherapy research and affective science is cognitive–behavioral treatment of panic disorder (Barlow, Gorman, Shear, & Woods, 2000). The treatment itself translates findings from studies of physiological and cognitive mechanisms of vulnerability to panic into a coherent, systematic package that in turn allows clinical investigators to study whether changes in hypothesized causal processes underlying panic disorder predict clinical improvement and relapse prevention. The theory on which much of the treatment is based (Bouton et al., 2001) predicts that certain conditioning processes, along with higher level cognitive processes, are responsible for the onset and maintenance of chronic "false alarm" fear responses. The availability of this theory, in turn, raises the question of whether the treatment works by altering those processes. Although studies of the mechanism of action in panic control treatment are just beginning to be reported (e.g., Landon & Barlow, 2004), those studies will surely have implications for the underlying theory of fear as well as for further refinement of the treatment itself.

A third example of developments in psychological intervention having implications for affective science can be found in the work of Davis and colleagues on fear extinction in behavior therapy for specific phobia (see Ressler et al., 2004). In a double-blind, placebo-controlled clinical trial, they tested the efficacy of D-cycloserine for facilitating fear extinction in a virtual-reality treatment and then in in vivo exercises among patients with clinically significant fear of heights. Patients receiving the drug manifested significantly greater reduction in their fear of heights than did those receiving placebo. This program of research clearly illustrates the potential for biological facilitation of psychological interventions and provides valuable data regarding underlying psychological and neurobiological mechanisms for the onset and maintenance of phobic disorders.

Generic and Universal Theories of Psychotherapy Challenge Current Etiologic Theories of Disordered Emotion

Whether psychological intervention is conceptualized in terms of empirically supported treatments (Chambless & Ollendick, 2001), relationships (Ackerman et al., 2001), or both (Messer, 2004), there is now compelling evidence that psychotherapy for disorders such as depression has a characteristic dose–response curve that predicts outcome across a number of common treatment modalities (Lambert, Hansen, & Finch, 2001; Lueger et al., 2001). One interpretation of these findings, obtained in extraordinarily large samples, is that the aspects of psychotherapy that are shared across treatments may be at least as important in determining efficacy as those aspects that distinguish one treatment from another. In contrast, theories of the etiology of emotional disorders invariably focus on specific, and often single, pathological factors as determining both the onset and maintenance of the disorder. As such, those theories imply that successful treatment requires intervention that targets the pathological factor implicated in the disorder. Is it possible to find synergy between these two seemingly inconsistent literatures? What are the implications of psychotherapy dose–response studies for affective science?

To our knowledge, both affective scientists and psychotherapy researchers have yet to consider this challenge. Nonetheless, generic–universal models of psychotherapy process raise important questions for emotion theory. For instance, if one takes the position that many human emotional experiences are the result of interpersonal processes (e.g., Fischer, Manstead, & Zaalberg, 2003), then either the putative importance of universal psychotherapy processes such as the quality of the therapeutic bond must be explainable in terms of interpersonal theories of affect or those theories will need to be revised in the light of the available psychotherapy outcome and process findings. Similarly, theories linking emotion regulation with mental disorders (e.g., John & Gross, 2004) imply that patients learn to use more adaptive affect regulation strategies in a number of forms of psychotherapy. If we are unable to find evidence that psychotherapy alters affect regulation, then those theories would be called into question. It is unfortunate that so little research appears to be available that takes advantage of psychotherapy findings to challenge, and ultimately improve, theories in affective science.

IN WHAT WAYS DO AFFECTIVE SCIENCE AND PSYCHOTHERAPY DIVERGE?

In this final section, we take a brief and admittedly more speculative look at the ways in which affective science and psychotherapy research differ and comment on some possible limits to the synergies between the two fields. Rather than implying that one field is ultimately more important than the other, however, we approach this speculative exercise with strong beliefs in the value of both basic science and intervention science (Strauman & Merrill, 2004). To the extent that these approaches have some fundamental differences, acknowledging those differences can still allow for thoughtful integration between them at the same time it encourages researchers in both fields to understand the limitations of particular levels of analysis.

Recognizing that these comments reflect a broad level of generalization, we offer the following four assertions as a partial list of differences between affective science and psychotherapy research:

- *Affective science takes a mechanistic approach, whereas psychotherapy takes an agentic approach.* Although not all affective science relies on research designs intended to maximize internal validity, by its nature affective science seeks to identify causes and consequences of particular emotional phenomena. This stance involves a decision on the investigator's part to "reduce" the complexity of the phenomenon being studied to test hypotheses regarding causal connections. Not surprisingly, theories developed from this mechanistic approach to affective experience may not translate easily into psychotherapeutic contexts, which are (even in behavioral therapies) fundamentally interactions between people and therefore tend to embrace the assumption that people are causal agents who control and direct their own behaviors and experience. There is no doubt that some psychotherapy practitioners explicitly reject the applicability of basic science to psychological interventions (for a thoughtful discussion of the relations between psychotherapy and science, see Wampold, 2001). However, we view this as an extreme and ultimately self-defeating stance that reflects a misunderstanding of the scientific method.

- *Affective science proceeds by studying phenomena one at a time, whereas psychotherapy research proceeds by studying complex (and possibly irreducible) interactions.* As the preceding paragraph suggested, the subject matter and methods of affective science afford the luxury of controlled experimentation in which phenomena of interest can be studied in isolation, even if such isolation comes at the cost of external validity. In contrast, psychotherapy research almost never involves controlled experimentation, at least in the strict sense of varying a single mechanism of interest while holding all potential mechanisms constant. These differences, which reflect distinctions in level of analysis as well as subject matter, are both profound and entrenched. As a result, it would hardly be surprising if affective scientists and psychotherapy researchers did not read the same journals or attend the same professional conferences. Affective scientists would be likely to find fault in psychotherapy outcome and process research, in which many potential influences on outcome cannot be entirely controlled (Kazdin, 2003). Compared with experimental laboratory research, even the best-designed clinical trial might appear messy and unable to support a firm conclusion regarding when and how treatments work. For their part, psychotherapy researchers might be tempted to dismiss the experimental designs of affective scientists as so highly artificial as to be irrelevant to a complex human interaction. Although we suspect these divergences may be exaggerated, the differences between how the two fields conduct their inquiries are formidable and not easily bridged.

- *In affective science, theory typically drives research; in psychotherapy research, theory often follows research.* It is curious, but nonetheless true, that a number of approaches to psychotherapy that are widely used were developed largely in the absence of a formal underlying theory about the causes of particular disorders. This state of affairs is not completely illogical; for instance, IPT (Klerman et al., 1984) was originally designed as a treatment "package" that incorporated the accumulated wisdom of experienced clinicians who worked with depressed people. There is as yet no theory in the strict sense to account for the efficacy of IPT, but its status as an efficacious treatment for depression is well established empirically. Nonetheless, treatments often are developed and implemented before basic research regarding their hypothesized mechanisms of action is ever conducted. Of course, exceptions to this trend can be found (perhaps the most notable being behavior therapy itself), but the tendency for psychotherapies to be promulgated in the absence of or independent from support in the basic science literature appears to be a significant incompatibility between the two fields. It has been argued elsewhere (Strauman & Merrill, 2004) that this trend is unfortunate and creates additional obstacles to the already challenging task of understanding why particular treatments are effective for particular problems.

- *Affective scientists are trained to advance knowledge; psychotherapists are trained to help people.* Our final assertion may represent the most challenging obstacle to integration of basic science and intervention science. Although many doctoral training programs in clinical psychology offer science-based training in assessment and intervention, most psychotherapy is still provided by practitioners who did not have substantial graduate-level training in behavioral science (Olfson, Marcus, Druss, & Pincus, 2002). On the other hand, most affective scientists are not trained as clinicians. The differences in training lead to distinct, and frequently incompatible, priorities, with affective scientists focusing on advancement of knowledge per se rather than translation and psychotherapists unfamiliar with the relevant science and seemingly uninterested in applying such knowledge. Given the increasing pressure from third-party payers to provide psychotherapy services with masters' level clinicians (Scheffler, Ivey, & Garrett, 1998), how can this divide be bridged? Most likely progress in the translation of affective science into psychotherapy will require both greater efforts on the part of scientists to collaborate with researchers who develop and test new treatment approaches and policies that encourage (if not mandate) such integration.

CONCLUSIONS AND RECOMMENDATIONS:
SYNERGIES LOST AND FOUND

Following Veblen's dictate, we began with a single topic—the implications of affective science for psychotherapy—and turned it into multiple points of inquiry. Rather than seeking definite answers (which are likely to be premature), we instead sought potential synergies between affective science and psychotherapy research. Of course, ultimately the two fields represent different and highly specialized viewpoints on the same phenomena, and so the challenge in integrating them is to balance their strengths and limitations and (ideally) to facilitate two-way translation of knowledge that allows both fields to develop and mature.

The history of clinical psychology in the latter half of the 20th century provides a sobering tale for efforts to translate basic science into better treatment. The field began squarely within academic psychology but soon became a separate, applied branch of psychology that gradually lost much of its connection with behavioral science—synergies lost. Yet, as we hope this chapter has illustrated, there remain numerous potential synergies to be nurtured between the two fields. We urge our basic science colleagues to bring their ideas into the clinic and our therapist colleagues to invite them in and apply those ideas to the complex dynamic of psychological intervention. Only by such bilateral efforts can we finally derive satisfactory answers to the single question that is most pressing from a public health standpoint: How does psychotherapy work to help people experience healthy emotions?

REFERENCES

Ackerman, S. J., Benjamin, L. S., Beutler, L. E., Gelso, C. J., Goldfried, M. R., Hill, C., et al. (2001). Empirically supported therapy relationships: Conclusions and recommendations of the Division 29 Task Force. *Psychotherapy: Theory, Research, Practice, Training, 38*, 495.

Badgio, P. C., Halperin, G. S., & Barber, J. S. (1999). Acquisition of adaptive skills: Psychotherapeutic change in cognitive and dynamic therapies. *Clinical Psychology Review, 19*, 721–737.

Barlow, D. H. (2004). Psychological treatments. *American Psychologist, 59*, 869–878.

Barlow, D. H., Gorman, J. M., Shear, M. K., & Woods, S. W. (2000). Cognitive-behavioral therapy, imipramine, or their combination for panic disorder. *Journal of the American Medical Association, 283*, 2529–2535.

Bartlett, F. J. (1932). *Remembering*. Cambridge, England: Cambridge University Press.

Beck, A. T. (2005). The current state of cognitive therapy: A 40-year retrospective. *Archives of General Psychiatry, 62*, 953–959.

Beck, J. S. (1995). *Cognitive therapy: Basics and beyond*. New York: Guilford Press.

Beevers, C. G., & Miller, I. W. (2005). Unlinking negative cognition and symptoms of depression: Evidence of a specific treatment effect for cognitive therapy. *Journal of Consulting and Clinical Psychology, 73,* 68–77.

Beutler, L. E., Clarkin, J. F., & Bongar, B. (2000). *Guidelines for the systematic treatment of the depressed patient.* New York: Oxford University Press.

Beutler, L. E., Machado, P. P., & Neufeldt, S. A. (2004). Therapist variables. In A. E. Bergin & S. L. Garfield (Eds.), *Handbook of psychotherapy and behavior change.* New York: Wiley.

Beutler, L. E., & Martin, B. R. (2000). Prescribing therapeutic interventions through strategic treatment selection. *Cognitive and Behavioral Practice, 7,* 1–17.

Bouton, M. E., Mineka, S., & Barlow, D. H. (2001). A modern learning theory perspective on the etiology of panic disorder. *Psychological Review, 108,* 4–32.

Brent, D. A., & Kolko, D. J. (1998). Psychotherapy: Definitions, mechanisms of action, and relationship to etiological models. *Journal of Abnormal Child Psychology, 26,* 17–25.

Brewin, C. R. (1996). Theoretical foundations of cognitive–behavior therapy for anxiety and depression. *Annual Review of Psychology, 47,* 33–57.

Chambless, D. L., & Ollendick, T. H. (2001). Empirically supported psychological interventions: Controversies and evidence. *Annual Review of Psychology, 52,* 685–716.

Davidson, R. J., Jackson, D. C., & Kalin, N. H. (2000). Emotion, plasticity, context, and regulation: Perspectives from affective neuroscience. *Psychological Bulletin, 126,* 890–909.

DeRubeis, R. J., & Feeley, M. (1990). Determinants of change in cognitive therapy for depression. *Cognitive Therapy and Research, 14,* 469–482.

Doss, B. D. (2004). Changing the way we study change in psychotherapy. *Clinical Psychology: Science and Practice, 11,* 368–386.

Drevets, W. C. (1999). Prefrontal cortical–amygdalar metabolism in major depression. In J. F. McGinty (Ed.), *Annals of the New York Academy of Sciences: Vol. 877. Advancing from the ventral striatum to the extended amygdala: Implications for neuropsychiatry and drug use: In honor of Lennart Heimer* (pp. 614–637). New York: New York Academy of Sciences.

Fischer, A. H., Manstead, A. S. R., & Zaalberg, R. (2003). Social influences on the emotion process. *European Review of Social Psychology, 14,* 171–201.

Goldapple, K., Segal, Z., Garson, C., Lau, M., Bieling, P., Kennedy, S., & Mayberg, H. (2004). Modulation of cortical–limbic pathways in major depression. *Archives of General Psychiatry, 61,* 34–41.

Greenberg, L. S., & Paivio, S. C. (1997). *Working with emotions in psychotherapy.* New York: Guilford Press.

Hansen, N. B., Lambert, M. J., & Forman, E. M. (2002). The psychotherapy dose–response effect and its implications for treatment delivery services. *Clinical Psychology: Science and Practice, 9,* 329–343.

Higgins, E. T. (1987). Self-discrepancy: A theory relating self and affect. *Psychological Review, 94,* 319–340.

Higgins, E. T. (1997). Beyond pleasure and pain. *American Psychologist, 52,* 1280–1300.

Howard, K. I., Leuger, R. J., Maling, M. S., & Martinovich, Z. (1993). A phase model of psychotherapy outcome: Causal mediation of change. *Journal of Consulting and Clinical Psychology, 61,* 678–685.

Ingram, R. E. (2003). Twenty-five years of inquiry and insight. *Cognitive Therapy and Research, 27,* 1–17.

James, I. A., Southam, L., & Blackburn, I. M. (2004). Schemas revisited. *Clinical Psychology and Psychotherapy, 11,* 369–377.

John, O. P., & Gross, J. J. (2004). Healthy and unhealthy emotion regulation: Personality processes, individual differences, and life span development. *Journal of Personality, 72,* 1301–1333.

Kazdin, A. E. (1999). Current (lack of) status of theory in child and adolescent psychotherapy research. *Journal of Clinical Child Psychology, 28,* 533–543.

Kazdin, A. E. (2003). Psychotherapy for children and adolescents. *Annual Review of Psychology, 54,* 253–277.

Kelly, G. A. (1955). *The psychology of personal constructs.* New York: Norton.

Klerman, G. L., Weissman, M. M., Rounsaville, B. J., & Chevron, E. S. (1984). *Interpersonal psychotherapy of depression.* New York: Basic Books.

Kolden, G. G., Chisholm-Stockard, S. M., Strauman, T. J., Tierney, S. C., Mullen, E. A., & Schneider, K. L. (2006). Universal session-level change processes in an early session of psychotherapy. *Journal of Consulting and Clinical Psychology, 74,* 327–336.

Kopta, S. M., Lueger, R. J., Saunders, S. M., & Howard, K I. (1999). Individual psychotherapy outcome and process research: Challenges leading to greater turmoil or a positive transition? *Annual Review of Psychology, 50,* 441–469.

Lambert, M. J., Hansen, N. B., & Finch, A. E. (2001). Patient-focused research: Using patient outcome data to enhance treatment effects. *Journal of Consulting and Clinical Psychology, 69,* 159–172.

Landon, T. M., & Barlow, D. H. (2004). Cognitive–behavioral treatment for panic disorder: Current status. *Journal of Psychiatric Practice, 10,* 211–226.

Levant, R. F. (2004). The empirically validated treatments movement: A practitioner/educator perspective. *Clinical Psychology: Science and Practice, 11,* 219–224.

Levenson, R. W. (1999). The intrapersonal functions of emotion. *Cognition and Emotion, 13,* 481–504.

Linehan, M. M. (1993). *Cognitive–behavioral treatment of borderline personality disorder.* New York: Guilford Press.

Linehan, M. M. (2000). The empirical basis of dialectical behavior therapy: Development of new treatments vs. evaluation of existing treatments. *Clinical Psychology: Science and Practice, 7,* 113–119.

Lisanby, S. H., & Sackeim, H. A. (2000). Therapeutic brain interventions in mood disorders and the nature of emotion. In J. C. Borod (Ed.), *The neuropsychology of emotion* (pp. 456–491). New York: Oxford University Press.

Lueger, R. J., Howard, K. I., Martinovich, Z., Lutz, W., Anderson, E. E., & Grissom, G. (2001). Assessing treatment progress of individual patients using expected treatment response models. *Journal of Consulting and Clinical Psychology, 69*, 150–158.

Lutz, W., Martinovich, Z., & Howard, K. I. (1999). Patient profiling: An application of random coefficient regression models to depicting the response of a patient to outpatient psychotherapy. *Journal of Consulting and Clinical Psychology, 67*, 571–577.

Mayberg, H. S. (2003). Modulating dysfunctional limbic–cortical circuits in depression: Towards development of brain-based algorithms for diagnosis and optimised treatment. *British Medical Bulletin, 65*, 193–207.

McFall, R. M. (2000). Elaborate reflections on a simple manifesto. *Applied and Preventive Psychology, 9*, 5–21.

Mennin, D. S. (2004). Emotion regulation therapy for generalized anxiety disorder. *Clinical Psychology and Psychotherapy, 11*, 17–29.

Messer, S. B. (2004). Evidence-based practice: Beyond empirically supported treatments. *Professional Psychology: Research and Practice, 35*, 580–588.

Mikulincer, M., & Florian, V. (2004). Attachment style and affect regulation: Implications for coping with stress and mental health. In M. B. Brewer & M. Hewstone (Eds.), *Applied social psychology* (pp. 28–49). Malden, MA: Blackwell.

National Institute of Mental Health. (1999). *Translating behavioral science into action: Report of the National Advisory Mental Health Council Behavioral Science Workgroup.* Bethesda, MD: Author.

Norcross, J. C. (Ed.). (2002). *Psychotherapy relationships that work: Therapist contributions and responsiveness to patient needs.* New York: Oxford University Press.

Norcross, J. C., Beutler, L. E., & Caldwell, R. (2002). Integrative conceptualization and treatment of depression. In M. A. Reinecke & M. R. Davison (Eds.), *Comparative treatments of depression* (pp. 397–426). New York: Springer Publishing Company.

Olfson, M., Marcus, S. C., Druss, B., & Pincus, H. A. (2002). National trends in the use of outpatient psychotherapy. *American Journal of Psychiatry, 159*, 1914–1920.

Orlinsky, D. E., & Howard, K. I. (1975). *Varieties of psychotherapeutic experience.* New York: Teachers' College Press.

Ressler, K. J., Rothbaum, B. O., Tannenbaum, L., Anderson, P., Graap, K., Zimand, E., et al. (2004). Cognitive enhancers as adjuncts to psychotherapy: Use of D-cycloserine in phobic individuals to facilitate extinction of fear. *Archives of General Psychiatry, 61*, 1136–1144.

Rychlak, J. (2001). Psychotherapy as practical teleology: Viewing the person as agent. In B. D. Slife, R. N. Williams, & S. H. Barlow (Eds.), *Critical issues in psychotherapy: Translating new ideas into practice* (pp. 195–204). Thousand Oaks, CA: Sage.

Salkovskis, P. M. (2002). Empirically grounded clinical interventions: Cognitive–behavioural therapy progresses through a multi-dimensional approach to clinical science. *Behavioral and Cognitive Psychotherapy, 30*, 3–9.

Samoilov, A., & Goldfried, M. R. (2000). Role of emotion in cognitive–behavior therapy. *Clinical Psychology: Science and Practice, 7*, 373–385.

Scheffler, R. M., Ivey, S. L., & Garrett, A. B. (1998). Changing supply and earning patterns of the mental health workforce. *Administration in Policy and Mental Health, 26*, 85–99.

Siegle, G. J., Steinhauer, S. R., Thase, M. E., Stenger, V. A., & Carter, C. S. (2002). Can't shake that feeling: Event-related fMRI assessment of sustained amygdala activity in response to emotional information in depressed individuals. *Biological Psychiatry, 51*, 693–707.

Singer, J. L., & Salovey, P. (1991). Organized knowledge structures and personality: Person schemas, self-schemas, prototypes, and scripts. In M. J. Horowitz (Ed.), *Person schemas and maladaptive patterns* (pp. 33–79). Chicago: University of Chicago Press.

Strauman, T. J. (1992). Self-guides, autobiographical memory, and anxiety and dysphoria: Toward a cognitive model of vulnerability to emotional distress. *Journal of Abnormal Psychology, 101*, 87–95.

Strauman, T. J. (2002). Self-regulation and depression. *Self and Identity, 1*, 151–157.

Strauman, T. J., Kolden, G., Davis, N., Stromquist, V., Kwapil, L., & Heerey, E. (2001). The effects of treatments for depression on failure in self-regulation. *Cognitive Therapy & Research, 25*, 693–712.

Strauman, T. J., & Merrill, K. A. (2004). The basic science/clinical science interface and treatment development. *Clinical Psychology: Science and Practice, 11*, 263–266.

Strauman, T. J., Vieth, A. Z., Merrill, K. A., Woods, T. E., Kolden, G. G., Klein, M. H., et al. (2006). Self-system therapy as an intervention for self-regulatory dysfunction in depression: A randomized comparison with cognitive therapy. *Journal of Consulting and Clinical Psychology, 74*, 367–376.

Vieth, A., Strauman, T. J., Kolden, G., Woods, T., Michels, J., & Klein, M. H. (2003). Self-system therapy: A theory-based psychotherapy for depression. *Clinical Psychology: Science and Practice, 10*, 245–268.

Wampold, B. E. (2001). *The great psychotherapy debate: Models, methods, and findings.* Mahwah, NJ: Erlbaum.

Watson, D., Wiese, D., Vaidya, J., & Tellegen, A. (1999). The two general activation systems of affect: Structural findings, evolutionary considerations, and psychobiological evidence. *Journal of Personality and Social Psychology, 76*, 820–838.

Whelton, W. J. (2004). Emotion processes in psychotherapy: Evidence across therapeutic modalities. *Clinical Psychology and Psychotherapy, 11*, 58–71.

AFTERWORD:
BRIDGES YET TO COME—FUTURE DIRECTIONS FOR INTEGRATING AFFECTIVE AND CLINICAL SCIENCE

JONATHAN ROTTENBERG, SHERI L. JOHNSON, AND JAMES J. GROSS

The effort to build bridges between basic emotion processes and clinical research is well underway. Exciting translational findings are appearing each month in journals, books, and the media, with strong support across funding sources. Although welcome, the speed of these developments can make it difficult to get a foothold on key methods and findings. We hope that this book has provided that foothold by presenting crucial developments in the synthesis of affective and clinical science. This is still a new venture, however, and many bridges remain to be built. In this afterword, we consider five directions for the future integration of affective and clinical science.

Perhaps the most obvious future direction is to fill in gaps in our knowledge base—affective science has not been applied evenly across disorders. For example, bipolar disorder is characterized by some of the most dramatic affective disturbances in all of psychopathology, yet it is one of the least studied disorders from an emotion perspective. There are many other areas where this unevenness in coverage needs to be redressed: We know far more about the emotions of adults with psychopathology than about the emotions of children with psychopathology; we know far more about abnormalities in emotion in people suffering from Axis I clinical disorders than in people who suffer from Axis II personality disorders.

A second important future direction is to rethink diagnostic systems. For example, some have argued that a diagnostic system that is based on dimensions of etiology could produce a more elegant link between models of etiology and clusters of symptoms than category-based systems (Krueger, Watson, & Barlow, 2005). Emotion may provide crucial probative data for refining schemes for classifying psychopathology. For example, researchers have proposed that we could consider anxiety and depressive disorders as disorders involving excessive negative emotions (Barlow, Chorpita, & Turovsky, 1996) or as disorders that could be defined by relative levels of positive affect, negative affect, and arousal (Clark, Watson, & Mineka, 1994). Alternatively, Berenbaum, Raghavan, Le, Vernon, and Gomez (2003) suggested an emotion-based typology for a broad range of disorders based on (a) emotional valence disturbances, (b) emotional intensity and regulation disturbances, and (c) emotion disconnections. It is interesting that several chapters in this volume buttress these distinctions. For example, in schizophrenia, there is considerable evidence of emotion disconnections—that is, deficits in the behavioral channel of emotion but not in other channels of response (e.g., self-report of emotion experience, emotion-related physiology). By contrast, generalized anxiety disorder appears to be characterized by pronounced deficits in the regulation of emotion. However diagnostic systems are ultimately refined, we expect affect science to play an important role: By differentiating the key emotional features of a given disorder, we will be in a stronger position to identify commonalities and differences across symptom patterns.

A third direction for future research is to build additional bridges between emotion research findings and interventions. One challenge is simply to understand how existing efficacious treatments operate on motivation and emotion. In their chapter on pharmacotherapy for depression, for example, Tomarken and colleagues (chap. 12) build a model for considering somatic treatments more generally, drawing on evidence that dopaminergic systems may modulate positive affect whereas serotonergic systems may play a stronger role in modulating negative affect. They suggest how medication and sleep deprivation treatments for depression may differentially influence these two motivational systems. In a broader overview, Straumann and colleagues (chap. 13) provide a road map for considering various types of treatment research and how each type of treatment development and research could gain by considering emotion research findings. There is no doubt that the integration of emotion and treatment research represents a complex endeavor. In a recent review, Beutler et al. (2004) noted that a focus on emotion did not consistently predict better therapeutic outcomes. One reason for this may be that "emotion" is too broad and heterogeneous a construct. The question is how to focus treatments on the more specific models of emotion deficits described in this book. Despite the gains from applying emotion research, such as those that result from emotion-focused treatments for anxiety disorders described by Mennin and colleagues (see chap. 11, this volume), few psychopathologies have been targeted with an intervention that specifically addresses a key deficit drawn from careful emotion research.

Indeed, across treatment development efforts, a fourth future research direction involves an explicit focus on treatments designed to correct problems in *emotion regulation*, a term that refers to people's attempts to influence which emotions they have, when they have them, and how these emotions are experienced and expressed (Gross, in press). In work on transdiagnostic approaches to treatment, Barlow, Allen, and Choate (2004) drew on the idea that emotional reactivity and regulation difficulties are central to a range of disorders. They suggested three basic therapeutic targets to be considered across diagnoses: "(a) altering antecedent cognitive reappraisals . . . (b) preventing emotional avoidance," and "(c) facilitating action tendencies not associated with the emotion that is disordered" (p. 217).

Thus far much of the translation in translational research has been in one direction—applying findings and methods from basic research to the clinical realm. Although much of this volume reflects this favored flow of information, a fifth direction for future research is to address this imbalance: Affective science has much to gain by integrating insights from clinical science. Indeed, understanding how emotion systems "break" can be tremendously informative about function. For example, elucidating anhedonic deficits in schizophrenia, Kring and Neale (1996) have shown important distinctions between anticipatory and consummatory pleasure, providing important clues about the very nature of pleasure. In our view, the health of this synthesis between affective and clinical science depends on attending equally to both sides of the translation.

In sum, we hope our readers have reached this afterword with new insights into the best ways to measure emotion as well as with examples of how these methods influence our models of psychopathology. We are particularly excited about the bridges yet to come: The further integration of affective and clinical science promises to enrich understanding of both adaptive and maladaptive emotional functioning and to lay a foundation for rethinking diagnostic systems, etiology, and emotion-based treatments, a series of developments that will provide new tools for alleviating human misery.

REFERENCES

Barlow, D. H., Allen, L. B., & Choate, M. L. (2004). Toward a unified treatment for emotional disorders. *Behavior Therapy, 35*, 205–230.

Barlow, D. H., Chorpita, B. F., & Turovsky, J. (1996). Fear, panic, anxiety, and the disorders of emotion. In D. A. Hope (Ed.), *Nebraska Symposium on Motivation: Vol. 43. Perspectives on anxiety, panic, and fear* (pp. 251–328). Lincoln: University of Nebraska Press.

Berenbaum, H., Raghavan, C., Le, H.-N., Vernon, L. L., & Gomez, J. J. (2003). A taxonomy of emotional disturbances. *Clinical Psychology: Science and Practice, 10*, 206–226.

Beutler, L. E., Malik, M., Alimohamed, S., Harwood, T. M., Talebi, H., Noble, S., & Wong, E. (2004). Therapist variables. In M. J. Lambert (Ed.), *Bergin and Garfield's handbook of psychotherapy and behavior change* (5th ed., pp. 227–306). New York: Wiley.

Clark, L. A., Watson, D., & Mineka, S. (1994). Temperament, personality, and the mood and anxiety disorders. *Journal of Abnormal Psychology, 103*, 103–116.

Gross, J. J. (Ed.) (in press). *Handbook of emotion regulation*. New York: Guilford Press.

Kring, A. M., & Neale, J. M. (1996). Do schizophrenic patients show a disjunctive relationship among expressive, experiential, and psychophysiological components of emotion? *Journal of Abnormal Psychology, 105*, 249–257.

Krueger, R. F., Watson, D., & Barlow, D. H. (2005). Introduction to the special section: Toward a dimensionally based taxonomy of psychopathology. *Journal of Abnormal Psychology, 114*, 491–493.

AUTHOR INDEX

Numbers in italics refer to listings in the references.

SUBJECT INDEX

and depression, 152, 266
emotions vs., 14–15, 124
Mood Adjective Check List (MACL), 21, 22
Mood and Anxiety Symptom Questionnaire (MASQ), 271–274
Mood diaries, 277
Motivation, 245–246
Multiple Affect Adjective Check List (MAACL), 23
Multiple Affect Adjective Check List—Revised (MAACL–R), 22, 23

NA. *See* Negative affect
Narratives, 40–41
National Institutes of Health, 6, 287, 294
Naturalistic stimuli response, 276–277
Naturalistic techniques, 83
Negative affect (NA), 18–19
    and bipolar disorder, 126
    and depression, 266–268, 271–276
    depressive potentiation of, 154–156
    and schizophrenia, 108–109
Negative potentiation hypothesis, 154–156
Neuroimaging, 275–276
Neurotransmitters, 265
Nicotine, 207
Nonconscious fear activation, 179–180
Nonspecificity of affect, 16
Norepinephrine, 58, 271
Nortriptyline, 270, 271
No sleep deprivation plus nortriptyline (MED), 270, 272
Notable absences in emotional behavior, 44–46

Obsessive–compulsive disorder (OCD), 169, 181
Ohm's law, 55
Olfaction, 112
Orbicularis oculi, 68
Orbitofrontal region of frontal lobes, 44

PA. *See* Positive affect
PANAS. *See* Positive and Negative Affect Schedule
PANAS–X. *See* Positive and Negative Affect Schedule—Expanded Form
Panic disorder, 14–15, 169, 294–295
Parasympathetic activity, 58, 60–61, 170, 172
Parent–child interaction
    and depression, 45

and facial expression, 37
and touch, 42
Paroxetine, 274
PCL–R. *See* Psychopathy Checklist—Revised
PEP. *See* Preejection period
Personal construct theory, 293
Phobia(s)
    bodily responses to phobic stimuli, 172–173
    brain responses to phobic stimuli, 173
    social, 168–169
    specific, 168
Physiological reaction, 14
PLAC. *See* Sleep deprivation plus pill placebo
Pleasure, 42
POMS. *See* Profile of Mood States
Positive affect (PA), 18, 19
    and bipolar disorder, 125–126
    and depression, 266–275
    depressive attenuation of, 153–154
    and dopaminergic activity, 269–270
    effects of antidepressants on, 270–273
    and schizophrenia, 108–109
Positive and Negative Affect Schedule (PANAS), 22, 25–29, 271–273
Positive and Negative Affect Schedule—Expanded Form (PANAS–X), 22, 23, 25
Positive attenuation hypothesis, 153–154
Posttraumatic stress disorder (PTSD), 169, 174, 178, 182, 183
PPI. *See* Psychopathy Personality Inventory
Preejection period (PEP), 61–62
Preparedness hypothesis, 175–176, 178
Priming methodologies, 84–86
Profile of Mood States (POMS), 21–23
Promotion goals, 290, 291, 293
Psychogalvanic reflex, 198
Psychopathology, bridging emotion and, 3–6
Psychopathy, 215–235
    characteristics of, 215
    clinical implications of, 233, 235
    diagnostic criteria for, 216–217
    and PCL–R. *See* Psychopathy Checklist—Revised
    and PPI. *See* Psychopathy Personality Inventory
Psychopathy Checklist—Revised (PCL–R), 215, 217–229

and antisocial personality/externalizing spectrum, 228–229
development of, 217–219
distinctive factors of, 219–221
and emotional reactivity deficits, 221–228
Psychopathy Personality Inventory (PPI), 215, 229–234
affective–physiological response, 232–234
development of, 229–230
personality/behavioral measures, 230–232
Psychophysiology of emotion, 53–71
cardiovascular activity, 58–62
electrodermal activity, 54–58
electroencephalogram, 62–68
facial electromyography, 68–70
Psychotherapy
affective science as basis for understanding, 286–288
affective science benefited by, 293–296
affective science for improving outcomes from current, 288–290
definition of, 285
differences between affective science and, 296–298
etiologic theories of disordered emotion challenged by theories of, 295–296
Psychotic patients, 110
PsycINFO, 13
PTSD. *See* Posttraumatic stress disorder

Questionnaires, 83

Recency effect, 27
Reciprocity reinforcement, 42
Remission, bipolar, 127, 139–141
and approach stimuli, 127, 139–140
and threat stimuli, 140–141
Renewal of the CR, 177
Research, theory and, 297–298
Resistance, 55
Respiratory cycle, 60
Respiratory sinus arrhythmia (RSA), 60–61
Resting EEG activity, 67
Retrieval of emotional information, 89–91
Retrospective recall, 27–28
Rewards
and alcohol consumption, 192
and bipolar disorder, 126, 127, 144, 145
and depression, 276

and dopaminergic systems, 269, 275
Risk, 54
Romantic partners, 37
RSA. *See* Respiratory sinus arrhythmia
Russell's model, 17, 18

Samples, 19–21
Schema, 291
Schizohypohedonia, 105
Schizophrenia, 103–116, 306
clinical implications of, 115–116
diminished emotional expression in, 46–47
and experience sampling method, 109–110
historical/theoretical perspectives on, 103–105
hypoactive SCRs in, 57
integration/future study for, 112–115
laboratory studies of, 110–112
phenomenology/diagnosis of, 105–106
and trait dimensions of emotion, 106–109
Schizotype, 104
Schizotypy, 104, 107, 108
SCL (skin conductance level), 55
SCRs. *See* Skin conductance responses
SD. *See* Sleep deprivation
Secondary hypohedonia, 104
Security needs, 254
Selective encoding of emotional information, 86–89
Selective processing biases, 91–94
Selective retrieval of emotional information, 89–91
Selective serotonin reuptake inhibitors (SSRIs), 264, 268
Self-conscious emotions, 45–46
Self-discrepancy theory, 289–290
Self–other agreement, 25–26
Self-regulation, 291–292
Self-report measures
of affect, 21–25
of thought content, 83–84
Self-system therapy (SST), 290–293
September 11, 2001 terrorist attacks, 249
Serotonergic (5-HT) systems, 268–269, 274, 277
Serotonin receptor modulators, 268
Serotonin transporter gene, 268, 269
Shifting attention, 181
Signal safety, 42

ABOUT THE EDITORS

Jonathan Rottenberg, PhD, was born in Massachusetts and raised in Connecticut. He graduated magna cum laude from Harvard College in 1990 and received a master's degree in history from the Johns Hopkins University. He did his graduate work in psychology at Stanford University, where he was a National Institute of Mental Health predoctoral fellow in affective science. Since receiving his PhD in 2003, Dr. Rottenberg moved to the University of South Florida, where he is currently an assistant professor, director of the Mood and Emotion Laboratory, and teacher of graduate and undergraduate courses in abnormal psychology. In his research, he and his students apply methods and insights drawn from basic research on emotion to further the understanding of important clinical conditions, such as major depressive disorder.

Dr. Rottenberg is a member of the Society for Research in Psychopathology, the Society for Psychophysiological Research, and the Emotion Research Group. Dr. Rottenberg's research has been supported by a New Researcher Grant at the University of South Florida, and he has reviewed grants for the National Science Foundation and the Institute for Mental Health Research. He has published his work on emotion and psychopathology in journals such as the *Journal of Abnormal Psychology*, *Psychophysiology*, *Emotion*, *Current Directions in Psychological Science*, and *Cognition & Emotion*. This book is his first edited volume.

Sheri L. Johnson, PhD, received her BA from Salem College in 1982 and her PhD from the University of Pittsburgh in 1992. She completed an internship and postdoctoral fellowship at Brown University, and she was a clinical assistant professor at Brown from 1993 to 1995. Since 1995, she has been teaching in the Department of Psychology at the University of Miami, where she is currently a professor of psychology with a joint appointment in the Department of Psychiatry and Human Behavior.

In 1993, Dr. Johnson received the Young Investigator Award from the National Alliance for Research in Schizophrenia and Depression, and her work has also been funded by the National Institute of Mental Health and the National Cancer Institute. She has authored more than 70 articles and chapters. Dr. Johnson's previous books include *Psychological Treatments of Bipolar Disorder* and *Stress, Coping, and Depression*. She was a coauthor on the textbook *Abnormal Psychology*. She is an associate editor for the journals *Applied & Preventive Psychology* and *Cognition & Emotion*, and she serves on the editorial board of *Psychological Bulletin*, *Psychology and Psychotherapy*, and the *Journal of Cognitive Psychotherapy*. Dr. Johnson's research is focused on processes that contribute to episodes of mania, including emotional reactivity and goal dysregulation.